INSIDE COUNSEL

Practices, Strategies, and Insights

Second Edition

Marc I. Steinberg

Rupert and Lillian Radford Professor of Law
Director, Corporate Counsel Externship Program
SMU Dedman School of Law

Stephen B. Yeager

Adjunct Professor
Faculty Supervisor, Corporate Counsel Externship Program
Assistant Dean for Student Affairs
SMU Dedman School of Law

WEST
ACADEMIC
PUBLISHING

© 2015 LEG, Inc. d/b/a West Academic
© 2020 LEG, Inc. d/b/a West Academic
    444 Cedar Street, Suite 700
    St. Paul, MN 55101
    1-877-888-1330

West, West Academic Publishing, and West Academic are trademarks of West Publishing Corporation, used under license.

Printed in the United States of America

ISBN: 978-1-64020-701-1

FOREWORD

Veta T. Richardson[*]

As CEO of the Association of Corporate Counsel (www. acc.com), I am honored to have been invited to pen the foreword to this important new textbook on the in-house practice of law and to congratulate its esteemed co-authors, Marc Steinberg and Stephen Yeager, upon this much-anticipated second edition.

Founded more than three decades ago, ACC is the preeminent global bar association for in-house counsel and the voice of the international in-house bar. ACC's membership spans more than 85 countries, six continents, and over 10,000 unique law departments.

My position as CEO affords a unique bird's eye view of the issues and trends that are top-of-mind with this key sector of the legal profession.

As such, I have witnessed the evolution of the in-house counsel role from gatekeeper to trusted advisor to key business strategist. Whether the company's top lawyer holds the title, "general counsel" or "chief legal officer," the position carries an increasing level of responsibility and influence within the C-suite, the boardroom and beyond. As companies expand globally, the breadth of laws and regulations with which in-house counsel must keep abreast becomes increasingly complex and harder to track.

Long gone are the days when going in-house meant relinquishing the driver's seat to outside counsel or sitting on the sidelines while law firms handle the more interesting or sophisticated legal work. Today, outside counsel work at the direction of in-house counsel, who are choosing to take the reins and set the strategy. In addition, the fast pace of technology and the speed at which information is communicated have ushered in a brand new set of challenges, particularly for in-house

---

[*]   President and Chief Executive Officer, Association of Corporate Counsel.

counsel who work for publicly held companies accountable to shareholders and investors.

The role of in-house counsel has never been more interesting or more challenging. In ACC surveys, a majority of in-house counsel consistently report high levels of career satisfaction. Yet, there has been a dearth of academic resources to assist an aspiring law student, new graduate, or freshly-hired in-house counsel to get up to speed on the range of basic issues that in-house counsel must address.

Therefore, I applaud Professors Marc Steinberg and Stephen Yeager for filling this void with *Inside Counsel—Practices, Strategies and Insights*.

Like Professor Yeager, my career includes a stint in-house—eleven years at a Fortune 200 energy corporation where I focused on securities disclosure, governance, corporate finance, and transactions. In fact, I went in-house immediately upon graduating from the University of Maryland School of Law, where I had the good fortune to build a strong foundation thanks to my former law professor, Marc Steinberg.

The cumulative wealth of knowledge that Professors Steinberg and Yeager bring to the table as co-authors has made for a wonderful collaboration. I am confident that this new textbook will quickly become a "go-to" reference for all those who seek an in-depth understanding of the in-house practice of law.

Veta T. Richardson
President and Chief Executive Officer
Association of Corporate Counsel

ABOUT THE AUTHORS

Marc I. Steinberg—The Rupert and Lillian Radford Professor of Law at Southern Methodist University (SMU) Dedman School of Law. He is the Director of SMU's Corporate Counsel Externship Program. He is the former Senior Associate Dean for Academics and former Associate Dean for Research at SMU. Prior to becoming the Radford Professor, Professor Steinberg taught at the University of Maryland School of Law, the Wharton School of the University of Pennsylvania, the National Law Center of the George Washington University, and the Georgetown University Law Center. His experience includes appointments as a Visiting Professor, Scholar and Fellow at law schools outside of the United States, including at Universities in Argentina, Australia, Canada, China, England, Finland, France, Germany, Israel, Japan, New Zealand, Scotland, South Africa, and Sweden. In addition, he has been retained as an expert witness in several significant matters, including Enron, Martha Stewart, Belnick (Tyco), and Mark Cuban.

Professor Steinberg received his undergraduate degree at the University of Michigan and his law degrees at the University of California, Los Angeles (J.D.) and Yale University (LL.M.). He clerked for Judge Stanley N. Barnes of the U.S. Court of Appeals for the Ninth Circuit, was an extern law clerk for Judge Anthony J. Celebrezze of the Sixth Circuit, was legislative counsel to U.S. Senator Robert P. Griffin and served as the adviser to former U.S. Supreme Court Justice Arthur J. Goldberg for the Federal Advisory Committee on Tender Offers.

Professor Steinberg was an enforcement attorney at the U.S. Securities and Exchange Commission, and thereafter became special projects counsel. In that position, he directly assisted the SEC's General Counsel in a wide variety of projects and cases and served as the General Counsel's confidential legal adviser.

Professor Steinberg has authored approximately 40 books and 150 law review articles, is editor-in-chief of The

International Lawyer, editor-in-chief of The Securities Regulation Law Journal, and an adviser to The Journal of Corporation Law. He previously served as a member of the FINRA National Adjudicatory Council (NAC). Professor Steinberg is a member of the American Law Institute.

Stephen B. Yeager—The Faculty Supervisor of the Corporate Counsel Externship Program at SMU Dedman School of Law, an innovative academic program for third-year law students that combines a corporate counsel course with externships in corporate legal departments. Now in its seventh year, this program has grown into the premier corporate externship program in the nation. This past fall, 90 students worked with 90 different companies where they were placed based on their practice area or industry interests. He also teaches the corporate counsel classroom component of the Program and serves as the Assistant Dean for Student Affairs at SMU Dedman School of Law.

Dean Yeager serves on the Faculty Advisory Committee for the Robert B. Rowling Center for Business Law & Leadership. Outside the law school, he sits on the board of the SMU Faculty Club, where he serves as treasurer. He also serves as an SMU Deputy Title IX Coordinator, on the President's Commission on the Needs of Persons with Disabilities, and on the Training Board for the SMU Police Department.

Before SMU, Mr. Yeager was in private practice at Jones Day for approximately nine years and general counsel of a private financial services company for almost seven. He received his undergraduate and law degrees at Southern Methodist University, where he was a student in one of Professor Steinberg's first Business Enterprises classes.

NOTE FROM THE AUTHORS

In writing this book, we relied heavily on our own accumulated experiences. For Professor Steinberg, this includes his work in the academic and practical spheres—as a law professor, expert witness, counsel at law firms, and author. And Dean Yeager brought his real-world experiences from a large firm and corporation, as well as his knowledge gained from teaching law students about in-house practice, serving as a career counselor to law students and recent graduates, working closely with corporate counsel in connection with SMU's Corporate Counsel Externship Program, and helping place law student interns and full-time attorneys in corporations.

In addition to our own experiences, we have included insights, wisdom and perspectives from corporate counsel, either directly from interviews with us or from lectures and panel discussions throughout the years at the Corporate Counsel Symposium and corporate counsel courses here at SMU. We also visited with attorneys who practice in firms to ensure the book is balanced with perspectives of outside counsel. The personal insights and wisdom of these individuals further developed our own understanding of inside counsel and provided an enhanced framework for the book.

SUMMARY OF CONTENTS

FOREWORD...III

ABOUT THE AUTHORS V

NOTE FROM THE AUTHORS VII

Introduction... 1

Chapter 1. The Role of Inside Counsel.................................... 5
Inside Counsel—"Wedded" to His/Her Client 6
Challenges Facing Inside Counsel 7

Chapter 2. Identifying Who Is Inside Counsel's Client 35
Principle of Confidentiality 35
Counsel's Communications with the Company's Constituents........ 36
Closely-Held Corporations.. 37
The "Entity" Rule 39
Avoidance of Conflicting Interests 40

Chapter 3. What It's Really Like to Work In-House and
      How to Find In-House Job Opportunities 49
What Do In-House Lawyers Do and Why? 50
What Else Can Attorneys Do in Corporations?.......................... 52
Common Perceptions About In-House Practice 52
Pathways to In-House Practice 65
What Are Corporations Looking for in Corporate Counsel?............. 75
Tips for Law Students Who Want to Work In-House 95

Chapter 4. Corporate Governance 105
Board of Directors 107
Committees of the Board 111
Corporate Executive Officers... 115
Loans.. 115
Conclusion... 116

Chapter 5. Client Confidentiality.................................... 137
Applicable Rules.. 137
Withdrawal and Its Consequences.. 140
The Ostrich Approach 142

Chapter 6. Working with Your "Internal Clients" 173
In-House Counsel as Business Partner 174
Becoming a Trusted Legal Advisor and Business Partner 176
Helping Internal Clients Identify and Evaluate Risk 191
Allocating Resources 195
In-House Counsel in Business Meetings 197
Corporate Minutes 200

Chapter 7. Law Compliance **205**
Law Compliance—Inside Counsel's Role 205
Advising Regarding Law Compliance 205
Impact of Sound Law Compliance Programs on Government
    Prosecution 207
Overseeing the Compliance Function 208

Chapter 8. Working with Outside Counsel **227**
Why Use Outside Counsel? 227
What Type of Work Is Typically Sent to Outside Counsel? 231
Criteria for Selecting Outside Counsel 232
Methods Used to Select Outside Counsel 242
Is a Bigger Firm Better than a Smaller One? 246
"Pet Peeves" 247
What Should Outside Counsel Do? 264

Chapter 9. Focusing on the Securities Laws **271**
Meaning of "Material" and "Non-Public" Information 272
Insider Trading 274
SEC Filings 276
Resales of Securities 278
State Securities Laws 279
Conclusion 279

Chapter 10. Corporate Internal Investigations **301**
Factors to Be Evaluated 301
Client Confidentiality 302
Purposes of Internal Investigations 304
Components of an Internal Investigation 306
Need for *Miranda*-Type Warning 309
Disclosing the Internal Investigation 311

Chapter 11. Early Case Assessments **331**
What Is an "Early Case Assessment Program"? 331
Using ECA to Develop a Roadmap 332
An Important Lesson from the Plaintiff's Perspective 332

Know 80% of What You Will Ever Know in 60 Days 333
The ECA Program—Defined 333
The Early Case Assessment Checklist.................................... 334
Putting the Checklist into Action...................................... 336
Better Settlements from Better Information 337
Better Docket Management Through Early Case Assessments 339

Chapter 12. Inside Counsel as Director 345
Potential Drawbacks.. 346
Benefits of the Dual Role 346
Ethical Rules 347
Risks of Serving as Attorney-Director 349
Suggested Alternative.. 353

TABLE OF CASES 355

TABLE OF CONTENTS

FOREWORD..III

ABOUT THE AUTHORS V

NOTE FROM THE AUTHORS VII

Introduction.. 1

Chapter 1. The Role of Inside Counsel....................................... 5
Inside Counsel—"Wedded" to His/Her Client 6
Challenges Facing Inside Counsel 7
    Client Identification 7
    Duty to Inquire 9
    Dealing with "Suspected" Employees................................... 11
    Inside Counsel's Liability Exposure................................... 13
    Role Within the Boardroom 13
    Law Compliance Role... 15
        Becoming In-House Counsel.. 17
        The 'Dark Side' Of Going In House 27

Chapter 2. Identifying Who Is Inside Counsel's Client 35
Principle of Confidentiality 35
Counsel's Communications with the Company's Constituents......... 36
Closely-Held Corporations.. 37
The "Entity" Rule 39
Avoidance of Conflicting Interests 40
    In the Matter of Carter and Johnson 40
    Restatement of the Law (Third) Governing Lawyers 41
    New York City Bar Association Task Force Report on the
    Lawyer's Role in Corporate Governance (2006) 44

Chapter 3. What It's Really Like to Work In-House and
How to Find In-House Job Opportunities 49
What Do In-House Lawyers Do and Why? 50
What Else Can Attorneys Do in Corporations?............................ 52
Common Perceptions About In-House Practice 52
    In-House Attorneys Work Less... 53
    In-House Jobs Are More Stable.. 57
    In-House Jobs May Be Less Prestigious 59
    It Is Better to Be a Generalist 61

In-House Counsel Cannot Be Lonely 63
In-House Attorneys Do Not Have to Worry About
    Malpractice 64
Pathways to In-House Practice 65
    The General Rule... 65
    The Exceptions to the Rule.. 69
        Opportunities with Very Large Legal Departments 69
        Opportunities with Smaller Companies............................ 72
What Are Corporations Looking for in Corporate Counsel?............. 75
    Starting Your In-House Job Search 77
        Identifying Your Experience and Skill Sets..................... 77
        Focusing on an Industry 81
        Identifying "Target" Companies 81
        The Active Job Search 83
        The Passive Job Search.. 88
    Application Materials—*Your Resume* 90
        Cover Letters 91
        LinkedIn.. 92
    Professional Organizations.. 95
Tips for Law Students Who Want to Work In-House 95
    Internships with Corporate Legal Departments....................... 97
    Externships and Practicums.. 100

Chapter 4. Corporate Governance **105**
Board of Directors 107
    Functions of the Board of Directors 107
    Business Judgment Rule and Related Principles 108
    Dual Role as CEO and Chair of Board of Directors;
        Lead Director 110
    Independent Directors 110
Committees of the Board 111
    Audit Committee 112
    Compensation Committee... 113
    Nominating/Corporate Governance Committee....................... 114
Corporate Executive Officers.. 115
Loans... 115
Conclusion... 116
    The Federalization of Corporate Governance (2018) 116
    American Law Institute, Principles of Corporate
        Governance: Analysis and Recommendations (1994)....... 120
    Certification of Disclosure in Companies' Quarterly and
        Annual Reports 133

Chapter 5. Client Confidentiality **137**
Applicable Rules 137
Withdrawal and Its Consequences 140
The Ostrich Approach 142
    Remarks before the Spring Meeting of the Association of
        General Counsel 144
    SEC v. Jordan H. Mintz and Rex R. Rogers 153
    SEC v. John E. Isselmann, Jr. 155
    SEC v. Nancy R. Heinen 156
    SEC v. David C. Drummond 158
    Trustee's Report in OPM Leasing Services, Inc. (1983) 159
    Independent Examiner's Report in Spiegel, Inc. (2003) 166

Chapter 6. Working with Your "Internal Clients" **173**
In-House Counsel as Business Partner 174
Becoming a Trusted Legal Advisor and Business Partner 176
    Develop Strong Relationships 176
    Communicate Effectively 182
    Know the Business 185
    Be a Facilitator Whenever Possible 189
Helping Internal Clients Identify and Evaluate Risk 191
Allocating Resources 195
In-House Counsel in Business Meetings 197
Corporate Minutes 200

Chapter 7. Law Compliance **205**
Law Compliance—Inside Counsel's Role 205
Advising Regarding Law Compliance 205
Impact of Sound Law Compliance Programs on Government
    Prosecution 207
Overseeing the Compliance Function 208
    The General Counsel as a Corporate Culture Influencer
        (2017) 209
    Compliance Programs for Insider Trading 219
    Minimizing Corporate Liability Exposure When the
        Whistle Blows in the Post Sarbanes-Oxley Era 225

Chapter 8. Working with Outside Counsel **227**
Why Use Outside Counsel? 227
What Type of Work Is Typically Sent to Outside Counsel? 231
Criteria for Selecting Outside Counsel 232
    Top Quality Legal Work 233
    Specialization 234
    Cost 235

Willingness to Enter into Alternative Fee Arrangements 236
Personal Relationships 237
Diverse Staffing 239
Key Relationships with Third Parties 241
Geography and Other Local Considerations 241
Methods Used to Select Outside Counsel 242
Requests for Proposals 242
Referrals 243
"Inherited" Outside Counsel 245
Discovered Through Networking or Speaking
Engagements 245
Management and Board Member Recommendations 246
Is a Bigger Firm Better than a Smaller One? 246
"Pet Peeves" 247
Poor Communication 248
Unresponsiveness 250
Not Being Accessible 252
Missing Deadlines 252
Billing Surprises 253
Sharing Confidences 253
Not Listening 253
Being Arrogant 255
Spotting Problems but Not Providing Solutions 255
Ineffective Law Firm Marketing 256
Putting the Law Firm's Interests Ahead of the Client's
Interests 257
Going over Budget 257
Delivering Poor Invoices 259
Staffing up 261
Doing More than the Client Wants 262
What Should Outside Counsel Do? 264

Chapter 9. Focusing on the Securities Laws **271**
Meaning of "Material" and "Non-Public" Information 272
Material Information 272
Non-Public Information 273
Insider Trading 274
SEC Filings 276
Resales of Securities 278
State Securities Laws 279
Conclusion 279
The "Work" of the SEC 279
SEC v. Andrew S. Marks 296

SEC v. Mitchell S. Drucker... 297
SEC v. Gene D. Levoff.. 298

Chapter 10. Corporate Internal Investigations 301
Factors to Be Evaluated... 301
Client Confidentiality 302
Purposes of Internal Investigations... 304
Components of an Internal Investigation...................................... 306
Need for *Miranda*-Type Warning... 309
Disclosing the Internal Investigation 311
    In Re: Kellogg Brown & Root, Inc. 312
    Law School Didn't Prepare You for This: Tips for the
    Internal Investigation 319

Chapter 11. Early Case Assessments 331
What Is an "Early Case Assessment Program"? 331
Using ECA to Develop a Roadmap... 332
An Important Lesson from the Plaintiff's Perspective 332
Know 80% of What You Will Ever Know in 60 Days...................... 333
The ECA Program—Defined 333
The Early Case Assessment Checklist.. 334
Putting the Checklist into Action.. 336
Better Settlements from Better Information 337
Better Docket Management Through Early Case Assessments 339

Chapter 12. Inside Counsel as Director 345
Potential Drawbacks.. 346
Benefits of the Dual Role 346
Ethical Rules 347
Risks of Serving as Attorney-Director 349
Suggested Alternative... 353

TABLE OF CASES 355

INSIDE COUNSEL

Practices, Strategies, and Insights

Second Edition

INTRODUCTION

This book provides a wide-ranging account of in-house practice. As the title suggests, the content generally falls into three main categories—practices, strategies and insights. The book includes best practices for corporate counsel, including ones on conducting internal investigations, performing early case assessments, and instituting compliance programs. It also contains practical strategies that in-house counsel can implement, such as effectively working with outside counsel, interfacing with your "internal clients" and the practice of "preventive" law. Finally, the book offers practical insights into a variety of topics, including what it is really like to work in a corporate legal department, what skill sets are valued by corporate counsel, and the potential liability concerns that face in-house counsel.

Audiences

We anticipate that this book will be useful resources for a wide variety of audiences. The first is law students. Many law schools, including the University of Chicago, Stanford Law School, Georgetown Law, and our own SMU Dedman School of Law, have developed business law curricula with courses and academic programs focused extensively on in-house practice. To the best of our knowledge, however, few texts on the market exist today for such classes. Prior to the publication of this book's first edition, most professors relied on articles written by corporate counsel—a less-than-ideal substitute for a good textbook. This book hopefully has filled this void, by combining substantive topics with practical insights that give law students a glimpse of what in-house lawyers actually do and the challenges they face.

Another audience is attorneys joining corporate legal departments for the first time, either right out of law school or from a firm. It used to be that corporations relied solely on large law firms to train lawyers for five to seven years before hiring them for in-house positions. But now an increasing number of corporations are charting a new course, and hiring recent law school graduates or attorneys with only one to two years of firm experience. This phenomenon is driven in large part on the increased budgetary pressures placed on corporate legal departments, which are in turn insourcing more work and hiring cheaper entry- and junior-level attorneys to handle the work. These attorneys who are new to in-house practice are being trained in a variety of ways, both formally and informally. This book hopefully is useful to train these new in-house lawyers about in-house corporate lawyering, which is a very specific type of practice and one that requires very different skill sets than those used in law firms or schools.

The book also serves as a key reference for experienced corporate counsel who need quick access to information on the broad spectrum of topics covered in the text. As the multifaceted subjects addressed illustrate, this book should provide useful guidance on issues that corporate counsel face every day.

Finally, although titled "Inside Counsel", the book serves as a useful resource for outside counsel—those who represent or hope to represent corporations. Our collective experience has been that many outside practicing attorneys do not understand what in-house lawyers do or want because they never worked as in-house counsel. This book hopefully allows outside counsel to view themselves from the perspective of their "clients." By understanding the expectations of in-house counsel and avoiding the common "pet peeves" outlined in this book, outside counsel will hopefully become more effective counselors to their clients—the corporations.

Acknowledgments

We are extremely grateful to our friends in the corporate counsel and law firm worlds who graciously provided wisdom, perspective, support or guidance in this project. We extend our appreciation to Veta T. Richardson, President and CEO of the Association of Corporate Counsel, for writing the Foreword to the first edition as well as the second edition of this book.

We are extremely grateful to the attorneys who have guest lectured in the Corporate Counsel courses at SMU Dedman School of Law as well as other inside and outside counsel who have contributed to our own understanding and appreciation of different aspects and challenges of serving as in-house counsel. Quotations from many of these attorneys are used in this book.

In addition, we thank Cullen (Mike) Godfrey for his insights, administrative assistants Ms. Jan Spann and Ms. Carolyn Yates for their excellent assistance, student research assistants Ms. Brenda Balli, Mr. Casey Fraser, Ms. Vanessa Murra-Kapon, and Mr. Logan Weissler for their diligence, and the John C. Biggers Faculty Research Fund for providing financial support for this project.

Stephen Yeager thanks his wife Amy, whom he met on their first day of law school at SMU and is now SVP and General Counsel for Children's Health, for her support. In addition, he thanks his twin brother, Douglas, also an SMU Dedman School of Law alumnus and a real estate partner at Winston & Strawn LLP for his input on the law firm perspective.

Dedications

Marc Steinberg dedicates this book to his terrific children—Alex, Avi, and Phillip (Bear)—as well as to our wonderful dog Teddy.

Stephen Yeager dedicates this book to his best friend and wife Amy, his fabulous children—Carson and Alexandra—and his loving parents, Patricia and Stan Yeager.

CHAPTER 1

THE ROLE OF INSIDE COUNSEL

Today, employment as inside counsel in a reputable and profitable company is coveted. Attractive compensation and related benefits, relatively reasonable working hours, and lawyering on interesting issues without the stress of client development that arises in the law firm setting are meaningful attributes. In this respect, the role of inside counsel has changed dramatically as compared to several decades ago. As Irving Shapiro, former general counsel of DuPont, remarked:

> In the past, businessmen wore blinders. After hours, they would run to their club, play golf with other businessmen, have a martini—and that was about it. . . . In a world where government simply took taxes from you and did not interfere with your operations, maybe that idea was sensible. In today's world, it is not.[1]

H.J. Aibel, then chief legal officer of ITT, upon reflecting on the status of inside counsel in the times of yesteryear, commented that "then the generally accepted wisdom [was] that jobs in corporate law departments were for second raters, or lawyers who had failed to make partner at some of the better firms."[2] This situation today is fundamentally different. The responsibility and prestige of inside counsel have dramatically increased.[3] Indeed, the issues facing in-house attorneys have become as multifaceted and challenging as those arising in law firms. Inside attorneys now play an active role in shaping corporate events, in assessing corporate policies, and in establishing the tone and standard for corporate conduct.[4]

---

[1]   Loeb, *The Corporate Chiefs' New Class,* Time, Apr. 14, 1980, at 87 (quoting Irving Shapiro).

[2]   Aibel, *Corporate Counsel and Business Ethics: A Personal Review,* 59 Mo. L. Rev. 427, 427 (1994).

[3]   Former SEC Chairman Harold Williams reflected on this dramatic change over three decades ago. See Williams, *The Role of Inside Counsel in Corporate Accountability,* [1979–1980 Transfer Binder] CCH Fed. Sec. L. Rep. ¶ 82,318, at 82,369 (1979).

[4]   *See Guide for In-House Counsel—Practical Resource to Cutting-Edge Issues* (ABA L. Berkoff ed. 2019); M. Steinberg, *Corporate Internal Affairs: A Corporate and*

Today, for example, there are many corporate legal departments with hundreds of in-house attorneys.

INSIDE COUNSEL—"WEDDED" TO HIS/HER CLIENT

As a full-time employee of his/her own client, in-house counsel faces the unique situation of being "wedded" to the client. As such, inside counsel is likely to encounter difficult questions of professional independence.[5] For example, when outside counsel has a "difficult" client (such as one that fails to timely pay its bills or one that engages in improper conduct), the attorney may "walk" from that client.[6] Although the attorney certainly may miss the revenues that the client otherwise would have generated, she normally has the economic leeway to resign from the engagement. However, when inside counsel's client is unduly "difficult" or behaves improperly, counsel must either tolerate such conduct or find another job. Hence, being in-house counsel makes separation and divorce far more onerous.

On the other hand, inside counsel's "marital" relationship to his client has key attributes. One particularly attractive one, for example, is that inside counsel is very much at the center of the key legal functions of the enterprise. Moreover, inside lawyers in many corporations are involved in business strategy. As a result, it is prevalent that in-house attorneys have the financial acumen to understand the benefits and risks of a prospective venture and the opportunity to communicate with management regarding the economic aspects of a contemplated "deal." In these functions, inside counsel seeks to be perceived within the

---

Securities Law Perspective 251 (1983); E. Veasey & C. Di Guglielmo, *Indispensable Counsel—The Chief Legal Officer in the New Reality* (2012). *See also* Symposium, *The Changing Role and Nature of In-House and General Counsel,* 2012 Wis. L. Rev. No. 2 (2012); Atherton-Ely, *Demonstrating Value to a Corporation as In-House Counsel,* 43 Mitchell-Hamline L. Rev. 1003 (2017); Veasey & Di Guglielmo, *General Counsel Buffeted by Compliance Demands and Client Pressures May Face Personal Peril,* 68 Bus. Law. 57 (2012); Williams, note 3 *supra.* There are tens of thousands of in-house lawyers in the United States. *See* 44 Sec. Reg. & L. Rep. (BNA) 1157 (2012).

[5]   *See* DeMott, *The Discrete Roles of General Counsel,* 74 Fordham L. Rev. 955, 956 (2005).

[6]   *See generally* Model Rules of Prof. Conduct, Rule 1.16 & cmts.; Hemmer, *Resignation of Corporate Counsel: Fulfillment or Abdication of Duty?,* 39 Hastings L.J. 641 (1988).

enterprise as a "can do yes person," while retaining the leverage to effectively say "no" when appropriate.[7]

H.J. Aibel, while discussing his experience as corporate counsel for ITT, elaborated upon this view:

> Early involvement of the lawyer often depends upon the prior establishment of a reputation for being a 'team player,' a 'can do lawyer'. . . . Although it is not easy for inside counsel to bring to the attention of the corporation's Board of Directors situations in which senior management is failing to take appropriate action, in the end, his or her career may depend upon doing so.[8]

CHALLENGES FACING INSIDE COUNSEL

As the following discussion illustrates, in-house attorneys often confront many challenging issues, such as: (1) client identification and loyalty; (2) the general duty to inquire when offering advice; (3) the obligation to take appropriate action when a corporate fraud or crime is discovered; (4) liability arising under applicable laws; and (5) the implementation of law compliance policies (including prohibitions against insider trading).

Client Identification

Client identification is key to understanding the role of inside counsel. Stated succinctly, who is inside counsel's client? The answer is that inside counsel's client is the corporate entity.[9]

In this regard, ABA Model Rule 1.13(a) provides that "[a] lawyer employed or retained by an organization represents the organization acting through its duly authorized constituents."[10]

---

[7]   See Creedon, *Lawyer and Executive—The Role of the General Counsel*, 39 Bus. Law. 25 (1983); *How Agile is Your Legal Department?*, Corp. Legal Times, Aug. 1995, at 1, 5 (quoting statements by McDonald's Corp. assistant general counsel Ira S. Feldman that "[a]ll of the lawyers at McDonald's become intimately involved on the business side" and that "lawyer[s] . . . wear two hats: a business hat as well as [a] legal hat"); Fuith, *Creating the Lawyer as Business Leader*, 43 Mitchell Hamline L. Rev. 1095, 1097 (2017) ("More and more lawyers are transitioning from roles as business attorneys and advisors into business leaders, managers, and chief executive officers.").

[8]   Aibel, *supra* note 2, 59 Mo. L. Rev. at 431.

[9]   *See, e.g.,* Model Rules of Prof. Conduct, Rule 1.13(a); ABA Model Code of Prof. Responsibility EC 5–18.

[10]   *See* Model Rules of Prof. Conduct, Rule 1.13(a).

The American Law Institute's (ALI) Restatement of the Law Governing Lawyers likewise states that "the lawyer represents the interests of the organization as defined by its responsible agents acting pursuant to the organization's decision-making procedures."[11]

The seeming simplicity of these rules often breaks down in practice, however, because the organizational entity can "speak" and make decisions only through its "authorized constituents," including the corporation's directors, officers, employees, and shareholders.[12] Due to the close working relationship that develops between in-house counsel and corporate executives, counsel may be forced to choose between her obligations to the corporate client and conflicting orders given by a superior; in other words, counsel may be faced with following an executive officer's directions or being fired from her only client.[13] To alleviate this dilemma, the general perception is that, so long as the board of directors and senior management are acting in a lawful manner, inside counsel should look to these constituents as the "spokespersons" for the corporate entity.[14] In this regard, if practicable, the inside general counsel should meet with the independent directors (or the lead independent director) in executive session on a regular basis to address pertinent issues.[15]

In certain situations, however, the perception that the lawyer may rely on a company's management or board of directors may prove problematic.[16] For instance, the Fifth Circuit in *Garner v. Wolfinbarger*,[17] in determining whether a corporation could invoke the attorney-client privilege to preclude

---

[11]   *See Restatement of the Law Governing Lawyers* § 96(1)(a). *Accord,* Report of the New York City Bar Association Task Force on the Lawyer's Role in Corporate Governance, 62 Bus. Law. 427, 481 (2007).

[12]   *See* Olson, *The Potential Liabilities Faced by In-House Counsel,* 7 U. Miami Bus. L. Rev. 1 (1998).

[13]   *Id.* at 5. *See* Steinberg, *The Role of Inside Counsel in the 1990s: A View From Outside,* 49 SMU L. Rev. 483 (1996).

[14]   *See* Taylor, *The Role of Corporate Counsel,* 32 Rutgers L. Rev. 237, 241–245 (1979).

[15]   *See* NYC Bar Association Task Force Report, *supra* note 11, 62 Bus. Law. at 487.

[16]   Taylor, *supra* note 14, 32 Rutgers L. Rev. at 241–245.

[17]   430 F.2d 1093 (5th Cir. 1970).

shareholders in a derivative suit from obtaining requested documents, stated:

> [I]t must be borne in mind that management does not manage for itself and that the beneficiaries of its action are the stockholders. Conceptualistic phrases describing the corporation as an entity separate from its stockholders are not useful tools of analysis. They serve only to obscure the fact that management has duties which run to the benefit ultimately of the stockholders. . . . There may be situations in which the corporate entity or its management, or both, have interests adverse to those of some or all stockholders. But when all is said and done management is not managing for itself.[18]

Duty to Inquire

Additional concerns may arise from the in-house lawyer's duty to inquire when offering advice. Generally, inside counsel regularly provides advice to employees and management concerning law compliance and consults with management as to what steps to take when possible violations are uncovered. In this context, the question arises as to whether counsel should accept the facts as they are presented or, alternatively, whether she has a duty to inquire. Not surprisingly, the facts and circumstances of a particular situation will determine the proper course of action.[19]

Particularly when "red flags" are raised, inside counsel should be cautious when advising on the basis of facts furnished by a corporate manager with whom he deals. In other words, certain circumstances should call for a duty to inquire. If in-house counsel conducts the necessary inquiry and renders advice accordingly, it normally is implemented. However, in instances where such advice is disregarded and the situation at hand

---

[18] *Id.* at 1101. Another issue related to client identification is whether in-house counsel may represent corporate constituents in addition to the corporate entity. Although the organization is technically the counsel's client, dual representation is generally allowed pursuant to Model Rule 1.7. *See also, infra* notes 27–30 and accompanying text.

[19] *See* Ferrara & Steinberg, *The Role of Inside Counsel in the Corporate Accountability Process,* 4 Corp. L. Rev. 3, 12 (1981); Williams, note 3 *supra.*

involves a crime or fraud likely to result in substantial harm to the business enterprise, counsel must take affirmative action. In such situations, as set forth in ABA Model Rule 1.13, "the lawyer shall refer the matter to higher authority in the organization, including, if warranted by the circumstances, to the highest authority [i.e., the corporation's board of directors] that can act on behalf of the organization as determined by applicable law."[20] If the board of directors insists upon action that constitutes a clear violation of law and that is likely to cause substantial injury to the corporation, the attorney would be prudent to resign.[21] Additionally, the ABA Model Rules, the SEC Standards of Conduct for Attorneys, and many state ethical rules permit counsel to disclose the corporate client's illegality to a shareholder or to a third party, such as a government regulatory authority (e.g., the SEC, EPA, FTC) under certain circumstances.[22]

It should be noted that resignation in such circumstances certainly is a drastic step, resulting in loss of employment, but nonetheless may be required under the ethical standards discussed above. Proceedings against in-house attorneys brought by the Securities and Exchange Commission (SEC) illustrate this dilemma. As the SEC has pointed out, inside counsel may be charged with both ethical and supervisory responsibilities under the federal securities laws. In such circumstances, in-house counsel cannot simply advise corporate personnel and then decline to ascertain whether such advice is being implemented. Rather, counsel must remain alert to

---

[20]   Model Rules of Prof. Conduct, Rule 1.13(b). Pursuant to the Sarbanes-Oxley Act of 2002 (SOX), the SEC by rule must:

> (1)   requir[e] [a subject] attorney to report evidence of a material violation of securities law or breach of fiduciary duty or similar violation by the company or any agent thereof, to the chief legal counsel or the chief executive officer of the company (or the equivalent thereof); and
>
> (2)   if the counsel or officer does not appropriately respond to the evidence (adopting, as necessary, appropriate remedial measures or sanctions with respect to the violation), requir[e] [such] attorney to report the evidence to the audit committee of the board of directors of the issuer or to another committee of the board of directors comprised solely of directors not employed directly or indirectly by the issuer, or to the board of directors.

This statute and the SEC Standards of Conduct for Attorneys, implemented pursuant to SOX's directive, are discussed in another chapter of the book.

[21]   *See* Model Rule 1.16(a)(1).

[22]   *See id.* Rule 1.13(c).

developments and, if corrective measures are not taken, must climb the corporate ladder. If the ultimate decision-maker embodying the corporate client—the board of directors—fails to take appropriate action, counsel's practical recourse is resignation.[23]

In sum, inside counsel must be careful not to become a participant in the client's illegality.[24] Generally, provided that the client listens in good faith to the advice given, counsel should not be obligated to resign when a legitimate question exists regarding the legality of corporate conduct. In such circumstances, inside counsel's "energies should be channeled into advising and prompting corporate management and the board of directors to engage in conduct that is both legal and ethical."[25]

Dealing with "Suspected" Employees

Another troubling issue arises when inside counsel learns that a corporate employee has allegedly violated the law. In this context, counsel may give the employee "quasi-Miranda" warnings to the effect that:

> (a) [counsel's] role is to represent the organization; (b) an actual or potential conflict of interest may exist between the organization and the individual; (c) [counsel] cannot represent the individual; (d) their conversation may not be confidential and any information the individual provides may be used

---

[23]   *See In re Gutfreund,* [1992 Transfer Binder] CCH Fed. Sec. L. Rep. ¶ 85,067 (SEC 1992); *In re Carter,* [1981 Transfer Binder] CCH Fed. Sec. L. Rep. ¶ 82,847 (SEC 1981).

[24]   *See, e.g., SEC v. National Student Mktg. Corp.,* 457 F. Supp. 682 (D.D.C. 1978); Callcott & Slonecke*r, A Review of SEC Actions Against Lawyers,* 42 Rev. Sec. & Comm. Reg. 71 (2009); Kim, *Inside Counsel: Friends or Gatekeepers?,* 84 Fordham L. Rev. 1867 (2016).

[25]   Ferrara & Steinberg, *supra* note 19, at 22. *See* M. Steinberg & R. Ferrara, *Securities Practice: Federal and State Enforcement* §§ 4:27–4:28 (2d ed. 2001 & 2019–2020 supp.); Millstein, *The Professional Board,* 50 Bus. Law. 1427, 1431 (1995) ("Lawyers . . . understand that in most circumstances they render advice, and that taking or leaving that advice is the client's role. The limit is when the lawyer's professional responsibilities require him or her to act when the advice is ignored.").

against [such individual]; and (e) he [or she] may wish to retain independent counsel.[26]

Decades ago, a number of inside counsel argued against conveying these warnings to a suspected erring employee, reasoning that so doing would not be in the corporation's interest.[27] Today, the clearly prevailing approach posits that failure to provide these warnings may subject counsel to increased liability exposure, particularly where the employee has a reasonable belief that counsel is personally representing the employee. For example, according to ABA Model Rule 1.13(f), counsel has the responsibility of explaining to a non-client constituent the identity of her client (namely, that she represents the corporation) when such counsel knows or reasonably should know that the corporation's interests are adverse to those of such non-client constituent. Counsel also may be obligated to expressly communicate to the non-client that she does not represent such individual.[28] Failure to provide such disclosure may subject the attorney to liability for failure to warn.[29] Moreover, in certain jurisdictions—if the employee reasonably believes that the corporation's lawyer represents the employee personally—an attorney-client relationship may be implicated, thereby signifying that such communications between counsel and the employee may be deemed confidential.[30]

---

[26]   Martin, *When Corporate Counsel Get Caught in the Middle*, Cal. Law., Dec. 1989, at 75.

[27]   *See, e.g.,* Aibel, *supra* note 2, 59 Mo. L. Rev. at 438–439.

[28]   *See* Model Rules of Prof. Conduct, Rule 1.13(f).

[29]   *See Parker v. Carnahan*, 772 S.W. 2d 151, 157 (Tex. App. 1989) (stating that "an attorney can be held negligent where he fails to advise a party that he is not representing him . . . where the circumstances lead the party to believe that the attorney is representing him").

[30]   *See, e.g., Westinghouse Elec. Corp. v. Kerr-McGee Corp.,* 580 F.2d 1311 (7th Cir. 1978). *Cf. United States v. Ruehle,* 583 F.3d 600, 609 (9th Cir. 2009) (stating that employee-interviewee's statements made to corporate counsel during an internal investigation interview not within the attorney-client privilege due to that the "statements made to the [attorneys] were not made in confidence but rather for the purpose of disclosure to outside auditors"); *In re Grand Jury Subpoena Under Seal,* 415 F. 3d 333 (4th Cir. 2005) (concluding that employee interviewed in internal investigation did not have an attorney-client relationship with legal counsel who was conducting the interview).

Inside Counsel's Liability Exposure

In addition to the issues arising from in-house counsel's unique employment relationship, counsel also should be aware of potential liability concerns under common and statutory (e.g., securities) law. Indeed, securities law claims, as well as malpractice, negligent misrepresentation, aiding and abetting, and breach of fiduciary duty allegations may be of significant concern, due to in-house counsel's principal involvement in drafting key corporate documents (such as transactional documents, corporate filings, lending agreements, and legal opinions).[31] Obviously, counsel should seek to ensure that the information which she uses to draft the documents is correct. In certain situations, this objective may signify that counsel has an affirmative duty of inquiry.[32] For example, in *FDIC v. O'Melveny & Myers*,[33] a case involving outside counsel who had prepared securities offering documents and who had relied solely on information provided by the client company's internal participants, the Ninth Circuit held that under the circumstances presented securities counsel was to have made a reasonable, independent investigation in order to detect and correct materially false or misleading statements.[34]

Role Within the Boardroom

It is also important to consider in-house counsel's role within the boardroom. Generally, it is essential for counsel to comprehend the business dynamics of the enterprise and possess the acumen to understand the economics of the transaction or

---

[31]   *See generally* M. Steinberg, *Attorney Liability After Sarbanes-Oxley* (2018); Webb et al., *Understanding and Avoiding Corporate and Executive Criminal Liability*, 49 Bus. Law. 617 (1994). Note also that in-house attorneys, unlike outside counsel, may incur liability as aiders under state law pursuant to the Uniform Securities Act. *See* Steinberg & Ames, *From the Regulatory Abyss: The Weakened Gatekeeping Incentives Under the Uniform Securities Act*, 35 Yale L. & Pol. Rev. 1 (2016).

[32]   Olson, *supra* note 12, 7 U. Miami Bus. L. Rev. at 4 (quoting Snow, et. al, *Defending Securities Class Actions*, C123 A.L.I.-A.B.A. Course of Study, June 2, 1995, at 710). In-house counsel may have a greater duty to inquire than outside counsel because in-house lawyers have greater access to corporate information. *Id.*

[33]   969 F.2d 744 (9th Cir. 1992), *rev'd on other grounds*, 512 U.S. 79 (1994).

[34]   *See* 969 F.2d at 748–749. *See also,* Olson, *supra* note 12, 7 U. Miami Bus. L. Rev. at 32.

other matter being considered.[35] Counsel's role also encompasses the implementation of internal governance procedures to reduce the threat of subsequent litigation. In this regard, the business judgment rule serves as an impressive shield to deflect otherwise successful challenges to board action.[36]

In this context, process is key. If the board abides by an acceptable procedural framework, courts will be reluctant to second-guess a deliberative decision reached in good faith by a reasonably informed and independent board.[37] Hence, inside counsel's role here is to guide the board through this process, building a fortress that will protect the decision from successful attack.

In conflict of interest transactions,[38] such as interested director transactions with a controlling shareholder, parent-subsidiary mergers, and leveraged buy-outs engineered by incumbent management, even more attention to process frequently will be necessitated. In such situations, establishment of a committee comprised of the disinterested directors may be called for, as well as appointment of special outside counsel for the committee.[39] As decisions such as

---

[35]   See Creedon, *Lawyer and Executive—The Role of the General Counsel*, 39 Bus. Law. 25 (1983); *How Agile is Your Legal Department?*, Corp. Legal Times, No. 45, Aug. 1995, at 40. See generally Symposium, *Business Lawyering and Value Creation for Clients*, 74 Or. L. Rev. No. 1 (1995).

[36]   Stated succinctly, the business judgment rule has four components. First, the board of directors must focus on the issue and make a deliberative decision. Second, the board's decision must be adequately informed (with gross negligence being the applicable standard). In this regard, the board should be provided with adequate information, including pertinent reports, appraisals, and other material documents central to the transaction or other matter at issue. Once having such information before it, the board should take the time necessary to reach an informed decision. Third, directors making the board's determination must be independent and disinterested, signifying that they are not engaged in self-dealing, do not have a disproportionate financial stake in the transaction, and are not under the control or domination of a director who has such a disabling conflict of interest. Last, the decision must have a rational basis or, stated differently, must be made without gross negligence. See, e.g., *Aronson v. Lewis*, 473 A.2d 805, 812 (Del. 1984); American Law Institute, *Principles of Corporate Governance: Analysis and Recommendations* § 4.01 (1994).

[37]   See *ALI Principles of Corporate Governance*, supra note 36, § 4.01 & cmts. See also, *In re Walt Disney Company Derivative Litigation*, 906 A.2d 27 (Del. 2006).

[38]   In conflict of interest transactions, the intrinsic fairness test generally is the applicable standard. See, e.g., *Weinberger v. UOP, Inc.*, 457 A.2d 701 (Del. 1983).

[39]   See, e.g., *Flood v. Synutra International, Inc.*, 195 A.3d 754 (Del. 2018); *Kahn v. M&F Worldwide Corp.*, 88 A.3d 635 (Del. 2014); *Rosenblatt v. Getty Oil Co.*, 493 A.2d 929 (Del. 1985).

THE ROLE OF INSIDE COUNSEL

Weinberger v. UOP, Inc.[40] illustrate, deficiency in process accompanied by the specter of overreaching by the control group heightens the risk that the transaction (or its terms) will be successfully challenged. To allay this prospect, participation by reasonably informed outside directors who have sufficient leverage to negotiate with the control group in an effective manner will dissuade a court from upsetting the subject transaction.[41] Playing a key role in this setting, inside counsel orchestrates the process in such a manner as to hopefully further the best interests of the corporation, shareholders, and other affected constituencies.[42]

Law Compliance Role

In-house lawyers also play a pivotal role in the practice of preventive law by facilitating the implementation of effective and operational law compliance programs. In corporations with multifaceted operations, law compliance programs may cover such diverse areas as antitrust, environmental policies, FCPA (Foreign Corrupt Practices Act), employment and hiring practices, intellectual property, and corporate/securities.[43] When rendering advice with respect to law compliance, inside counsel may consider the following:

1. Although no system is "bullet-proof," the corporation should keep in mind that, if a violation were to occur, it would have the burden of showing that its law compliance program (Program) is reasonably effective.

2. The corporation's board of directors should adopt the Program, and the Program should be administered under the board's supervision as an integral part of its monitoring function. On a periodic basis, the board should review the Program for possible revision.

---

[40] 457 A.2d 701 (Del. 1983).

[41] *See* M. Steinberg, *Securities Regulation: Liabilities and Remedies* § 15.04 (2019); cases cited note 39 *supra*.

[42] With respect to the interests of other constituencies, *see, e.g., Symposium, Corporate Malaise—Stakeholder Statutes: Cause or Cure?*, 21 Stetson L. Rev. No. 1 (1991).

[43] American Bar Association, *Corporate Director's Guidebook—Sixth Edition*, 66 Bus. Law. 975, 999–1000 (2011).

3. The Program's scope should reflect the nature of the enterprise's business and the legal issues such enterprise realistically may face. Given the economic practicalities involved and with the proviso that the law must be obeyed, an objective cost/benefit analysis normally is appropriate. Certainly, an enterprise engaged in several different businesses with operations abroad should be expected to develop a more extensive program than one with purely local operations specializing in a particular product market.

4. The Program (such as a Code of Conduct) should be disseminated to and understood by all affected company personnel.

5. To integrate the Program into the corporation's culture and to help ensure continued personnel compliance, educational sessions should be conducted on a periodic basis. Moreover, consideration should be given to the question whether affected personnel should be required to certify annually that they have complied with the applicable Code of Conduct.

6. The Program should be effectively administered. In this regard, the enterprise should not adopt any non-essential aspect of a prospective Program that it cannot feasibly implement.

7. The Program should be subject to adequate internal enforcement, such as spot checks, board of director (or delegated committee) review, "whistleblower" procedures, and the taking of meaningful disciplinary action against those who fail to comply.[44]

In sum, inside counsel's role in helping to administer and oversee an enterprise's law compliance program is critical and reduces the risk of significant liability exposure.

---

[44] Steinberg, 19 Sec. Reg. L. J. 323 (1992); Aibel, *supra* note 2, at 59 Mo. L. Rev. at 435–439; McLucas, Wertheimer & June, *Preparing for the Deluge: How to Respond When Employees Speak Up and Report Possible Compliance Violations,* 44 Sec. Reg. & L. Rep. (BNA) 922 (2012); Pitt & Groskaufmanis, *Minimizing Corporate Civil and Criminal Liability: A Second Look at Corporate Codes of Conduct*, 78 Geo. L.J. 1559 (1990). Note that the federal criminal sentencing guidelines deem a subject company's establishment and implementation of a reasonably effective law compliance program to be a mitigating factor in the assessment of an appropriate sentence. *See* United States Sentencing Commission, U.S. Sentencing Guidelines Manual §§ 8B2.1, 8C2.5. While the guidelines were declared unconstitutional in *Blakely v. Washington,* 542 U.S. 296 (2004), they nonetheless continue to be persuasive with the federal courts.

The following materials focus on the role of inside counsel.

BECOMING IN-HOUSE COUNSEL*

Association of Corporate Counsel

I. An Introduction to Serving as In-House Counsel

The CEO of Reebok once quipped to his general counsel, "I hate lawyers—not you, Jack; you don't count." This anecdote typifies the widely held notion that corporate counsel is a breed apart from other attorneys. This begs the question, "What exactly is an in-house lawyer?" Are they attorneys or are they merely corporate employees? What is their function within the corporate structure and to whom do they owe a duty of loyalty? What is their correct title? This [discussion] will answer these questions, and address common notions and misperceptions about the identity of in-house counsel and their role in a corporate entity.

A. What is an In-House Lawyer?

Simply stated, an in-house lawyer is an employee who works as an attorney for the corporation. The in-house lawyer, like any other employee, serves primarily to advance the needs of the business. The in-house counsel acts in a professional capacity as an attorney and, as such, is subject to the rules and regulations governing the practice of law.

[In a number of] corporate law departments, attorneys fall within one of two groups: senior counsel (including general counsel and other senior level attorneys with oversight responsibilities) and staff attorneys. The law department is headed by the General Counsel (GC), who [often] also serves as the Chief Legal Officer of the company. The GC typically advises the Board of Directors and the corporation's officers in all legal proceedings. The GC often reports directly to the Chief Executive Officer and is considered an essential component of the management team.

---

*   Association of Corporate Counsel, "Becoming In-House Counsel: A Guide for Law Students and Recent Graduates", ACC InfoPAK (December 2013). Reprinted with the permission of the Association of Corporate Counsel, www.acc.com/.

Senior attorneys are charged with supervising lower-level staff attorneys, advising the company in one particular field of law, or supporting the GC in coordination with outside counsel on litigation matters. Staff attorneys . . . are typically assigned research-oriented tasks or are asked to provide support for the senior staff attorneys. A [number of] law departments have removed this hierarchy by eliminating these titles. . . .

. . . In-house counsel is more than just a legal adviser to a corporation or entity; in-house attorneys affect the full range of that body's decisions. While counsel will typically have a greater investment in the legalities of the decision-making process than with the substantive implications of the companies' business strategy, knowledge of the latter is essential for counsel to effectively protect the company's legal interests.

B. Who is the Client?

Unlike lawyers at a typical law firm, in-house counsel have one and only one client—the corporation. They do not represent the board of directors, principal officers or other individuals, even though those individuals act on behalf of the corporation. As Model Rule 1.13(a) provides, "A lawyer employed or retained by an organization represents the organization acting through its duly authorized constituents."

The parameters of counsel's representation is clear, and the Model Rules take pains to emphasize that the in-house counsel must advance the interests of the corporation above those of the individual officers. Model Rule 1.13(b) goes so far as to impose an affirmative obligation on in-house counsel to advance the needs of the corporation over that of an individual officer or director if the latter is in conflict with the corporations' best interests. . . .

In light of [federal] legislation such as the Sarbanes-Oxley Act, in-house counsel is now, more than ever, being held responsible for actions taken by corporate officers or directors that cause harm to the corporation and/or outside entities or individuals.

C. What Are the Duties of In-House Counsel?

Until the 1970's, corporate counsel functioned essentially as conduits between their employer, the corporation, and outside law firms. With work confined primarily to corporate housekeeping and other routine matters, the corporate attorney was little more than glorified middle management with a law degree. However, the rising cost of legal services has seen an expansion of corporate counsel's responsibilities to the point where in-house counsel now are able to cherry-pick what they want to do and give the "boring stuff" to outside firms. Now, as many organizations have legal departments that rival law firms in both size and qualification, more and more corporate matters are being handled in-house.

In-house counsel in small legal departments of less than ten lawyers may be exposed to a practice that encompasses a wide range of issues on a regular basis. In contrast, lawyers in large in-house departments are usually assigned to work in a single practice area within a specific practice group.

In-house attorneys affect the full range of corporate law. Practice areas include antitrust law, international trade, corporate securities, tax, real estate, government contracts, ethics, privacy, and intellectual property as well as the standard contracts and employment law issues. The in-house counsel serves as a trusted advisor in areas that may extend beyond a strictly legal role. The exact role that counsel will play within the corporation often varies depending on the individual relationships formed between counsel and corporate officers.

Without the guarantee of more and new business around the corner, the primary duties of in-house counsel take on greater importance as a company's ability to manage risks is jeopardized. Experts state that four of the biggest issues on the minds of in-house counsel [include]: controlling litigation costs; satisfying new corporate governance rules, including Sarbanes-Oxley; diminished insurance coverage and rising premiums; and potential liabilities arising from workforce terminations.

[The] primary duties of in-house counsel [include:]

- Foster [the company's] corporate conscience and set the tone for its ethical culture;

- Implement legal educational responsibilities of management and employees;

- Handle day-to-day corporate legal affairs;

- Select and supervise outside counsel;

- Effect corporate housekeeping; [and]

- Supervise the relationship with outside auditors.

1. Legal Duties

The goal of the in-house counsel [includes] to plan for the future of the corporation, institute measures to prevent future litigation, and monitor the activity of the organization and its employees. In-house counsel endeavors to ensure that the organization is in compliance with all applicable laws and protects the legal rights of the corporation from abuse by others. Recent corporate scandals and the passage of the Sarbanes-Oxley [and Dodd-Frank] Act[s] have made these responsibilities among the most significant of the tasks performed by in-house counsel.

While much of the in-house counsel's work is to avoid litigation, sometimes it cannot be avoided. Whether it is in pursuit of protecting the corporation's rights or defending it from lawsuits, in-house counsel must be prepared to oversee all litigation matters. Often, counsel will work with outside law firm attorneys preparing and defending the company from suits. However, the in-house counsel is usually involved in all stages of litigation, from the discovery process through settlement negotiations or trial.

2. Business Duties

It is imperative that in-house counsel fully understand the complexities of a company's business as well as the respective industry to best serve their client. In-house counsel has the luxury of being able to approach business problems without having ultimate responsibility for resolving the matters. This objectivity enables counsel to contribute meaningful suggestions to be used in resolving complicated business questions. In-house counsel can utilize their unique position within the organization's structure to play an integral role in the strategic planning of the company's business. Counsel can provide legal insight that might otherwise never be addressed from more business-oriented directors.

D. Non-Legal Function Within the Corporation

In-house counsel are not constrained in their opportunities for advancement within a corporation. The significance of a legal degree in today's corporate environment is invaluable, enabling counsel to move from a strictly legal position to one in the upper levels of corporate management such as Chief Executive Officer (CEO), Chief Financial Officer (CFO) or a member of the Board of Directors. In [an] ACC poll, 11 percent of in-house counsel respondents served as CEO, six percent served as CFO, and another seven percent served as Chief Operating Officer. In addition, 5 percent served as head of a business unit and almost 25 percent served as head of a Human Resources Department. By combining knowledge and understanding of the legal side of the business with a strong grasp for the business operations of a company, in-house lawyers can maximize their own value to the corporate entity. It is this value which eventually leads to advancement outside of the legal department.

II. Why Become an In-House Attorney?

Flexibility and predictability are factors that make working for a corporation more attractive than the lifestyle common to the large firm attorney. As one ACC member said, "The beauty of in-house counsel is that every day brings new challenges and experiences" without the stress of billable hours.

A. Hands-on Law Experience

While first-year associates at a law firm are likely to be placed in a group specializing in one area of law, [many] in-house counsel have the opportunity to handle matters that cross the spectrum of legal issues. Whether it involves a relatively simple contract law issue or complex civil litigation, an in-house attorney must be prepared for the multitude of legal issues that present themselves. Corporate legal departments offer substantial opportunities for hands-on experience in litigation matters. Even in situations where a corporate entity retains outside counsel, the in-house lawyer continues to play a substantive role in the matter.

B.   Concentration on the Client

Corporate counsel is responsible for one client—the corporation. The lack of divergent and/or conflicting alliances benefits both counsel and the corporation. Individual attorneys never need to assume the role of rainmaker, or concern themselves with bringing new business into the firm. Eliminating this responsibility allows attorneys to focus their energy and efforts completely on the corporate client. Not only does this create a less stressful working environment for counsel, it benefits the corporation because it receives the full attention of its attorneys. This focus also allows counsel to understand the dynamics of the company, and fosters an intimate familiarity with the full range of issues faced by the corporation. This insight is integral to counsel's ability to proactively protect the company's legal interest and craft the most aggressive and effective defense in the event of litigation.

C.   Opportunities for Growth

Attorneys working in a firm are often driven by their desire to become a partner. "Seven [or more] years or out" is a common phrase young attorneys hear as they advance up the firm ladder. Failure to make partner means that a young attorney will be forced to move on, as the firm will prefer to focus on more "promising" attorneys. Unlike firm attorneys however, the career advancement of corporate attorneys does not follow such a rigorous and inflexible schedule. Because corporations and businesses do not organize their legal departments in hierarchies that require employees to rise to the top of one particular field, in-house attorneys tend to have more varied promotional opportunities. This potential for advancement is due in large part to counsels' direct and daily working relationship with corporate officers.

As corporations seek to reduce legal costs, they are increasingly turning to in-house counsel to handle legal issues. The reliance has, in turn, led to a greater need for corporate counsel, who now handle more complex matters. While junior associates may spend their first few years working on large document reviews or writing memos for more senior attorneys, even the most junior in-house counsel will enjoy the dual benefits of having daily contact with the client and working on substantive issues. Engaging in the legal side of the business allows young in-house counsel to gain greater insight into the corporation itself, while also increasing their knowledge of the business world. While law firm attorneys restrict their focus to legal issues, in-house counsel must be aware of the business ramifications when providing advice. The multi-faceted nature of corporate counsel's responsibilities allows counsel to enhance their experience base and foster their ability to meet the needs of their corporate client.

D. Women as Corporate Counsel

The opportunity for women to rise to positions of prominence within corporate legal departments has never been greater than it is today. According to ACC's In-House Counsel census, [approximately one-third] of in-house attorneys are women. Currently, of ACC's members who serve as their respective organization's General Counsel or Chief Legal Officer, . . . [approximately one-quarter] are women. . . .

. . . .

E. Quality of Life

In general, the greatest benefit that corporate attorneys possess over their firm brethren is the high "quality of life." The predictability of in-house counsel's work environment is invaluable: the lack of mandatory billable hours, the absence of responsibility for cultivating new clients and the elimination of a partner track distinguish the in-house profession from that experienced by attorneys at firms.

Don't be fooled, however. Working as in-house counsel is no cakewalk. Depending on the particular corporate entity, some in-house counsel's hours may rival those of any law firm associate. The increase in the use of email, voicemail and [other electronic means of communication] has led clients and senior attorneys to demand answers to their questions or concerns 24 hours a day, seven days a week. The use of technology has led to increased pressure for lawyers to provide a fast turn-around to legal questions. In the end though, as many counsel have reported, it is the ability to have more control over those hours that separates the life of an in-house counsel from that of a law firm associate.

With the parity between some in-house positions and firm life in some cases, why don't more in-house counsel jump ship? While the lure of six figure salaries and expense accounts may seem to be a natural draw for those working in corporate legal departments, the fact is that only seven percent of in-house counsel would leave their corporate position to become a partner at a large law firm.

While in-house counsel do not necessarily work fewer hours than attorneys in firms as a rule, they do function in a work environment free from the pressing demands of billable hours that drive law firms. In an informal survey of ACC members, in-house counsel reported working on average 50 hours a week.

This ability to predict and control a work schedule makes an in-house corporate position particularly attractive to individuals with families. The growing acceptance in the corporate culture of alternative work schedules—flex-time, telecommuting, part-time and job sharing—makes in-house counsel positions particularly attractive.

Again, however, avoid painting all corporate counsel opportunities with a broad brush. While this more relaxed environment is common for many in-house attorneys, it is by no means standard for all in-house positions. Thus, when researching possible corporate legal positions, it is important to talk with attorneys currently employed by the company and explore whether the corporate expectations comport with your own goals. These individuals can provide valuable insight into the lifestyle and work environment fostered by the corporation. . . .

The best testament to the quality of life of an in-house counsel can be found in the words of in-house counsel:

- "A typical day involves so many different facets of law and management that it makes the job fun."

- "I spend most of my working time in the office. Very little travel or outside meetings."

- "I will work until Noon and then I try to head to the gym for an hour. I have a light lunch at my desk and leave at about 5:00 P.M."

III. The Downside of In-House Practice

A. Lower Pay

On average, in-house attorneys earn less than their law firm counterparts. . . .

A further drag on in-house counsel salaries is the fact that, unlike firm partners, corporate attorneys do not share in the profits of the corporation. While their salary and bonus structure may earn them significant compensation, their salaries will never rival those earned by top attorneys in private practice. Companies used to offer stock options as an incentive to attract and retain quality in-house counsel; however, such offerings are now [less common]. . . .

B. Isolation from Other Lawyers

A majority of corporate law departments maintain a legal staff that numbers in the single digits. In fact, almost 22 percent of law departments are staffed by a solo practitioner; 38 percent of departments have between two to five attorneys; nearly 25 percent of organizations employ between six to 20 in-house counsel; and 15 percent of law departments have 21 or more attorneys.

Perhaps the greatest disadvantage of being the sole attorney for a corporation is that such an arrangement has the potential to foster a sense of isolation from other attorneys. Because counsel's ability to bounce ideas off other attorneys may be limited by the size of the corporate legal department, it is wise for in-house counsel to secure membership in organizations such as ACC. The ACC Chapters and Committees provide forums through which members (and non-members) can network with their peers. Utilizing ACC's database of sample forms, articles and informational packages allows a single attorney or small law department to operate as if they had a large legal research group at their fingertips.

C. Moving On—Once In-House, Always In-House?

Attorneys who become in-house counsel after leaving private firms often worry about whether they will be able to transition back to a law firm. While it is unclear what percentage of lawyers seek to move back to firms after serving as in-house counsel, the desire to move back can be daunting for mid-level attorneys. Law firms are designed around "the partner-track"—that mythical career path that ends with attorneys becoming partners in the firm. For lawyers who leave a firm to serve as in-house counsel, this path is not easily retraced. While the individual attorney may be gaining valuable experience working within the corporate environment, he or she will need to demonstrate an ability to bring clients, and thus revenue, into the firm.

Senior-level corporate attorneys may face less difficulty moving back into [a law] firm as they are often brought on as either a partner or a senior attorney. Their knowledge base, contacts, and expertise are assets sought by law firms, and make them valuable lateral additions to any legal staff.

Of course, in-house counsel's decision to leave his or her position may not be a matter of election, but one of necessity. While some law firms do go out of business, it is more common for a corporation to fold. Thus, it is important to thoroughly investigate the long-term stability of any corporation before accepting a position in its in-house legal department.

[In summary:]

Advantages of Becoming In-House Counsel:

- Close to the business management and decisions;
- Increasingly complex and more sophisticated practice than private practice;
- Broader practice, generally speaking (this can vary);
- Hours can be better regulated (though not necessarily less than private firm hours);
- Greater direct exposure for advice and decisions; [and]
- Less stress and pressure due to lack of billable hours, [client development, and] partner track.

Disadvantages of In-House Counsel:

- Compensation is generally less;

- Perceptions of the quality of the practice and of the practitioners can vary widely;

- Resources are usually not as great as in a large firm;

- Isolation—[may have] fewer colleagues to consult on ideas; [and]

- Career tied to the fortune of the company.

. . . .

The following critique provides a distinctly less optimistic portrayal of practicing as an in-house lawyer.

THE 'DARK SIDE' OF GOING IN HOUSE*
By Harrison Barnes (BCG Attorney Search)

The purpose of this article is to provide you with insight as to whether or not you should go in-house. Many attorneys claim that going in-house was their best career move. Conversely, some attorneys claim it was their biggest career mistake. In the end, going in-house is entirely up to you. You need to understand, however, that the decision to go in-house is one of the most significant career decisions you will ever make as an attorney.

On the plus side, many attorneys go in-house for more interesting work, shorter hours, potentially lucrative stock options, and the opportunity to be on the business side in a corporate environment. Depending upon the in-house environment, these reasons for going in-house may be entirely justified in all respects, and you may find yourself in an ideal situation. Yet, there are several little-known facts about going in-house that may not necessarily make it the best career decision for you:

- It is extremely difficult to get another law firm job once you have gone in-house;

---

* Reprinted with the permission of Harrison Barnes and BCG Attorney Search.

- The overwhelming majority of attorneys do not reap an economic windfall when they go in-house;

- It is very difficult to move to another in-house job once you have gone in-house;

- Your legal skills are likely to deteriorate once you go in-house; and,

- You may have to work as hard in-house as you did in a law firm.

A. *It is extremely difficult to get another law firm job once you have gone in-house*

A significant portion of the attorneys contacting us [an attorney search firm] are attorneys whose most recent experience is in an in-house legal department. We rarely are able to help these attorneys transition into a law firm because law firms simply do not want them, regardless of how good of a law school they went to or how stellar their last law firm was. The market tells the story: Once you go in-house, you had better understand that you will be very unlikely to ever practice law with a large law firm ever again.

. . . .

We . . . estimate that at least 60% of . . . attorneys attempted to return to law firms after losing their jobs inside corporations. Out of this 60%, we estimate that less than 20% landed at law firms even arguably approaching the prestige level of the law firms they left to go in-house and that less than 50% were successful in getting another job with a law firm at all. . . .

While there are certainly exceptions, once you go in-house, you are likely to become more of a generalist than a specialist. While the idea of being a generalist may be something that appeals to you, you also need to understand that the skills of a generalist will certainly not serve you well if you ever choose to go back to a law firm. Most law firms demand their attorneys specialize very early in their careers and continue as specialists in one practice group or another throughout their careers. As a generalist, you will be an expert in nothing. While you may find it more interesting to participate in several different types of work, over time, you will simply be making yourself increasingly unmarketable to law firms.

Going in-house is something that jeopardizes the type of growth law firms expect attorneys to demonstrate throughout their careers. In short, law firms want attorneys to be committed to their methods of practicing law. Going in-house is not an action that law firms consider something that demonstrates your commitment to their method of practicing law. When you decided to go in-house, you radically put yourself off the track of training, growth, and development from a law firm's perspective. More significantly, you have sent the message to future potential law firm employers that you are not committed to their way of practicing law.

None of this is to say that you will never work in a law firm again if you go in-house. Many patent prosecutors, real estate attorneys, and other types of attorneys can become extremely specialized and receive excellent training in an in-house environment. There are, in fact, some very well respected in-house legal departments throughout the United States. In addition, if you reach the role of a General Counsel in an important corporation (like Disney or General Motors), you may actually become an extremely hot commodity among law firms because of your connections and the fact that you will likely be able to parlay this into significant business for the law firm once you join it. Many attorneys have successfully moved from important in-house legal environments to partner roles within the most significant international law firms after several decades in-house.

B.   *You Are Unlikely to Reap an Economic Windfall if You Go In-House*

Many attorneys who went in-house during the tech boom were under the impression that they were invincible. Some were. It was not uncommon for third- or fourth-year associates in the Bay Area who went in-house from 1997–1999 to have cashed out stock options worth $1,000,000 or several times more after less than two years in an in-house environment. In fact, this happened enough times that many attorneys were under the impression that if they went in-house, this result was all but inevitable. The results these attorneys were able to achieve with their careers in such a short period of time are nothing less than remarkable. These results were also unparalleled at any other time in the history of the legal profession.

Corporate attorneys, in particular, were in massive demand, and these attorneys were receiving calls—often several times per day—from recruiters seeking to place them in both corporations and law firms. Wanting fewer hours and stock options and having a certain vision of what going in-house meant, attorneys flocked to start-up companies (often companies with no revenue model) in the belief that they would quickly be rich. The fact is, however, that these success stories were (and continue to be) less common than believed.

We would estimate that fewer than 1 in 50 attorneys who left prestigious law firms ever ended up making more in their time in-house (through a combination of stock options and salary) than they would have made had they remained in their respective law firms and not gone in-house. None of this even takes into account that a substantial number of these attorneys who did not experience fortune after going in-house left the practice of law completely after being unable to successfully find alternative legal employment after losing their in-house positions. In terms of a cost-benefit analysis, if you were to analyze the potential incomes these attorneys gave up over the courses of their legal careers by going in-house, the differential between the numbers would likely be staggering.

. . . .

C. *It is Very Difficult to Get Another In-House Job Once You Go In-House*

The difficulty of getting a job in another law firm once you have gone in-house may be surpassed only by the difficulty of getting another in-house counsel position. Typically, some of the most attractive candidates to in-house employers are the attorneys inside the law firms that handle their legal work. These attorneys are already familiar with the Company, have established relationships with key players inside the Company, and are trusted legal advisors who cost the Company a great deal of money. The idea of bringing these already trusted attorneys inside the Company and saving the Company money is something that is certainly an attractive prospect to many companies. In our experience, most attorneys who go in-house are hired by their former clients.

In theory, it would be excellent if everyone could go to work for one employer and remain there until retirement. Nevertheless, this is not a socialistic or communist country, and companies go out of business, legal departments are downsized, and companies decide they no longer want an in-house legal department. The fact is that you will be extremely unlikely to remain in the same in-house job throughout your career and will in all probability need to seek alternative in-house employment at some point in time. In searching for your next in-house legal job, you will not have the luxury of being a bright-eyed attorney being wooed by your client. Instead, you will need to hit the street and start tracking down these jobs on your own. When you have a family, friends in the area, kids in a local school, and a mortgage, this may not be something that appeals to you all that much.

. . . .

D.   Once You Go In-House, Your Skills Are Likely to Deteriorate

Very few attorneys realize just how much their skills are likely to deteriorate once they go in-house. A large portion of the responsibility of many in-house attorneys is to farm out challenging work to the appropriate law firms. Therefore, once you go in-house, you will often cease doing sophisticated legal work and instead merely hand off work to law firms. For some attorneys, this is the ideal job. For other attorneys, this is not an ideal job because they no longer work directly on challenging legal work.

If you are at a Company doing an IPO, an outside law firm— and not you—will likely be responsible for the IPO. If your company is involved in significant litigation, almost always an outside law firm—and not you—will be the one drafting the motions, doing discovery, and going to court. All of this should make it obvious that a great deal of the learning and refinement of your legal skills that occurs inside a law firm stops once you go in-house. It is unlikely you will stay abreast of the law once you are in-house because you will have no reason to. Because you will be doing less hands-on work and will be exposed to fewer nuts and bolts of practicing law, your skills will gradually deteriorate.

E.   *You May Have to Work as Hard In-House as in a Law Firm*

With some exceptions, in-house attorneys most often do not have to work as hard as their counterparts at firms. This is one of the better reasons for going in-house. It is your life, and being in-house can release you from much of the pressure of the billable hour requirement and other stresses of being in a law firm. In addition, being in-house typically has more predictable hours. We have no doubt that working in a law firm can often be incredibly stressful. In large law firms, many attorneys are plagued by divorce or substance abuse and spend little time with their children. Indeed, many attorneys in large law firms consider anything that does not relate directly to the practice of law as something that is a distraction, even if it is spending time with family. An in-house environment can often give you your life back.

However, a job in-house is often not the utopian environment described above. We often encounter lawyers whose primary goal in a career change is to reduce the pressure of billable hour requirements that seem to be only associated with private practice. Depending on your career and life goals, it is often perfectly reasonable to seek situations that will require something less than the typical billable hour requirements of an associate at a busy law firm. However, we do not agree that private practice necessarily means an unreasonable grind, nor should one expect a laid-back lifestyle in every in-house position.

General Counsel and Associate General Counsel of large corporations often work the same hours as lawyers in private practice, which sometimes includes late-night and weekend work. Many in-house departments of corporations are set up like law firms, where different departments within the company are considered clients, and in-house counsel are required to bill and record how they spend their time with the internal clientele. For the companies that do not require their lawyers to bill their time, a lawyer working long hours has no record for the purpose of year-end productivity bonuses, as law firms do.

Additionally, the typical in-house work environment is changing and may no longer be everything an attorney fleeing firm life is seeking. [A] most recent annual survey of in-house attorneys by Corporate Counsel shows that despite myths to the contrary, the in-house environment is slowly morphing into somewhat of a friendlier law firm grind over the last few years. . . .

With corporate budgets going down, more pressure is being put on in-house attorneys to bring work in-house rather than farm it out to law firms. When that work comes in, though, fewer attorneys are being asked to handle it. In-house downsizing is one way that corporations are choosing to trim the budget fat. . . . Those in-house attorneys surveyed by Corporate Counsel say that this piling on of work has led to the late nights and weekends that many seek to avoid by making the in-house decision.

While the work is increasing and the perks are decreasing, in-house attorneys surveyed in the article overwhelmingly still enjoy their positions. Many who are currently employed are not looking for new positions. . . . Also, the work is able to hold the interest of the majority of employees, and the client contact and increased sense of camaraderie among colleagues still remains.

On the other hand, law firms are increasingly amenable to flextime, reduced hours, or telecommuting situations for valued lawyers. In the end, it is impossible to generalize what the time and billable hour requirements are for either law firms or corporations, and it is simply incorrect to assume that the grass is greener on the other side. At the end of the day, the fact of the matter is that most lawyers with sophisticated practices work hard, whether in private practice or in-house. There are as many distinctions to be made between lawyers practicing with law firms as there are differences in the day-to-day lives of prosecutors, general counsel, and large-firm associates.

Conclusions

. . . .

You need to carefully weigh your options before going in-house. There is a chance that going in-house could be the perfect career decision for you. Like everything in life, you need to maximize your long-term self-interest. If, when all is said and done, going in-house is likely to maximize your self-interest, then it is probably the right thing to do.

A number of in-house attorneys disagree with the positions taken in the foregoing critique. Two "posts" follow:

[1] "I have had in-house positions with 4 companies [in] 20+ years. I would have to say that each of the general propositions advanced in the article is fundamentally incorrect. The possible exception may be the one about not getting rich in-house. Compensation is generally lower, especially at the entry level, but as you move up the ladder, particularly with equity participation, there are many opportunities for financial reward in-house."

[2] "This is spectacularly bad advice, especially the part about not being able to find another job in-house. Most in-house postings seek prior in-house experience. This sounds like you were paid by large firms."

CHAPTER 2

IDENTIFYING WHO IS INSIDE COUNSEL'S CLIENT

Serving as inside counsel to a corporation or other business enterprise raises the subject of client identification. By its nature, entity representation renders the attorney's client-identification process more complex.

The importance of ascertaining the identity of the client is underscored by the American Bar Association's (ABA) Model Rules of Professional Conduct. These Rules, representing the universal position embraced by the practicing bar and applicable ethical mandates, impose certain obligations that run from the attorney to the client. For example, Rule 1.7 focuses on the loyalty owed by the attorney to each client.[1] Similarly, Rule 1.6, with certain exceptions, requires the attorney to maintain confidentiality with respect to information relating to the representation of a client.[2] This confidentiality is premised on two separate, but related, legal doctrines.[3]

PRINCIPLE OF CONFIDENTIALITY

The first principle of confidentiality is based on the attorney-client privilege and the work product doctrine.[4] The second principle premised on lawyer-client confidentiality is found in the ABA's Model Rules themselves.[5] Lawyer-client confidentiality is more encompassing than the attorney-client privilege: Regardless whether the information is protected from disclosure under the attorney-client privilege,[6] the ethical rules mandate (with certain exceptions) that all information relating

---

[1]   As comment 1 to Model Rule 1.7 states: "Loyalty and independent judgment are essential elements in the lawyer's relationship to a client."

[2]   *See* Rule 1.6 of the Model Rules.

[3]   *Id.* Rule 1.6 cmt. 3.

[4]   *Id. See Upjohn Co. v. United States*, 449 U.S. 383 (1981).

[5]   *See* Model Rule 1.6.

[6]   *See generally* ABA Task Force on the Attorney-Client Privilege, *Report of the American Bar Association's Task Force on the Attorney-Client Privilege*, 60 Bus. Law. 1029 (2005).

to the representation of that client, regardless of its source, be kept confidential.[7]

Both the privilege and the attorney's confidentiality obligation contain certain exceptions. For example, the client may give informed consent to the disclosure of the otherwise protected information.[8] As another example, a lawyer under the prevailing view may reveal client information to the extent necessary "to prevent the client from committing a crime or fraud that is reasonably certain to result in substantial injury to the financial interests or property of another and in furtherance of which the client has used or is using the lawyer's services."[9]

COUNSEL'S COMMUNICATIONS WITH THE COMPANY'S CONSTITUENTS

An entity, such as a corporation, clearly cannot speak for itself; rather, it must rely on and speak through its representatives.[10] These corporate representatives are often called "constituents."[11] Constituents include directors, officers, employees, members, and shareholders.[12] The communications between the attorney and a constituent of the organization relating to the giving of legal advice to the organization normally are within the principle of confidentiality, so long as the communications concern the constituent's role or position within the organization.[13]

In a situation where inside counsel becomes aware of a constituent's contemplated course of action that is a violation of law that reasonably may be imputed to the organization, the Model Rules set forth specified actions that the attorney should take, depending on the severity of the potential harm.[14] In the most extreme situation, inside counsel may find it necessary to refer the matter to the organization's highest authority (namely,

---

[7] *See* Rule 1.6 cmt. 3.

[8] *Id.* Rule 1.6(a).

[9] Rule 1.6(b)(2). For other exceptions to the principle of confidentiality, *see e.g.,* Rules 1.6(b), 1.13(c) & cmt. 6.

[10] *See, e.g.,* Rule 1.6(a), 1.6(b)(2).

[11] *Id.* Rule 1.13.

[12] *Id.* Rule 1.13(f).

[13] *Id.* Rule 1.13 cmt. 2.

[14] *Id.* Rule 1.13(b) & cmt. 4.

the board of directors).[15] In the event that the corporation's highest authority—the board of directors—insists upon conduct that violates the law and that likely will result in substantial harm to the company, inside counsel may be obligated to withdraw from the representation, thereby signifying (in practical effect) the likely resignation from one's employment. In addition, in such circumstances, the attorney may under nearly all ethical rules (except, for example, California) reveal information to appropriate sources (including the SEC) concerning the representation to the extent the attorney reasonably views is necessary to prevent substantial harm to the organization.[16]

CLOSELY-HELD CORPORATIONS

A number of successful closely-held corporations and other such business enterprises (for example, limited liability companies) have in-house counsel, normally comprised of the general inside counsel and perhaps additional legal counsel who work under his or her direction. Closely-held corporations (such as family corporations) may present complex scenarios. The in-house attorney for such an enterprise often has significant contact with many, if not all, of the corporation's constituents.[17] As a result, some of the constituents may think that the attorney is representing them as individuals, in addition to the business enterprise.[18] Indeed, some sources argue that due to the close nature of these enterprises, the attorney's actions have a direct effect on each constituent and consequently, the attorney's obligations should run not only to the company, but to each constituent as well.[19] In a family corporation, for example, the constituents are generally the employees, shareholders, officers

---

[15]   *Id.* Rule 1.13(b)(3) & cmt. 5.

[16]   *Id.* Rules 1.13(c), (d), 1.16(a), (b). *See* C. Wolfram, *Modern Legal Ethics* § 13.7 (1986). But see Cal. Bus. & Prof. Code § 6068(e).

[17]   *See* Mitchell, *Professional Responsibility and the Close Corporation: Toward a Realistic Ethic,* 74 Cornell L. Rev. 466 (1989); Comment, *Once You Enter This Family There's No Getting Out: Ethical Considerations of Representing Family-Owned Businesses,* 75 UMKC L. Rev. 1085 (2007).

[18]   *See* Haynsworth, *Competent Counseling of Small Business Clients,* 13 U.C. Davis L. Rev. 401 (1980); Mitchell, note 17 *supra.*

[19]   Mitchell, *supra* note 17, at 506. *See In re Brownstein,* 602 P.2d 655 (Or. 1979). *But see Skarbrevik v. Cohen, England & Whitfield,* 282 Cal. Rptr. 627 (Ct. App. 1991).

and directors of the enterprise.[20] In addition, the business operations of a closely-held corporation are oftentimes the sole source of livelihood for its shareholders. In such a situation, the corporation's success takes on paramount importance to each shareholder; if things go sour, such shareholders frequently have no viable exit from their investment.[21] These problems are exacerbated when individual shareholders have different personal interests, and each attempts to implement her individual goals within the company's policies and corporate framework.

It should be noted that in the partnership context, some courts have found that the attorney representing the organization also represents the individual partners.[22] As one court explained: "In the context of the representation of a partnership, the attorney for the partnership represents all the partners as to matters of partnership business."[23]

Nonetheless, several courts adhere to the "entity" theory of representation in the partnership setting which may be viewed as consistent with the Uniform Partnership Act's position that "[a] partnership is an entity distinct from its partners."[24] Consequently, depending on the jurisdiction and the underlying circumstances, it may be uncertain whether inside counsel for a partnership represents only the enterprise, or, absent an agreement otherwise, is deemed to represent the individuals as well.

Accordingly, inside counsel for a closely-held enterprise should monitor the situations in which significant adverse interests may arise. The need for caution results from the fact

---

[20]   *See, e.g., Galler v. Galler*, 203 N.E. 2d 577 (Ill. 1964); *Triggs v. Triggs*, 385 N.E. 2d 1254 (N.Y. 1978).

[21]   *See* D. Branson, J. Heminway, M. Loewenstein, M. Steinberg & M. Warren, *Business Enterprises: Legal Structures, Governance and Policy* 431–516 (3d ed. 2016).

[22]   *See, e.g., Metropolitan Life Insurance Company v. The Guardian Life Insurance Company of America,* 2009 WL 1439717 (N.D. Ill. 2009); *Adell v. Sommers, Schwartz, Silver and Schwartz,* 428 N.W.2d 26 (Mich. Ct. App. 1998).

[23]   *Wortham & Van Liew v. Superior Court,* 233 Cal. Rptr. 725, 728 (Ct. App. 1987). *See also, Law v. Harvey,* 2007 WL 1280585, at *5 (N.D. Cal. 2007) (holding that attorney was representing the partnership and the partners in their individual capacity).

[24]   *See, e.g.,* § 201(a) of the Uniform Partnership Act (1997); *Hopper v. Frank,* 16 F.3d 92 (5th Cir. 1994) (applying Mississippi law); *Eurycleia Partners, LP v. Seward & Kissel, LLP,* 12 N.Y. 3d 553, 910 N.E. 2d 976, 883 N.Y.S. 2d 147 (Ct. App. 2009).

that in closely-held enterprises the interests and rights of the organization and the constituents who control the organization often start off as consistent with one another.[25] Perhaps because of this alignment of interests, some courts take the position that, unless the parties agree otherwise, the attorney for a closely-held enterprise represents the constituents in their individual capacities as well as the organization.[26] This approach, however, is contrary to the prevailing "entity" rule, according to which the entity (or the business organization) is the client, and not the individual equity holders.[27]

THE "ENTITY" RULE

Under the entity rule, "where a lawyer represents a corporation, the client is the corporation, not the corporation's shareholders."[28] As explained by one court:

> [W]here an attorney represents a [corporation, including a] closely held corporation, the attorney [normally] . . . owes no separate duty of diligence and care to an individual shareholder. . . . [A]n attorney representing a corporation does not become the attorney for the individual stockholders merely because the attorney's actions on behalf of the corporation may also benefit the stockholders. The duty of an attorney for a corporation is first and foremost to the corporation, even though the legal advice rendered to the corporation may affect the shareholders.[29]

Contrary to the "entity" theory of representation, some courts take the position that in the close corporation setting counsel represents individual shareholders in addition to the

---

[25]   See, e.g., Wilkes v. Springfield Nursing Home, Inc., 353 N.E. 2d 657 (Mass. 1977).

[26]   See, e.g., In re Brownstein, 602 P.2d 655 (Or. 1979), citing, In re Banks, 584 P.2d 284 (Or. 1978).

[27]   See, e.g., Skarbrevik v. Cohen, England & Whitfield, 282 Cal. Rptr. 627 (Ct. App. 1991); Egan v. McNamara, 467 A.2d 733 (D.C. 1983); Jesse v. Danforth, 485 N.W.2d 63 (Wis. 1992); Carnegie Associates Ltd. v. Miller, 2008 WL 4106907 (N.Y. Sup. Ct. 2008).

[28]   McKinney v. McMeans, 147 F. Supp. 2d 898, 901 (M.D. Tenn. 2001). See also, Model Rule 1.13(a) ("A lawyer employed or retained by an organization represents the organization acting through its duly authorized constituents.").

[29]   Brennan v. Ruffner, 640 So. 2d 143, 145–146 (Fla. Dist. Ct. App. 1994). See SEC. v. Credit Bancorp, Ltd., 96 F. Supp. 2d 357 (S.D.N.Y. 2000).

organization, based on that shareholder's reasonable expectation of being separately represented.[30] As one court explained: "Although, in the ordinary corporate situation, corporate counsel does not necessarily become counsel for the corporation's shareholders . . .where, as here, the corporation is a close corporation consisting of only two shareholders with equal interests in the corporation, it is indeed reasonable for each shareholder to believe that the corporate counsel is in effect his own individual attorney."[31]

AVOIDANCE OF CONFLICTING INTERESTS

If inside counsel is deemed to be concurrently representing the company as well as an individual constituent, the attorney may be in a precarious position. As clients, each is owed the duties of loyalty and confidentiality.[32] Accordingly, where practicable, inside counsel should avoid representing the corporation and one or more of its constituents. When undertaking assignments that may implicate these concerns (such as the drafting of an employment agreement or stock option provision), inside counsel would be prudent to inform the constituent in writing that he is not that constituent's attorney.

With the foregoing discussion in mind, consider the following.

IN THE MATTER OF CARTER AND JOHNSON
Securities Exchange Act Release No. 17597 (SEC 1981)

We are mindful that, when a lawyer represents a corporate client, the client—and the entity to which he owes his allegiance—is the corporation itself and not management or any other individual connected with the corporation. Moreover, the lawyer should try to "insure that decisions of his client are made

---

[30]   *See e.g.,* Comment, *An Expectations Approach to Client Identity,* 106 Harv. L. Rev. 687 (1993).

[31]   *Rosman v. Shapiro,* 653 F. Supp. 1441, 1445 (S.D.N.Y. 1987), *citing, Westinghouse Electric Corp. v. Kerr-McGee Corp.,* 580 F.2d 1311 (7th Cir. 1978), *Glover v. Libman,* 578 F. Supp. 748 (N.D. Ga. 1983), *Bobbitt v. Victorian House, Inc.,* 545 F. Supp. 1124 (N.D. Ill. 1982). *But see United States v. Graf,* 610 F. 3d 1148, 1159 (9th Cir. 2010); cases cited notes 28–29 *supra.*

[32]   *See* Model Rules 1.6, 1.7.

only after the client has been informed of relevant considerations." These unexceptionable principles take on a special coloration when a lawyer becomes aware that one or more specific members of a corporate client's management is deciding not to follow his disclosure advice, especially if he knows that those in control, such as the board of directors, may not have participated in or been aware of that decision. Moreover, it is well established that no lawyer, even in the most zealous pursuit of his client's interests, is privileged to assist his client in conduct the lawyer knows to be illegal. The application of these recognized principles to the special role of the securities lawyer giving disclosure advice, however, is not a simple task.

The securities lawyer who is an active participant in a company's ongoing disclosure program will ordinarily draft and revise disclosure documents, comment on them and file them with the [Securities and Exchange Commission—the SEC]. He is often involved on an intimate, day-to-day basis in the judgments that determine what will be disclosed and what will be withheld from the public markets. When a lawyer serving in such a capacity concludes that his client's disclosures are not adequate to comply with the law, and so advises his client, he is "aware," in a literal sense, of a continuing violation of the securities laws. On the other hand, the lawyer is only an adviser, and the final judgment—and, indeed, responsibility—as to what course of conduct is to be taken must lie with the client. . . . [D]isclosure issues often present difficult choices between multiple shades of gray. . . .

RESTATEMENT OF THE LAW (THIRD)
GOVERNING LAWYERS*
American Law Institute (ALI), § 96 Comment

A lawyer who has been employed . . . to represent an organization as a client owes professional duties of loyalty and competence to the organization. By representing the organization, a lawyer does not thereby also form a client-lawyer

---

relationship with all or any individuals employed by it or who direct its operations or who have an ownership or other beneficial interest in it, such as its shareholders. However additional circumstances may result in a client-lawyer relationship with constituents while the lawyer concurrently represents the organization.

A lawyer representing only an organization does not owe duties of care, diligence, or confidentiality to constituents of the organization. . . . Correspondingly, although a lawyer for the organization acts at the direction of its officers, the lawyer for an organization does not possess, solely in that capacity, power to act for officers as their lawyer. Thus, third persons may not reasonably conclude, solely from that capacity, that a lawyer for the organization represents officers individually. . . . Similarly, a lawyer representing only a constituent does not, by virtue of that representation, owe either to the organization employing the constituent or to other constituents obligations that would arise only from a client-lawyer relationship with the organization.

The so-called "entity" theory of organizational representation . . . is now universally recognized in American law, for purposes of determining the identity of the direct beneficiary of legal representation of corporations and other forms of organizations. . . . Pursuant to the entity theory, the rights and responsibilities of the client-lawyer relationship [are] between the organization and the lawyer.

A lawyer representing an organization deals with individuals such as its officers, directors, and employees, who serve as constituents of the organization. Such individuals acting under the organization's authority retain and direct the lawyer to act on behalf of the organization. Nonetheless, personal dealings with such persons do not lessen the lawyer's responsibilities to the organization as client, and the lawyer may not let such dealings hinder the lawyer in the performance of those responsibilities.

. . . A constituent includes an officer, director, or employee of the organization. A shareholder of a stock corporation or a member of a membership corporation is also a constituent. . . .

A lawyer may represent an organization either as an employee of the organization (inside legal counsel) or as a lawyer in private practice retained by the organization (outside legal counsel). In general, a lawyer's responsibilities to a client organization are the same in both capacities. . . . However, the nature of the lawyer's work and greater or less access to an organization's channels of information can affect the lawyer's knowledge and thus, for example, the reasonableness of the lawyer's reliance on a constituent of the organization for information and direction.

. . . .

Persons authorized to act for the organization make decisions about retaining or discharging a lawyer for the organization, determine the scope of the representation, and create an obligation for the organization to compensate the lawyer. . . . [S]uch persons also direct the activities of the lawyer during the course of the representation. Unless the lawyer withdraws, the lawyer must follow instructions and implement decisions of those persons, as the lawyer would follow instructions and decisions of an individual client. A constituent of the organization authorized to do so may discharge the lawyer. . . . [A] lawyer is not bound by a constituent's instruction to a lawyer to perform, counsel, or assist future or ongoing acts that the lawyer reasonably believes to be unlawful. Such an instruction also does not remove the lawyer's duty to protect the best interests of the organizational client. . . .

A lawyer representing an organization is required to act with reasonable competence and diligence in the representation and to use care in representing the organizational client. The lawyer thus must not knowingly or negligently assist any constituent to breach a legal duty to the organization. However, a lawyer's duty of care to the organization is not limited to avoidance of assisting acts that threaten injury to a client. A lawyer is also required to act diligently and to exercise care by taking steps to prevent reasonably foreseeable harm to a client. . . .

The lawyer is not prevented by rules of confidentiality from acting to protect the interests of the organization by disclosing within the organization communications gained from constituents who are not themselves clients. That follows even if disclosure is against the interests of the communicating person, of another constituent whose breach of duty is in issue, or of other constituents. Such disclosure within the organization is subject to direction of a constituent who is authorized to act for the organization in the matter and who is not complicit in the breach. The lawyer may withdraw any support that the lawyer may earlier have provided the intended act, such as by withdrawing an opinion letter or draft transaction documents prepared by the lawyer.

NEW YORK CITY BAR ASSOCIATION TASK
FORCE REPORT ON THE LAWYER'S ROLE
IN CORPORATE GOVERNANCE (2006)*

It is a matter of critical importance . . . that the client be identified as the company itself, and not its individual officers or directors. The lawyer for the client company must be alert to conduct by management that is in conflict with the best interests of the company. Such conduct or conflicts, when perceived, may require a report to the Board.

This essential ethical orientation is in tension with the practical reality that a lawyer's contacts will be with management. In the opinion of the court-appointed examiner of Enron, one explanation for the alleged failure of Enron's attorneys to alert [Enron's] Board [of Directors] to management misconduct "may be that they lost sight of the fact that the corporation was their client. It appears that some of these attorneys considered the officers to be their clients when, in fact, the attorneys owed duties to Enron."

. . . .

A strong General Counsel is an important participant in a good corporate governance process. He is a key advisor to senior management. He is uniquely positioned to bring relevant matters to the Board of Directors. He often participates in the negotiation, structuring and documentation of significant business transactions, as well as in the preparation of SEC

---

* Reprinted with permission of the New York City Bar Association.

disclosure and other regulatory filings. He is expected to bring to the table a broad view in his role as a counselor, giving advice based not only on the letter of the law, but also on broad ethical considerations and a "public" perspective, including how a particular action might be viewed by third parties, such as potential investors, shareholders, government officials and the public in general.

As a result, the General Counsel has been described as the "guardian of the corporate reputation." The SEC has made clear its expectations that the General Counsel play an essential leadership role in promoting an appropriate "tone at the top" or corporate culture to support rigorous compliance with the law. The SEC views General Counsel as generally better able than other employees to "push back" on senior management when difficult legal issues arise and to assure an appropriate level of protection for whistleblowers and others who identify potential legal problems at a company. However, the General Counsel cannot single-handedly instill a culture of compliance and integrity in an organization. These values must be embraced and communicated by corporate management at all levels, especially the CEO and the Board of Directors. A lawyer would be well-advised to be sure that this is the case before accepting a position as General Counsel of a corporation.

There is an inherent tension in the role of General Counsel and other internal lawyers that must be recognized and managed. To be effective, the General Counsel and his top lieutenants must maintain a close, open relationship with the CEO and other senior executives, and have a thorough understanding of the client's business and other objectives. To be "welcomed in," these high-ranking legal officers must be seen as trusted advisors, partners to the business and advocates for the corporation. If a culture is promoted in which they are seen only as the enforcers of the law, the General Counsel and other senior internal lawyers risk creating "an atmosphere of adversity, or at least arm's length dealing, between the lawyer and the corporate client's senior executive officers that is inimical to the lawyer's essential role as a counselor promoting the corporation's compliance with the law." The tension, in short, is "between giving independent judgment and advice and securing the trust and confidence" of management and the Board.

In reconciling their potentially conflicting roles, the General Counsel and other internal lawyers must always keep in mind that their client is the corporation, not its directors, officers or other corporate agents. They must be able to recognize, and have sufficient status and independence to deal with, situations in which the interests of the corporation may not align with the individual desires of senior management or even the Board of Directors. Such independence must include a willingness to speak privately to appropriate Board members [such as the members of the audit committee who, pursuant to the Sarbanes-Oxley Act of 2002, must be comprised of all independent directors] about issues that trouble the General Counsel or even to resign when important interests of the corporation, the ultimate client, are not being served.

The risks to the corporation inherent in the absence of a strong legal function has been noted in Congressional testimony, investigative reports and articles regarding several recent corporate scandals. According to the WorldCom investigative report, its legal department was "not structured to maximize its effectiveness as a control structure upon which the Board could depend." The report states that "at [CEO Bernard] Ebbers' direction, the Company's lawyers were in fragmented groups, several of which had General Counsels who did not report to WorldCom's General Counsel for portions of the relevant period; they were not located geographically near senior management or involved in its inner workings and they had inadequate support from senior management." Ebbers did not include the Company's lawyers in his "inner circle" and appeared to have dealt with them only when he felt it was necessary"; he "let them know his displeasure with them personally when they gave advice—however justified—that he did not like," and generally "created a culture in which the legal function was less influential and less welcome than in a healthy corporate environment."

Similarly, in HealthSouth, the General Counsel would appear at Board meetings only if the CEO, Richard Scrushy, invited him to discuss a particular issue. Normally he did not even see the Board agendas. There were no clearly established procedures to refer to the internal legal department allegations of criminal conduct. It was clear that Scrushy (like Ebbers) created a culture of intimidation and made it personally difficult for anyone, including the General Counsel, to give advice that Scrushy did not like.

Articles about Enron have noted that the Enron lawyers were insulated in "silos," with little contact or direction from the General Counsel. A climate was created where the "worst thing you could do was be viewed as an obstructionist," a situation exacerbated by a structure that allowed business managers effectively to determine lawyers' compensation. In his Final Report, the Court Appointed Examiner for Enron outlined numerous situations where Enron's General Counsel or other internal lawyers failed to analyze, elevate, or adequately advise Enron management or its Board of known issues, including significant conflicts of interest. Among other things, he noted that it "appeared some of these attorneys considered officers to be their clients when, in fact, the attorneys owed duties to Enron." In other cases, he noted this possible explanation for the attorney's behavior:

> "[S]ome of these attorneys saw their role in very narrow terms, as an implementer, not a counselor. That is, rather than conscientiously raising known issues for further analysis by a more senior officer or the Enron Board or refusing to participate in transactions that raised such issues, these lawyers seemed to focus only on how to address a narrow question or simply to implement a decision (or document a transaction)."

Strengthening the role of the General Counsel should be a high priority in efforts to promote compliance with laws. . . .

CHAPTER 3

WHAT IT'S REALLY LIKE TO WORK IN-HOUSE AND HOW TO FIND IN-HOUSE JOB OPPORTUNITIES

In-house positions are in greater demand now than ever before. This is not surprising given the very real and tangible benefits associated with an in-house practice. Most corporate counsel will tell you that the benefits of their jobs far outweigh the negatives and that their work/life balance is better in a corporation. After all, they no longer have to keep track of their time in 6- or 15-minute increments and meet an annual minimum billable hour requirement. Former law firm associates are now off the high-pressured partnership track. And gone is the difficult task of developing new clients in a highly competitive legal market.

Not surprisingly, many law students and junior associates view corporate counsel positions as the "be all and end all," saying they would rather work in a corporate legal department than in a law firm. But many in-house lawyers will tell you that it is actually more difficult to work in-house than in a law firm. Although they do not have the pressures associated with billable hours, client development, and making partner, other burdens keep them stressed, worried, and awake at night. This chapter explores many of the common perceptions of in-house practice and outlines specific strategies for landing an in-house job opportunity, if that is what you want.

One caveat: This chapter speaks in generalities about the roles and challenges corporate counsel face because there is no conventional legal department or stereotypical chief legal officer. Indeed, in-house law departments vary greatly in terms of practice area, size, organization, corporate culture, and expertise. Similarly, the legal, regulatory, and business issues facing corporations vary greatly. Corporate counsel are no different. Some are "solo GCs"—generalists, handling a wide variety of legal issues and depending more on outside counsel.

Others work in law departments that rival global law firms in terms of size—their in-house attorneys focus on discrete practice areas, much as their law firm counterparts do, and handle much of their work internally.

WHAT DO IN-HOUSE LAWYERS DO AND WHY?

Law students, and frankly, many practicing lawyers have a limited understanding of what attorneys within corporations actually "do." This is not unexpected because the work in-house attorneys handle can be very different than the work attorneys in firms handle. And most law students are never exposed to an in-house law department during law school and do not take any classes on in-house practice.

Generally speaking, in-house attorneys typically provide legal counseling to a corporation's core business units. Depending on the particular company and industry, corporate legal departments usually handle the following types of matters internally:

- Contracts

- Labor/Employment

- Compliance/Ethics

- Real Estate

- Corporate Governance[1]

In-house attorneys handle these types of matters for at least three reasons. First, these types of matters are usually enough to keep an in-house attorney busy. For example, large companies have thousands of employees, leading to a steady flow of labor

---

[1]   See Ass'n of Corp. Couns., *2015 ACC Global Census: A Profile of In-House Counsel* (Dec. 2015), at 27–28, https://www.acc.com/sites/default/files/resources/vl/purchaseOnly/1411926_2.pdf, *archived at* https://perma.cc/4JUR-PD42; *see also* Eagle, *Becoming In-house Counsel: A Guide for Law Student and Recent Graduates*, Ass'n of Corp. Couns. at 5 (Dec. 2013), https://www.acc.com/sites/default/files/resources/vl/membersonly/InfoPAK/19654_2.pdf, *archived at* https://perma.cc/2L6T-H55Z ("In-house. . . [p]ractice areas include antitrust law, international trade, corporate securities, tax, real estate, government contracts, ethics, privacy and intellectual property as well as the standard contracts and employment law issues."); Chan, *From Private Practice to In-House—Making the Transition*, Int'l In-House Couns. J. 654, 656 (Autumn 2008) (listing employment; basic intellectual property rights; general company, contract and tort law; and laws and regulations relevant to the company's business).

and employment issues. Similarly, technology companies, for instance, have many legal issues connected with Research and Development, including patent preparation and technology licensing. Accordingly, hiring full-time attorneys to handle these types of matters internally is justifiable and more cost-effective than sending all this work to attorneys who bill by the hour.

Second, attorneys who counsel core business units must be readily available to business people because their matters are central to the business and are often time-sensitive. For this reason, law departments do not isolate attorneys in back rooms; they are on the front-line, attending meetings with colleagues at all levels of their organization, from board members and executives to sales people, engineers, scientists, and those in advertising.[2] To give advice based on a thorough understanding of how the business works, in-house counsel must be available and accessible.[3] Having an attorney "down the hall" whom the business person can call or meet with, is critical.[4]

Third, core counseling work often requires more "institutional knowledge" than other areas of the law. In-house attorneys embedded in the company are privy to formal and informal flows of information, including business meetings, conference calls, and "water cooler" conversations. They also know the personalities of the business people with whom they work, how past situations were handled, and what is important to their corporate client.

This institutional knowledge also adds to predictability of decision-making. When in-house counsel encounter similar fact situations, they are better able to provide more-consistent advice based on past experience. This leads to a more profound understanding of the business and legal challenges facing the

---

[2]   Fontaine, *So You Want to Go In-House?*, NALSC.org (Fall 2013), http://www. nalsc.org/wp-content/uploads/2018/05/NALSC-Newsletter-Fall-2013.pdf, *reprinted from* Corp. Couns. (Sept. 30, 2013) (noting that "[m]ost lawyers make the move in-house while mid- to senior-level associates, or later, having garnered solid law firm training. New law school graduates typically lack sufficient business experience and exposure to a variety of practice areas and legal tasks to immediately step into an in-house role.").

[3]   *Id.*

[4]   *See* Seckler, *Hiring Your First In-House Counsel*, BCG Att'y Search, https://www.bcgsearch.com/article/60614/Hiring-your-first-in-house-counsel/, *archived at* https://perma.cc/3T9P-35J5 ("A key advantage of having an in-house GC is that he or she is 'living with the client' during the initial thinking about projects . . . .").

internal client, resulting in greater efficiency, more effective counseling, better risk management, and better overall results. Value like this cannot usually be supplied by an attorney from an outside firm.

WHAT ELSE CAN ATTORNEYS DO IN CORPORATIONS?

Corporations may also hire attorneys to handle other law-related duties, such as:

- Risk Management
- Contract Administration, Management, and Negotiation
- Compliance
- Labor Relations
- Government Affairs
- Investor Relations
- Corporate Finance
- Fraud Investigations
- Human Relations[5]

Many times, attorneys who handle these non-legal duties will not work in the law department. Rather, they will be in a department like compliance, human resources, or risk management. Typically, these jobs are "JD Advantage," meaning that they do not require bar passage, an active law license, or involve practicing law in the traditional sense.[6]

COMMON PERCEPTIONS ABOUT IN-HOUSE PRACTICE

In-house counsel may be the happiest section of the legal profession. According to one source, an astonishing 96 percent of

---

[5]   *See* Robert Half Legal, *Career Options for In-House Counsel Info PAK*, Ass'n of Corp. Couns. at 11–12, 14, 20, 40 (Sept. 2013), https://www.acc.com/sites/default/files/resources/vl/membersonly/InfoPAK/19669_3.pdf, *archived at* https://perma.cc/HZH6-DYT2.

[6]   National Association for Law Placement: The Association for Legal Career Professionals, *What is the JD Advantage?*, https://www.nalp.org/0513research?s=jd%20advantage, *archived at* https://perma.cc/GER7-ETRK.

general counsels say they are very satisfied in their jobs or that there are more aspects of their jobs they like than dislike.[7] Only seven percent of in-house counsel would leave their corporate position to become a partner at a large law firm.[8]

Being in-house counsel definitely has its benefits. Generally speaking, in-house attorneys have a better work/life balance. With some exceptions, inside counsel do not have to work the extremely long hours their counterparts at large law firms do and have more control of their schedules, including having most weekends off. Other aspects of their jobs that many in-house counsel enjoy include the work environment, autonomy, being part of the business, and practicing as generalists in a profession that increasingly demands specialization from lawyers.[9]

Those on the outside looking in—law students and experienced attorneys at firms—perceive in-house practice as more satisfying and less demanding than working in private practice. And in many corporations this perception is reality. In other corporations, however, this perception is not reality. Working as in-house counsel is not a cake walk.[10] Some in-house counsel may work as much or more than their law firm counterparts. And, for some in-house attorneys, certain aspects of the job debunk the numerous perceptions about corporate legal departments being more attractive places to work than law firms. This section addresses many common beliefs about in-house practice and presents how, at least in some cases, these perceptions may not be true.

In-House Attorneys Work Less

One common perception is that in-house attorneys work less than attorneys in firms. In many companies, they do. According to an informal survey of Association of Corporate Counsel (ACC) members, in-house counsel reported working on average fifty hours a week versus lawyers in large firms who reported an

---

7   Lyne, *The Pressure Is On: Though Happy in Their Jobs, General Counsels Surveyed Feel Squeezed by Management over Legal Costs*, Nat'l L. J. 24 (Sept. 9, 1991).

8   *Id.*

9   *See id.; see also* Aman, *Topping Out*, 5 Corp. Couns. 63 (Dec. 2005).

10   *See* Lyne, *supra* note 7.

average six-day work week, billing sixty to seventy hours per week.[11]

Some inside counsel, however, work just as many (or more) hours than attorneys in law firms.[12] Their workloads may be greater for a host of reasons. One is that the volume of work is picking up. A recent survey found that in-house counsel work 49 hours per week on average.[13] Almost half of the in-house lawyers in the survey reported an increase in workload over the prior 12 months, citing "new laws and regulatory changes, mergers and acquisitions activity, staffing changes and business needs as explanations for the changing workload."[14] Another reason for increased workloads may be that many companies, forced to reduce budgets across the board, are pressuring their law departments to do more with less.[15] As a result, inside counsel are handling more matters internally (a concept known as "insourcing") and, therefore, sending less work to outside counsel.[16] Despite the additional work created by insourcing, however, many companies are not hiring more in-house

---

[11]   Nicholson, *Making In-Roads to Corporate General Counsel Positions: It's Only a Matter of Time?*, 65 Md. L. Rev. 625, 652 (2006); *see also* Eagle, *supra* note 1, at 7.

[12]   Nicholson, *supra* note 11, at 660; *see also* Larry Smith, *Inside/Outside: How Businesses Buy Legal Services* 283 (2001) (describing how in-house work has become just as demanding as working at a law firm).

[13]   *See 2015 ACC Global Census, supra* note 1, at 21.

[14]   *Id.*

[15]   Maleske, *How to Cut Outside Counsel Spend: How Pressured Law Department Leaders Have Cut Costs and Stuck to Budgets,* Inside Couns. (July 1, 2011)), https://www.law.com/almID/4e09f528150ba0562c000248/ (last visited Sept. 19, 2019) (quoting Michael Wu, then general counsel of Rosetta Stone, "[I]nsourcing legal work has become standard operating procedure for legal departments across the United States. It seems like the No. 1 priority in many companies [is] in terms of cutting back on outside counsel spend, because of rates and the economy. It's something that's quite normal—of course you insource when you can. The trend toward insourcing is alive and well.").

[16]   *See* Williams-Alvarez, *Legal Departments Keep Huge Percentage of Work In-House,* Law.com (June 28, 2017), https://www.mlaglobal.com/en-sg/knowledge-library/in-the-news/legal-departments-keep-huge-percentage-of-work-in-house?byconsultantor author=michael-sachs, *archived at* https://perma.cc/AZ8R-75YD ("[n]early 75 percent of work for legal departments is handled internally" due to control, cost and efficiency); Wald, *In-House Myths,* 2012 Wis. L. Rev. 408, 414 (2012) (noting that "the rise and growth of in-house legal departments allowed corporate clients to handle some of their basic legal and corporate paperwork internally and more effectively manage their overall legal needs, cutting costs and eliminating a significant income source for large law firms").

lawyers.[17] The result is that each lawyer has more work than ever before.

In addition to a greater volume of work, the pace of an in-house practice can at times be faster, more constant, and less predictable than a law firm practice. A new legal crisis or urgent phone call can change the day corporate counsel already had planned and force him to put his other work on hold. Being in-house counsel is somewhat akin to being an emergency room doctor. Although legal decisions are not life and death, projects come from all directions and fast. Inside counsel may not have the luxury of focusing on any one thing for an extended period of time like her counterparts in a firm.[18] She must prioritize, make decisions, and act quickly. Paul M. Jolas, the Chief Legal Officer of U.S. Concrete, Inc., compares the high-level, consistent workload to "drinking water from a fire hose."[19]

While law firm associates and partners may work around the clock preparing for trial or drafting documents in connection with a transaction, they can take a well-deserved break when the case settles or the deal closes. Litigators typically find that their summers are slower because judges and opposing counsel take vacation then; transactional attorneys tend to be busier at year-end for tax reasons but slower in the beginning of the year.

---

[17]   Barnes, *The "Dark Side" of Going In House*, BCGSearch.com, https://www.bcg search.com/article/60637/The-dark-Side-Of-Going-In-House/, *archived at* https://perma.cc/9EBS-B55N.

[18]   *See* Cannon, *A View from the Other Side: My Life as an In-House Attorney*, BCG Attorney Search, https://www.bcgsearch.com/article/60692/A-View-from-the-Other-Side-My-Life-as-an-In-House-Attorney/, *archived at* https://perma.cc/4Z8H-TKGJ (noting that "each day was incredibly busy, and there never seemed to be any downtime or days where I could just relax and log in seven hours of 'professional reading' as I did at the law firm between deals. This was due to the fact that instead of working on one or two big deals, I typically handled approximately 20 to 30 different matters at a time"); *see also* Sachs, *Law Firm to In-House: A Different Type of Mountain But Not Insurmountable*, Corp. Couns. Connect Collection (Nov. 2013), https://store.legal.thomsonreuters.com/law-products/news-views/corporate-counsel/law-firm-to-in-house-a-different-type-of-mountain-but-not-insurmountable, *archived at* https://perma.cc/Y2EN-QEGZ (noting that "the pace of things in-house is so much quicker and less precise; a law firm attorney might very quickly yearn for the days of drafting ten-page memos and having all night to proofread and mark up a complicated agreement. That skill set, which is so appropriately valuable at a law firm, can sometimes be completely disregarded in-house").

[19]   Interview with Paul M. Jolas, Vice President, General Counsel and Corporate Secretary, U.S. Concrete, Inc., in Dallas, Tex. (Mar. 5, 2014).

One reason for the frantic and unending pace of in-house practice is that there is no "buffer" between in-house counsel and her internal client.[20] In-house counsel typically office in the same building or complex as their internal constituents, who may just show up on their doorstep if in-house counsel does not respond to their phone calls or emails.[21] On the other hand, lawyers in firms, are physically "removed" from their clients in a different building or even a different city, and it would be extremely unlikely for a client to just "show up" unannounced.

Moreover, in-house lawyers are consulted on a whole host of matters on which the company would likely not spend outside legal fees.[22] In the case of an employed, in-house lawyer, the company's cost is largely set no matter how many matters are brought to the lawyer's attention and, thus, there is an incentive to maximize the use of the in-house attorney's services. Clients of law firm attorneys, on the other hand, ordinarily contact their outside counsel only when a need arises. The primary pricing model used by outside lawyers is to charge by the hour. Under that model, the more communications with and projects sent to outside counsel, the higher the bill. This actually creates a disincentive to send routine or non-specialized matters to outside counsel.

Technology has also compounded the demands on their time. The use of technology has led to increased pressure for lawyers to provide a fast turnaround to legal questions.[23] Indeed, the increased use of email, text messaging, smartphones, and voicemail have led internal "clients" to demand answers 24 hours a day, seven days a week.

To make matters more problematic, the practice of law is not getting any easier or less stressful. Instead, the practice of law, like the practice of medicine, is becoming more specialized, and companies are now more heavily regulated than ever.[24] Staying

---

[20]   *See* Cannon, *supra* note 18.

[21]   *See id.*

[22]   *See* Seckler, *supra* note 4 ("[I]n-house counsel may identify and focus on issues that management might never have brought to the attention of outside counsel . . . .").

[23]   *See* Eagle, *supra* note 1, at 7.

[24]   *LL.M. Degrees Explode as Law Gets More Specialized*, Nat'l Jurist (Oct. 25, 2013), http://www.nationaljurist.com/national-jurist-magazine/llm-degrees-explode-law-gets-more-specialized, *archived at* https://perma.cc/2D9A-A65H; Goad & Hattem,

apprised of new laws and regulations, facilitating compliance, counseling with respect to ethics matters, and investigating and remediating any violations are all significant sources of stress.[25]

In-House Jobs Are More Stable

Another common perception is that corporate counsel jobs are more stable. But "stable" is not the word many in-house counsel would use to describe their jobs. Some say they actually have less job security than law firm lawyers.

In-house lawyers, unlike lawyers in a firm, are employed by only one client: the corporation or other form of business enterprise (e.g., limited liability company). If an in-house lawyer is terminated or her employer is acquired or otherwise goes out of business, she is out of a job. A lawyer in a law firm, on the other hand, typically has many clients. If one of his clients fires him, he still has other clients.

Moreover, corporations are not immune to lay-offs. In fact, some would argue that in-house lawyers are at a greater risk of being laid off since they do not generate any revenue for their client. Inside counsel may be viewed as expendable overhead that can be replaced with less costly counsel if the company runs into financial difficulty and has to downsize its operations.[26]

Besides termination and business closures, other corporate changes that are beyond in-house counsel's control can jeopardize her livelihood. Consider the following possibilities that could leave her with a job one day and out of a job the next:

- Carl Icahn takes over her company and brings in his own management team.

- In a corporate merger, the general counsel of the other company is named chief legal officer of the surviving entity.

Businesses Hire Up to Deal with More Regs, The Hill (Nov. 9, 2013), https://thehill.com/ regulation/business/189770-businesses-hire-up-to-deal-with-mounting-regulations, *archived at* https://perma.cc/K42Q-QNZC.

[25]   *See Stress, Compliance, and Ethics Survey*, Soc'y of Corp. Compliance & Ethics & Health Care Compliance Ass'n (Jan. 2012), https://www.anti-corruption.com/files/ 2013/03/11/194_0_2011stresssurvey_report.pdf, *archived at* https://perma.cc/V6R9-QGEP.

[26]   *See* Cannon, *supra* note 18.

- The CEO who hired her retires, and the new CEO names his long-time friend as general counsel.

- She is forced to resign rather than become a participant in an illegal course of conduct by her client.

- The board outsources the general counsel function to outside counsel as a cost-saving measure.

- The corporate headquarters relocates to a different city and, although she is offered a job in the new location, she does not want to (or cannot) move.[27]

While the displaced attorney may receive a severance payment under the organization's severance or change-in-control plans as a result of some of these events, she nevertheless lost her job and a regular paycheck. And it is not unusual for many in-house job searches to take twelve months or longer.[28]

There are limited career development opportunities in many legal departments. Many departments are fairly flat with little to no room to move up the department hierarchy.[29] Unlike associates in law firms who move up class levels each year and enjoy significant pay raises, in-house attorneys may find themselves in the same position for many years to come, with pay raises averaging 3–5 percent per year.[30]

Moreover, an AGC (assistant or associate general counsel) at a large, publicly-traded corporation is unlikely to be named general counsel of her company.[31] More likely, an outside legal

---

[27] *See id.* ("Thus, your job could quickly disappear if the company runs into financial difficulties"); *see also* Barnes, *supra* note 17 ("Even in the best of times, companies may cut back on their legal departments, go out of business, merge, or relocate."); *see also* Robert Half Legal, *Career Options for In-House Counsel Info PAK*, Ass'n of Corp. Couns. at 7 (Aug. 2008) ("Of course, the reality of today's corporate environment is that some in-house lawyers are presented with no choice about a career move; a corporate downsizing or office closure could suddenly place legal professionals in transition involuntarily.").

[28] *See* Vidal, *In Search of That In-House Spot*, EsquireRecruiting.com (2011), http://esquirerecruiting.com/wp-content/uploads/2011/11/In-Search-of-That-In-House-Spot160.pdf, *archived at* https://perma.cc/ULY5-PXMR ("If you are looking for a GC-level position with a publicly traded Fortune 500 company . . . a good rule of thumb is anywhere between six months to a year, and in many cases a lot more.").

[29] *See Are You Ready to Go In-House?*, In-House Insider: Forum, News and Career Center for In-House Counsels (Jan. 14, 2013).

[30] *Id.*

[31] Aman, *supra* note 9.

officer from another company in the same or similar industry will be recruited.[32] In order to progress, she may need to move to the legal department of another company.[33]

According to a survey conducted by *Corporate Counsel*, nearly seventy-five percent of in-house counsel surveyed described overall opportunities for advancement in their departments as either "limited" or non-existent.[34] Although many of the 1,278 respondents reported receiving promotions since going in-house, they said they were unlikely to get much further:[35] 19% saw no opportunities for advancement for them in their department, while 56% said opportunities were limited.[36]

In-House Jobs May Be Less Prestigious

The transition from law firm to corporation can be a humbling experience for many new in-house attorneys. Unlike a law firm where lawyers are the center of the universe, in-house lawyers are not. Law firms exist because of their attorneys: attorneys bill time, generating revenue for the firm. Non-lawyers in the firm (executive assistants, word processors, and legal assistants) support the attorneys and make them more productive.[37]

Companies, on the other hand, exist to make a profit from effective, non-legal business operations. The law department is one of many departments in the corporation, and it is viewed by many employees as a cost center, an obstacle to be avoided, or a necessary evil.[38]

The transition to in-house from a law firm may mean a smaller paycheck. An inside attorney's base salary normally will

---

[32]   *Id.*

[33]   *See Are You Ready to Go In-House?*, *supra* note 29; *see generally* Wald, *supra* note 16, at 432–34.

[34]   Aman, *supra* note 9.

[35]   *Id.*

[36]   *Id.*

[37]   *See* Legg, *In-House Lures: Should You Take the Bait?*, The Legal Times (2011), http://www.firmadvice.com/articles/article_inhouse.html, *archived at* https://perma.cc/TTC9-7SHX.

[38]   *See* Wald, *supra* note 16 at 429 ("[I]n-house lawyers are often thought of within the entity as cost centers, commonly perceived as naysayers who do not generate profit and therefore value.").

not be as high as at a law firm. In-house salaries vary greatly depending on the particular company, industry, and geographical location; however, as a general guideline, the median base salaries for in-house attorneys with 0–3 years of experience range between $91,750 and $171,750 per year, without consideration to bonuses, incentives, or other benefits.[39] For those with four to nine years of experience, the median range is $110,000 to $193,000.[40] The most experienced group, with more than 10 years of work under their belts, make median earnings ranging from $139,750 to more than $257,000.[41]

In addition to base salary, annual bonuses are common for in-house attorneys and typically average 20–30% of base.[42] In one survey, some 61% of in-house professionals received a bonus, and 81% of those were satisfied with their bonus.[43] Other benefits for in-house counsel include retirement programs (52%) and stock options (25%).[44]

Contrast in-house base salaries and bonuses with the fact that the going rate for first-year associates at major law firms is $190,000 a year and many equity partners at large law firms earn upwards of $1,136,000 per year.[45] As stated by one source:

> [I]f a law firm attorney [will not] accept a cut in his or her base pay, it will be extremely difficult for [him] to move over to a corporate client. A law firm attorney would have to accept and acknowledge that [her] future compensation might come in many different buckets, including base pay, target bonus, equity and other corporate benefits, and that the total of these buckets

---

[39] *2019 Salary Guide*, Robert Half Legal, at 13.

[40] *Id.*

[41] *Id.*

[42] *Are You Ready to Go In-House?, supra* note 29.

[43] *Id.*

[44] *See 2015 ACC Global Census, supra* note 1, at 14.

[45] Press Release, National Association for Law Placement, First-Year Associate Salaries on the Rise at Large Law Firms (May 22, 2019), https://www.nalp.org/associate salarysurvey2019, *archived at* https://perma.cc/62PH-89RS; Lowe, *2018 Partner Compensation Survey*, Major Lindsey & Africa, https://www.mlaglobal.com/en/ knowledge-library/research/2018-partner-compensation-report, *archived at* https:// perma.cc/F4H2-YDDH.

will be close to or maybe even higher than [her] current compensation at a firm.[46]

The transition may also mean a smaller office. While attorneys in firms typically work in individual windowed offices with high end finishes, in-house attorneys may find themselves sharing offices, in cubicles, or in internal offices with no windows.

Efficiency and cost-cutting measures are factors causing corporate law departments to move some or all their lawyers into cubicles. The move also appears to be driven by a concern for equity, as many business managers and executives are moving, or have moved, to cubicles. Because business members may be viewed as "siblings" of the law department, there is concern that some animosity might be created if lawyers, with equivalent status within the corporation, are in private offices, while the business "siblings" are in cubicles.[47] A significant drawback to working in a cubicle is that an attorney's personal and business conversations may be overheard. In order to maintain confidentiality, an attorney may have to reserve a conference room when discussing confidential matters.[48]

It Is Better to Be a Generalist

Many in-house counsel, particularly those in smaller legal departments, are generalists.[49] Although the idea of being a generalist is appealing to many junior attorneys who seek

---

[46]   Sachs, *supra* note 18.

[47]   DiLucchio, *In-House Lawyers: Cubicles Versus Offices*, Altman Weil Rep. Mgmt. (Nov./Dec. 2004), http://www.altmanweil.com/dir_docs/resource/24ddb354-95cc-4dc8-896d-efe18e791f05_document.pdf, *archived at* https://perma.cc/EJ6Q-YTAP.

[48]   Legg, *supra* note 37.

[49]   On the other hand, lawyers in large corporations can be assigned to specific practice areas, much like attorneys in large firms, and their practice areas can be very specific. For example, the attorneys in the Corporate Securities, Mergers & Acquisitions (CSM&A) group at Hewlett-Packard Company handle a variety of complex corporate legal matters, including corporate governance, securities compliance, treasury and tax transactions, mergers, acquisitions, divestitures and equity investments. The M&A legal team there works closely with the HP Strategy and Corporate Development team to negotiate and execute acquisitions on behalf of HP's business units. They provide legal advice with respect to divestitures, joint ventures and integration of acquired companies. In addition, attorneys in the CSM&A team are exposed to financial and asset management transactions through HP Financial Services. *See* Job Description, *HP Corporate, Securities, Mergers and Acquisitions—1st Year Attorney Program* (Oct. 2, 2013).

variety in their work, there can be significant drawbacks to being one. On any given day, corporate counsel may be juggling multiple projects, such as reviewing a licensing agreement, finalizing packets for the next board meeting, and working on a Form 10-Q that must be filed with the SEC the following week. He must be conversant on many issues but obviously cannot be expert on them all.[50]

Knowing a little about a lot adds to the stress level. In-house lawyers worry that they are opining about something on which they may not be qualified or missing an important red flag that an expert in the area would clearly see. Or they are afraid they will be asked a question at a board meeting to which they do not know the answer. Inside counsel typically have a hard time saying, "I don't know," because they feel they should know the answer. Most law firm lawyers, on the other hand, specialize and have the "luxury" of becoming experts in their particular areas.[51]

Being a generalist may also make corporate counsel less marketable to law firms should she want to return. In the current market, law firms favor expertise because the law has become more specialized and complex. The number of practice areas has increased dramatically since the 1970s and the globalization of business has made transactions more complex. Moreover, governmental regulation and oversight (in the U.S. and abroad) have mushroomed. Some of the more specialized areas of private practice involve, by way of example, government relations, energy and regulated industries, health care, securities practice, telecommunications and intellectual property, and financial regulation. Sophisticated clients and the firms they use demand lawyers with expertise in very specific areas over lawyers with a more general practice. Generalists simply cannot compete with specialists.[52]

Michael Raoufpour, Associate Corporate Counsel with Smoothie King, offers the following insight about making the "reverse commute" from corporation to law firm:

---

[50]   *See* Barnes, *supra* note 17.

[51]   *Id.*

[52]   *See id.*

Once you go in-house, the likelihood of ever working at a firm greatly diminishes. It's a different world, and most law firms prefer someone who is very well versed in a niche area compared to the typical in-house attorney who is more of a generalist. Even if you find a firm willing to take you on, the years in-house may not be fully considered when joining the firm. For example, a third-year in-house attorney may only be able to join as a first- or second-year associate.[53]

In-House Counsel Cannot Be Lonely

Although surrounded by hundreds or thousands of other employees, corporate counsel can be lonely. An in-house attorney, unlike an attorney in a law firm, may find himself handling issues alone, with no guidance. This isolation can be terrifying for a junior attorney.

Law firms, on the other hand, have experts in many different areas of the law brought together in one place (e.g., tax, real estate, ERISA, securities, etc.)—attorneys to exchange ideas, and senior attorneys to mentor junior attorneys. If a law firm lawyer needs assistance or additional resources to evaluate an issue outside her area of expertise, she has a "bullpen" of other lawyers to call upon. A general counsel, particularly one in a small or mid-sized department, however, lacks those resources and may feel isolated.[54]

Another aspect of the job that may contribute to the "loneliness factor" is that a general counsel, as a result of her role, will often be privy to confidential information about her co-workers and supervisors that she cannot share with others in the company. Such information may include plans to terminate a member of the senior management team, details on executive compensation, board member evaluations, and internal investigations into suspected criminal activity. In compensation committee meetings, the general counsel may hear what the board members like (and do not like) about a particular

---

[53]   Interview with Michael Raoufpour, Associate Corporate Counsel, Smoothie King, in Dallas, Tex. (July 2, 2019).

[54]   *See* Eagle, *supra* note 1 at 10; *see generally* Kiang, *Isolation: Surviving Being Solo In-House Counsel*, Law. Wkly. In-House Couns. (Fall 2009).

executive, what he or she is currently paid relative to other executives in the company as well as what her future compensation package will be. Sometimes this information concerns individuals with whom the general counsel works closely. Absent client consent, the general counsel may not, however, disclose any of this information.[55] Possessing such sensitive information about colleagues, some of whom may be superiors, only contributes to the loneliness factor.[56] As observed by one source,

> Within the corporation [in-house lawyers may] often [be] perceived as outsiders, working alone, removed from non-lawyers, from corporate colleagues, especially vis-a-vis lower-ranked executives who often see only one goal, generating profit, and thus little use for lawyers, as opposed to higher-up executives who have been tested in decision-making entailing complex legal elements who might better appreciate the value lawyers can generate. . . . In-house attorneys must bridge the gap, prove themselves valuable to the entity, and overcome the outsider perception.[57]

In-House Attorneys Do Not Have to Worry About Malpractice

Until fairly recently, in-house counsel were not named as defendants. But today, some inside counsel find themselves named individually as defendants in civil and criminal matters and even malpractice suits by their own clients.[58] In the post-Enron/Sarbanes Oxley/Dodd-Frank world, companies and their general counsel have come under enhanced scrutiny. Several general counsel have been the subject of SEC enforcement actions, government investigations, prosecutions, defendants in

---

[55]   *See* Turner & Floyd, *In-House Counsel and Confidentiality*, For the Defense (Feb. 2007), at 59, https://www.bakerdonelson.com/files/Uploads/Documents/Emerging %20Technologies%20-%20In-House%20Counsel%20and%20Confidentiality2007.pdf, *archived at* https://perma.cc/7C33-CD6Q.

[56]   *See* Martin, *The GC's Role in Ethics Can Be Lonely*, Inside Couns. (Oct. 30, 2012).

[57]   Wald, *supra* note 16, at 437–38.

[58]   *See* Friedman, *Most Claims Against In-House Counsel Don't Make the Front Page*, Corp. Couns. (July 23, 2007).

civil litigation, and even disbarred for ethical transgressions.[59]
There may also be conflicts of interest within the corporation.[60]
Indeed, at times, the general counsel may be forced to resign
rather than become complicit in illegal activity.[61]

---

*No job is 100% perfect. And despite the challenges and
tensions described above, most in-house counsel will tell you that
they enjoy their jobs and would not do anything else. If working
in-house sounds right for you, there are concrete steps you can
take to increase your chances of obtaining an in-house position.*

PATHWAYS TO IN-HOUSE PRACTICE

The General Rule

Traditionally, lawyers make the move to in-house practice
after spending at least 2 to 3 years as an associate in a law
firm.[62] In fact, the Association of Corporate Counsel reports that
the vast majority of in-house attorneys had some prior, private
practice experience prior to becoming in-house counsel.[63] Most
corporations do not hire right out of law school simply because
they do not have the resources or desire to train new lawyers.

---

[59]   *Id.* (noting high-profile cases involving in-house counsel, particularly those
involving the Securities and Exchange Commission and investigations or enforcement
actions, shareholder class actions, misbranding or marketing misstatements regarding
pharmaceuticals, and backdating of stock options); *see also* DeMott, *The Discrete Roles
of General Counsel*, 74 Fordham L. Rev. 955, 974–75 (2005); *see generally* M. Steinberg,
Attorney Liability After Sarbanes-Oxley (2018) (analyzing lawsuits against inside
counsel); Pera & Faughnan, *Paradise Tarnished: Today's Sources of Liability Exposure
for Corporate Counsel*, Ass'n of Corp. Couns. (Mar. 1, 2005) (concluding that corporate
counsel will more often be focus of government enforcement actions, shareholder
derivative claims, securities fraud class actions and maybe even malpractice suits by
their own clients); Epstein, *So You Want to Depose Opposing Counsel?*, American Bar
Association National Conference on Professional Responsibility (Aug. 27, 2012) (courts
increasingly reluctant to quash a subpoena for an in-house attorney to testify).

[60]   Friedman, *supra* note 58 (discussing action against an associate general
counsel alleging, among other things, conflict of interest).

[61]   *See* DeMott, *supra* note 59, at 976–77 (noting that "[s]olidarity between a
general counsel and other members of senior management can compromise counsel's
service as a legal adviser).

[62]   Alexander, *Straight to In-House: P&G's Tara Rosnell on Rising to the Ranks of
Hiring Attorney*, ACC Docket (Feb. 21, 2018), https://www.accdocket.com/articles/
straight-to-in-house-p-g-tara-rosnell-hiring.cfm?_ga=2.166448702.1081831929.1561122
899-2141563396.1559055313, *archived at* https://perma.cc/4Q42-PA6Y.

[63]   *See 2015 ACC Global Census, supra* note 1, at 26.

Rather, they prefer to let recent law school graduates learn and hone their skills at law firms. Most large firms have excellent formal training programs where junior associates receive training in specialized areas of the law as well as informal training from attorneys with technical and real-world experience.[64] Michael Raoufpour, Associate Corporate Counsel at Smoothie King, offers the following insight:

> In-house attorneys also do not receive the same training many law firm attorneys obtain right out of law school. When you go in-house, you are typically thrown right in and most companies don't have a Westlaw/Lexis subscription, so you utilize past contracts and/or independent research for much of what you'll be working on. You learn by doing.[65]

There is no hard and fast rule on how much experience is needed to go in-house. Data from the Association of Corporate Counsel indicates that 41% of in-house counsel worked 5 years or less in a law firm prior to becoming in-house counsel.[66]

A notable trend is the growth of new in-house attorneys who never worked in a law firm: 14% of in-house counsel never worked in a firm or outside legal position before going in-house.[67] "This growth may be the result of converging market forces that see new law graduates migrating in-house directly from law school."[68]

Staying in a law firm for more than seven years may reduce an in-house candidate's marketability for more junior level in-house positions.[69] More senior in-house positions, and particularly general counsel positions, normally require ten or more years of significant experience at a law firm, corporation, or both.[70] Some larger companies require more experience, such

---

[64]   *See* Barnes, *supra* note 17.

[65]   Interview with Michael Raoufpour, Associate Corporate Counsel, Smoothie King, in Dallas, Tex. (July 2, 2019).

[66]   *See 2015 ACC Global Census, supra* note 1, at 26.

[67]   *Id.*

[68]   *Id.*

[69]   *See* Barnes, *supra* note 17.

[70]   *See* Legg, *supra* note 37.

as nine to twenty years of experience, for associate general counsel positions.[71]

Attorneys transition to corporate counsel roles in a variety of different ways, with no single one standing out from the others. Many times, a corporation will hire an attorney they have used as outside counsel with whom they are impressed and have a requisite level of trust. Such a hire is viewed as "safe" because the in-house lawyers are already familiar with the attorney; his skills and work ethic are known as a result of his interaction with the legal department. Moreover, the transition is smoother because the attorney already understands the corporation's business and the legal issues it faces as a result of serving as its outside counsel.[72]

Once an attorney leaves a law firm for a corporation, it is unlikely she will ever go back to private practice, both because of personal choice and business reality.[73] Consider a lawyer who leaves a law firm after three years and works in-house for four years. He will likely be less attractive to a law firm than a seven-year associate who has a book of business, unless he has the ability to bring work from his corporate employer with him.[74]

Other attorneys learn of in-house positions through corporate job boards, networking with other attorneys, or legal recruiters. Some attorneys transition in-house from legal jobs with government agencies. The skills and knowledge acquired while working in agencies such as the Securities and Exchange Commission, Environmental Protection Agency, Federal Trade Commission, Federal Communications Commission, or the Department of Agriculture can prove invaluable, especially when a lawyer moves to a company whose industry is regulated

---

[71]   See, e.g., Assistant General Counsel posting for global biopharmaceutical company (seeking 9+ years of experience in a pharmaceutical law—in-house or law firm; Executive Level Bank Regulatory Counsel posting (requiring "[n]o less than 15 to 20 years [of] experience as an attorney in the financial services sector"); Deputy General Counsel posting by publicly-traded leading supplier of advance wireless systems for the mobile Internetworking market ("ideal candidate will have at least 12 years of strong transactional experience in commercial sales and licensing (both direct and indirect)").

[72]   See generally Fontaine, supra note 2.

[73]   Sachs, supra note 18; see also Cannon, supra note 18 (noting that once an attorney makes the jump, it can be very difficult to return to private practice primarily because law firms will question the attorney's commitment to returning on a long-term basis).

[74]   See Barnes, supra note 17.

by his prior employer. Another route to in-house is through a "secondment," an arrangement between a law firm and a company (usually one of the firm's clients) where a lawyer is seconded, or temporarily loaned, to work for that company. The lawyer is an employee of the law firm, but works at the client's offices under the supervision of the client. When the secondment period ends, the attorney usually goes back to the law firm, but sometimes secondments turn into permanent in-house positions.[75]

Fahad Juneja is a good example of the traditional path to in-house practice. As a third-year law student at SMU Dedman School of Law, he externed with the legal department at Lennox International Inc. After graduation, he began his legal career at Sidley Austin LLP where he worked in both the Dallas and Los Angeles (Century City) offices. He was a litigator for the first six months of his legal career but later switched to Sidley's Corporate and M&A practice group. Almost 4 years later, he joined Paramount Pictures as Counsel focusing on worldwide digital distribution and television licensing in Los Angeles, California. Fahad offers the following advice based on his experience:

> One of the most tried and true methods of going in-house is by working at a law firm for at least two to three years (generally in a transactional role), making client connections through your law firm experience and leveraging those connections or your experience to move in-house. However, if you have a sense of industry or type of company where you wish to exit in-house, it is advantageous to start making connections in that industry or type of company. As I was not in an entertainment-specific practice group at Sidley, I made an effort to attend entertainment law conferences in the area and also attended networking events for the entertainment industry whenever possible, ultimately making a connection through a Viacom Business and Legal Affairs mixer that led to my current job at

---

[75] Allison, *In-House Counsel, Firms Turn to Secondments,* Law360 (Sept. 16, 2009) (noting that Clay Mingus accepted position of general counsel at Hooters of America Inc. while on secondment from Elarbee Thompson Sapp & Wilson LLP, a labor and employment firm in Atlanta).

Paramount. Other potential pathways include joining specialized bar membership groups, presenting CLEs, or writing articles on specialized topics or networking with in-house attorneys who have a career path that you wish to explore.[76]

The Exceptions to the Rule

Although the typical in-house career starts at a law firm, signs indicate this is changing. According to the latest statistics from the National Association for Law Placement, 13.9% of recent law school graduates obtained jobs in business and industry.[77] This means that law students are contemplating in-house careers earlier, and more companies—both large and small—seek to attract and hire more junior lawyers.

The required experience level has trended downward significantly over the last decade. William Kruse, author of "The Corporate Counsel Survival Guide," says "recent law school grads can become in-house attorneys if they come to the table with marketable training. Because many corporations are trying to reduce the amount of money they spend on legal costs, these corporations are expanding the number of full-time, in-house attorneys on staff, so they can avoid paying the hefty fees charged by big law firms."[78]

Opportunities with Very Large Legal Departments

Large companies with legal departments the size of large law firms have a head start on hiring and training new grads.[79]

---

[76]   Interview with Fahad Juneja, Counsel, Paramount Pictures, in Los Angeles, Cal. (July 2, 2019).

[77]   Collins, Jobs & JDs: Employment for the Class of 2017—Selected Findings, National Association for Law Placement (Oct. 2018), *archived at* https://perma.cc/BCW9-8Y2N.

[78]   Kowarski, *How to Find Law Schools That Lead to In-House Counsel Jobs*, US News.com (Dec. 24, 2018), https://www.usnews.com/education/best-graduate-schools/top-law-schools/articles/2018-12-24/how-to-find-law-schools-that-lead-to-in-house-counsel-jobs, *archived at* https://perma.cc/963P-2SMH.

[79]   Hechler, *The Art of Hiring: Three Savvy Law Departments Take Different Approaches to Choosing and Training, But Each Yields Excellent Results*, Corp. Couns. (May 2014), at 86 (discussing hiring and training at International Business Machines Corporation, Google, Inc. and Microsoft Corporation); O'Connell, *Cut the Law Firms, Keep the Lawyers*, Wall St. J. (Aug. 12, 2011), at B1 (hiring of recent law school graduates by legal departments at Hewlett-Packard Company and Pfizer Inc.); Strom, *Some Law School Grads Find Their Place In-House*, Chi. Law. (Mar. 1, 2012) (discussing recent law

For example, since 2010, Hewlett-Packard Company (now HP Inc.) has hired attorneys directly out of law school.

In fall 2009, the leaders of Hewlett-Packard's legal department saw an opportunity and took it.[80] Many law firms were deferring or rescinding offers to new associates, leaving top graduates from the nation's leading law schools in the lurch. "We could pluck the top talent whose opportunities had been taken away," says Amy Schuh, Hewlett-Packard Legal Department's former Chief of Staff and Deputy General Counsel, both of students willing to work for less money than top law firms pay because they didn't have a job and of those who wanted the work-life balance associated with an in-house career. "It was an opportunity to bring in lawyers we can train in the Hewlett-Packard way who will have long, successful careers in this department."

That year, Hewlett-Packard recruited four law school students who started work at Hewlett-Packard's Palo Alto, California, headquarters in September 2010. The following year, the program expanded to five new graduates hired in the U.S. and four in India. The Hewlett-Packard class of 2012 includes six students hired to work domestically, and additional hiring overseas is under consideration.

Hewlett-Packard's training includes two, weeklong "boot camps" that have been so successful that they are now offered to all new Hewlett-Packard lawyers, regardless of level. The first-year associates must also complete a curriculum of practical training, including research memos, document review, and a day spent with the government relations team and with a salesperson. Two weeks of face-to-face training includes seminars on writing and negotiation, and is supplemented with web-based training. Intermittent training continues into the second year, with experiences such as visiting Hewlett-Packard's contracting site to learn how to negotiate a contract.

---

school graduates hired by Solo Cup Co., McDonalds, Ace Hardware, and RNA), https://www.chicagolawyermagazine.com/elements/pages/print.aspx?printpath=/Archives/2012/03/19197&classname=tera.gn3article, *archived at* https://perma.cc/LA3E-URDW.

[80]   The following discussion, through *infra* note 81, is taken from Swanton, *Some Law School Grads Head Directly In-House,* Inside Couns. (Mar. 1, 2012), https://www.law.com/almID/4f4be167150ba0f041000079/, *archived at* https://perma.cc/Q6SG-CBEU. Reprinted with permission. All rights reserved.

"We looked at the basics of lawyering—the things every junior associate [at a law firm] should do—and said let's make sure they have that opportunity here as well," Schuh says.

The new hires are immediately assigned to a practice group where they are given real legal work, though often the kind more senior attorneys don't want to do, such as 50-state surveys on a legal issue. "They are getting work done that desperately needed to get done," Schuh says, thereby freeing up more senior attorneys to work on more complicated matters. They have quickly exceeded expectations. "Every one of them is a rising star," Schuh says. "All four [who started in 2010] are doing the work of mid-level associates already, and very high-quality work. It's been a real pleasant surprise for all of us," says Schuh

Another surprise is the impact the new lawyers' energy and enthusiasm have had on the department's culture. "They are incredibly engaged and happy to be here. They really appreciate the opportunity they have, and that has been contagious," she says. Hewlett Packard recruits at 13 top law schools from coast to coast and receives many more resumes from students across the nation.

While Hewlett-Packard has one of the world's largest legal departments, with 450 to 500 attorneys worldwide, Schuh believes any department with 50-plus attorneys could start such a program—but only with commitment from the department's leadership to provide the resources for a robust training program. "We had commitment from the top that we would run our program better than law firms," she says. "It's been a priority cascaded down through the organization. Without that, you are set up to fail."[81]

Early career attorneys at larger companies typically specialize in a particular area as they would in a law firm. "Examples of these types of roles include in-house corporate counsel, transactional counsel, employment and benefits counsel, litigation counsel, tax counsel, intellectual property counsel, and privacy counsel."[82] Bradshaw Hawkins, Associate

---

[81]   See Swanton, *supra* note 80.

[82]   *How to Go In-House Straight from Law School*, The Girl's Guide to Law School, Newstex (Feb. 20, 2018).

General Counsel at AZZ, Inc., says, "We've seen many companies, particularly larger companies, adding junior counsel to handle matters typically assigned to junior associates at outside law firms. Especially if a company primarily uses large law firms, the cost of a junior in-house attorney can be easily justified after discounting the NDAs, simple contracts, and document review handled by attorneys of similar experience at high hourly rates. It is a great opportunity for a young attorney to gather direct experience on a wide variety of practice areas."[83]

Hawkins himself is an example of this trend. After graduating from SMU Dedman School of Law in 2014, he spent approximately two years with a mid-sized firm. Hawkins then transitioned to an in-house role at Goldman Sachs and then to his current role with a publicly-traded global enterprise. He says there is a "huge upside potential for an in-house attorney. Corporate counsel who add value beyond mere legal review can really pop on the radar of senior management. This could mean additional responsibilities, more business involvement, or even a career pivot. At larger companies, compensation comes with better bonuses and equity participation. Combined with a better lifestyle and broader practice areas, in-house work can be attractive for attorneys at any level."[84]

Opportunities with Smaller Companies

Smaller companies are seeing more quality applicants and are now selectively hiring attorneys with zero to three years of experience. Melanie Trostel Terrell may be the new face of in-house counsel. She began her legal career in-house at Rug Doctor, LLC, where she was hired before passing the bar in 2017. As a first-year attorney, she took notes and asked lots of questions. Everyone at the company knew she was right out of law school and did not expect her to know the answers to all the questions just starting out. But they expected her to take the initiative and learn. Trostel had the support of a highly-skilled general counsel who was there when she was unsure about how to proceed on a matter. "Fortunately, Amy Osteen, our general

---

[83]   Interview with Bradshaw Hawkins, Associate General Counsel, AZZ Inc. in Ft. Worth, Tex. (July 16, 2019).

[84]   *Id.*

counsel, is an excellent role model who invested the time to mentor and train me. She made sure I was provided opportunities to do real legal work at an early stage in my career ranging from contract drafting and negotiating to international employment law issues. I also made it a priority to get involved with and learn as many aspects of the business as I could, which allowed me to work collaboratively with individuals from other departments and find areas where our internal legal processes could be improved upon."[85]

Trostel says, "I don't know whether I would have received this breadth and depth of legal experience as a first-year associate with a law firm. I am very fortunate that I started my legal career in-house and have had the opportunity to learn and work with an excellent legal department at a rapidly-growing company."[86] So how can law students take advantage of this trend and best prepare themselves to begin their legal careers in-house like she did? Trostel says:

> Take courses in the following areas: corporations or business enterprise, sale of goods, social media law, advanced legal research, employment law, advanced contracts drafting, and creditor's rights. If your school offers an externship program in corporate counsel offices, take full advantage of that opportunity. As a third-year law student, I externed with the Dean Foods legal department in Dallas, Texas. This experience exposed me to the realities of in-house practice, and I was able to translate this practical experience to my legal position at Rug Doctor. The connections students make in corporate externships like mine can also be instrumental in landing highly-coveted, entry-level roles.[87]

Karen Sargent, dean of career services at SMU Dedman School of Law, says she has seen an increasing number of recent graduates talk with companies about in-house or other law-related positions, such as compliance and contracts

---

[85] Interview with Melanie Trostel Terrell, Assistant General Counsel, Rug Doctor, LLC, in Plano, Tex. (Sept. 19, 2019).
[86] *Id.*
[87] *Id.*

management. "With the recruiting mantra to do more with fewer resources, in-house legal departments are seeking new ways to create efficiencies in all areas of their practice while increasing their effectiveness. Indeed, since late 2011, companies are considering lawyers with fewer than three years of experience. Gone are the days when landing an in-house position requires several years of law firm experience."[88]

Marcus Bahena, acting General Counsel of Emerus in The Woodlands, Texas, has never worked anywhere except at this developer of fully operational micro-hospitals. He credits his law school externship with the legal department at Parkland Health & Hospital System with giving him a "competitive advantage" when he applied for a job with Emerus as Corporate Counsel straight out of law school.[89] With the healthcare knowledge he obtained at Parkland, Emerus was eager to hire him because they did not have to start from scratch like they would for most new hires.

A recent law graduate, Bahena joined the company in 2017 right out of law school and immediately started doing "a little bit of everything from reviewing contracts to developing social media policies." Due to the smaller size of the company, he interacted daily with senior executives and members of every department in the company, working with some of the biggest non-profit healthcare systems across the country to develop multi-million dollar joint venture partners.

Bahena points out that in-house counsel are in a unique position to "connect" people across departments. He credits a large part of his success within the company to developing relationships with his fellow coworkers. He considers the legal department not as a closed door but as a department that sparks business development. His internal "clients" who come to him with various issues sometimes forget to connect with one another. "I can then ask, 'Have you checked with this person because she may be working on the same project or issue?' " says Bahena. Beyond just performing legal work, new in-house

    [88]   Interview with Karen C. Sargent, Assistant Dean for Career Services, SMU Dedman School of Law, in Dallas, Tex. (Sept. 20, 2019).
    [89]   Interview with Marcus Bahena, Acting General Counsel, Emerus, in The Woodlands, Tex. (July 19, 2019).

counsel can add value in this way. "As a generalist, I have information from multiple departments that may be helpful to others in advancing their project," says Bahena, "making improvements, or driving better results for the company." And his hard work and ability to connect business partners has paid off. Bahena moved up quickly through the small legal department: he was promoted to Associate General Counsel and then acting General Counsel when his boss left the company.

WHAT ARE CORPORATIONS LOOKING FOR IN CORPORATE COUNSEL?

Large law firms and corporate legal departments have very different hiring criteria. While the largest firms value degrees from top law schools, top 25% GPAs, law review, and post-graduate judicial clerkships, corporations focus primarily on a candidate's experience.[90]

Corporations have very specific needs based on their particular industry, the legal issues they face, and their regulatory environment. For example, a midstream energy company may have very specific needs for a new Associate General Counsel. The job requirements may look something like this:

> *Seeking attorney with seven or more years of legal experience related to interstate pipelines, including work with the Federal Energy Regulatory Commission. Management experience of staff of at least 10 other lawyers also required.*

As much as the general counsel may like a candidate with significant experience in another industry or practice area, he

---

[90]   *See* Fontaine, *supra* note 2 ("In-house employers usually don't value academic credentials such as law school prestige and the candidate's class rank as highly as law firms do; rather, they weigh experience and interpersonal skills much more heavily"); Sachs, *supra* note 18 (Corporations "want to find someone to join their legal department who already has the appropriate industry experience. Retail clients want retail experience, oil and gas clients want oil and gas experience, hospitality clients want. . . you get the picture. It's one thing to say that you have worked on some (or even many) matters for retail clients as part of your law firm portfolio; it's quite another to say that you go to work every day at a retail company and one hundred percent of your job is retail-focused"); *see generally* Henderson & Zahorsky, *The Pedigree Problem: Are Law School Ties Choking the Profession?*, ABA J. (July 1, 2012), http://www.abajournal.com/magazine/article/the_pedigree_problem_are_law_school_ties_choking_the_profession/, *archived at* https://perma.cc/J3W5-M46G.

must have an attorney who can "hit the ground running" and work autonomously on the complex legal and regulatory issues facing the company.[91]

Another key consideration for corporations is interpersonal skills.[92] Corporations need counsel who "fit" into the corporate culture and can gain a high level of trust with the business people. Other characteristics and skill sets that general counsel identify as important when hiring an in-house attorney include:

- Strong critical thinking skills
- Integrity and diplomacy
- Sound business judgment and common sense
- Specific industry experience
- Demonstrated analytical skills
- Intellectual curiosity for other areas of the law
- Confidence
- Creative problem solver
- Detail-oriented
- Solid communication and writing skills[93]

The following job posting for an entry-level attorney position with a regional insurance company illustrates some of the

---

[91]   *See, e.g., Job Watch: Fast-Moving Consumer Goods and Retail*, Lawyer (Mar. 18, 2013).

[92]   *See* Robert Half Legal, *supra* note 5, at 17.

[93]   *See* Roellig & Love, *So You Want to Be a General Counsel: How to Maximize Your Chances*, ACC Docket (Jan./Feb. 2012) (listing following attributes and skills: good and tested judgment; specific industry experience; confidence; impeccable ethics and integrity; leadership; hardworking; ability to develop relationships; first-class communication skills; ability to be strategic, to anticipate issues and estimate risks; and creative in identifying proactive solutions to eliminate or mitigate risks and advance the business), https://www.spencerstuart.com/~/media/PDF%20Files/Research%20and%20 Insight%20PDFs/So-You-Want-To-Be-A-General-Counsel_31Jan2012.pdf, *archived at* https://perma.cc/E4CS-WB9G; *see also* Fontaine, *supra* note 2 ("You need confidence and strong negotiating skills, not just for deal-making across the table, but also to advocate for your recommendations within the company"); Ass'n of Corp. Couns. Executive Series, *Skills for the 21st Century General Counsel* (2008 Report) (listing curiosity and drive to understand the organization and its business; strategic thinking ability; strong emotional intelligence; and broad-based legal experience as necessary skill sets); *See generally The Criteria In-House Counsel Use to Hire and Fire Outside Lawyers: A Roundtable Discussion*, N.J.L.J. (June 16, 1997) (listing chemistry, long-term working relationships, efficiency, good business judgment and knowledge of the law).

characteristics that such a company may value in a new in-house attorney:

> *ABC Company, specializing in life, health, and accident coverage has an immediate opening for an Attorney. This position will be responsible for tasks including, but not limited to, insurance claim review, regulatory compliance, litigation management, contract drafting, and general corporate legal work.*

> *Ideal candidates will have a law degree with 0–5 years' experience and strong academic record. Recent law school graduates will be considered. Excellent communication skills and the ability to manage multiple priorities and deadlines required. Must be highly self-motivated with the ability to start a project and see it to fruition. Prior insurance experience preferred but not required. Candidate should have strong adaptable, interpersonal skills as well as the ability to work independently. Must be detail-oriented with the ability to analyze information and make logical conclusions.*

Starting Your In-House Job Search

Many believe that a broad search incorporating virtually every practice area, industry, and geographical location will increase a candidate's chances of finding an in-house job, but this approach does not work as well with in-house placements. Rather, an active, focused job search as outlined below is likely to be more successful.

Identifying Your Experience and Skill Sets

The first step in any in-house job search is to identify the practice areas for which you are legitimately qualified. Start by taking a hard, objective look at your private practice experience and educational background to identify your area(s) of specialization and the amount of your experience. Specialized areas such as intellectual property, employment law, health law, securities law, environmental law, and tax law demand more experience and may require significant prior law firm experience, while areas like general contract and drafting work may require less experience.[94]

Consider whether your background is such that it lends itself to a more-generalized practice. Generalist credentials can be helpful in going in-house, particularly with smaller companies that value attorneys with a more-general knowledge than knowledge in a particular area of the law.[95] According to one expert:

> In-house legal departments primarily hire lawyers with transactional expertise, especially in corporate, securities, mergers and acquisitions, and—depending upon the company's business—real estate or intellectual property; labor and employment expertise also is desirable. While litigation management skills are valuable, most corporations other than those with the largest law departments send active litigation matters to outside lawyers. Consequently, law department positions for pure litigators are few and far between.[96]

Another corporate counsel offers the following perspective with respect to background experience:

> If you are fairly certain that you want to go in-house in the future (or to have that option readily available), choosing a litigation-focused practice group is generally not advised. Most in-house roles are transactional focused and having contract drafting experience and knowing what terms are 'market' versus aggressive positions is valued. There are some former litigators who go in-house and a handful of in-house positions require litigation experience as well as the ability to manage the company's ongoing litigation matters. On a pure numbers basis, however, the available in-house jobs for litigators are much fewer than the positions open to lawyers with transactional backgrounds. Therefore, if you eventually want to go in-house and are

---

[94]   *See* Strom, *supra* note 79.

[95]   *See* Posting of Russeth to *Lessons from #LawJobChat: @richard_russeth on Landing In-House Counsel Jobs* (Aug. 28, 2010), *archived at* https://perma.cc/NHT5-GPAJ.

[96]   Fontaine, *supra* note 2.

on the fence about selecting a litigation or transactional practice group at a law firm, I would suggest starting with a transactional practice group (ideally corporate, M&A or technology transactions).[97]

The Association of Corporate Counsel recently reported that the most prominent practice areas in an in-house counsel practice are, in descending order:

1. General Commercial/Contracts

2. Corporate transactions

3. Generalist

4. Employment/HR

5. Compliance

6. Litigation

7. Intellectual Property

8. Mergers/Acquisitions

9. Real Estate

10. Personnel management

11. Securities

12. International

13. Finance[98]

Other primary disciplines included Labor, Antitrust/Trade, Environmental, Health, Banking, ERISA/Pension, Insurance Defense, Bankruptcy/Creditor issues, Non-Profit, Energy, Tax, Retail, Franchising, Insurance/Risk Management, Government Affairs, Investment Banking, Technology/E-commerce, Corporate Governance/Ethics, and Construction.[99]

The desired experience and skill set will vary by company. An attorney with trademark experience or labeling requirements may be highly sought after by companies in the

---

[97]   Interview with Fahad Juneja, Counsel, Paramount Pictures, in Los Angeles, Cal. (July 2, 2019).

[98]   *2015 ACC Global Census, supra* note 1, at 23; *see also* Robert Half Legal, *supra* note 5, at 12.

[99]   *2015 ACC Global Census, supra* note 1, at 23.

consumer-packaged goods industry, such as Keurig Dr Pepper or Dean Foods Company. Consumer intensive companies (not business-to-business) are more likely to hire litigators. Experience with real estate leasing and construction law can be very useful in companies in the retail or hospitality industries, such as Michaels Stores, JCPenney, and Omni Hotels & Resorts, that lease and/or build properties across the country. Companies in the biotechnology and life sciences industries seek attorneys with industry experience and the ability to communicate legal concepts in layperson's terms for scientists and other non-legal professionals.[100] And, of course, securities law experience can be a real plus in publicly traded companies. As domestic corporations continue to expand their footprints globally, "the demand for native fluency and cultural awareness can also spell opportunity for bilingual or multilingual attorneys."[101]

Companies want attorneys with sound business judgment. To this end, consider what business education, know-how, or specific technical or industry knowledge you possess. An attorney with video game and entertainment software know-how would be valued at a company like GameStop, whereas knowledge of cloud computing would be extremely helpful at a company like SoftLayer Technologies, Inc. Similarly, a chemistry background may be valued for lawyers working with chemical and life sciences companies.[102]

Litigation can be a perfect training ground for in-house lawyers because they are forced to learn complex sets of facts and law (e.g., banking, trademark, products liability) quickly and then "teach" those areas to juries and judges. Like litigators, corporate counsel must not be afraid to jump in and learn something new. Commercial litigators also have a unique perspective of seeing how poorly-drafted contracts can result in litigation, and they may be more attuned to resolving issues quickly before they become claims. Finally, some very large

---

[100]   Robert Half Legal, *supra* note 5, at 12.

[101]   Bechet, *The Language of Law: The Demand for Bilingual Attorneys in Corporate Law Departments,* Minority Corp. Couns. Ass'n Diversity & the Bar (May/June 2006),   http://archive.mcca.com/index.cfm?fuseaction=page.viewpage&pageid=1048, *archived at* https://perma.cc/22GG-JNYP.

[102]   *Chemistry and the Law: Opportunities for Chemists in the Legal Profession,* ACS,   https://www.acs.org/content/acs/en/careers/college-to-career/chemistry-careers/chemistry-law.html, *archived at* https://perma.cc/UUZ9-38GL.

companies have large dockets of litigation matters and will hire in-house attorneys solely to handle smaller, single-plaintiff cases and/or manage outside counsel in larger, high-stakes litigation matters.[103]

Focusing on an Industry

One job search strategy for recent law school graduates is to focus on a particular industry. Ashley Yen, Associate In-House Counsel for Methodist Health System in Dallas, interned with a healthcare services company during law school and was offered a job with the same company upon graduation. She is now an attorney with a major health care system. Yen advises young lawyers to figure out what industry they would like to work in before applying in-house:

> Interviewing and being interviewed at various places, I've realized that companies will sometimes overlook the 'years of experience' requirement if they see that you have applicable industry-specific experience listed on your resume. Therefore, as a law student, I would aim to gather some internship/externship experience in the area of law that you would like to go into and reach out to the attorneys at those companies in that specific industry.[104]

Identifying "Target" Companies

Because there are so many prospective employers, searching for an in-house job can be overwhelming. For example, there are public companies, privately-held enterprises, non-profit corporations, start-up firms, and educational institutions. And these companies operate in hundreds of different industries. For example, hundreds of companies exist in the oil and gas industry alone in the United States. Where do you start?

The first step is to match your experience and skills with companies in your geographic location (or in the location where

---

[103] *See* Nicholas, *Companies Look for New Ways to Control Litigation Costs*, Inside Counsel (Aug. 30, 2013).

[104] Interview with Ashley Yen, Associate In-House Counsel, Methodist Health System, in Dallas, Tex. (July 1, 2019).

you would like to work).[105] Prepare a target list of companies in your area that have legal departments and have needs that match your background or industry focus. Corporate and in-house legal directories, particularly those limited to a major metropolitan area, can be very helpful in this process. For example:

- The Fortune 500 issue of *Fortune* magazine as well as the digital version at www.fortune.com list the largest companies and their data according to many variables, including revenue, profit, and percentage growth.

- The *Dallas Business Journal* publishes an annual Book of Lists which lists the largest public and private companies in the Dallas-Fort Worth area and categorizes companies by industry. Other cities have similar publications.[106]

- *Directory of Corporate Counsel* published by the *Texas Lawyer* includes the most complete list of in-house attorneys in Texas legal departments. The directory lists the names, titles, addresses, and phone numbers of general counsel and other in-house counsel in alphabetical order by company.[107]

---

[105]   *See* Rubin & Williams, *Seven Secrets of Landing Your Next In-House Job*, Inside Counsel.com (June 2009) ("[P]ick 10–20 companies where you'd like to work, which are geographically convenient and where your existing legal expertise and experience are valued."). Where are most of the in-house jobs located? The jobs with sizeable in-house law departments are located in the states with the largest corporate headquarters. There are 54 Fortune 500 companies in California. New York and Texas are tied for second place with 52 companies apiece and Illinois takes third place with 32 corporations. Therefore, a large company, corporate counsel career path in California, Texas, New York or Illinois would be a reasonable one, whereas there will be fewer in-house job opportunities in states that are not home to many major corporations. *See, e.g., Fortune 500 Headquarters in Texas*, Off. Governor Econ. Dev. & Tourism (identifying the 49 Fortune 500 corporate headquarters in Texas) (citing Fortune Magazine, June 2019), https://gov.texas.gov/uploads/files/business/TXfortune500-2019.pdf, *archived at* https://perma.cc/2JAL-T3B6.

[106]   *See Dallas Business Journal Book of Lists*, https://www.bizjournals.com/dallas/ecommerce/product/bookoflists, *archived at* https://perma.cc/YXR8-Z399; *see e.g., Book of Lists Online* (noting over 150 Books of Lists produced by business journals across the United States. From New York to LA, from Florida to Charlotte), http://www.bookoflists online.com/2014/08/2015-book-of-lists_20.html, *archived at* https://perma.cc/DV6P-JSEW.

[107]   *2018 Directory of Corporate Counsel*, Tex. Law. (Dec. 30, 2018).

Other states have publications that likewise comprehensively list this information.

The following online resources are also very good for researching companies:

- *Glassdoor*: Employees anonymously review their companies, post salary information, rate CEOs, and much more.[108]

- *LinkedIn*: LinkedIn company profiles provide great insight into a particular company, and you can even "follow" companies that interest you. Company profiles also allow you to see new hires, posted jobs, promotions, company statistics, and your connections at the company.[109]

- *Association of Corporate Counsel's Members Only Directory*: ACC members can find contact information for more than 45,000 in-house peers and tailor searches by company name, area of expertise, local chapter, or country.[110]

Include the companies you initially identify in a spreadsheet, but recognize that your list is not static. It should be revised often as you learn of new companies and contacts or rule certain companies out of your search.[111]

The Active Job Search

Once you have identified your areas of experience and matched them with appropriate companies, you are ready to begin your search. A large part of your job search should be "active"—that is networking, and meeting people face to face. Indeed, many of the best in-house job leads are passed among

---

[108] http://www.glassdoor.com.

[109] http://www.linkedin.com.

[110] https://www.acc.com/member-directory.

[111] *See* Morgan, *How to Find Target Companies for Your Job Search*, Career Sherpa (Jan. 29, 2013), https://careersherpa.net/how-to-find-target-companies-for-your-job-search/, *archived at* https://perma.cc/73A8-LFX2.

contacts (and coincidentally, so are recommendations and endorsements).[112]

The first step many corporations take in the hiring process is to ask attorneys in the law department and attorneys at their outside firms for referrals. These provide companies with easy access to a short list of potential candidates who have been recommended by a trusted contact. Additionally, referrals are usually faster, cheaper, and more effective than delegating the search to an outside legal search firm. Many times, corporate jobs are filled through "word of mouth" and are never posted.[113]

In order to hear about job openings, you must put yourself out there and connect with your network.[114] Go through your LinkedIn connections, address book, and resume—anywhere you can identify potential contacts—and compile a list of contacts who may be able to help you with your search. By using the Advanced Search option on LinkedIn, you can identify alumni of your undergraduate and law school who might be willing to assist you. It may help to organize the list into categories, based on how well you know the people or how you hope to work with them, such as:

- Family and friends
- Former employers or co-workers
- Prospective informational interviews
- Possible liaisons to desired employers
- People with whom to brainstorm
- Law school alumni
- Undergraduate alumni

[112] *See* Smith, *When and How to Consider Hiring In-House IP Counsel*, Law360 (May 16, 2013) (suggesting to "rely heavily on word of mouth when considering candidates").

[113] *See* Weber & Kwoh, *Beware the Phantom Job Listing: Jobs Go Unadvertised as Managers Rely on Their Own Contacts*, Wall St. J. (Jan. 8, 2013) (estimating that around 50% of positions are currently filled on an informal basis); Rubin & Williams, *supra* note 105, at 1 ("Many in-house jobs never make it to the newspaper's classifieds, Web job boards or a recruiter's Web site. They are part of the 'hidden job market,' which can be accessed only by networking.").

[114] Many times, jobs come from the most unexpected contacts, so never discount the ability of someone to help you. Your in-house job may be found at the grocery store, church, fundraising event, social function, or the gym.

- Professors
- Social acquaintances
- Strangers to whom you were referred

Contact those people who know you best, are familiar with your work, and can recommend you to others. These individuals may or may not be attorneys—sometimes the best contacts for in-house legal positions are business executives. Ask these contacts for a short meeting over coffee or lunch at a location near their office.

During the meeting, let your contact know your goal of working in-house, if you have not done so already. And remember you are not asking them for a job (that goes unsaid) but rather for advice on your search. Below are some suggestions for topics of conversation and questions to ask during your meeting:

- Show your contact the list of companies you are targeting. Your contact will appreciate that you have done your homework and are being strategic in your search. Ask if she knows anyone at your targeted companies who may be willing to speak with you.

- Can he think of any other companies that should be added to your targeted company list?

- Can he recommend a legal recruiter who handles corporate placements with whom you should visit?

- Definitely ask her to keep you in mind and to let you know if she hears of any in-house opportunities.

- If the connection is a close one, consider asking her to review your resume or LinkedIn profile from the impression of an in-house practitioner and to give you her impressions.[115]

As a result of this meeting, you are now on your connection's "radar screen." He or she knows that you are in the market and

---

[115]   *See* Posting of Pollak to LinkedIn Blog, *How to Tap Your LinkedIn Network for Your Next Opportunity* (Apr. 29, 2013), https://blog.linkedin.com/2013/04/29/how-to-tap-your-linkedin-network-for-your-next-opportunity, *archived at* https://perma.cc/9ACK-Q9EX.

hopefully will let you know of any opportunities at their company or otherwise. And, of course, be sure to send your contact a thank you note to show your gratitude for her courtesy, time, and support.[116]

In addition to networking, go to conferences or meetings attended by in-house counsel. Putting yourself in places where in-house attorneys frequent makes you more likely to make new connections who can help you in your search and hear about potential opportunities. Attend CLEs about corporate practice, local bar section meetings or trade association meetings for a particular industry that interests you. Consider joining your local chapter of the Association of Corporate Counsel, the Minority Corporate Counsel Association, local and state bar associations and their in-house or corporate sections, and the American Bar Association.[117] When you introduce yourself to other attorneys at these meetings, if feasible, tell them you are interested in working in-house and ask them about their company and particular practice area.[118]

Experienced attorneys should also contact a legal search firm that concentrates on in-house placements. These firms are hired by corporations on either an exclusive or non-exclusive basis to source candidates, and they are paid a certain percentage of a successful hire's salary, provided the candidate stays at the corporation for a minimum duration, usually between three and six months.[119] Although their client is the employer, they need viable candidates. If practicable, focus primarily on search firms that principally handle corporate placements. Some search firms purport to handle law firm and corporate counsel placements; however, this arrangement can lead to conflict situations if the firm places an attorney with a firm only to recruit another lawyer away from the firm for a corporate position.

---

[116]   *See* Doyle, *Sample Thank You Letter for Networking*, About.com: Job Searching,   https://www.thebalancecareers.com/networking-thank-you-letter-example-2063995, *archived at* https://perma.cc/2RNP-R2GT.

[117]   Rubin & Williams, *supra* note 105, at 2.

[118]   *See generally* Robert Half Legal, *supra* note 5, at 33.

[119]   *See* Sundberg, *Just How Much Do Recruiters Earn?* Undercover Recruiter, https://theundercoverrecruiter.com/just-how-much-do-recruiters-earn/, *archived at* https://perma.cc/4CJ2-CKNE.

Newhouse + Noblin, with its home office in Dallas, Texas, is an example of a firm that handles mostly in-house placements with corporate legal departments. Russell Newhouse, one of the co-founders of the established firm, says that corporations typically retain Newhouse + Noblin to either fill a very specific placement or to screen and identify the best candidates for a more general position:

> We usually work directly with the General Counsel of the company, at least at the initial stages of the engagement when the requirements for the particular position are established. Other times, we work directly with individuals in the human relations department, such as the head of HR or an assigned internal recruiter.[120]

Once they know the parameters of the search, Newhouse sources potential candidates in several ways:

> We have an internal database of over 30,000 attorneys whom we know are at least open to new opportunities. We also rely on other online resources, along with proprietary methods, and our own extensive networks and relationships to find viable candidates. Our client is the corporation, and we strive to find the perfect candidate for them so that they will retain Newhouse + Noblin for their next search.[121]

Although Newhouse + Noblin places almost exclusively experienced attorneys, Newhouse is always willing to visit with junior attorneys or recent law graduates about their job searches. And he offers the following practice tip to junior associates at law firms or attorneys new to in-house practice who receive calls from recruiters about new opportunities:

> Don't be too quick to ignore or discount a professional recruiter's call, even if you're currently not interested in a new position. Even if you're professionally content now, build a relationship with a few reputable recruiters for the future. At some point, all lawyers will

---

[120]   Interview with Russell Newhouse, Newhouse + Noblin, in Dallas, Tex. (June 24, 2019).

[121]   *Id.*

wonder if they are on the right professional path, or
they may have a family member or friend needing
guidance. That's when it helps to have a relationship
established with a knowledgeable recruiter you trust.[122]

The Passive Job Search

Your job search should not be spent solely responding to job
postings. While this is an important part of any job search,[123] it
is too easy to sit at home in front of the computer and apply for
jobs. As already mentioned, some in-house jobs are never posted
and are filled through word of mouth, and more jobs are secured
through networking than from applying to postings. Reliable
websites that post available in-house positions include the
following:

- The Association of Corporate Counsel website
  (http://www.acc.com), has one of the most extensive
  lists of job postings for in-house positions by state.

- Check the company websites of the companies you
  identified in your initial research. Many companies
  do not want to pay fees to legal search firms, so they
  usually post open attorney positions on their
  websites.

- The Minority Corporate Counsel Association,
  MCCA, has an extensive job bank (https://jobbank.
  mcca.com/).

- The Goinhouse.com (https://www.goinhouse.com/)
  job board focuses solely on in-house counsel
  positions.

- Lawjobs.com (https://lawjobs.com) includes over
  1,200 jobs daily.

- Relevant industry websites—like the Society of
  Corporate Compliance and Ethics (https://www.
  corporatecompliance.org/) for those seeking a
  compliance job or the National Association of
  College and University Attorneys (https://www.

---

[122]   *Id.*

[123]   *See* Adams, *How to Make Them Respond When You Apply for a Job Online,*
Forbes (Jan. 24, 2012), *archived at* https://perma.cc/SW89-NUZ8.

nacua.org/) for those seeking a job in higher education law—provide specific job postings, contacts, new and events.

- Job search aggregators, like Indeed.com (www.indeed.com), are efficient sites for surveying job listings, since they aggregate information from job boards, news sites, and company listings.[124] An advanced search function enables users to drill down on a location, specific company, keywords, and salary range. Indeed claims that 75% of job seekers use its site, which adds 3.2 million jobs each month.[125]

- SimplyHired (www.simplyhired.com) is another good job search aggregator.

- LinkedIn (www.linkedin.com), not only provides company information, *supra*, it allows you to apply for jobs directly on its website. You can also view your LinkedIn connections who may be able to refer you for an available position. Search for jobs on LinkedIn by keyword, country, and postal code.[126] Use the Advanced Search option to refine your search and to search by date posted, industry, job function, experience level, salary, location, miles from a location, and date posted.[127]

When you find a job of interest, do not just press the "apply now" button. Rather, use LinkedIn to find those persons in your network connected to the company—perhaps as an employee, outside counsel, or legal recruiter—handling the search. Rather than simply sending in a resume, consider whether your relationships can tell you more about the opportunity, get your resume to the correct person, or put in a good word for you. One of the best ways to get hired is to become an employee referral.

---

[124] *See* Kauflin, *12 Websites to Jump-Start Your Career in 2018*, Forbes.com (Oct. 19, 2017), *archived at* https://perma.cc/FW86-6FYY.

[125] https://www.indeed.com/hire?hl=en&cc=US, *archived at* https://perma.cc/Z3F9-8QFE.

[126] Doyle, *How to Optimize Your Job Search Using LinkedIn*, About.com: Job Searching (June 25, 2019), https://www.thebalancecareers.com/how-to-use-linkedin-to-job-search-2062600, *archived at* https://perma.cc/5MFN-VMGE.

[127] *Id.*

Your chances of being hired increase substantially when one of the company's own employees recommends you because the Human Resources department knows that it will have to respond to that employee.[128]

Application Materials—*Your Resume*

Your resume is your chance to make a great first impression. The goal of creating a successful resume is to convey your qualifications to a prospective company in a concise and well-organized manner while highlighting the most favorable aspects of your background. On average, employers spend about thirty seconds reviewing a resume, so it is crucial that upon first glance your resume be both aesthetically pleasing and easy to read.[129] Tailor your resume to the particular in-house position you are seeking: if you are applying for a generalist position, for example, be sure to demonstrate your diverse experience.

Many large corporations use applicant tracking systems, which scan submitted resumes for certain keywords.[130] You can increase the odds of your resume rising to the top of the stack and surviving the first cut by using keywords from the job description—just make sure the keywords you use accurately describe your actual experience. For example, if the job posting seeks a lawyer with experience in federal pesticide registration and in-depth knowledge of the Federal Insecticide, Fungicide, and Rodenticide Act (FIFRA), consider revising your work description from "experienced in all aspects of environmental law" to add these specific areas—provided you actually have the experience.[131]

---

[128] Sullivan, *Why You Can't Get a Job . . . Recruiting Explained by the Numbers*, ere.net (May 20, 2013), https://www.ere.net/why-you-cant-get-a-job-recruiting-explained-by-the-numbers/, *archived at* https://perma.cc/G79J-UWUE; *see also* Schwartz, *In Hiring, a Friend in Need Is a Prospect, Indeed*, N.Y. Times (Jan. 27, 2013), at A1.

[129] Allen, *The Resume Makeover* (2001); Tucker et al., *Paving the Way: Directing Your Legal Career Search*, Georgetown University Law Center (1992).

[130] *See* Weber, *Your Résumé vs. Oblivion: Inundated Companies Resort to Software to Sift Job Applications for Right Skills*, Wall St. J. (Jan. 24, 2012).

[131] *See Job Hunting*, Ass'n of Corp. Couns., https://www.acc.com/services-initiatives/legal-operations/careers/job-hunting, *archived at* https://perma.cc/WK59-B75X.

Cover Letters

Your cover letter or email is critical to your job search. It is the first document of your job application materials that a corporate recruiter will read and often the only opportunity to engage an employer. It is also the key document that you will use to convince a corporation to look at your resume. Do not give an employer a reason to reject your application because you have not taken the time to draft a well-written, concise cover letter which highlights how your experience and skills would be beneficial to that particular employer.[132]

Generally speaking, you should always include a cover letter with your resume when applying for a position or responding to an advertisement, even when it is not expressly requested. Drafting a cover letter, especially individual cover letters to each particular company, can be a painstaking process but may well be worth the effort.[133]

Your cover letter is the vehicle by which you can directly address qualifications that specifically match the in-house position for which you are applying. Corporate recruiters are looking to understand why you would be the right person for the position. Accordingly, demonstrate how your strengths and accomplishments match the job requirements. All too often, cover letters spell out what the applicant wants and not what the employer needs. Employers want to read about how you can help them and not what they can do for you.[134]

Below are some tips for writing an effective cover letter:

- Find out the name and title of the recipient. Never use "To Whom it May Concern."

---

[132] *See* AllBusiness.com, *Get the Job with a Tailored Cover Letter and Unbeatable Resume* (Aug 15, 2012), https://smallbusiness.yahoo.com/advisor/job-tailored-cover-letter-unbeatable-090000809.html, *archived at* https://perma.cc/XJR4-FZ6V.

[133] *See* Greenawald, *4 Ways to Make Writing Cover Letters Less Painful,* Forbes.com (Apr. 16, 2013), https://www.forbes.com/sites/dailymuse/2013/04/16/4-ways-to-make-writing-cover-letters-less-painful/, *archived at* https://perma.cc/XCV8-3ZNQ; Ass'n of Corp. Couns., *supra* note 131.

[134] *See* Douthwaite, *5 Ways Your Cover Letter Lost You the Job,* Forbes.com (May 9, 2013), https://www.forbes.com/sites/dailymuse/2013/05/09/5-ways-your-cover-letter-lost-you-the-job/, *archived at* https://perma.cc/DL54-5MDK.

- Use simple language and uncomplicated sentence structure.

- Use active voice, as it conveys a much stronger, more positive impression than passive voice.

- Project confidence, but not arrogance.

- Keep it brief—never more than one page.

- Try to answer the question employers will be asking themselves as they read your letter: "Why should I hire this person?"

- Do not send out mass mailings of your cover letter and resume.[135]

Avoid simply rehashing your resume in the cover letter. Look at your letter and resume as separate but related documents. They should complement each another without being overly repetitive. Although you will undoubtedly need to mention past positions, employers, or experiences in your introductory letter, use slightly different wording and a more conversational style than you would typically use in a resume. Your cover letter is the perfect opportunity for you to explicitly state how your skills will be beneficial to this particular employer.[136]

Keep it brief. Cover letters should always be concise. Your letter does not have to be lengthy to be compelling enough to interest the hiring manager to study your resume in more detail and, ultimately, to invite you for an interview. A good rule of thumb is to keep the communication to two to three paragraphs for e-mail and three to five paragraphs for a letter in printed form.[137]

LinkedIn

The value of social media cannot be underestimated, and LinkedIn is the social media site for professionals. With over 610 million users in more than 200 countries, it includes executives with every Fortune 500 company. And according to one source,

---

[135]   *Id.*

[136]   *Id.*

[137]   Ass'n of Corp. Couns, *supra* note 131.

LinkedIn is the social media source in-house counsel use most to obtain information and expand their contacts.[138]

Many corporate recruiters, hiring managers, and legal recruiters use a subscription-based product offered by LinkedIn called "LinkedIn Recruiter" to search for attorneys with specific skill sets, flag them, and add a dossier to their profile—all without that person knowing.[139] The ability to source passive candidates (that is, people who are not actively looking for a job but may be most qualified) is very valuable. Instead of relying solely on a job posting, recruiters use LinkedIn to find exactly who they want with the skills and experience they want and then reach out to candidates through LinkedIn's messaging service, InMail. More than 16,000 companies pay to use LinkedIn Recruiter, including Google, BP, and L'Oréal, as well as thousands of other large, medium, and small business and recruiting firms.[140]

If you are not on LinkedIn, employers and search firms will never find you. And even if they did, some employers view candidates without a LinkedIn profile as a red flag. Thus, if you are serious about your career, you must have a detailed LinkedIn profile with your job history that looks like your resume. Make sure that your LinkedIn profile is 100% complete:

- Include your full name and a professional photograph, preferably a head shot.

- Personalize your LinkedIn URL with your name.

- Use a headline that properly describes you. Usually, this is simply your current title and company (or law school). If you are seeking an in-house position, use the terms "attorney" or "counsel" in your headline since these are the most commonly searched terms by recruiters handling corporate placements.

---

[138]   See Kennedy & Shields, *Making the Most of LinkedIn*, Your ABA (Mar. 2014).

[139]   LinkedIn Talent Solutions, Introducing Recruiter, https://business.linkedin.com/content/dam/me/business/en-us/talent-solutions/products/pdfs/LinkedIn-datasheet-Recruiter-Oct2018.pdf, *archived at* https://perma.cc/S3UU-8VT2.

[140]   Chang, *The Most Important LinkedIn Page You've Never Seen*, Wired (April 15, 2013 9:30 AM), https://www.wired.com/2013/04/the-real-reason-you-should-care-about-linkedin/, *archived at* https://perma.cc/W6GR-N249.

- Consider status updates to show that you are relevant. Going to an in-house event or conference? share it. Did you recently read something that is relevant to your brand? mention it. Have you written a relevant article or blog or been mentioned in a recent news article? include it. If you use updates, try to update at least once a week.

- Describe what you are doing now and what you have done in the past with sufficient detail. Your LinkedIn profile needs to contain detailed descriptions under your current and past jobs so that someone reviewing your profile will understand who you are, your current role, depth of experience, and skill set. You also want to make sure that your descriptions contain "hot" (but accurate) keywords likely to be searched by recruiters or search firms in your industry.[141] Back to the example of a midstream energy company, such "key" words might include "pipelines," "interstate regulation," and "FERC."

- Be sure to include your undergraduate college and law school on your profile. This makes your profile complete and also allows former classmates and alumni to find you.

- Try to get at least one recommendation from each position you have held. Law students can get recommendations from professors or summer employers. Having someone else recommend you helps give you credibility.

- Connect with people you know. You can search your connection's connections in the LinkedIn database.

- Include your contact settings.[142]

After your resume and LinkedIn profile are complete, run both by a recruiter or human resources professional to make

[141]   *See* Kennedy & Shields, *supra* note 138.

[142]   Svei, *3 Places to Feature Your Contact Info on Your LinkedIn Profile*, AvidCareerist (Apr. 22, 2013), https://avidcareerist.com/2013/04/22/linkedin-contact-information/, *archived at* https://perma.cc/5689-YTBR.

sure that someone who scans them for fifteen seconds will be able to actually find each of the key points that recruiters need to find.[143]

Professional Organizations

Once you are in-house, it is important to join in-house professional organizations to continue growing your personal network so you will be ready for your next career move. As mentioned before, consider joining the Association of Corporate Counsel (ACC). The ACC was founded in 1982 and currently includes more than 45,000 members from over 10,000 corporations in 85 countries around the world. The group provides its members with excellent resources through its website as well as through events that address a wide variety of topics relevant to the in-house experience and networking opportunities.[144]

In Texas, the Texas General Counsel Forum (Forum) is another great organization for relationship building. The Forum is a community of more than 650 general counsel and senior managing counsel representing over 450 companies and organizations. It hosts networking and educational events in chapter cities, in a multitude of venues, and program formats. Events include breakfast, lunch, and dinner meetings with and without speakers; cocktail parties in the homes of prominent general counsel; sporting events; awards dinners; and conference meetings.[145]

TIPS FOR LAW STUDENTS WHO
WANT TO WORK IN-HOUSE

What are the most important things to do in law school if you want to work in-house? A good starting point is to look at people who are 20 years older than you who currently work in-house. Examine their backgrounds either on LinkedIn or, even better, through an informational interview. Determining how they got to where they are will give you a good idea of at least

---

[143]   See Sullivan, *supra* note 128.

[144]   *See Get Connected by In-House Counsel, For In-House Counsel*, Ass'n of Corp. Couns.

[145]   *About the Forum*, Gen. Couns. Forum: Legal Best Prac. Comm., https://www.tgcf.org/about/, *archived at* https://perma.cc/YP96-QL89.

one educational and career path that worked successfully. Below are some questions that you might ask in an informational interview of in-house counsel:

- What advice do they have for you as a law student interested in working in-house one day?

- Did they specialize in law school? If so, in what?

- Is a business background helpful for what they do?

- Is there any advantage to having a Master of Business Administration or Master of Law degree?

- How much law firm experience do they recommend?

- What classes would they recommend you take in law school?

- What do they wish they had known their first year as in-house counsel?

- When did they go in-house? Many in-house counsel will advise against going in-house too early in your career.[146]

Law students considering an in-house position as a career goal would be wise to keep abreast of business news in one or more industries. When possible, they should cultivate connections in that field.[147]

Two of the most important skills a successful in-house counsel can possess are strong writing and communication skills. Accordingly, law students interested in an in-house practice should concentrate on improving their skills in these areas by taking advanced legal writing courses and participating in advocacy programs.[148] Students should also consider taking business classes outside the law school, or obtaining a JD/MBA degree, so they can better understand the businesses within which they will work.[149] Although what interested students

---

[146]   *See generally* Tucker, *Transitioning to an In-House Legal Position*, Georgetown University Law Center, http://law2.wlu.edu/deptimages/career%20planning/In_House_Quick_Tips.pdf, *archived at* https://perma.cc/RZ9L-5GS2.

[147]   In-House (Law Departments of Corporations), Berkeley Law.

[148]   Eagle, *supra* note 1, at 15.

[149]   *Id.*

learn in these relevant courses will not substitute for on-the-job training, these skills and experiences may help distinguish these students from candidates without such coursework.[150]

Internships with Corporate Legal Departments

Some corporations will hire law student interns to assist their in-house lawyers during the summer or on a part-time basis during the school year. These internships generally offer broad exposure to a number of practice areas and can provide great opportunities for law students to gain experience and make connections. Students may be able to secure a legal internship with companies after their first year of law school. Second-year students interested in a corporate practice may consider combining a first-half law firm clerkship with a second-half corporate counsel internship.

Part-time law students currently working for companies with in-house legal departments may consider exploring internship opportunities with that department. The in-house legal departments may be able to provide students with projects that can be completed on a flexible schedule, including evenings or weekends. Moreover, depending on the time of year and a student's workload in his current position, a student may be able to structure a part-time schedule with the in-house legal department and his own department.

Corporate internships can provide law students with valuable training and practical experience that will benefit them when they start practicing law. While many law students work as summer associates in law firms or serve as judicial interns with state and federal courts, relatively few get the chance to see a corporate legal department during their law school careers. Corporate internships provide students with a unique perspective of the practice of law from the client's standpoint.

Michael Raoufpour, Associate Corporate Counsel with Smoothie King, recommends the following:

> I think the best thing one can do in law school to obtain
> an in-house position right out of school is to find in-
> house internships or externships during law school. In-

---

[150]   *Id.*

house experience and displaying a desire early on to go in-house made a huge difference for me in my first in-house interview right out of school. The interviewers were really impressed that I already had almost a year of experience in-house before graduating and felt that I would understand the responsibilities and culture better than someone who may not have experienced the same.[151]

Ashley Yen was introduced to in-house practice during law school at SMU Dedman School of Law, where she interned or externed with (no less than!) seven different companies, including Hewlett Packard Enterprise, Dr Pepper Snapple Group, Allegro Development, Sun Holdings, Rug Doctor, TXU Energy, and Alliance Family of Companies. As early as her 1L summer internship with Hewlett Packard Enterprise, she knew she wanted to go in-house as quickly as possible. Yen says she decided to show her dedication to going in-house by gaining as much in-house experience as she could during law school and as her school schedule would permit.

Through her various internships, Yen says:

I gained useful in-house experience in a wide array of practice areas ranging from contract review to employment litigation to mergers and acquisitions. Even if I weren't able to work directly on a project, it was still extremely beneficial to be able to shadow experienced attorneys because I was able to see the legal thought process that goes into a project as well as become familiar with the jargon that is used in that specific area of law. Consequently, I developed skills that directly transferred over or related to the job requirements of in-house counsel positions. During interviews, interviewers consistently said that I had the experience necessary to successfully do the job. I know they only reached that conclusion because of the experiences that I received at these internships and externship. I believe my internships and externship are what opened up the door for a company to take a risk

---

[151] Interview with Michael Raoufpour, Associate Corporate Counsel, Smoothie King, in Dallas, Tex. (July 2, 2019).

and hire a 'baby attorney' like me coming right out of law school.[152]

Similarly, Lindsey Rattikin worked with legal departments with three companies as a law student.

> Participating in in-house legal externships and clerkships while in law school is an invaluable way to get a feeling for the pace and feel of an in-house legal office and to get to know members of the in-house legal community in your city. I appreciated the experience of how the different legal departments interacted within themselves and with corporate partners. In my last year of law school, I was offered a full-time position in one of the offices I had clerked in, and I attribute my hiring to my varied corporate experience and my commitment to the in-house practice.[153]

Interns may also be more attractive candidates to other legal employers as a result of the substantive experience, broader networks, and stronger resumes they build. The relationships interns form with in-house counsel may be valued by law firms, which realize that students who have gained the respect and trust of in-house attorneys may provide valuable introductions to those attorneys. Corporate counsel may even consider a student connection at a law firm when deciding where to send their legal work.

Legal recruiter Jeffrey Lowe agrees that in-house experience can give law students an advantage. He says, "One benefit of getting early in-house experience is the ability to work on a lot of different things under relatively short deadlines that are outside any one area. It teaches young lawyers to be more versatile and aggressive in thinking out answers, which I think is really positive development."[154]

---

[152]   Interview with Ashley Yen, Associate In-House Counsel, Methodist Health System, in Dallas, Tex. (July 18, 2019).

[153]   Interview with Lindsey K. Rattikin, Assistant University Counsel and Higher Education Law Fellow, Southern Methodist University, in Dallas, Tex. (July 22, 2019).

[154]   Alvarez, *Program Places Law Students in Paid Internships that Help Them See the Business Picture*, ABA Journal (Mar. 15, 2018), http://www.abajournal.com/news/article/institute_for_the_future_of_law_practice, *archived at* https://perma.cc/NR2H-665K.

Students who perform well in corporate counsel internships could also receive good references from inside counsel at major corporations based on first-hand knowledge of the students' work product, work ethic, and personality. Solid recommendations by corporate counsel to their outside law firms and/or counterparts at other companies can be instrumental in a student's job search and may tip the scales in her favor.

Externships and Practicums

An increasing number of law schools are offering classes, externship programs, and practicums focused on training future corporate counsel.[155] These courses and programs can be invaluable for students who are interested in learning about the role of inside counsel and what in-house attorneys actually "do."

Many of the courses focus on the unique aspects of working as a lawyer within a corporation. Topics often covered in such classes include the roles and history of in-house counsel, how corporate legal departments are structured, working with outside counsel, conducting an internal investigation, corporate compliance and legal risk management, as well as ethical issues confronting corporate counsel. Sometimes, practice areas common for in-house counsel are also covered. In-house practitioners are often invited to guest lecture in certain classes or serve on panel discussions with other attorneys. The personal insights and knowledge that these individuals offer students can contribute a great deal to their learning experiences and make the classes more practical.

SMU Dedman School of Law added a Corporate Counsel Externship Program to its corporate law curriculum in 2013.[156] The academic program combines a corporate counsel class with externships in corporate legal departments. Approximately ninety students are assigned to the same number of corporate legal departments each year where they serve as externs.

---

[155] *See* Reisinger, *Law Schools Offering More Courses for In-House Careers*, Corp. Couns. (Oct. 19, 2012); Day, *Teaching Students How to Become In-House Counsel*, 51 J. Legal Educ. 503 (Dec. 2011); Martin, *Law Students Learn In-House Counsel Responsibilities with Role Playing*, Inside Couns. (July 2011).

[156] *See* Yeager, *Inside a Law School's In-House Training Program,* Corp. Couns. (July 9, 2014), https://perma.cc/D42S-EDSS; Browning, *The Proving Ground*, D CEO (July-Aug. 2015), https://perma.cc/2HV6-CDGY; Posgate, *From Law School to the Corporate Suite*, Dallas Morning News (July 2013), https://perma.cc/Q6SE-DDTM.

Corporate participants have included American Airlines, AT&T, Boeing, Dallas Cowboys Football Club, Fluor Corporation, Interstate Batteries, J.C. Penney Company, Inc., Lennox International Inc., Mark Cuban Companies, PepsiCo, and Toyota Motor North America, Inc.

In their externships, students have the opportunity to observe lawyers dealing with legal issues and business problems in context and learn from corporate counsel. Externs' projects and experiences are as broad and varied as the different companies participating in the program. As an example, one student assisted attorneys with a credit agreement and observed the agreement evolve from the first draft to the closing. Another student worked on compliance checklists and schedules, allowing her to delve into regulations governing public companies and to review the company's policies for compliance. A different student worked on a project involving both legal and accounting issues. As a CPA, she said that the project allowed her to learn how the legal and accounting departments within the company worked together to formulate an approach to solving the issue.

The students also attend a corporate counsel class each week in which they learn about substantive areas encountered in an in-house legal department, such as corporate governance practices, intellectual property, employment law, and securities filings, as well as the ethical responsibilities of in-house counsel. Other classes focused on practical skills, such as working with outside counsel, conflicts of interest, litigation management, contract drafting, and conducting internal investigations. In-house counsel at area corporations served as guest lecture in some classes, adding yet another opportunity for students to learn from and interface with corporate counsel.

The program served as a capstone learning experience for many students. Stacy Phillips, a third-year student assigned to Reddy Ice Holdings, Inc., describes the experience as the "icing on the cake" of her legal education. "Property law was my Achilles heel in law school because I really didn't have a frame of reference for any of the topics we covered," she said. "It all suddenly made sense after working on a project involving real estate titles, title insurance policies, and land survey plats."

Other law schools are offering similar programs. For example, Northwestern Pritzker School of Law's Corporate Counsel Practicum places students as externs in general counsel offices of Chicago-area businesses where they commit one day a week to the corporate law department under the direct supervision of in-house counsel.[157] Students earn two semester credits during the academic year and four credits during the summer program. Students attend a weekly seminar taught by an adjunct professor (former general counsel), complete a reflective journal, and write a 10–15 page paper which relates to externship or class readings and discussion. Participating corporations have included Abbott Labs, Mittal Steel, and Chicago Board of Options Exchange.

The University of Chicago Law School offers the Kirkland & Ellis Corporate Lab, which provides students with the opportunity to work on projects in collaboration with the legal departments at leading corporations.[158] Groups of five to eight students are assigned to a company. The students then work on issues similar to those that await them during summer internships and after they graduate. Corporate participants have included Accenture, Baxter International, IBM, Microsoft, Nike, 3M, Ulta Beauty, Verizon, and Walmart.

Cornell University Law School's semester externship program allows students to extern full-time with in-house counsel offices in media or sports. Participating companies have included News Corp., Fox News, Harper and Collins, Warner Brothers Studios, and the NFL Management Group.[159] During the semester, students participate in a weekly web-based discussion with the faculty member and other students enrolled in the externship. They also write weekly, reflective journal entries that are shared with the instructor. Normally, the

---

[157] Northwestern Law, Bluhm Legal Clinic, Center for Externships, Corporate Counsel Practicum, Professor Pete Wentz, http://www.law.northwestern.edu/legalclinic/externships/studentopps/courses/#corporate, *archived at* https://perma.cc/B6JZ-RY58.

[158] The University of Chicago Law School, Corporate Lab, Professor David Zarfes and Lecturer Sean Z. Kramer, https://www.law.uchicago.edu/corporatelab, *archived at* https://perma.cc/CF9Y-FN39; *see also* Reisinger, *Send in the Externs*, Corp. Couns. (Mar. 2012).

[159] Cornell University Law School, Full-Term Externships, https://www.lawschool.cornell.edu/academics/clinicalprogram/externships/full-term-externship.cfm, *archived at* https://perma.cc/L78J-8ALF.

instructor visits the student at his or her placement during the semester and receives evaluations from the placement site supervisors.

Other schools offer similar programs.[160] These programs can be invaluable for students looking to gain insight into the skills necessary to thrive as corporate counsel.

Chances are you will work with a number of different employers between the time you graduate from law school until you retire at the end of what is hopefully a long, successful legal career. Whether you work as outside counsel in a law firm for your entire career, go in-house counsel after several years in private practice, or join a corporate legal department right out of law school, knowing what corporations look for in their corporate counsel is valuable information to have. Likewise, it is always useful for attorneys to focus on how to find and best present themselves for external opportunities during the course of their careers.

------

[160] *See, e.g.,* Boston University School of Law's Corporate Counsel Externship Program provides the opportunity for second- and third-year students to train for academic credit in a number of corporate counsel offices, including Boston Children's Hospital, State Street, TripAdvisor, and Wayfair. https://www.bu.edu/law/files/2015/07/ BU-Law-Corp-Counsel-Externships-Program-Info-2018.pdf, *archived at* https://perma. cc/6AT9-CJ7V; UCLA School of Law allows students in their second and third years to apply to do part-time externships with in-house corporate counsel. https://www.law.ucla. edu/~/media/Assets/Externships/Documents/parttimeexternships.ashx, *archived at* https://perma.cc/C97S-ZVBN; The University of Minnesota Law School's Corporate Externship Program familiarizes students with the working connections between law and business in corporate counsel settings. Placements have included: Best Buy, Regis Corporation, Target and U.S. Bank. Students receive three hours credit for 150 on-site hours and may work up to 20 hours per week. https://www.law.umn.edu/corporate-institute/externship-companies, *archived at* https://perma.cc/MM8P-XKHZ; Washington University School of Law has a New York City Regulatory and Business Externship that places law students in a semester-long clinical experience in New York City. The externship allows third-year law students, and qualified second-year law students, to spend their fall or spring semester in New York City and work under the direction of attorneys in a variety of in-house counsel offices for investment banks and other large financial institutions. https://law.wustl.edu/academics/clinical-education-program/new-york-regulatory-and-business-externship/, *archived at* https://perma.cc/FW85-2TA6; Indiana University Robert H. McKinney School of Law's In-House Corporate Counsel Externship places students with the in-house legal departments of Anthem, Inc., CMG Worldwide, Eli Lilly and Company, Finish Line, and Old National. Students draft and review contracts, engage in legal research and prepare memoranda regarding business law issues confronting the corporation, and otherwise assist in legal work typical of that performed by corporate counsel. https://mckinneylaw.iu.edu/courses/official-descriptions/externships.html, *archived at* https://perma.cc/3LQR-HZQ8.

CHAPTER 4

CORPORATE GOVERNANCE

For those in-house attorneys who provide legal advice to the company's board of directors, committees of the board, and executive officers, knowledge of corporate governance principles is fundamental to their practice. For other in-house lawyers, although not requiring the detailed knowledge that legal corporate governance specialists have, familiarity with basic corporate governance principles should prove helpful.

The objective of this chapter is to address key aspects of corporate governance the in-house lawyer may face. An in-depth analysis is not intended to be provided here. For that, other sources should be consulted.[1]

The term "corporate governance" has been defined in a number of ways. As defined by the International Organization of Securities Commissioners (IOSCO), corporate governance "describe[s] a system of overlapping legal, regulatory, organizational, and contractual mechanisms designed to protect the interests of a company's owners (the shareholders) and limit opportunistic behavior by corporate managers who control the company's operations."[2] In publicly-held companies, corporate governance entails "a reaction to agency problems, associated with the separation [of control] between owners and managers."[3] A sound corporate governance structure focuses on such characteristics as: the adequacy of internal controls; appropriate conduct by the board of directors, committees thereof, and

---

[1]   *See, e.g.,* American Law Institute (ALI), *Principles of Corporate Governance: Analysis and Recommendations* (1994); The Conference Board, Commission on Public Trust and Private Enterprise, *Corporate Governance—Findings and Recommendations* (2010); M. Steinberg, *The Federalization of Corporate Governance* (Oxford Univ. Press 2018).

[2]   IOSCO, Final Report of the Task Force, *Protection of Minority Shareholders in Listed Issuers* (June 2009); IOSCO, Final Report of the Task Force, *Strengthening Capital Markets Against Financial Fraud* (Feb. 2005).

[3]   *Id.*

officers of the company; and transparency to enable shareholders and other stakeholders to be sufficiently informed.[4]

Today, under certain circumstances, the interests of certain stakeholders, in addition to stockholders, are proper considerations under the corporate governance umbrella. These constituencies may include, for example, employees, customers, the environment, affected communities, and the general public. Indeed, a majority of states have enacted "benefit" corporation and "constituency" statutes which authorize a company's board of directors to consider these non-shareholder interests.[5] Construed flexibly, these statutes give boards of directors wide-ranging discretion to take into account constituent interests, provided that shareholders are not unduly prejudiced.[6] Nonetheless, the prevailing view is that, in ascertaining a corporation's best interests (which may be a short or long-term perspective), the collective interests of the shareholders remain paramount.[7]

In-house lawyers look to several sources when identifying appropriate corporate governance standards. These include, for example, requirements set forth in the Sarbanes-Oxley Act (SOX) of 2002 and the Dodd-Frank Act of 2010, Securities and Exchange Commission (SEC) rules implementing the SOX and Dodd-Frank mandates, stock exchange (e.g., New York Stock Exchange) rules setting forth minimum standards to be met as a condition for listing, and state law, particularly statutes and court decisions focusing on the duties of care and loyalty owed by corporate fiduciaries. In addition to these mandatory requirements, bar associations (e.g., the American Bar

---

    [4]   *See* M. Steinberg, *Developments in Business Law and Policy* 143 (2012).

    [5]   See, e.g., Fla. Stat. Ann. ch. 607.0830; N.Y. Bus. Corp. Law § 717; Ohio Rev. Code Ann. § 1701.59; About B Corps, *available at* http://www.bcorporation.net/about; Corporate Law Committee, American Bar Association Business Law Section, *Benefit Corporation White Paper*, 68 Bus. Law. 1083 (2013); Hansen, *Other Constituency Statutes: A Search for Perspective*, 46 Bus. Law. 1355 (1991); Loewenstein, *Benefit Corporations: A Challenge in Corporate Governance*, 68 Bus. Law. 1007 (2013).

    [6]   *See* Steinberg, *supra* note 4, *Developments in Business Law and Policy*, at 144.

    [7]   *See, e.g., Revlon, Inc. v. MacAndrews & Forbes Holdings*, 506 A. 2d 173 (Del. 1986). Some experts disagree. *See, e.g.,* L. Stout, *The Shareholder Value Myth: How Putting Shareholders First Harms Investors, Corporations and the Public* (2012) (criticizing the perceived duty to maximize shareholder value and opining that shareholder primacy causes corporate fiduciaries unduly to focus on short-term earnings, impedes innovation, and injures customers, employees and communities).

Association), corporate voluntary associations or groups (e.g., the Business Roundtable), and other bodies (e.g., the American Law Institute) set forth corporate governance principles in their quest to enhance accountability and oversight in U.S. corporations.

This chapter now will address a number of key corporate governance concepts that impact the legal practice of in-house attorneys.

BOARD OF DIRECTORS

A company's board of directors, irrespective whether the company is publicly or privately-held, should make the fundamental decisions for the enterprise and act as the overseer of managerial conduct.[8] In a publicly-held company listed on a national stock exchange, a majority of the directors must be independent.[9]

Functions of the Board of Directors

From a general perspective, the board of directors in a publicly-held company has several key responsibilities, encompassing: strategic planning; overseeing the implementation of reasonably adequate internal controls; risk assessment; appointment (and termination) of executive officers; oversight of senior management; succession planning; shareholder communications; and adoption and implementation of reasonably effective law compliance programs.[10] In this regard, the Business Roundtable identifies the following key functions that boards of directors should undertake:

1. Select, regularly evaluate and, if necessary, replace the chief executive officer. Determine management compensation. Review succession planning.

---

[8] Note that in certain closely-held corporations, the shareholders may manage the corporation directly, with little input from the board of directors. Indeed, in many states, pursuant to a unanimous shareholder agreement, the board of directors may be eliminated, with the shareholders acting in lieu of the board. *See, e.g.,* § 7.32 of the Model Bus. Corp. Act.

[9] NYSE, Inc., Listed Company Manual § 303A.01; NASDAQ, Inc., Manual Rule 4350(c).

[10] *See* Steinberg, *Developments in Business Law and Policy, supra* note 4, at 145.

2.   Review and, where appropriate, approve the financial objectives, major strategies, and plans of the corporation.

3.   Provide advice and counsel to top management.

4.   Select and recommend to shareholders for election an appropriate slate of candidates for the board of directors; evaluate board process and performance.

5.   Review the adequacy of systems to comply with all applicable laws/regulations.[11]

Business Judgment Rule and Related Principles

In exercising its responsibilities, the board of directors is entitled to rely on information supplied by the company's lawyers, accountants, officers, employees, and others who merit such reliance. As an example, in regard to the corporation's financial statements, the board of directors (as well as the audit committee) relies on information furnished by the company's financial officers (e.g., the chief financial officer), internal accounting personnel, and the outside auditors. Accordingly, to effectively carry out its responsibilities, the board of directors should seek to ensure that the internal control procedures and practices that are implemented are sufficient to effectuate the flow of pertinent and accurate information.[12]

When counseling the board of directors (and committees thereof), the in-house lawyer should focus on the parameters of the business judgment rule. When its conditions are met, the business judgment rule provides an impressive shield to protect decisions made by the board of directors from successful challenge. Stated succinctly, the business judgment has four components: *First,* the board of directors must focus on the issue and make a deliberative decision. *Second,* the board's decision must be sufficiently informed (with gross negligence being the applicable standard). In this regard, the board should be provided with adequate information, including pertinent

---

[11]   The Business Roundtable, *Corporate Governance and American Competitiveness* (New York, The Business Roundtable 1990, 2002).

[12]   *See* Steinberg, *Developments in Business Law and Policy, supra* note 4, at 146–147; The Conference Board, *Conference Board Commission on Public Trust and Private Enterprise* (Jan. 9, 2003).

reports, appraisals, and other material documents that are central to the transaction or other matter being considered. Upon having this information, the board should take the time necessary to reach an informed decision. *Third*, directors making the board's decision must be disinterested, generally meaning that they are not engaged in financial self-dealing and are not under the control of a director who is herself conflicted with respect to the matter at hand. *Fourth*, as held by some courts, the decision made by the board of directors must have a rational basis; stated somewhat differently, the decision made must not be grossly negligent.[13]

In addition to the shield of the business judgment rule, directors also may avail themselves of the director limitation of liability (exculpation, or "raincoat") provisions enacted by state legislatures. In most states, to be applicable, these provisions must be contained in the subject corporation's articles of incorporation. Any validity incorporated company, whether privately or publicly-held, may adopt these provisions. Although the degree of director protection provided by these statutes varies among the states, the majority approach generally protects a director from personal monetary liability unless he breaches the duty of loyalty, acts in bad faith, knowingly authorizes an unlawful distribution, engages in intentional misconduct, or knowingly violates the law.[14] Because of the broad protection that these statutes provide, with respect to those corporations that do not have such a "raincoat" provision, inside counsel should consult with the board of directors about whether the company's articles of incorporation ought to be amended to contain such a provision.

Moreover, inside counsel should assess the availability and scope of insurance coverage as well as indemnification for the company's directors and officers. With some frequency, these protective mechanisms benefit the subject director or officer by providing advancement or reimbursement of attorneys' fees and other litigation costs as well as amounts paid in settlement or by adverse judgment. The invocation of these arrangements,

---

[13]   *See, e.g., Aronson v. Lewis*, 473 A. 2d 805, 812 (Del. 1984); American Law Institute, *Principles of Corporate Governance, supra* note 1, at § 4.01.

[14]   *See e.g.,* Del. Gen. Corp. Law § 102(b)(7).

however, is subject to specified conditions, exceptions, and limits. Accordingly, if appropriate, inside counsel should evaluate the subject company's insurance and indemnification policies and practices to ascertain the breadth of coverage and to recommend any needed changes.

Dual Role as CEO and Chair of Board of Directors; Lead Director

Today, there is much debate about whether the company's chief executive officer (CEO) should also serve as chair of its board of directors. Indeed, the Dodd-Frank Act of 2010 requires a publicly-held company to set forth in its annual proxy statement why it has decided for the same person to serve both as CEO and chair of the board, or in the alternative, why it has decided that different persons serve as CEO and chair of its board of directors. An evident increasing number of publicly-held companies have different individuals serving as CEO and chair of the board of directors.[15]

Nonetheless, many publicly-held companies continue to have the CEO also serve as chair of its board of directors. The apparent majority of such companies opt to have an independent director serve as "lead" director of the board. Among the roles that the lead director may assume are: interfacing with committees of the board (e.g., audit, compensation, and nomination committees); taking steps to help ensure that there is an appropriate flow of information from management to the board; playing a key role in setting the agenda for board meetings; meeting separately with internal personnel, including in-house counsel; and overseeing the process by which special committees of the board (e.g., a special litigation committee) are appointed.[16]

Independent Directors

Clearly, the presence of the "independent" director is a fundamental corporate governance principle in publicly-held

---

[15]   Section 14B of the Securities Exchange Act. *See* Item 407 of SEC Regulation S–K, 17 C.F.R. § 229.407; Corporate Governance by the Numbers—Ernst & Young, Board Leadership Structure (2019).

[16]   *See* The Conference Board, *Corporate Governance—Findings and Recommendations,* note 1 *supra*; Ernst & Young Report, note 15 *supra*.

corporations today. Generally, an independent director is one who, for example, is not (and has not recently been) employed by the company, does not have an immediate family member who is (or recently was) an executive officer of the company, does not receive consulting fees exceeding a specified amount (e.g., $120,000 annually per NYSE rules), is not an employee of an entity that made payments to or received payments from the corporation exceeding a specified amount or percentage (e.g., greater than $1 million or 2% of gross revenues per NYSE rules), and is not under the control or domination of the CEO, chair of the board, or other corporate fiduciary.[17] The strong role played by independent directors in corporate governance has been recognized by the U.S. Congress, the SEC, and the courts.[18] With guidance from in-house counsel, reasonably informed decisions made by independent directors normally will be insulated from successful challenge in a myriad of situations, ranging from interested director transactions to termination of shareholder derivative suits to defensive measures taken in response to a hostile takeover bid by a prospective acquirer.

COMMITTEES OF THE BOARD

Publicly-held corporations today have several committees of the board, including, for example, the audit, compensation, and nominating/corporate governance committees. These committees should be comprised entirely of independent directors. Indeed, in order to have its securities listed for trading on a national securities exchange (e.g., the NYSE), a corporation must appoint solely independent directors to its audit and compensation committees.[19]

---

[17]   See NYSE, Inc., Listed Company Manual § 303A.02; NASDAQ, Inc., Manual Rule 4200(a)(15). Aside from financial or family grounds for lack of director independence, under established case law, a director who is under the control of a dominant CEO or other fiduciary is likewise not independent. See, e.g., Aronson v. Lewis, 473 A. 2d 805 (Del. 1984).

[18]   See, e.g., In re Cox Communications, Inc. Shareholders Litigation, 879 A. 2d 604, 647 (Del. Ch. 2005) (recognizing "the strong role that our law gives to independent directors").

[19]   See §§ 10A, 10C of the Securities Exchange Act; NYSE, Inc., Listed Company Manual § 303A.07(a); NASDAQ, Inc., Manual Rule 4350(d)(2)(A)(i). With respect to the audit committee, directors serving on that committee can receive only director fees (and thus may not receive any other remuneration, such as consulting fees, from the corporation).

Much of the preceding discussion about the business judgment rule also applies to board committees. Counseling by in-house counsel to enable committee members to invoke the business judgment rule is critical. The providing of sufficient facts and other supporting information with adequate time for deliberation by the committee's members are key determiners for an independent committee's successful invocation of the business judgment rule.

In-depth treatment of the roles of the various board committees is beyond the scope of this book. Tellingly, many of these committees play an essential role in effectuating a sound corporate governance framework.

Audit Committee

The audit committee has general oversight responsibility in the review of the processes and practices that are adhered to by the company for producing financial data and for establishing and monitoring corporate internal controls.[20] In performing these functions, the audit committee serves as an important overseer of corporate management: "Because the corporation's financial data concerns the performance of management, it is important to have an independent forum for discussing this data [both with the corporation's internal staff as well as with the outside audit firm] and the manner of its preparation, in which management participates only on request."[21]

The audit committee also will oversee certain internal corporate investigations as well as issues relating to employee whistleblower complaints. Another key audit committee function is to oversee the external auditor's performance and provide a forum for discussion between the corporation's senior internal accounting personnel and the external auditor.[22] As stated by one respected source:

An independent audit committee provides a forum for regular, informal, and private discussion between the external auditor and directors who have no significant

---

[20]   *See* Steinberg, *Developments in Business Law and Policy, supra* note 4, at 149.
[21]   American Law Institute, *Principles of Corporate Governance, supra* note 1, at § 3.05 comment c(i).
[22]   *See* Steinberg, *Developments in Business Law and Policy, supra* note 4, at 149.

relationships with management. In the absence of such a forum, an external auditor would often be reluctant to call for a meeting at the board level unless a problem of great magnitude had arisen. In contrast, the provision of an institutionalized forum facilitates and indeed encourages the external auditor to raise potentially troublesome issues at a relatively early stage, allows the auditor to broach sensitive problems in an uninhibited and private fashion, and gives the auditor assurance that it can readily get a hearing in the event of a disagreement with management.[23]

Compensation Committee

Another key board committee is the compensation committee. A decade ago, in response to perceived unduly lucrative compensation practices as well as fraudulent stock option backdating,[24] Congress acted by requiring (with certain exceptions) that any publicly-held corporation whose stock is listed on a national securities exchange must have solely independent directors on its compensation committee.[25] Moreover, in publicly-held companies, an advisory shareholder vote must be conducted with respect to executive compensation.[26] This non-binding shareholder vote, called "Say on Pay," is proving somewhat influential in determining the level of executive remuneration.[27] In providing disclosure in this context, the company must provide a compensation and disclosure analysis (CD&A). The CD&A must meaningfully address the company's executive compensation policies and determinations.[28] Undoubtedly, in-house (as well as perhaps

---

[23] American Law Institute, *Principles of Corporate Governance, supra* note 1, at § 3.05 comment c(iii).

[24] Stock option backdating generally "involves a company issuing stock options to an executive on one date while providing fraudulent documentation asserting that the options were actually issued earlier." *Ryan v. Gifford*, 918 A. 2d 341, 345 (Del. 2007).

[25] Section 10C of the Securities Exchange Act. *See* SEC Rule 10C, 17 C.F.R. § 240.10C; Securities Exchange Act Release No. 67220 (2012) (Stock Exchange Listing Standards for Compensation Committees).

[26] Section 14A of the Securities Exchange Act. *See* Securities Exchange Act Release No. 63768 (2011).

[27] *See* Brady, *Say on Pay: Boards Listen When Shareholders Speak,* Bloomberg BusinessWeek, June 7, 2012. *But see Chasan, Companies Say 'No Way' to 'Say on Pay'*, Wall St. J., Aug. 26, 2014, at B1.

[28] *See* Securities Exchange Act Release No. 63768 (2011).

outside) counsel will provide meaningful input and advice with respect to this disclosure obligation.

A truly independent compensation committee functions to lessen the conflict of interest that executive officers have (either expressly or by implied "coercion") with respect to their compensation packages. Along with independence, the committee must be adequately informed when making its determinations. In this respect, the committee should keep itself updated regarding the current executive remuneration trends and practices in the industry in which the company is engaged. In-house counsel often plays an important role in this process by placing before the committee sufficient data and sources (which frequently includes the retention of an outside compensation firm) to enable the committee to make informed judgments.[29]

Nominating/Corporate Governance Committee

An independent nominating/corporate governance committee is essential to the composition of an independent and competent board of directors. A principal function of this committee is to select director-nominees for the company's board of directors and its committees, applying sound selection criteria. In addition, the committee periodically should assess each director's performance and determine whether such director's continued service should be recommended. The committee also may oversee corporate governance issues. Consistent with customary practice, all members of the committee should be independent directors.[30] As stated by The Conference Board, "each [publicly-held] corporation [should] establish a committee of independent directors to oversee corporate governance issues, including the statement of corporate governance principles and the performance evaluations of the board, its committees, and each director, as necessary."[31]

---

[29]   *See* Steinberg, *Corporate Developments and Policy, supra* note 4, at 151; American Law Institute, *Principles of Corporate Governance, supra* note 1, at § 3A.05 comment d.

[30]   *See* Steinberg, *Developments in Business Law and Policy, supra* note 4, at 167.

[31]   The Conference Board, *Corporate Governance—Findings and Recommendations,* note 1 *supra. See* SEC Regulation S–K Item 407, 17 C.F.R. § 229.407 (focusing, inter alia, on disclosure in regard to nominating committees).

CORPORATE EXECUTIVE OFFICERS

In many companies, on a regular basis, the inside general counsel interacts with the chief executive officer, chief operating officer, chief financial officer, and other executive officers. Depending on the structure and formality of the particular company, other in-house lawyers also will render assistance with some frequency to the executive officers.

With respect to daily operations, the CEO and other executive officers make major business and strategic decisions for the company. On this basis, in-house lawyers routinely provide legal counsel to corporate officers and other personnel. The in-house attorney's level of performance in her interactions with these individuals is instrumental in determining the degree of her success within the company.

An important function for CEOs and CFOs is the certifications that they must provide in SEC reports as required by the Sarbanes-Oxley Act. Miscommunication and errors in judgment (if negligent or worse) in completing these certifications can result in liability. In many companies, in-house lawyers play a meaningful role in this certification process. The contents of this certification are addressed later in this chapter.

LOANS

Prior to the Sarbanes-Oxley Act, publicly-held companies routinely extended low or no interest loans to corporate officers. Such loans are no longer legally permissible. SOX generally prohibits a publicly-held company from making loans to its directors and executive officers. An exception is made with respect to limited types of loans that are made in the ordinary course of the company's business if the terms of such loans are on the same basis as loans extended to the general public.[32] In-house lawyers must be aware of this limitation and accordingly render appropriate legal advice to executive officers and the board of directors.

---

[32]   Section 402 of the Sarbanes-Oxley Act, *amending,* § 13(k) of the Securities Exchange Act.

CONCLUSION

Adequacy of corporate governance today is not a luxury; it is an essential component of profitable companies that comply with the law and that desire to maintain the support of their institutional shareholders. In-house lawyers play an important role in the quest to achieve and maintain sound corporate governance practices.

Traditionally, the states (particularly, Delaware) have been and continue as the principal regulators of corporate governance. Nonetheless, corporate governance has become increasingly federalized. This journey is succinctly described below by one of the authors of this book.

THE FEDERALIZATION OF CORPORATE GOVERNANCE (2018)
Marc I. Steinberg[*]

In my recently published book, T*he Federalization of Corporate Governance* (Oxford University Press 2018) (ISBN 978-0-19-993454-6), I explore the process of federalization in the United States from 1903 to the present. Clearly, the states, particularly Delaware, traditionally have been and continue as principal regulators of the sphere of corporate governance. Nonetheless, to an increasing degree, the federal government, the SEC, and the national stock exchanges impact corporate governance standards. The book views this federalization as an evolutionary process that commenced at the beginning of the twentieth century. Going through periods of activism, gradual transition, and stagnation, the process intensified with the enactment of the Sarbanes-Oxley and Dodd-Frank Acts.

To view these Acts as representing a revolutionary transformation with respect to federal oversight of corporate governance is an exaggeration. Rather, they symbolize a period of enhanced activism whereby this federalization process was accentuated. From a historical perspective, between 1903 and 1914, 24 bills were introduced in Congress which sought to

---

[*]   The above is from the Harvard Law School Forum on Corporate Governance & Financial Regulation (June 21, 2018), *available at* https://corpgov.law.harvard.edu/2018/06/21/the-federalization-of-corporate-governance/.

require federal chartering and/or the implementation of federal minimum substantive standards. During that era, both Presidents Roosevelt and Taft favored federal incorporation. Between 1914 and 1930, another seven bills were introduced in Congress seeking to effectuate similar objectives—with one such bill requiring that the Federal Trade Commission approve executive officer remuneration. [During the past few decades, a small number of bills have been introduced seeking to mandate federal minimum standards.] Although hearings were held through the years, none of these bills were enacted.

This effort to implement federal minimum standards was not confined to the legislative arena. Indeed, for years, attempts were made to achieve such federalization through judicial construction of the federal securities laws, particularly Section 10(b) [of the Securities Exchange Act] and SEC Rule 10b–5. Although achieving some fleeting success, the U.S. Supreme Court in *Santa Fe Industries* (430 U.S. 462 (1977)) thoroughly rejected this effort—holding that a disclosure deficiency must be present to implicate these federal provisions. The substantive fairness of fiduciary conduct, the Court reasoned, is a matter of state corporate law.

Although not becoming law, these legislative and judicial efforts have modern day relevance. For example, many of the bills introduced early in the twentieth century sought to exclude corporate insiders from serving as directors or officers at competing companies. With certain exceptions, this prohibition was codified in the Clayton Antitrust Act of 1914. A number of other bills mandated that a subject company's independent auditor certify such company's financial statements as a requisite for the issuance of a federal charter. Today, audited financial statements, CEO and CFO certifications, and independent audit committees are firmly established. And, as mentioned above, one such bill required federal regulatory approval of executive officer compensation. Although this mandate has not been enacted, today we have extensive disclosure with respect to executive remuneration, the prohibition on loans to officers and directors, and shareholder advisory votes on executive compensation (say-on-pay).

Perhaps surprising to some observers, the initial implementation of federal corporate governance standards occurred with the Securities Exchange Act of 1934. Although not its primary focus, that Act prohibited short-selling by insiders as well as requiring, based on strict liability, that short-swing profits (made from purchases and sales or sales and purchases of an equity security within a six-month period) be disgorged. Seven years later, the SEC took its first significant foray in this sphere by promulgating the shareholder proposal rule. As stated by the author, "The SEC shareholder proposal rule represents an early 'intrusion' by the Commission—dating back to 1942— with respect to federalizing an area traditionally within the purview of state company law. Today, the Rule is well entrenched as an accepted facilitator of shareholder activism and of dialogue between management and institutional shareholders." (Federalization of Corporate Governance at page 190).

Also stunning in this context is the federalization of insider trading which commenced in 1961 with the SEC's administrative decision in *In re Cady, Roberts* (40 SEC 907 (1961)). Displeased with state court refusal to rectify this perceived misconduct, SEC Chairman William Cary made this subject a key item of his agenda. Seven years thereafter, the Second Circuit in *Texas Gulf Sulphur* (401 F.2d 833 (2d Cir. 1968) (en banc)) reinforced that the insider trading prohibition is a matter of federal corporate governance. Although subsequent U.S. Supreme Court decisions have confined the scope of *Texas Gulf Sulphur*, nonetheless federal law continues to govern this area of substantive fiduciary conduct.

The shareholder proposal rule and *In re Cady, Roberts* are two early examples of the SEC's activism impacting the federalization of corporate governance. This SEC activism has continued with frequency, such as: (1) with respect to insider trading, adopting SEC Rules 10b5–2 and 14e–3 as well as Regulation FD; (2) seeking to mitigate the impact of the U.S. Supreme Court's decision in *Santa Fe* by promulgating Rule 13e–3 that requires a subject party to disclose whether it has a reasonable belief that the going-private transaction is fair or unfair to unaffiliated shareholders and the reasons supporting that belief; (3) adopting the all holders rule prohibiting exclusionary tender offers, thereby, in practical effect, abrogating the Delaware Supreme Court's decision in *Unocal* (493 A.2d 945 (Del. 1985)), that upheld the use of selective tender offers; (4) seeking to deter fiduciary self-dealing through the guise of disclosure (*In re Franchard Corporation* (42 SEC 163 (1964)); (5) levying officer and director bars against miscreant fiduciaries; (6) ordering Undertakings in Commission enforcement actions (including such expansive measures as the appointment of independent directors, retention of special counsel, appointment of independent consultants, and retention of independent monitors—see. e.g., *In re Occidental Petroleum Corporation*, Securities Exchange Act Release No. 16950 (1980); and (7) bringing disciplinary proceedings against gatekeepers, including attorneys, for engaging in allegedly unethical conduct, thereby declining to relegate this area solely to state bar associations. These actions exemplify that the Commission is an active participant in the federalization of corporate governance process.

From this perspective, the Sarbanes-Oxley and Dodd-Frank Acts reflect a continuation on this federalization path. Focusing on such subjects as independent directors, the composition, roles and functions of board committees (such as the audit and compensation committees), codes of conduct, and say-on-pay advisory shareholder votes, these Acts meaningfully impact normative conduct. These Acts reinforce that federal corporate governance is a strong presence. They also serve as a reminder to the states that lax regulation may induce the passage of federal legislation, particularly during times of crisis.

Lastly, the national stock exchanges play a prominent role in this federalization process. Indeed, at the SEC's behest, the New York Stock Exchange in 1977 adopted a rule requiring that the members of a listed company's audit committee be comprised solely of independent directors. Several of the provisions contained in the Sarbanes-Oxley and Dodd-Frank Acts condition the eligibility of a subject company to list on a national stock exchange by requiring that the subject company adhere to the Acts' mandates. Through this process of government mandates and SEC "persuasion," the Exchanges have facilitated the effectuation of this federalization process. . . .

In conclusion, federal law today impacts the governance of publicly-held corporations to a greater extent than ever before in our country's history. . . .

The following excerpt from the American Law Institute's Restatement of the Law of Corporate Governance provides a useful overview of key corporate governance principles.

AMERICAN LAW INSTITUTE, PRINCIPLES OF CORPORATE GOVERNANCE: ANALYSIS AND RECOMMENDATIONS (1994)*

§ 2.01   *The Objective and Conduct of the Corporation*

(a) Subject to the provisions of Subsection (b) and § 6.02 (Action of Directors That Has the Foreseeable Effect of Blocking Unsolicited Tender Offers), a corporation should have as its objective the conduct of business activities with a view to enhancing corporate profit and shareholder gain.

(b) Even if corporate profit and shareholder gain are not thereby enhanced, the corporation, in the conduct of its business:

(1) Is obliged, to the same extent as a natural person, to act within the boundaries set by law;

(2) May take into account ethical considerations that are reasonably regarded as appropriate to the responsible conduct of business; and

(3) May devote a reasonable amount of resources to public welfare, humanitarian, educational, and philanthropic purposes.

Comment:

Corporate objective and corporate conduct. The subject matter of these Principles is the governance of business corporations. The business corporation is an instrument through which capital is assembled for the activities of producing and distributing goods and services and making investments. These Principles take as a basic proposition that a business corporation should have as its objective the conduct of such activities with a view to enhancing corporate profit and shareholder gain. . . . The basic proposition is qualified in the manner stated in Subsection (b), which speaks to the conduct of the corporation. The provisions of Subsection (b) reflect a recognition that the corporation is a social as well as an economic institution, and accordingly that its pursuit of the economic objective must be constrained by social imperatives and may be qualified by social needs.

The economic objective. In very general terms, Subsection (a) may be thought of as a broad injunction to enhance economic returns, while Subsection (b) makes clear that certain kinds of conduct must or may be pursued whether or not they enhance such returns (that is, even if the conduct either yields no economic return or entails a net economic loss). In most cases, however, the kinds of conduct described in Subsection (b) could be pursued even under the principle embodied in Subsection (a). Such conduct will usually be consistent with economic self-interest, because the principle embodied in Subsection (a)—that the objective of the corporation is to conduct business activities with a view to enhancing corporate profit and shareholder gain—does not mean that the objective of the corporation must be to realize corporate profit and shareholder gain in the short run. Indeed, the contrary is true: long-run profitability and shareholder gain are at the core of the economic objective. Activity that entails a short-run cost to achieve an appropriately greater long-run profit is therefore not a departure from the economic objective. An orientation toward lawful, ethical, and public-spirited activity will normally fall within this description. The modern corporation by its nature creates interdependencies with a variety of groups with whom the corporation has a legitimate concern, such as employees, customers, suppliers, and members of the communities in which the corporation operates. The long-term profitability of the corporation generally depends on meeting the fair expectations of such groups. Short-term profits may properly be subordinated to recognition that responsible maintenance of these interdependencies is likely to contribute to long-term corporate profit and shareholder gain. The corporation's business may be conducted accordingly.

. . . .

Compliance with legal rules. Under § 2.01(b)(1), the corporation is obliged, to the same extent as a natural person, to act within the boundaries set by law. It is sometimes maintained that whether a corporation should adhere to a given legal rule may properly depend on a kind of cost-benefit analysis, in which probable corporate gains are weighed against either probable social costs, measured by the dollar liability imposed for engaging in such conduct, or probable corporate losses, measured by potential dollar liability discounted for likelihood of detection. Section 2.01 does not adopt this position. With few exceptions, dollar liability is not a "price" that can properly be paid for the privilege of engaging in legally wrongful conduct. Cost-benefit analysis may have a place in the state's determination whether a given type of conduct should be deemed legally wrongful. Once that determination has been made, however, the resulting legal rule normally represents a community decision that the conduct is wrongful as such, so that cost-benefit analysis whether to obey the rule is out of place.

Accordingly, in conducting its business, the corporation, like all other citizens, is under an obligation to act within the boundaries set by law. . . .

Ethical considerations. Section 2.01(b)(2) provides that a corporation may take into account ethical considerations that are reasonably regarded as appropriate to the responsible conduct of business. It is sometimes argued that because adherence to ethical principles typically involves long-run financial benefits, the concept of the long run dissolves any apparent tension between financial and ethical considerations. Certainly, a long-run profit motive may often explain conduct that appears to be based on ethical grounds. Furthermore, when ethical considerations enter into corporate decisions, they are usually mixed with, rather than opposed to, long-run profit considerations. Nevertheless, observation suggests that corporate decisions are not infrequently made on the basis of ethical considerations even when doing so would not enhance corporate profit or shareholder gain. Such behavior is not only appropriate, but desirable. Corporate officials are not less morally obliged than any other citizens to take ethical considerations into account, and it would be unwise social policy to preclude them from doing so.

This does not mean that corporate officials can properly take into account any ethical consideration, no matter how idiosyncratic. Because such officials are dealing with other people's money, they will act properly in taking ethical principles into account only where those considerations are reasonably regarded as appropriate to the responsible conduct of business. In this connection, however, it should be recognized that new principles may emerge over time. A corporate official therefore should be permitted to take into account emerging ethical principles, reasonably regarded as appropriate to the responsible conduct of business, that have significant support although less-than-universal acceptance.

The ethical considerations reasonably regarded as appropriate to the responsible conduct of business necessarily include ethical responsibilities that may be owed to persons other than shareholders with whom the corporation has a legitimate concern, such as employees, customers, suppliers, and members of the communities within which the corporation operates. The content of these responsibilities may vary according to the type of business in question and the history and established standards of the particular corporation. For example, a manufacturer of consumer goods may owe an ethical obligation to produce safe products, while newspapers may owe ethical obligations that are defined in part by the moral standards of journalism. Similarly, the content of the fairness obligation owed to groups such as employees may depend in part on past statements and practices that have engendered reasonable reliance or legitimate expectations. . . .

Public welfare, humanitarian, educational, and philanthropic purposes. Section 2.01(b)(3) permits the corporation to devote a reasonable amount of resources to public welfare, humanitarian, educational, and philanthropic purposes, even if corporate profit and shareholder gain are not thereby enhanced. As in the case of ethical considerations, conduct that appears to be based on public welfare, humanitarian, educational, or philanthropic considerations may be intended to enhance corporate profit and shareholder gain. For example, a donation to public television may be made for reasons comparable to those for sponsoring a commercial, and a contribution to local Red Cross or Community Chest activities may be made for reasons of employee well-being and morale. Furthermore, when considerations of the type described in § 2.01(b)(3) enter into corporate decisions, they are usually mixed with, rather than separable from, considerations of profitability and ethics. In such cases the activity may be justified under § 2.01(a) or § 2.01(b)(2).

Section 2.01(b)(3) goes beyond these justifications and allows corporate resources to be devoted to public welfare, humanitarian, educational, and philanthropic purposes even without a showing of expected profits or ethical norms. It is now widely accepted that the corporation should at least consider the social impact of its activities, so as to be aware of the social costs those activities entail. By implication, the corporation should be permitted to take such costs into account, within reason. For example, the corporation may take into account, within reason, public-welfare concerns relevant to groups with whom the corporation has a legitimate concern, such as employees, customers, suppliers, and members of the communities within which the corporation operates. Furthermore, because of the central position of corporations in the economic structure, the cooperation of corporations in furthering established governmental policies is often critical to the success of such policies. Social policy also favors humane behavior by major social institutions. Finally, social policy favors the maintenance of diversity in educational and philanthropic activity, and this objective would be more difficult to achieve if corporations, which control a great share of national resources, were not allowed to devote a portion of these resources to those ends. . . .

The determination whether the amount of resources used for purposes stated in § 2.01(b)(3) is reasonable in any given case, like other questions of reasonableness in the law, depends on all the circumstances of the case. . . .

*§ 3.01   Management of the Corporation's Business: Functions
         and Powers of Principal Senior Executives and Other
         Officers*

*The management of the business of a publicly held
corporation should be conducted by or under the supervision
of such principal senior executives as are designated by the
board of directors, and by those other officers and employees
to whom the management function is delegated by the board
or those executives, subject to the functions and powers of the
board under § 3.02.*

Comment:

a.   *Comparison with present law.* The formation of § 3.01
differs from the literal terms of the older statutory formulations
(which commonly provided that the business of the corporation
"shall be managed by [its] board") and, to a much lesser extent,
from the more modern formulations, such as Delaware Gen.
Corp. Law § 141 ("[t]he business and affairs of every corporation
. . . shall be managed by or under the direction of" the board), or
Model Act § 8.01(b) ("[a]ll corporate powers shall be exercised by
or under authority of, and the business and affairs of a
corporation shall be managed under the direction of," the board).
However, § 3.01 reflects long-established corporate practice
under both types of statutory formulation. For example, the
Corporate Director's Guidebook states:

> It is generally recognized that the board of directors
> is not expected to operate the business. Even under
> statutes providing that the business and affairs shall be
> "managed" by the board of directors, it is recognized
> that actual operation is a function of management. The
> responsibility of the board is limited to overseeing such
> operation. . . .

> It is important to emphasize that the role of the
> director is to monitor, in an environment of loyal but
> independent oversight, the conduct of the business and
> affairs of the corporation on behalf of those who invest
> in the corporation.

Similarly, the *Business Roundtable Statement* (pp. 2094–98)
comments:

It is plainly impossible for a board composed [largely] . . . of persons who are not full-time employees, to conduct . . . day-to-day [corporate] affairs. . . .

Although the board cannot effectively conduct day-to-day operations, the board does have a major role in, and a major accountability for, the financial performance of the enterprise. This clearly requires a continuing check on corporate financial results and prospects, including profit and loss and cash flow by major business segments.

. . . .

§ 3.02   *Functions and Powers of the Board of Directors*

Except as otherwise provided by statute:

(a) *The board of directors of a publicly held corporation should perform the following functions:*

(1) *Select, regularly evaluate, fix the compensation of, and, where appropriate, replace the principal senior executives;*

(2) *Oversee the conduct of the corporation's business to evaluate whether the business is being properly managed;*

(3) *Review and, [as a general matter], approve the corporation's financial objectives and major corporate plans and actions;*

(4) *Review and, [as a general matter], approve major changes in, and determinations of other major questions of choice respecting, the appropriate auditing and accounting principles and practices to be used in the preparation of the corporation's financial statements;*

(5) *Perform such other functions as are prescribed by law, or assigned to the board under a standard of the corporation.*

(b) *A board of directors also has power to:*

(1) *Initiate and adopt corporate plans, commitments, and actions;*

(2) Initiate and adopt changes in accounting principles and practices;

(3) Provide advice and counsel to the principal senior executives;

(4) Instruct any committee, principal senior executive, or other officer, and review the actions of any committee, principal senior executive, or other officer;

(5) Make recommendations to shareholders;

(6) Manage the business of the corporation;

(7) Act as to all other corporate matters not requiring shareholder approval.

(c) Subject to the board's ultimate responsibility for oversight under Subsection (a)(2), the board may delegate to its committees authority to perform any of its functions and exercise any of its powers.

Comment:

a. Comparison with present law. Section 3.02 differs from the literal terms of statutory formulations of the role of the board (see Comment *a* to § 3.01), but provides an articulation of the board's basic functions and powers that almost certainly would be arrived at by the courts in light of the language of these statutes read in the context of modern corporate practice. Although the statutes literally seem to require the board to either manage or direct the management of the corporation, it is widely understood that the board of a publicly held corporation normally cannot and does not perform those functions in the usual sense of those terms. . . .

Accordingly, it seems clear that, as provided in § 3.02, the board can normally satisfy the requirements of present statutes without either actively managing or directing the management of the corporation, as long as it oversees management and retains the decisive voice on major corporate actions. As stated by the New Jersey Supreme Court in Francis v. United Jersey Bank, 87 N.J. 15, 432 A.2d 814 (1981), "Directorial management does not require a detailed inspection of day-to-day activities, but rather a general monitoring of corporate affairs and policies." . . .

The oversight function. In the publicly held corporation, the management function is normally vested in the principal senior executives. A basic function of the board is to select these executives and to oversee their performance (using the term "oversee" to refer to general observation and oversight, not active supervision or day-to-day scrutiny) to determine whether the business is being properly managed. . . . This oversight function is usually performed, not directly by actively supervising the principal senior executives, but indirectly by evaluating the performance of those executives and replacing any who are not meeting reasonable expectations concerning job performance. . . .

The board's obligation to oversee the performance of the principal senior executives does not imply an antagonist relationship between the board and the executives. Rather, it contemplates a collegial relationship that is supportive as well as watchful. To paraphrase the *Business Roundtable Statement,* the relationship between the board and the executives should be challenging yet positive, arm's length but not adversary.

A significant aspect of oversight by the board is continuing attention to the [law compliant] conduct of the corporation's business. As stated in the *Corporate Director's Guidebook:*

> The corporate director should be concerned that the corporation has programs looking toward compliance with applicable laws and regulations, both foreign and domestic, that it circulates (as appropriate) policy statements to this effect to its employees, and that it maintains procedures for monitoring such compliance.

Similarly, the Business Roundtable's *Corporate Governance and American Competitiveness* lists as one of the board's five primary functions: "Review the adequacy of systems to comply with applicable laws/regulations."

Selection, evaluation, compensation, and replacement of principal senior executives. Section 3.02(a)(1) provides that the board should select, regularly evaluate, fix the compensation of, and, where appropriate, replace the principal senior executives. . . . The evaluation of the principal senior executives need not be formal. In determining the compensation of and in evaluating principal senior executives, the board or its committee is entitled to rely on the chief executive officer's formal or informal evaluations of principal senior executives who are the chief executive officer's subordinates.

In most cases, recommendations of candidates for principal senior executive offices will be initiated by the chief executive. The board will normally be entitled to rely on such recommendations, and in any event the board should normally give great weight, or even defer, to such recommendations. However, ultimate responsibility for the selection of principal senior executives rests with the board, unless otherwise provided by statute.

The process of selecting and evaluating officers below the level of the principal senior executives is normally conducted by the principal senior executives, but the board should oversee that process, or its results, both as part of its general oversight function and to help ensure that the ranks of top management are capably staffed and that lines of succession are adequately maintained.

Review of major corporate plans and actions. Section 3.02(a)(3) provides that the board should review and, [as a general matter], approve the corporation's financial objectives and major corporate plans and actions. What constitutes a major corporate plan or action is a matter of business judgment. Moreover, as a functional matter these judgments will normally be made, at least in the first instance, by the principal senior executives, and more particularly the chief executive officer, because in most cases the executives shape the board's agenda. . . .

Examples of major corporate *plans* would normally include long-term strategic and investment plans, annual capital and operating budgets, and targeted rates of return. Examples of major corporate *actions* would normally include the creation or retirement of significant long-term debt, programs for the issuance or reacquisition of significant amounts of equity, significant capital investments, significant acquisitions of stock in other corporations, business combinations including those effected for cash, and the disposition of significant businesses. In general, the board should also address any matters that would in its judgment, or in the judgment of the principal senior executives, expose the corporation to significant litigation or significant new regulatory problems, or have or promise to have major public impact.

As a practical matter, the initiation and formulation of major corporate plans and actions must depend in large part on an intimate knowledge of the business of the corporation, and this knowledge is more likely to be possessed by the senior executives than by the board. Section 3.02(a)(3) therefore contemplates that, while ultimate responsibility for approving major corporate plans and actions is vested in the board, and the board also has power to initiate their formulation, in practice these plans and actions will usually be initiated and formulated by the senior executives. By the same token, the board may properly approve several options and leave it to the senior executives to decide, in light of emergent conditions, which option to execute. In making such determinations, the board and the senior executives would be entitled to the protection of the business judgment rule when they satisfy the standards of that rule. . . . [As explained in other chapters of this book, the business judgment rule generally protects a determination made by a board of directors from successful challenge. The rule is a presumption that the Board made an adequately informed deliberative decision in good faith without a disabling conflict of interest. The standard for rebutting the presumption of the business judgment rule is that of gross negligence.]

Delegation of board powers and functions. It is commonly provided by statute that the board may delegate to a committee the authority to exercise any of its powers, subject to certain limitations. Section 3.02(c) recognizes the permissibility of such delegation, within the limitations imposed by those statutes. Section 3.02(c) also recognizes that the board's functions can be delegated to its committees. Although the board can (and normally will) delegate to committees the performance of parts of the oversight function, and employ committees to implement and support that function, this delegation and employment is subject to the constraint that, because of the critical nature of the oversight function, the board must maintain a continuing presence in and ultimate responsibility for the overall performance of that function. . . .

Certain powers and functions, most notably the power to manage the business of the corporation, may also be delegated to officers, as is made clear by § 3.01.

As a matter of corporate practice, actions taken by a committee to which a significant part of the authority of the board has been delegated should be reported to the board at its next meeting, usually by distribution of committee minutes or by a written or oral report. This procedure is intended . . . to give the board a means of [being informed and] supervising its committees. . . .

    . . . .

§ 3.05   *Audit Committee in Large Publicly Held Corporations*

Every . . . publicly held corporation [must] have an audit committee to implement and support the oversight function of the board by reviewing on a periodic basis the corporation's processes for producing financial data, its internal controls, and the independence of the corporation's external auditor. The audit committee should consist of at least three members, and should be composed exclusively of [independent outside] directors. . . .

    . . . .

Comment:

Rationale and operation. An independent audit committee serves to implement and support the oversight function of the board in several ways.

(i)   Such a committee provides a means for review of the corporation's processes for producing financial data, its internal controls, and the independence of the corporation's external auditor, and a forum for dialogue with the corporation's external and internal auditors. In theory, the full board might execute these functions itself, because the board is obliged in any event to be conversant with those matters. In practice, however, there are several reasons why an audit committee would normally constitute a preferable location for these functions. For one thing, a focused review and detailed discussion of the corporation's processes for producing financial data, its internal controls, and the independence of its external auditor might be too time-consuming for the full board. For another, because the corporation's financial data concerns the performance of management, it is important to have a forum for [the independent outside directors who comprise the entire membership of the committee to] discuss this data, and the manner of its preparation, in which management participates only on request.

(ii) An independent audit committee reinforces the independence of the corporation's external auditor, and thereby helps assure that the auditor will have free rein in the audit process. This reinforcement is achieved in part by conferring, on an organ that is independent of the management whose financial results are being audited, a vital role in the retention, discharge, and compensation of the external auditor. In addition, such a committee provides tangible embodiment of the concept that, within the framework of corporate relationships, the external auditor is responsible to the board and to the shareholders.

(iii) An independent audit committee provides a forum for regular, informal, and private discussion between the external auditor and directors who have no significant relationships with management. . . .

(iv) An independent audit committee reinforces the objectivity of the internal auditing department. If that department reports primarily to management . . . and has no regular access to the board or to a board committee, it may encounter resistance to recommendations that do not meet with management's approval. Regular access to an audit committee may help ameliorate such resistance. A working relationship with an audit committee is also likely to increase the status and therefore the effectiveness of the internal auditing department.

. . . .

The CEO and CFO certifications in SEC reports were discussed earlier in this chapter. The following SEC release focuses on this subject. In-house lawyers frequently render counsel in connection with the certification process.

CERTIFICATION OF DISCLOSURE IN COMPANIES' QUARTERLY AND ANNUAL REPORTS
Securities Act Release 8124 (SEC 2002)

On July 30, 2002, the Sarbanes-Oxley Act of 2002 (the "Act") was enacted. Section 302 of this Act, entitled "Corporate Responsibility for Financial Reports," requires the Commission to adopt final rules . . ., under which the principal executive officer or officers and the principal financial officer or officers, or persons providing similar functions, of an issuer each must certify the information contained in the issuer's quarterly and annual reports. Section 302 also requires these officers to certify that: they are responsible for establishing, maintaining and regularly evaluating the effectiveness of, the issuer's internal controls; they have made certain disclosures to the issuer's auditors and the audit committee of the board of directors about the issuer's internal controls; and they have included information in the issuer's quarterly and annual reports about their evaluation and whether there have been significant changes in the issuer's internal controls or in other factors that could significantly affect internal controls subsequent to the evaluation.

. . . .

While Section 302 of the Act requires an issuer's principal executive and financial officers to make specific certifications regarding their responsibilities to establish and maintain internal controls, it does not directly address the issuer's responsibility for controls and procedures related to the issuer's Exchange Act reporting obligations. The [Rule] Proposals included requirements that companies maintain sufficient procedures to provide reasonable assurances that they are able to collect, process and disclose, within the time periods specified in the Commission's rules and forms, the information required to be disclosed in their Exchange Act reports. We have adopted this requirement largely as proposed. Because of the broad scope of Section 302 of the Act, the new rules are applicable to all types of issuers that file reports under Section 13(a) or 15(d) of the Exchange Act [i.e., publicly-held reporting enterprises]. . . .

Certification of Quarterly and Annual Reports Requirements

... Exchange Act Rules 13a–14 and 15d–14 require an issuer's principal executive officer or officers and the principal financial officer or officers, or persons performing similar functions, each to certify in each quarterly and annual report that:

- he or she has reviewed the report;

- based on his or her knowledge, the report does not contain any untrue statement of a material fact or omit to state a material fact necessary in order to make the statements made, in light of the circumstances under which such statements were made, not misleading with respect to the period covered by the report;

- based on his or her knowledge, the financial statements, and other financial information included in the report, fairly present in all material respects the financial condition, results of operations and cash flows of the issuer as of, and for, the periods presented in the report;

- he or she and the other certifying officers:

   [1] are responsible for establishing and maintaining "disclosure controls and procedures" . . .;

   [2] have designed such disclosure controls and procedures to ensure that material information is made known to them, particularly during the period in which the periodic report is being prepared;

   [3] have evaluated the effectiveness of the issuer's disclosure controls and procedures of a date within 90 days prior to the filing date of the report; and

   [4] have presented in the report their conclusions about the effectiveness of the disclosure controls

and procedures based on the required evaluation as of that date;

- he or she and the other certifying officers have disclosed to the issuer's auditors and to the audit committee of the board of directors (or persons fulfilling the equivalent function):

[1] all significant deficiencies in the design or operation of internal controls (a pre-existing term relating to internal controls regarding financial reporting) which could adversely affect the issuer's ability to record, process, summarize and report financial data and have identified for the issuer's auditors any material weaknesses in internal controls; and

[2] any fraud, whether or not material, that involves management or other employees who have a significant role in the issuer's internal controls; and

- he or she and the other certifying officers have indicated in the report whether or not there were significant changes in internal controls or in other factors that could significantly affect internal controls subsequent to the date of their evaluation, including any corrective actions with regard to significant deficiencies and material weaknesses.

For purposes of [these] rules, "disclosure controls and procedures" are defined as controls and other procedures of an issuer that are designed to ensure that information required to be disclosed by the issuer in the reports filed or submitted by it under the Exchange Act is recorded, processed, summarized and reported, within the time periods specified in the Commission's rules and forms. . . .

CHAPTER 5

CLIENT CONFIDENTIALITY

Inside counsel owes a duty of confidentiality to his or her client—a duty that, with certain exceptions, prohibits counsel from "reveal[ing] information relating to the representation of [the] client."[1] Nonetheless, the in-house attorney cannot assist a client "in conduct that the lawyer knows is criminal or fraudulent."[2] A tension between these principles may arise when counsel believes that she has a duty or wishes to remain silent regarding the representation, but is concerned that such silence may facilitate the client company's fraudulent or criminal act.

APPLICABLE RULES

Under ABA Model Rule 1.6(b), a version of which has been adopted by the vast majority of states, an attorney has discretion to disclose information concerning the representation of a client to the extent that such attorney reasonably believes is necessary:

(1) to prevent reasonably certain death or substantial bodily harm;

(2) to prevent the client from committing a crime or fraud that is reasonably certain to result in substantial injury to the financial interests or property of another and in furtherance of which the client has used or is using the lawyer's services; [or]

(3) to prevent, mitigate or rectify substantial injury to the financial interests or property of another that is reasonably certain to result or has resulted from the

---

[1]   Rule 1.6(a) of the ABA Model Rules provides: "(a) A lawyer shall not reveal information relating to representation of a client unless the client gives informed consent, the disclosure is impliedly authorized in order to carry out the representation or the disclosure is permitted by paragraph (b)."

[2]   Model Rule 1.2(d). Rule 1.2(d) states: "A lawyer shall not counsel a client to engage, or assist a client, in conduct that the lawyer knows is criminal or fraudulent, but a lawyer may discuss the legal consequences of any proposed course of conduct with a client and may counsel or assist a client to make a good faith effort to determine the validity, scope, meaning or application of the law."

client's commission of a crime or fraud in furtherance of which the client has used the lawyer's services.[3]

The Securities and Exchange Commission (SEC) in its Standards of Professional Conduct for Attorneys likewise permits an attorney, without the client's consent, to reveal to the SEC such confidential information.[4]

The issue of disclosure becomes further complicated when the attorney's client is an organization, such as a corporation. Because a corporation is an artificial entity, it must act through its duly authorized constituents. Thus, if inside counsel learns that an officer or employee of a corporate client is engaging in or is about to engage in fraudulent activity, the attorney must ascertain whether such person is acting on behalf of or independently from the corporation. In this situation, Model Rule 1.13 directs the attorney to "proceed as is reasonably necessary in the best interest of the organization" including, if warranted, referring the matter "to the highest authority that can act on behalf of the organization as determined by applicable law."[5]

A similar approach is taken by the Sarbanes-Oxley Act (SOX), enacted in 2002. Section 307 of SOX directs the SEC to adopt a rule:

(1) requiring a [subject] attorney to report evidence of a material violation of securities law or breach of fiduciary duty or similar violation by the company or

---

[3]   At least 42 states permit a lawyer to reveal a client's fraud or crime that threatens substantial financial loss. *See* American Law Institute, *Restatement (Third) of the Law Governing Lawyers* § 67, Reporter's Note at 514 (2000).

[4]   *See* 17 C.F.R. § 205.3(d)(2) of the SEC's Standards:

"(2)   An attorney appearing and practicing before the Commission in the representation of an issuer may reveal to the Commission, without the issuer's consent, confidential information related to the representation to the extent the attorney reasonably believes necessary:

(i)   To prevent the issuer from committing a material violation that is likely to cause substantial injury to the financial interest or property of the issuer or investors; . . . or

(iii) To rectify the consequences of a material violation by the issuer that caused, or may cause, substantial injury to the financial interest or property of the issuer or investors in the furtherance of which the attorney's services were used."

[5]   Model Rule 1.13(b). The highest authority within the organization ordinarily is the board of directors or similar governing body.

any agent thereof, to the chief legal counsel or the chief executive officer of the company (or the equivalent thereof); and

(2) if the counsel or officer does not appropriately respond to the evidence (adopting, as necessary, appropriate remedial measures or sanctions with respect to the violation), requiring [such] attorney to report the evidence to the audit committee of the board of directors of the issuer or to another committee of the board of directors comprised solely of directors not employed directly or indirectly by the issuer, or to the board of directors.[6]

Responding to this directive, the SEC's Standards of Conduct for Attorneys resemble existing ethical standards set forth in the ABA Model Rules. For example, the SEC's Standards:

require an attorney to report evidence of a material violation, determined according to an objective standard, 'up-the-ladder' within the issuer to the chief legal counsel or the chief executive officer of the company or the equivalent; [and] require an attorney, if the chief legal counsel or the chief executive officer of the company does not respond appropriately to the evidence, to report the evidence to the audit committee, another committee of independent directors, or the full board of directors.[7]

An important justification underlying the above pronouncements is that by bringing the potential fraud or illegality to light within the company, the attorney may be able to help prevent its occurrence.

---

[6]   SOX § 307, 15 U.S.C. § 7245. *See* Bainbridge & Johnson, *Managerialism, Legal Ethics, and Sarbanes-Oxley Section 307,* 2004 Mich. St. L. Rev. 299 (2004).

[7]   SEC Press Release No. 2003–13 (2003). *See* 17 C.F.R § 205.3. The SEC Standards, as an alternative, permit a subject company to establish a "qualified legal compliance committee" (QLCC) for reporting and responding with respect to evidence of a material violation. *See* 17 C.F.R. § 205.3(c). Thus far, the QLCC alternative has not been widely adopted. *See* Rosen, *Resistances to Reforming Corporate Governance: The Diffusion of QLCCs,* 74 Fordham L. Rev. 1251, 1252 (2005) (pointing out that "97.5% of issuers have not yet adopted" the QLCC).

Although the in-house lawyer may communicate with
constituents of the corporation (such as officers, directors,
shareholders and employees) in connection with learning about
the potential fraud, she will be limited in terms of what
information she may share with the constituents, particularly if
their interests are adverse to the corporate client. As a comment
to ABA Model Rule 1.13 states, the "lawyer may not disclose to
such constituents information relating to the representation
except for disclosures explicitly or implicitly authorized by the
organizational client in order to carry out the representation or
as otherwise permitted by Rule 1.6."[8] Thus, when
communicating with constituents associated with an
organizational client, the in-house lawyer must be able to
distinguish between those persons acting in their organizational
capacity on behalf of the company and those acting in their
personal constituent capacity, and must disclose confidential
information relating to her representation of the client only to
the former.

WITHDRAWAL AND ITS CONSEQUENCES

When the company, acting through its duly authorized
representative(s), such as its board of directors, uses or plans to
use the in-house attorney's work to perpetrate a crime or fraud,
the ABA Model Rules permit the lawyer to withdraw from the
representation.[9] Indeed, when continued representation will
result in counsel's violation of applicable law or ethical rules, the
attorney must withdraw.[10] For in-house lawyers, in practical
effect, this often means that the attorney must resign from his
employment—a much tougher consequence as compared to
outside lawyers who, while losing one client, carry on their law
practice.

When inside counsel withdraws, thereby leaving her
employment, a key issue becomes how much "noise" ("noisy"
withdrawal) the attorney can make in terminating the
representation—that is, what can or should the attorney do or
say to indicate that the client has acted or will act fraudulently

---

[8]   Model Rule 1.13 cmt. 2. *See generally,* Veasey & Di Guglielmo, *The Tensions,
Stresses and Responsibilities of the Lawyer for the Corporation,* 62 Bus. Law. 1 (2006).

[9]   Model Rule 1.16(b)(2).

[10]   *Id.* Rule 1.16(a)(1).

or illegally? For example, may the inside lawyer disaffirm legal advice she rendered based on materially false information provided by corporate executives? By disaffirming previously issued legal advice and making such a "noisy" withdrawal, a possible collateral consequence is the disclosure, inferentially, of information that relates to the representation.[11] "Unlike a silent, unexplained withdrawal, a lawyer's explicit disaffirmance of work product [such as the drafting of an offering document] by the lawyer in the course of the representation, may well be understood as amounting to a representation by the lawyer that the client information on which the disaffirmed document relied is untrustworthy, thereby necessitating the withdrawal."[12]

Today, the ABA Model Rules, the SEC Standards, and the vast majority of states allow counsel to make a "noisy" withdrawal when the client uses such lawyer's services to commit an ongoing or completed fraud or crime.[13] Although the SEC has declined to adopt a rule requiring that counsel make a

---

[11]   See N.Y. Rules of Prof. Conduct, Rule 1.6(b)(3).

[12]   *See* ABA Comm. on Ethics and Professional Responsibility, *Withdrawal When a Lawyer's Services Will Otherwise Be Used to Perpetrate a Fraud,* Formal Op. 92–366 (1992) (setting forth instances in which an attorney may "disaffirm documents prepared in the course of the representation that are being, or will be, used in furtherance of [a] fraud, even though such a "noisy" withdrawal may have the collateral effect of inferentially revealing client confidences").

Moreover, in certain circumstances, in many jurisdictions withdrawal from the representation is not sufficient where a lawyer knows that a document he drafted is materially false and is being relied upon by non-clients. In these situations, the attorney may be required to disaffirm her work product and thereupon make a noisy withdrawal. Comments to the ABA's Model Rules of Professional Conduct as well as an ABA Formal Opinion support this view. As the ABA Formal Opinion provides, "where the client avowedly intends to continue to use the lawyer's work product, this amounts to a *de facto* continuation of representation even if the lawyer has ceased to perform any additional work." Hence, "[t]he representation is not completed, any more than the fraud itself is completed." *See* Model Rules 1.2 cmt. 10, 4.1 cmt. 3. ABA Committee on Ethics and Professional Responsibility, Formal Opinion 92–366 (1992). *See also,* Jarvis & Rich, *The Law of Unintended Consequences: Whether and When Mandatory Disclosure Under Model Rule 4.1(b) Trumps Discretionary Disclosure Under Model Rule 1.6(b),* 44 Hofstra L. Rev. 421 (2016); Steinberg, *The Corporate Securities Attorney as a Moving Target— Client Fraud Dilemmas,* 46 Washburn L.J. 1 (2006).

[13]   *See, e.g.,* Model Rule 1.6(b)(2), (3), cmt. 10 to Model Rule 1.2, cmt. 3 to Model Rule 4.1; N.Y. Rules of Prof. Conduct, Rule 1.6(b)(3) (permitting an attorney "to withdraw a written or oral opinion or representation previously given by the lawyer and reasonably believed by the lawyer still to be relied upon by a third person, where the lawyer has discovered that the opinion or representation was based on materially inaccurate information or is being used to further a crime or fraud"); Texas Rules of Prof. Conduct, Rule 1.05(c)(7), (c)(8); SEC Standards, 17 C.F.R. § 205.3(d)(2).

noisy withdrawal,[14] a small number of states, such as Tennessee, mandate that counsel make a noisy withdrawal under specified circumstances.[15]

Not all jurisdictions are in agreement. California, for example, precludes attorney disclosure of client confidences to prevent or rectify financial harm.[16]

In this regard, the State Bar of California Standing Committee on Professional Responsibility and Conduct, in directly addressing the issue of what an attorney can and should do in light of a client's fraud, has stated that the lawyer is prohibited from disclosing anything regarding the fraudulent activity without the client's consent. The attorney, however, must try to persuade the client from furthering the fraud. If the client persists in the misconduct, the lawyer must withdraw from the representation.[17] In practical effect, in such circumstances, the in-house lawyer may be obligated to resign from his employment.

THE OSTRICH APPROACH

As attractive as it may sometimes seem, in-house counsel would be imprudent to adopt an "ostrich" approach toward his corporate client's fraudulent activity in the name of preserving its confidences. Consider, for example, *In re OPM Leasing Services, Inc.*,[18] which although involving a law firm, is pertinent for in-house lawyers. There, a law firm, after learning of its role in closing a fraudulent transaction for a client, received assurances from the client's principals that they would not commit any further fraud. Thereafter, the law firm continued to close fraudulent transactions for the client despite "numerous

---

[14]   *See* Securities Exchange Act Release Nos. 42726, 47282 (2003).

[15]   *See* Tenn. Rules of Prof. Conduct, Rule 4.1(b), (c). For further discussion, see M. Steinberg, *Attorney Liability After Sarbanes-Oxley* § 3.05 (2018); Cramton, Cohen & Koniak, *Legal and Ethical Duties of Lawyers After Sarbanes-Oxley,* 49 Vill. L. Rev. 725 (2004).

[16]   *See* Cal. Bus. & Prof. Code § 6068(e).

[17]   *See* State Bar of Cal. Standing Comm. on Prof. Responsibility and Conduct, Formal Op. 1996–146 (1996). *See also,* Cal. Bus. and Prof. Code § 6068(e)(1) ("It is the duty of an attorney . . . to maintain inviolate the confidence, and at every peril to himself or herself to preserve the secrets, of his or her client").

[18]   *In re OPM Leasing Services, Inc.* (1983) (Bankruptcy Trustee Report). *See also, In re O.P.M. Leasing Services, Inc.,* 40 B.R. 380 (S.D.N.Y. 1984); S. Taylor, "Ethics and the Law: A Case History," *N.Y. Times Magazine* at 31 (Jan. 9, 1983).

additional facts . . . that should have raised suspicions about the bona fides of" the transactions.[19] Although the law firm subsequently terminated its representation as outside general counsel, it agreed to mischaracterize the termination as a mutual decision between the firm and client.[20] After the law firm's resignation, the former client continued to close fraudulent transactions using in-house attorneys as well as another law firm—consequently, both inside counsel and the second law firm were oblivious regarding the actual reasons for the original law firm's resignation.[21]

The law firm's conduct in *OPM* "raise[d] issues beyond professional ethics. . . . No rule of professional ethics can or should exempt lawyers from the general legal proscriptions against willful blindness to the client's crimes or reckless participation in them."[22] Or, to put the issue another way, "a lawyer is not privileged to unthinkingly permit himself to be co-opted into an ongoing fraud and cast as a dupe or a shield for a wrong-doing client."[23]

The following materials focus on key issues for in-house attorneys with respect to client confidentiality and counseling ramifications.

---

[19] O.P.M. Bankruptcy Trustee Report, *supra* note 18, at 359. *See id.* at 372 (considering these "red flags," the attorneys "should have proceeded with extreme caution" in closing the financings).

[20] *See id.* at 399 (stating that the law firm retained two law professors to counsel it on the ethical issues involved). *See also, id.* at 378–379 (The trustee also noted the close relationship between the law firm and the client, including that the law firm received up to 65% of its revenues from the client and that one of the attorneys served on the client's board of directors).

[21] *Id.* at 417–421.

[22] *Id.*

[23] *Carter and Johnson,* [1981 Transfer Binder] CCH Fed. Sec. L. Rep. ¶ 82,847, at 84,172 (SEC 1981). *See In the Matter of Lapine,* [2010 Transfer Binder] CCH Fed. Sec. L. Rep. 89,039 (SEC 2010); Matthews & Johnson, *Prosecutors Probe Lawyers at GM,* Wall St. J., Aug. 22, 2014, at A1 ("Federal prosecutors are scrutinizing whether employees inside and outside General Motors Co.'s legal department concealed evidence from regulators about a faulty ignition switch . . . .").

REMARKS BEFORE THE SPRING MEETING OF
THE ASSOCIATION OF GENERAL COUNSEL
By SEC General Counsel Giovanni P. Prezioso (2005)

My topic tonight is attorney conduct. In particular, I would like to discuss some recent Commission enforcement actions involving lawyers, including in-house counsel at public companies. Then, I would like to describe generally the kinds of investigations involving lawyers that are on the horizon, and how those fit together with the Commission's mandate under the Sarbanes-Oxley Act of 2002. Finally, I would like to close with a few thoughts about the particular implications of Section 307 of that legislation for general counsel at public companies.

Consider a scenario:

Your company's CEO is a strong believer in new technologies and wants to replace some expensive bank loans with debt securities sold on the internet, but does not want to take the time and incur the cost of registering the securities. This practice, he believes, has become quite popular among your competitors, none of whom apparently has registered their debt securities with the Commission. You're out of the office at a conference, so the CEO calls his favorite outside counsel and asks for advice. After careful consideration, outside counsel advises that she sees little financial exposure to the company in private litigation—since the only remedy is likely to be rescission of the debt offering, which effectively will mean merely repaying the debt that is already owed, given that interest rates are rising. Nevertheless, she says that the overwhelming weight of the case law and SEC interpretations require compliance with the registration provisions of the Securities Act of 1933. The CEO hangs up the phone and says to himself, "Great, if we don't have any exposure to the plaintiffs' bar, I'll take my chances with the SEC." He then carries out the transactions, without informing outside counsel.

What happens when the SEC's Enforcement Division learns about this? Ordinarily, the staff would seek sanctions against the company and the CEO, and would not accept an advice-of-counsel defense on these facts. Your company's SEC enforcement counsel would tell you that the company should settle, and the company probably would, as would the now-chastened CEO.

Outside counsel gave accurate advice and had no reason to know it was being ignored—so she's off the hook.

Now, let's change the facts. Instead of being at a conference, you're in the office and the CEO calls you. He asks the same question. When you tell him you need to talk to outside counsel, he says, "Great, but I've got to go to a conference—so just take care of it while I'm away." You call outside counsel, get the same advice and make the same judgment as the CEO to proceed with the transaction. When the Enforcement Division shows up, should you [as an in-house attorney] be treated any differently than the CEO?

You can probably guess how I would answer that question. Just because you are a lawyer does not mean you get a pass to engage in conduct that would constitute a violation for anyone else at the company. At the same time, there is a sensitive issue here: not every case will present facts as clear as those in my scenario. Sometimes, a lawyer must make difficult legal judgments, and may well feel justified in taking a position with which the Commission or its staff might not agree.

The Commission has had to deal with these issues on several occasions. . . . Of particular note, the Commission has brought and settled significant enforcement cases against lawyers serving as general counsel at public companies for causing their corporate client's violation of the securities laws. These cases have provoked consternation among some lawyers, who have claimed that the SEC has changed direction in its enforcement policy toward the bar.

In my view, much of this consternation is misplaced. In fact, the principles underlying the enforcement proceedings . . . have been broadly consistent with the approach to lawyer liability that the Commission, and the courts, have taken for many years. I would like to review some of those principles, in a way that may be helpful in framing your obligations in day-to-day practice.

What are the guiding principles for sanctioning lawyers who violate the securities laws?

For over thirty years now, there has been an ongoing debate about whether and when the Commission should use its powers to sanction lawyers. The debate has generally been framed in terms of lawyers' role as "gatekeepers," since at least the Carter & Johnson case of the early 1980s, although the issues tend to go beyond lawyers acting purely in a "gatekeeping" capacity.

Two competing policy considerations have driven this debate. On one hand, the Commission has long recognized that many securities law violations could not occur without the participation of lawyers—who have professional responsibilities and knowledge that can often prevent misconduct harmful to investors. On the other hand, many lawyers—and the Commission itself—have identified the importance of zealous advocacy in securities law matters, and have thus resisted policies that might chill lawyers' capacity to advance that objective.

. . . .

One central and recurring point and one that I would like to focus on, is that the debate about lawyers as "gatekeepers" needs to be disentangled from consideration of the potential liability of lawyers as "principals." Put another way, while the two problems sometimes overlap in important ways, the Commission's approach to sanctioning lawyers who violate *professional standards of conduct* raises questions quite distinct from its approach to sanctioning lawyers for participating in *securities law violations*.

How has the Commission approached this latter question of securities law violations in the past? At the extremes, two propositions have become clear. At one end of the spectrum, to preserve an appropriate level of advocacy, the Commission ordinarily will not sanction lawyers under the securities laws merely for giving bad advice, even if that advice is negligent and perhaps worse. At the other end, the Commission will sanction a lawyer for conduct that—if carried out by any other person— would have given rise to an enforcement proceeding. This distinction has sometimes been characterized as a question of "when is a lawyer acting as a lawyer?"

To use the clearest example of the proposition, there is no serious doubt that when a lawyer engages in insider trading, the Commission should not have any reservations about instituting an enforcement action against that lawyer, simply because of his or her status as a member of the bar. A similar outcome can be expected for other securities law violations as well. These sanctions for violating the securities laws are separate from any professional disciplinary action . . . that might flow from the conduct [of] the lawyer.

. . . .

In considering this point, keep in mind that there are situations in which a lawyer—even in the course of practicing as a lawyer—can engage in conduct that constitutes a violation of the securities laws. For example, when a lawyer knowingly provides an opinion letter or knowingly drafts a disclosure document that contains a misstatement of fact or law that will be relied upon in the purchase or sale of securities, then that lawyer may be held liable for securities fraud. This, too, is consistent with the law more generally applicable to lawyers.

Factual difficulties often present themselves, of course. In some cases, a lawyer's actions may involve a mixture of conduct and advice. And those cases will often involve inside counsel—so they will have a special relevance to this audience. They will be further complicated by the fact that the securities laws [in SEC enforcement actions], like many other types of law, assign liability not only to primary violators, but also to secondary violators—those who aid and abet or cause violations by a company or other third party.

In cases involving a mixture of conduct and advice, what factors may be relevant? First, a critical issue will be the extent to which the decision-making process depended on the lawyer. Lawyers who serve in senior management roles, including in some cases as directors, often assume significant decision-making responsibility, even on matters that are not purely legal. If you are given responsibility for negotiating a contract, for example, you may find yourself making business decisions, not just legal ones. As a general counsel, you may find yourself particularly integrated into the management structure—and occasions for crossing the line from providing management with legal advice to making management decisions are likely to be more frequent. Further, especially difficult issues can arise in the disclosure context, given the often heavy reliance on lawyers to assist in the drafting process.

In thinking about whether a lawyer has crossed the line—becoming more of a decision-maker or counseling a course of conduct, rather than acting as a legal adviser—a key indicator, not surprisingly, will be the extent to which the lawyer in fact gave anyone else at the company legal "advice" on the relevant issue. If the lawyer provides the CEO with a balanced legal view and the CEO then disregards the implications of that view, there may be legitimate questions about the lawyer's obligations as a professional. In such a case, though, rarely will the lawyer be viewed as primarily, or even secondarily, liable under the securities laws absent further participation in the misconduct. On the other hand, if a lawyer makes a legal judgment about an issue that cannot fairly be viewed as immaterial and fails to inform anyone else at the company of the potential legal risks—in other words, if the lawyer doesn't advise anybody about anything—it will be much more difficult to argue that the lawyer played a purely advisory role. Rather, the lawyer's continuing participation in the activity without providing advice to others may, in some cases, constitute part of a course of conduct that effectively makes the ultimate business decision for the company.

A second significant factor in assessing the lawyer's responsibility for securities law violations will be the nature of the legal judgments made by the lawyer. In matters involving close or difficult judgment calls, I do not believe that the Commission has—or should—second guess those calls, even when the lawyer is close to the center of the decision-making process. The securities laws often are too complex—and involve too many questions on which reasonable lawyers legitimately can disagree—to permit 20/20 hindsight to be the Commission standard. Having said that, there are many cases where every securities lawyer ought to know the answer, or where a non-securities lawyer cannot in good faith fail to seek advice—and in those cases, the lawyer may properly be held responsible for corporate conduct in which he or she participated.

A third, and related factor, will also often come into play. Did the lawyer's activities occur in the context of an investigation or enforcement proceeding, or otherwise in direct representation of the client before the Commission or its staff?

Absent misrepresentations to the Commission or other unethical conduct, there is a strong countervailing policy consideration against sanctioning lawyers in these contexts—for this is where the adversarial nature of the lawyer's role most needs protection.

[In the past,] there have been a few settled enforcement actions in which these principles were applied to hold lawyers responsible for causing their corporate client's violation. While some among the bar have expressed surprise at these cases, I think they represent continuity, not change and are wholly consistent with prior Commission statements and cases on substantially similar facts over a long period of years. They do not impose sanctions on lawyers for the *advice* that they gave— but for their *actions* in situations where they in fact *failed to advise their* clients and became participants in the prohibited conduct.

What has changed?

Having spent a fair amount of your time trying to explain some of the elements that have not changed in the Commission's approach to sanctioning lawyers for securities law violations, let me turn to what I think has changed—and what those changes mean for you as the chief legal officers at your companies. What has changed—and this may seem obvious—is the law. The Sarbanes-Oxley Act, as you all know, significantly expanded the Commission's authority to adopt professional standards governing lawyers—and specifically required the Commission to adopt regulations mandating "up-the-ladder" reporting of evidence of certain material violations of law. There has been a great deal of attention devoted to the question of when to "report up," and the related but more difficult question of when and whether a lawyer may, or must, "report out." Much less attention has been devoted, however, to other aspects of the legislation that I think, over time, are likely to have an equally significant impact on lawyers.

First, Section 307 of the Sarbanes-Oxley Act went beyond mandating "up-the-ladder" reporting. It provided that the Commission should adopt "minimum standards of professional conduct for attorneys appearing and practicing before the Commission in any way in the representation" of public companies. . . . Further, the Sarbanes-Oxley Act included a little noted provision, Section 602, adding new Section 4C to the Exchange Act—a provision that explicitly confirms the Commission's authority to sanction all professionals appearing and practicing before it.

What are the implications of these legislative provisions? Most importantly, I think, they alter one of the key underpinnings of the Commission's traditional approach to oversight of lawyers—the lack of an explicit mandate from Congress to regulate the profession. Traditionally, the Commission and its staff regularly cited this lack of an express mandate as an important rationale for exercising restraint. As a legal matter, the absence of an express mandate counseled for care in determining which cases against lawyers—as professionals, rather than as principals—should be litigated, and where they should be litigated. As a policy matter, moreover, the Commission had long indicated its sensitivity to regulating professional conduct, an area where it claimed no special expertise.

With the enactment of the Sarbanes-Oxley Act, any lingering questions about the Commission's authority disappeared. And while the Commission cannot be expected miraculously to become expert overnight in the regulation of lawyers as professionals, there is no doubt that it can—indeed, given the mandate of Congress, really must—devote more time and resources to developing its expertise in this area. [Notably, during the past 15 years, the SEC has brought few enforcement actions against lawyers alleging fraudulent conduct by such attorneys when advising their corporate clients.]

. . . .

What do the new provisions of the Sarbanes-Oxley Act regarding attorneys mean for the General Counsel of a public company?

There is a second aspect of the changes growing out of the Sarbanes-Oxley Act that I think merits an additional moment of discussion in this forum: the heightened role now assigned to the chief legal officer (CLO) of public companies.

As you know, the "up-the-ladder" reporting provisions of Section 307 of the Act specify that the Commission's rules must require the reporting of evidence of material violations, in the first instance, to the CEO or to the CLO of a public company. The standards adopted by the Commission clarify and amplify this obligation. Subject to certain limitations, they provide that the report must be brought to the attention of the CLO in every case or to the CLO as well as to the CEO. Further, the Commission's rules impose an affirmative duty on the CLO to "cause such inquiry" into the evidence of a material violation as he or she "reasonably believes is appropriate." The rules also create an obligation, except where the CLO reasonably determines that there is no material violation, to "take all reasonable steps to cause the issuer to adopt an appropriate response" and to advise the reporting attorney thereof.

Before enactment of Section 307, no Commission rule or policy statement expressly imposed distinct responsibilities on a company's general counsel or other chief legal officer. The Commission had, of course, [previously] made clear that the general counsel at a regulated entity sometimes might serve in a supervisory role—and would be expected to discharge the same supervisory responsibilities as others—but in a sense this policy can be seen as nothing more than a variation on the proposition that an attorney must comply with the law just like anyone else.

The heightened responsibilities imposed under the Commission's Section 307 rules reflect, like the statute, the unique institutional role of a CLO. A system of reporting "up-the-ladder" cannot work well without a central clearinghouse through which the reports must flow. More importantly, from an accountability perspective—and strengthened accountability must be viewed as one of the primary goals of the Sarbanes-Oxley Act—it is essential for key corporate officials to know that they are personally expected to assume responsibility for doing the right thing.

More broadly, the responsibility of the CLO under the new rules flows from the primary point that Congress was making in Section 307: *that a lawyer's client, in a corporate context, is not senior management, but the entity itself.* The one lawyer who is responsible for all of the company's legal affairs—and whose only client is the company—is the CLO. Put another way, the

CLO can and must place the company's interests first. [emphasis supplied]

In doing this, the CLO can play an essential leadership role in assuring an appropriate "tone" and corporate culture that support rigorous compliance with all laws. The CLO generally can "push back" on senior management more forcefully than other employees when difficult legal issues arise, especially in light of the greatly heightened awareness among officers and directors today of the price of corporate malfeasance. Further, the CLO can serve as a bridge to the board on difficult legal matters. The CLO also can best assure an appropriate level of protection for whistleblowers and others who identify potential legal problems at the company, especially given the sometimes difficult task of sorting out potential cases of whistleblower retaliation from ordinary personnel disputes. Consider whether your company has given you the authority to perform these functions effectively.

Moreover, the responsibility under the Commission's Section 307 rules to conduct an inquiry, and to "cause" the company "to adopt an appropriate response" in cases where a violation has occurred, is a serious one. And I believe it has received insufficient attention in the public debate on our new rules. Congress gave us limited guidance in the statute, but it plainly expected some appropriate action to take place. Further, the basic mandate was, in many ways, already enshrined in prior professional responsibility requirements.

In my view, additional dialogue between the Commission and the bar on this issue could be quite constructive. CLOs must work within a delicate framework in assuring an appropriate corporate response. After all, this response may entail significant expenditures of company resources or have other important business implications that require input from managers and others. Moreover, the specific requirements of the rules often will lead CLOs, when in doubt, to bring particular matters and responses to the attention of their boards of directors, who will be seeking guidance as to the factual and legal considerations that should guide their decision. We all could benefit, I believe, from efforts by public company CLOs, who ultimately should have the greatest direct interest in the topic, to work with each other and the Commission in outlining the procedural and substantive elements that would typically characterize an appropriate response.

And while there are challenges presented in defining an appropriate response, I am confident that attorneys will rarely go wrong if they revert back to the central premise of Section 307 that I alluded to a moment ago: putting the interests of the company, and its shareholders, ahead of the interest of its management or other interested parties. Actions that are taken in good faith and in the company's best interests, I believe, will rarely raise any significant questions at the Commission, or in any other forum.

[Interestingly, since the enactment of Section 307 of the Sarbanes-Oxley Act of 2002 and the SEC's adoption of its Standards of Professional Conduct for attorneys in 2003, the Commission has declined to invoke these Standards against legal counsel on any occasion.]

Over the years, the SEC has brought scores of enforcement actions against in-house lawyers. The following SEC releases serve as useful examples.

SEC v. JORDAN H. MINTZ AND REX R. ROGERS
SEC Litigation Release No. 20866 (2009)

The Securities and Exchange Commission announced today that ... the U.S. District Court in Houston entered final judgments in the Commission's civil action against Jordan H. Mintz, a former Enron Vice President and General Counsel of Enron's Global Finance group, and Rex R. Rogers, Enron's former Vice President and Associate General Counsel. On March 28, 2007, the Commission charged Mintz and Rogers with, among other things, participating in a fraudulent scheme not to disclose Enron's related-party transactions with partnerships controlled by its Chief Financial Officer, Andrew Fastow, and compensation Fastow had received through those transactions. As part of the alleged scheme, Rogers further failed to disclose Enron's related-party transactions involving insider stock sales by its Chairman, Kenneth Lay.

The final judgments permanently enjoin Mintz and Rogers. . . . The final judgments also order Mintz and Rogers each to pay . . . disgorgement and a $25,000 civil money penalty. . . .

Mintz and Rogers further consented to the entry of an Administrative Order, pursuant to Rule 102(e)(3)(i) of the Commission's Rules of Practice, suspending each attorney from appearing or practicing before the Commission for a period of two years.

In settlement of this action, Mintz and Rogers neither admitted nor denied the allegations of the Commission's complaint. Among other things, the complaint alleged the following: In 1999, Enron sold an interest in a troubled power project in Cuiaba, Brazil to a related party called LJM1, a partnership controlled by Fastow, to deconsolidate the project and recognize related earnings. Under accounting rules, deconsolidation and earnings recognition were inappropriate because Enron did not transfer the risks and rewards of ownership in light of a secret side agreement promising that LJM1 would not lose money on Cuiaba. Satisfying the side agreement, Mintz helped Enron repurchase Cuiaba from LJM1 in 2001. Mintz then delayed signing and closing of the Cuiaba buyback in an effort to avoid reporting related-party transactions in Enron's 2000 Proxy Statement and 2001 Second Quarter Form 10-Q. Moreover, Mintz and Rogers failed to disclose in Enron's 2000 Proxy Statement millions of dollars Fastow received through related-party transactions between LJM and Enron. Rogers further failed to disclose in Enron's 2000 Proxy Statement at least $16 million in insider stock sales by Chairman Kenneth Lay to repay his Enron line of credit during 2000, and aided and abetted Lay's failure to disclose in SEC Form 4 filings an additional $70 million in insider stock sales by Lay during 2001.

SEC v. JOHN E. ISSELMANN, JR.
SEC Litigation Release No. 18896 (2004)

. . . .

[T]he Commission charged that John E. Isselmann, Jr., ESI's [Electro Scientific Industries, Inc.'s] former General Counsel, failed to provide important information to ESI's Audit Committee, Board of Directors, and independent auditors regarding the key accounting transaction that enabled ESI to report a profit rather than a loss in the quarter ended August 31, 2002. Without admitting or denying the Commission's allegations, Mr. Isselmann agreed to settle the enforcement action by paying a $50,000 civil penalty and consenting to an order prohibiting certain securities law violations.

. . . .

With respect to [ESI's] former General Counsel Isselmann, the Commission alleged that . . . Mr. Isselmann failed to provide important information to the Audit Committee, Board of Directors, and outside auditors relating to one of the restated accounting transactions. Isselmann attended a meeting with ESI's Audit Committee and independent auditors to review the financial results for the quarter ended August 31, 2002, where he did not question a false statement by [CEO] Dooley that the decision to eliminate the retirement benefits for employees in Asia had been reviewed by legal counsel. Isselmann also was provided a document written for ESI's independent auditors stating that ESI was under no legal obligation to provide retirement benefits to its Japanese employees. Isselmann later received written legal advice that contradicted what the Audit Committee and outside auditors had been told. The advice stated that the law prohibited the unilateral elimination of such benefits. Despite having opportunities to convey the advice to ESI's Audit Committee, Board, and independent auditors, Isselmann failed to do so. Isselmann's failure allowed [CEO] Dooley and [Corporate Controller] Lorenz to hide an ongoing fraud. Moreover, while in possession of the written legal advice stating that the law prohibited the unilateral elimination of the benefits, Isselmann was involved in the review process for ESI's quarterly report filed with the Commission describing the elimination of the benefits and the resulting impact on ESI's income. Isselmann's conduct was a cause of the Company reporting materially false financial results for ESI's first quarter ended August 31, 2002, and violated a Commission rule prohibiting officers of public companies from omitting to state material facts to independent auditors.

. . . .

SEC v. NANCY R. HEINEN
SEC Litigation Release No. 20683 (2008)

The Securities and Exchange Commission today announced that it has settled options backdating charges against Nancy R. Heinen, the former General Counsel of Apple, Inc. As part of the settlement Heinen, of Portola Valley, California, agreed (without admitting or denying the Commission's allegations) to pay $2.2 million in disgorgement, interest and penalties, be barred from serving as an officer or director of any public company for five years, and be suspended from appearing or practicing as an attorney before the Commission for three years.

The settlement stems from a complaint filed by the Commission in April 2007 in federal court in the Northern District of California. According to the complaint, Heinen caused Apple to fraudulently backdate two large options grants to senior executives of Apple—a February 2001 grant of 4.8 million options to Apple's Executive Team and a December 2001 grant of 7.5 million options to Apple Chief Executive Officer Steve Jobs—and altered company records to conceal the fraud. The complaint alleges that as a result of the backdating Apple underreported its expenses by nearly $40 million.

In the first instance, Apple granted 4.8 million options to six members of its Executive Team (including Heinen) in February 2001. Because the options were in-the-money when granted (i.e. could be exercised to purchase Apple shares at a below market price), Apple was required to report a compensation charge in its publicly-filed financial statements. The Commission alleges that, in order to avoid reporting this expense, Heinen caused Apple to backdate options to January 17, 2001, when Apple's share price was substantially lower. Heinen is also alleged to have directed her staff to prepare documents falsely indicating that Apple's Board had approved the Executive Team grant on January 17. As a result, Apple failed to record approximately $18.9 million in compensation expenses associated with the option grant.

The Commission's complaint also alleges improprieties in connection with a December 2001 grant of 7.5 million options to CEO Steve Jobs. Although the options were in-the-money at that time, Heinen—as with the Executive Team grant—caused Apple to backdate the grant to October 19, 2001, when Apple's share price was lower. As a result, the Commission alleges that Heinen caused Apple to improperly fail to record $20.3 million in compensation expense associated with the in-the-money options grant. The Commission further alleges that Heinen then signed fictitious Board minutes stating that Apple's Board had approved the grant to Jobs on October 19 at a "Special Meeting of the Board of Directors"—a meeting that, in fact, never occurred.

As part of the settlement, Heinen consented (without admitting or denying the allegations) to a court order that:

- enjoins her from violations of . . . the Securities Act of 1933 and . . . the Securities Exchange Act of 1934 . . .;
- orders her to pay disgorgement of $1,575,000 (representing the in-the-money portion of the proceeds she received from exercising backdated options) plus $400,219.78 in interest;
- imposes a civil penalty of $200,000; and
- bars her from serving as an officer or director of any public company for five years.

In addition, Heinen agreed to resolve a separate administrative proceeding against her by consenting to a Commission order that suspends her from appearing or practicing before the Commission as an attorney for three years.

SEC v. David C. Drummond
SEC Press Release No. 2005–6 (2005)

The Securities and Exchange Commission today charged Google, Inc. with failing to register the issuance of option grants to employees or provide required financial information to the option recipients. According to the Commission, the Silicon Valley search engine technology company issued over $80 million in stock options to its employees in the two years preceding its IPO, yet failed to register the securities or make financial disclosures mandated by federal securities law. To settle the charges, Google and its General Counsel, David C. Drummond, agreed to cease and desist from violating the registration and related financial disclosure requirements.

The Commission found that between 2002 and 2004, Google issued over $80 million worth of stock options to its employees as part of their compensation. The federal securities laws [at that time] require[d] companies issuing over $5 million in options during a 12-month period either to provide detailed financial information to the option recipients, or to register the securities offering with the Commission and thereby publicly disclose financial and other important information. According to the Commission, Google far exceeded the $5 million disclosure threshold, yet failed to register the options or provide the required financial information to employees. According to the Commission, Google—which, at the time, was still a privately-held company—viewed the disclosure of the information to employees as strategically disadvantageous, fearing the information could leak to Google's competitors.

The Commission's order further finds that Google's General Counsel David Drummond . . . was aware that the registration and related financial disclosure obligations had been triggered, but believed that Google could avoid providing the information to its employees by relying on an exemption from the law. According to the Commission, Drummond advised Google's Board that it could continue to issue options, but failed to inform the Board that the registration and disclosure obligations had been triggered or that there were risks in relying on the exemption, which was in fact inapplicable.

Stephen M. Cutler, Director of the Commission's Enforcement Division in Washington, D.C., said, "The securities laws exist to ensure full disclosure to investors, including employees accepting stock options as compensation. Companies cannot freely decide that they don't need to comply with the law."

Added Helane Morrison, District Administrator of the Commission's San Francisco District Office, "Attorneys who undertake action on behalf of their company are no less accountable than any other corporate officers. By deciding Google could escape its disclosure requirements, and failing to inform the Board of the legal risks of his determination, Drummond caused the company to run afoul of the federal securities laws."

. . . .

The following saga reflects the problems generated when inside or outside counsel is "co-opted" by constituents of the client.

TRUSTEE'S REPORT IN OPM LEASING SERVICES, INC. (1983)

James P. Hassett, Trustee of O.P.M. Leasing Services, Inc., submits this Report under section 1106(a)(4) of the Bankruptcy Code concerning fraud and other misconduct in the management of OPM's affairs.

. . . .

OPM: The Story in Brief

Mordecai Weissman founded his own leasing company in July 1970 at the age of twenty-three in hopes of prospering with a minimum investment of his own capital and effort. He called the new enterprise O.P.M. Leasing Services, Inc., a name whose mysterious initials often sparked curiosity as the company grew. Different explanations offered for the name wryly capture the different facets of the OPM debacle.

OPM's principals often told customers and others in the business and financial communities that "O.P.M." stood for "other people's machines." To the outside world that watched OPM grow into one of the nation's largest computer leasing companies, this explanation seemed to fit OPM's role as intermediary between computer manufacturers and computer users.

But the truth was that the initials stood for "other people's money." The name connoted the plan of Weissman and Myron S. Goodman, his brother-in-law and partner, to rely almost exclusively on funds advanced by others to run the business. But beyond that, the name reflected the pair's cynical, unscrupulous attitude toward financial and personal interests of other people. Seen from the inside, their business relied on corruption and deception from the start to create an illusion of success. Meanwhile OPM actually lost money at ever increasing rates. By the end Weissman and Goodman were able to continue operating only with other people's money they obtained by fraud of record proportions.

The fraud relied heavily on a factor identified in yet another explanation offered for the OPM initials—"other people's mistakes." Numerous financiers, businessmen, and professionals acted through ignorance, carelessness, poor judgment, or self-interest in ways that permitted the fraud to continue for years. This Report is not simply a story of the myth and reality of OPM; it is also a study of how outsiders who dealt with OPM allowed the fraud at OPM to occur.

. . . .

"Other People's Mistakes": The Outsiders

No less noteworthy than the remarkable saga of OPM from the inside is the combination of actions and inactions by various outsiders that permitted the fraud to occur and, in some instances, actively contributed to its success. Accountants, management consultants, lawyers, investment bankers, lessee representatives, bankers, and other businessmen all worked intimately with Goodman and Weissman in ways that exposed them to transactions used for the fraud. In the misguided belief that someone else was checking the bona fides of OPM's transactions or was acting to stop the fraud, all stood by while the fraud continued at an ever increasing pace.

. . . .

Lawyers

Lawyers played a critical role in the massive Rockwell lease fraud [involving the entering into of fraudulent computer leases]. Without their witting or unwitting assistance, the fraud simply could not have occurred.

The law firm of Singer Hutner Levine & Seeman (and its predecessor and successor firms) served as OPM's outside general counsel from 1971 to September 1980 and did not fully sever its relationship with OPM until December 1980. Singer Hutner closed all but seven of the fifty-four financings of fraudulent Rockwell leases.

Singer Hutner acquired OPM as a client in 1971 through Andrew B. Reinhard, the older brother of a close boyhood friend of Goodman. Reinhard was then a Singer Hutner associate and later became a partner. In 1972 Weissman and Goodman elected Reinhard the third director of OPM. As OPM's business expanded, Singer Hutner followed along, more than doubling in size to twenty-seven lawyers in 1980. By 1975 Singer Hutner participated in virtually every facet of OPM's business. Goodman likened the close relationship between OPM and Singer Hutner to a "bondage of the bookends."

From 1976 through 1980 Singer Hutner received legal fees of almost $7.9 million—sixty to seventy percent of its revenues—from OPM. Singer Hutner also received almost $2 million in reimbursement of expenses. While Singer Hutner lawyers, unlike Goodman, may not have regarded the firm as an adjunct to OPM, their prosperity was tied to OPM's success. The Trustee believes Singer Hutner was not sufficiently alert to the danger that its professional judgment might be impaired by its financial dependence on OPM.

One of the most difficult questions encountered during the Trustee's investigation was whether [attorney] Reinhard knowingly participated in any of the fraudulent activities at OPM. Although the United States Attorney's Office determined not to seek a grand jury indictment against him, the decision not to prosecute is not dispositive.

The principal witness against Reinhard is Goodman. Goodman testified that, having previously told Reinhard about the early frauds at OPM, he informed Reinhard in early 1979 of his intention to finance three phantom Rockwell leases and successfully enlisted Reinhard's assistance in the fraud. Goodman says he told Reinhard that the financing was necessary to keep OPM in business because of a temporary cash shortage, that he would buy out the financings within several weeks, and that he would never engage in fraudulent financings again. According to Goodman, Reinhard resisted but eventually agreed to help. Goodman testified that Reinhard reluctantly assisted in several subsequent fraudulent financings.

Through his lawyers Reinhard denies he had any knowledge of fraud at OPM apart from information obtained by his firm in June and September 1980. On advice of counsel, Reinhard invoked his Fifth Amendment privilege and refused personally to respond to any questioning by the Trustee concerning the fraud.

Despite a number of internal inconsistencies and anomalies, Goodman's testimony has a ring of truth. Statements by other members of the OPM fraud team and Marvin Weissman tend to corroborate Goodman's testimony. On the other hand, Goodman is an acknowledged master liar and may have hoped implicating Reinhard would endear Goodman to the United States Attorney's Office. While the issue is by no means free from doubt, the Trustee believes there is substantial evidence that Goodman led Reinhard to become, however reluctantly, a knowing participant in the Rockwell fraud.

Apart from Reinhard's probable complicity in the fraud from the outset, [the law firm] Singer Hutner's conduct as OPM's counsel in closing fraudulent Rockwell financings cannot be justified. By early 1979 Singer Hutner had received indications that Goodman and Weissman were capable of serious illegality. Some lawyers were aware that Weissman and Goodman had engaged in lease fraud and commercial bribery, and the firm knew that Goodman had recently perpetrated a $5 million check kiting scheme. Singer Hutner also had knowledge of facts showing that OPM was suffering severe cash shortages that provided a motive for further fraud.

In the sixteen months between the first financing of phantom Rockwell leases in February 1979 and Goodman's first confession to Singer Hutner of serious wrongdoing in June 1980, numerous facts came to Singer Hutner's attention that should have raised suspicions about the bona fides of OPM-Rockwell leases. . . . With all these red flags, Singer Hutner should have exercised extreme caution in closing OPM-Rockwell lease financings. Instead, until June 1980 the firm closed these transactions on a business as usual basis.

On June 12, 1980, Goodman met with Joseph L. Hutner, a Singer Hutner partner, and confessed that he had engaged in past "wrongful transactions" in an amount exceeding $5 million. During a break in the meeting, Goodman somehow retrieved the letter . . . describing the details of the Rockwell fraud. Goodman refused to return the letter or provide additional details of his acknowledged wrongdoing, citing his desire for assurances that Singer Hutner would keep the information secret under the attorney-client privilege.

Singer Hutner promptly retained Joseph M. McLaughlin, then dean of Fordham Law School, and Henry Putzel, III, formerly an associate professor of professional responsibility at Fordham, to advise the firm on its ethical responsibilities in dealing with Goodman's disclosure. Whether or not Singer Hutner's conduct based on their advice was "ethical" (a legal question the Trustee does not address), it was woefully inadequate to prevent further fraud. After June 1980 Singer Hutner closed fifteen additional fraudulent Rockwell transactions totaling $70 million.

Singer Hutner kept Goodman's misdeeds secret and continued closing OPM transactions on the basis of certificates from Goodman attesting to the legitimacy of the transactions. The Trustee believes Singer Hutner was wrong in relying on Goodman's representations that the fraud had stopped and ignoring substantial evidence that it had not. . . . [O]n two occasions in June and July Singer Hutner lawyers noticed peculiarities in title documents used in fraudulent Rockwell lease financings that should have led them to seek to confirm their authenticity with third parties.

For months Goodman resisted pressure to make full disclosure of the fraud to Singer Hutner by a series of gambits including a threat to jump out of a window in OPM's ninth story offices if pressed further. In September 1980 Goodman finally came clean, or so he claimed. At a meeting with the Singer Hutner partners, Goodman described the mechanics of the Rockwell fraud and quantified it at $30 million—only about $100 million short of the truth. Notwithstanding Goodman's continued insistence that the fraud had stopped by June 1980, and Goodman's hysterical threat to "bring down this firm," on September 23 Singer Hutner voted to resign as OPM's counsel.

With Putzel's approval, Singer Hutner agreed to characterize its resignation misleadingly as a "mutual determination of our firm and [OPM] to terminate our relationship as general counsel." Singer Hutner also agreed to continue rendering legal services over a two and one-half month transition period to avoid unnecessary injury to OPM.

In late September or early October Goodman dropped the bombshell that the fraud had in fact continued throughout the summer of 1980. Despite this shocking acknowledgment by Goodman that he had continued to use Singer Hutner as an instrument of fraud even after his initial confession of wrongdoing, Putzel advised Singer Hutner that it could not ethically warn successor counsel of the danger that Goodman would use them to help finance additional fraudulent transactions.

After Singer Hutner's withdrawal, OPM's young *in-house lawyers* and the law firm of Kaye, Scholer, Fierman, Hays & Handler represented OPM in its lease transactions. Kept in the dark by Goodman and Singer Hutner about the real reasons for the departure of Singer Hutner, *OPM's in-house staff* unwittingly closed six fraudulent financings of Rockwell leases and Kaye Scholer unwittingly closed one. [emphasis supplied]

Singer Hutner, of course, relies on the advice it received from McLaughlin and Putzel to justify its conduct during the summer and fall of 1980. While the Trustee does not attempt to resolve the question whether that advice was consistent with the legal profession's code of ethics, it is clear that McLaughlin and Putzel could have advised other courses, consistent with Singer Hutner's ethical responsibilities, that would have stopped the fraud. Although McLaughlin and Putzel in good faith considered their advice appropriate in the circumstances, the Trustee believes it was in fact the worst possible advice from the point of view of OPM, the third parties with whom it dealt, Singer Hutner's successor counsel, and Singer Hutner itself. Accordingly, McLaughlin and Putzel must shoulder significant responsibility for their client's conduct.

But Singer Hutner cannot properly shift all blame for its actions after Goodman's first confession of wrongdoing to McLaughlin and Putzel. While Singer Hutner relied on McLaughlin and Putzel for advice on its ethical obligations, McLaughlin and Putzel relied on the firm for the central factual predicate for their advice—whether the fraud was continuing. . . .

Viewed as a whole, the Trustee finds Singer Hutner's conduct nothing short of shocking, given the warnings it received before June 1980 and the remarkable events of the summer and early fall. Although Singer Hutner cites its ethical obligation not to injure its client unnecessarily, the most questionable aspects of Singer Hutner's conduct raise issues beyond professional ethics. Even after learning that Goodman had engaged in major wrongdoing, Singer Hutner continued to close OPM debt financings without obtaining prior disclosure of the nature of the wrongdoing and without independently verifying transaction facts. No rule of professional ethics can or should exempt lawyers from the general legal proscriptions against willful blindness to their clients' crimes or reckless participation in them.

The *OPM* saga, focusing on insider-constituents engaging in fraud, is a concern for both in-house and outside attorneys. Note that the law firm's financial success in *OPM* was dependent on keeping the company as its client. In that situation, the ability of the law firm to maintain its independence of professional judgment was compromised. Due to this conflicting interest, inside counsel may be prudent to advise that any law firm or outside attorney retained by the company not be unduly financially dependent on revenues generated by the engagement.

As set forth above in *OPM*, the law firm of Singer Hutner maintained a "closed-mouth" approach with respect to its resignation, apparently to preserve the former client's (OPM) confidences and secrets. As the Trustee found, this approach facilitated OPM's continuation of its fraudulent conduct, utilizing unknowing inside and outside legal counsel as a means to perpetuate the fraud. The better response would have been as follows:

> Former counsel should not stand idly by acquiescing in the former client's retention of successor counsel, thereby resulting in further injury to innocent victims. In such situations, predecessor counsel should send 'red flags' to the inquiring attorney. For example, predecessor counsel may state: 'I'm disinclined to explain why I resigned unless the former client gives me permission to tell you.' If the client refuses to give such permission, this should signal to the inquiring attorney that the prospective engagement should be declined. In any event, and particularly if the representation is undertaken by successor counsel, such counsel should draft a memorandum documenting the results of such inquiry and the information obtained. Moreover, it would be prudent for predecessor counsel to document the contents of communications with prospective successor counsel.[24]

The following Report reflects additional concerns generated by the problematic client.

INDEPENDENT EXAMINER'S REPORT
IN SPIEGEL, INC. (2003)

. . . .

Summary of Findings

Facing the need to improve poor sales performance in its retail subsidiaries, Spiegel embarked by 1999 on a program that

---

[24] Steinberg, *Attorney Liability for Client Fraud*, 1991 Colum Bus. L. Rev. 1, 21–22 (1991). *See* Brown, *Counsel with a Fraudulent Client*, 17 Rev. Sec. Reg. 909 (1984); Comment, *The Client-Fraud Dilemma: A Need for Consensus*, 46 Md. L. Rev. 436 (1987).

one of its audit committee members later called "easy credit to pump up sales." Through various techniques involving both its retail subsidiaries and its captive credit card bank subsidiary, Spiegel tilted its portfolio of credit card customers decidedly in the direction of high-risk subprime borrowers. These were customers who often could not get credit elsewhere and who could be counted on to respond to the opportunity to buy merchandise with the easy credit Spiegel offered them.

At the time, the "new economy" was booming, and Spiegel was getting these risky credit card receivables off its own balance sheet by selling them to various off-balance-sheet special purpose entities through an asset-backed securitization program. This use of "easy credit to pump up sales" worked in the short term, and Spiegel reported to its directors that it had achieved a "return to profitability." This result also personally benefited certain Spiegel senior executives who were entitled to performance-based compensation.

But then the economy soured, and many of Spiegel's subprime customers stopped paying their credit card bills. Charge-offs of uncollectible credit card receivables climbed dramatically. With Spiegel's portfolio of credit card receivables suffering under this barrage of charge-offs, its asset-backed securitizations came dangerously close to hitting a performance "trigger" that would have sent Spiegel's securitizations spinning into a "rapid amortization" that would have destroyed Spiegel. Specifically to avoid this disaster, beginning in 2001, Spiegel manipulated at least one of the components used to calculate this securitization performance trigger, and in doing so, staved off a Spiegel bankruptcy for almost two years.

As Spiegel's financial condition worsened in late 2001, it breached all four loan covenants contained in its bank loan agreements. Spiegel tried desperately to renegotiate its financing with a consortium of 18 banks, but a myriad of problems frustrated this effort. As Spiegel was preparing to file its 2001 Form 10-K annual report [with the SEC] due in March 2002, its auditor KPMG advised that it would have to give Spiegel a "going concern" opinion, based on Spiegel's inability to conclude its bank refinancing arrangements and other problems.

Spiegel decided not to file its Form 10-K with a going concern opinion. Soon afterwards, Nasdaq indicated that it would delist Spiegel. At the delisting hearing, Spiegel assured Nasdaq that it was only days away from concluding its refinancing arrangements, and that it would then be able to file its Form 10-K without a going concern opinion. After several days, Nasdaq advised Spiegel that it had a last chance to file its Form 10-K and that otherwise it would be immediately delisted.

Spiegel's Chicago-based management—supported by Spiegel's outside counsel Kirkland & Ellis and its outside auditors KPMG—strongly recommended that Spiegel file its Form 10-K in late May 2002. But the ultimate decision makers for Spiegel were in Germany. Spiegel was only 10% an American public company. About 90% of its equity and all of its voting stock were in the hands of Michael Otto and his family [hereinafter Otto] in Hamburg, Germany. Indeed, Spiegel operated in effect as the American division of Otto's huge multinational retail empire, including 89 companies with over 79,000 employees in 21 countries around the globe.

On May 31, 2002 in Hamburg, Spiegel's executive or "board" committee (consisting of Michael Otto and an executive of his private company Otto Versand GmbH) and Spiegel's audit committee (consisting of one present and one former Otto Versand executive) rejected the views of Spiegel's management, Kirkland & Ellis and KPMG, and directed Spiegel not to file its already-late first-quarter 2002 Form 10-Q. As time went by, they likewise directed Spiegel not to file its remaining 2002 Forms 10-Q.

Spiegel's German decision-makers had been fully briefed on the array of serious problems Spiegel faced, including at a seven-hour meeting with Spiegel's Chicago-based executives several weeks before. But they refused to allow Spiegel to file its reports with the SEC because they felt that a going concern opinion would cause Spiegel's suppliers to refuse to extend credit to Spiegel for the merchandise it purchased for resale. Such a result could lead Spiegel to bankruptcy. Likewise, Spiegel was concerned about the impact a going concern opinion would have on investors and employees.

It was only the prospect of an SEC Enforcement Division investigation that made Spiegel begin to belatedly file reports in February 2003—after not having filed a single periodic report since November 2001 (its third-quarter 2001 Form 10-Q). This 15-month hiatus in periodic reporting left investors without the disclosures and other protections mandated by the federal securities laws. All investors could do during this period was to attempt to piece together several incomplete pieces of information from a few press releases and news stories.

This matter involves not simply a failure to make required SEC filings. Rather, it involves a failure to make disclosure of material information about Spiegel's financial condition that investors needed to make their investment decisions about Spiegel. The SEC has already charged Spiegel with fraud for failing to disclose its auditors' going concern position. But . . . investors likewise failed to get a variety of other material information about Spiegel's financial condition. . . .

Ultimately, Spiegel was unable to dig itself out of this hole. Its financial condition just kept getting worse. On March 17, 2003, Spiegel filed a Chapter 11 bankruptcy case. . . .

Involvement of Spiegel's Professional Advisors

In the present case, the SEC charged Spiegel with fraud, and Spiegel consented (without admitting or denying liability) to a fraud injunction against the company. When a fraud charge hits a public company, the question naturally arises whether its professional advisers could have done anything to prevent this "train wreck" that hurt the company and its shareholders, creditors and employees.

Spiegel's Legal Advisers. In evaluating the performance of Spiegel's lawyers, it is useful to consider rules recently adopted and other rules recently proposed by the SEC under Section 307 of the Sarbanes-Oxley Act, even though these SEC rules were not in effect at the time of the conduct here. Under [the] SEC rules, [in-house and outside] lawyers representing a public company must report "up the ladder"—as high as the board of directors, if necessary—if the lawyers "become aware" of "evidence" of a "material violation" of federal or state securities law or a material breach of fiduciary duty by the company (or [any] officer, director, employee or agent).

In addition, the SEC has proposed [*but has declined to adopt*] so-called "noisy withdrawal" rules that would require lawyers to assess whether the company has made an "appropriate response within a reasonable time" to the matter the lawyer has reported up the ladder, and if not, whether "substantial injury" to the financial interest or property of the issuer or investors has occurred or is likely. An outside attorney [*under the proposed but not adopted rule*] must then "withdraw forthwith from representing the issuer," and tell both the company and the SEC that the withdrawal was for "professional considerations." *An inside attorney must cease participation in the matter. Both outside and inside attorneys must also disaffirm to the SEC any document the attorney assisted in preparing that "may be" materially false or misleading.* [emphasis supplied]

Robert Sorensen joined Spiegel as its [inside] general counsel at the end of June 2001. He brought in the firm of Kirkland & Ellis as principal outside counsel, in place of Rooks Pitts, to provide additional depth in corporate and securities matters. Rooks Pitts continued to represent Spiegel in securitization and other matters. As described above, by mid-May 2002, Kirkland & Ellis had plainly advised Spiegel that it was violating the law by not filing its Form 10-K, and that this illegal act could have serious consequences, including action by the SEC. Sorensen plainly concurred in this advice. The advice reached Spiegel's management, including its president Martin Zaepfel, who was also a member of Spiegel's board committee, which had the power to act for the full board. By the end of May, Zaepfel reported the advice to Michael Otto and Michael Cruesemann, the other two members of the board committee. Kirkland & Ellis also repeated this advice by phone to Spiegel's audit committee at the end of May. Plainly, Kirkland & Ellis and [in-house counsel] Sorensen reported "up the ladder" to Spiegel's audit committee and its board committee.

However, this was a case where reporting "up the ladder" was not enough. The advice from the lawyers here was rejected by Spiegel's audit and board committees, and the material information that should have reached investors was kept under wraps. White & Case became involved in Spiegel's affairs as counsel for Spiegel's "sole voting shareholder," Michael Otto and his corporate vehicles. Through its Hamburg partner Urs Aschenbrenner, White & Case "interpreted" for the Otto interests the advice received from Spiegel's U.S. legal advisors, and it clearly played a substantial role in helping Otto and the Spiegel board committee evaluate that advice. Aschenbrenner consulted with White & Case's New York office on Spiegel issues, and lawyers from the firm's New York office were substantively involved on various Spiegel matters—again as representatives of Spiegel's sole voting shareholder—during much of 2002.

Aschenbrenner began accompanying Cruesemann to meetings with Spiegel's lender banks in Spring 2002, and also attended Spiegel's delisting hearing before Nasdaq on May 17, 2002. On May 31, 2002, the day Spiegel's audit and board committees made the final decision not to file the Form 10-K, Aschenbrenner was invited to be present at the audit committee meeting, and the audit committee had Aschenbrenner phone Kirkland & Ellis on a speakerphone for the committee to get advice. Aschenbrenner was heard to challenge Kirkland and Ellis' advice on the need to file Spiegel's form 10-K and the consequences of non-filing. In the days following the May 31, 2002 meeting, it appears that neither Aschenbrenner nor his [White & Case] New York partners did anything to express their agreement with Kirkland & Ellis' advice.

Whatever the conclusion as to the lawyers' performance around the time of the May 31, 2002 audit and board committee meetings, the question naturally arises as to what the lawyers did to press Spiegel to make its required SEC filings through the balance of 2002—or otherwise to update, supplement or correct disclosures made in Spiegel's [SEC] Forms and/or its press releases. There does not appear to be a record of either Kirkland & Ellis or White & Case advising Spiegel of the dire consequences of its continuing failure to file its Form 10-K and make full disclosure to investors after May 31, 2002.

After May 2002, it appears that Spiegel's German directors considered Kirkland & Ellis and [in-house counsel] Sorensen, along with the rest of Spiegel's U.S. management, to be "black painters"—meaning pessimists who were exaggerating the seriousness of the situation. Over the summer, Cruesemann suggested that Kirkland & Ellis, and perhaps Sorensen, be replaced. The effort to replace Kirkland & Ellis failed only when U.S. management pointed out the cost of bringing in a new firm to draft documentation for the refinancing and other pending matters.

At the same time, while ostensibly still only counsel for Spiegel's sole voting shareholder, White & Case assumed a prominent role in negotiating on Spiegel's behalf with its banks on the refinancing effort, with the OCC on FCNB issues, and with the insurer of the Spiegel securitizations. While still not technically retained as Spiegel's counsel, White & Case clearly enjoyed the confidence of Spiegel's sole voting shareholder, and an effort by White & Case to report "up the ladder" to Spiegel's audit and board committees that it shared the views of the "black painters" Kirkland & Ellis and [in-house counsel] Sorensen could have well caused Spiegel to comply with its obligations and avoid a fraud charge from the SEC.

As the months went by, Kirkland & Ellis continued to prepare and file Spiegel's [SEC] Forms providing official notice of Spiegel's failure to file its remaining quarterly reports for the balance of 2002. All of these recited that Spiegel was not filing its periodic reports because it was "not currently in compliance with its 2001 loan covenants and is currently working with its bank group to amend and replace its existing credit facilities," and thus "not in a position to issue financial statements . . . pending resolution of this issue." Of course, as Kirkland & Ellis knew, the real reason why Spiegel was not filing its periodic reports was that it did not want to disclose KPMG's going concern qualification and other material bad facts and circumstances threatening Spiegel's survival.

None of Spiegel's legal advisers withdrew—"noisily" or otherwise—from representing Spiegel. If the SEC's proposed withdrawal rule [which has not been adopted] had then been in effect, the SEC would have been alerted to take action sooner, and investors would have received information they could have acted on to make informed investment decisions about Spiegel. In this case, the absence of a "noisy withdrawal" requirement allowed Spiegel to keep investors and the SEC in the dark.

CHAPTER 6

WORKING WITH YOUR "INTERNAL CLIENTS"

As previously discussed, one primary benefit of working in-house is that you no longer have to obtain and retain clients. After all, your employer, the company, is "the client" now. As corporate counsel, you have input in hiring and directing outside counsel; paying invoices; having the final word on strategy decisions; and setting deadlines. This client focus must be all encompassing. You now have one very important client: the company.

Your role requires you to interact with a variety of "constituents"[1] across the corporation, including in business units, human resources, finance, information technology, internal audit, sales and marketing, and research and development. For purposes of this chapter, these constituents will be referred to as your "internal clients." *Absent exceptional circumstances, however, these individuals are not your "clients."*[2]

If "internal clients" don't see you as a partner in the business, don't have confidence in you, or don't receive useful, practical advice from you on a timely basis, they may not involve you in projects early or often enough for you to do a proficient job. Internal clients may bring you in only at the "eleventh hour" so they can say they ran the project by legal, or they may circumvent you altogether by going to someone else in the legal department they trust. Your workload, performance, evaluations, and reputation within the company may suffer.

---

[1]   *See* ABA Model Rules of Prof. Conduct, Rule 1.13, cmt. 1 ("An organizational client is a legal entity, but it cannot act except through its officers, directors, employees, shareholders and other constituents. Officers, directors, employees and shareholders are the constituents of the corporate organizational client . . . . 'Other constituents' as used in this Comment means the positions equivalent to officers, directors, employees and shareholders held by persons acting for organizational clients that are not corporations.").

[2]   *See id.,* Rule 1.13(a) ("A lawyer employed or retained by an organization represents *the organization* acting through its duly authorized constituents.") (emphasis supplied).

This chapter addresses several topics central to working with your "internal clients." It begins by looking at the increasing role of in-house counsel as a business partner and it outlines four specific ways that inside counsel can become a trusted legal advisor and business partner. The second half of the chapter examines four important issues facing many in-house counsel: identifying and evaluating risk, allocating important resources, the role of inside counsel in business meetings, and preparing corporate board minutes.

IN-HOUSE COUNSEL AS BUSINESS PARTNER

The responsibilities and influence of corporate counsel has expanded greatly over time. Only a few years ago, many of them were relegated to a separate floor in their buildings, isolated from decision-making . . . .[3] That's no longer the case.

Today they are involved in every aspect of corporate operations, from helping determine a company's strategic growth plans and analyzing risk factors to framing the business's public image and even becoming a profit center. "The job has gone from being just a legal adviser to being much more of a business role," said Christopher Willis, EVP and Chief People and Corporate Affairs Officer at Dallas-based Interstate Batteries. "CEOs and business leaders have seen the value of a general counsel's contribution, and there's now an expectation that the corporate legal team has an in-depth business knowledge that wasn't there only a few years ago."

Melanie Wright, general counsel of Fujitsu Network Communications, said that in her past corporate legal jobs, she was "pretty much isolated" from the operational and finance departments. "The documents came in and the documents went out," said Wright, who was previously an assistant general counsel at Greyhound Lines Inc. and Southland Corp., now called 7-Eleven Inc. "It's definitely not like that anymore."

---

[3]   The following discussion, through *infra* text and accompanying note 5, is taken and edited slightly from Mark Curriden, *Corporate General Counsels: Not Just Attorneys Anymore*, The Dallas Morning News (Nov. 6, 2012), https://www.dallasnews.com/business/2012/11/07/corporate-general-counsels-not-just-attorneys-anymore/, *archived at* https://perma.cc/6FJ8-VB2P. Reprinted with permission. All rights reserved.

Wright said she started working "side-by-side with the sales guys negotiating contracts" soon after she was hired as Fujitsu Network's one-person legal department in 1992. "I believe in having more contact with business colleagues on the front end, which is much more fun," she said. "It's much less fun when you go into a situation on the back end when there's already a crisis."

According to experts, the passage of federal corporate compliance laws, such as the Sarbanes-Oxley Act in 2002 and the Dodd-Frank Wall Street Reform and Consumer Protection Act in 2010, account in part for the change.[4] "No doubt about it, Sarbanes-Oxley and Dodd-Frank have had a far-reaching and significant impact on the role of the general counsel in corporate America," said Jim Baldwin, Chief Legal Officer and General Counsel of Keurig Dr Pepper. "Today, GCs are involved in nearly every aspect of a business's operation, and those two laws are a big reason."[5]

Similarly, in-house attorneys are increasingly asked to advise on business decisions because of the wide range of legal, regulatory, and reputational risks facing companies—from data breaches to trade tariffs to activist shareholders.[6] A recent survey found that nearly 70% of chief legal officers say the executive team almost always seeks their input on business decisions.[7]

And timing is everything. Involving inside counsel in business decisions at the outset leads to better results. Alex Arellano, General Counsel of the American Airlines Center, advises, "Being an effective in-house counsel means that you have convinced the business team you add value to any transaction. Engagement of in-house counsel in the early stages of a transaction leads to higher success rates."[8] Similarly, Jason

---

[4]   Other compliance laws have been in existence for decades, such as the Foreign Corrupt Practice Act ("FCPA"). The FCPA, enacted 1977, requires issuers to maintain reasonably accurate books and records and prohibits the payment of bribes to foreign officials to assist in obtaining or retaining business.

[5]   Curriden, *supra* note 3.

[6]   2019 ACC Chief Legal Officers Survey, Association of Corporate Counsel at 8, https://www.acc.com/sites/default/files/resources/vl/membersonly/QuickReference/1294 863_1.pdf, *archived at* https://perma.cc/H53Z-2RTB.

[7]   *Id.*

[8]   Interview with Alex Arellano, General Counsel, American Airlines Center, in Dallas, Tex. (June 24, 2019).

Cohen, General Counsel of the Dallas Cowboys, says, "We need to be inserted into the business pipeline as soon as possible. We can help save a ton of time on the back end if [our business clients] bring us into the deal on the front end. Everything from licenses, permits, filings, registrations and insurance takes time!"[9]

BECOMING A TRUSTED LEGAL ADVISOR AND BUSINESS PARTNER

In-house counsel can be effective advisors within their organizations only if the business people seek them out for advice and counsel. And fortunately, most business people do. They understand the law department is a valuable resource available to them and know how and when to use it appropriately. This section addresses four specific ways in-house counsel can become a trusted legal advisor and business partner: (1) develop strong relationships; (2) communicate effectively; (3) know the business; and (4) be a facilitator, not a roadblock, whenever practicable.

Develop Strong Relationships

Because most internal clients assume their inside counsel have the requisite legal knowledge, skills, and experience to do their jobs,[10] they evaluate in-house counsel on relational and behavioral skills, such as customer service, communication, personality, and teamwork.[11] For this reason, in-house attorneys who practiced in law firms before transitioning to a corporate setting should apply their skills of cultivating and nurturing client relationships to constituents within the company.[12]

---

[9] Interview with Jason Cohen, General Counsel, Dallas Cowboys, in Frisco, Tex. (June 24, 2019).

[10] *See Evolving Role of In-House Counsel: Adding Value to the Business*, Gen. Couns. Consulting, at 6, http://www.gcconsulting.com/articles/pdf/120280.pdf, *archived at* https://perma.cc/L374-K5JT; *see also* Dan Currell, *What Other Departments Need From Legal*, In-House Tex., May 5, 2014, at 4.

[11] *Id.* at 6.

[12] Martin & Atteberry, *3 Ways to Ease the Leap from Firm to In-House Counsel*, Corp. Couns. (2014), http://www.corpcounsel.com/id=1202650989384/3-Ways-to-Ease-the-Leap-From-Firm-to-In-House-Counsel?slreturn=20140403105104, *archived at* https://perma.cc/GJ8U-Y4TP.

As with any relationship, interpersonal skills are paramount.[13] Inside counsel should get to know their internal clients on both an organizational and individual level.

At an organizational level, inside counsel should get out of the law department and visit their business colleagues in the environments in which they work. Making "the rounds" at the client site and regularly participating in key team meetings enable counsel to learn and understand the products, competition, technology, and challenges of the business units they counsel as well as the legal issues and key people in each unit.[14]

Inside counsel should strive to be part of the business team.[15] Many of the business people in a corporation come from specialized backgrounds, with focused education and experience in areas like engineering, sales and marketing, information technology, finance, and internal audit.[16] "Helping to generate cross-functional energy and synergy in defining problems, debating issues and developing positions with the CEO on a broad range of issues facing the company is a fascinating task open to curious, energetic, broad-gauged lawyers."[17]

On an individualized level, corporate counsel should also connect with their internal clients. Getting to know them as people, their personalities, personal goals, and priorities helps build strong working relationships. One consultant encourages her corporate clients to buy seats or sponsor a table at a volunteer fundraising event in order to invite co-workers so they can get to know each other better outside the work environment. "Creating and looking for more opportunities for informal interaction helps build those authentic relationships," she says.

---

[13] *See* Legg, *The In-House Life*, 24 Legal Times 46 (2001) ("In-house legal departments need counsel who can instill trust with the corporate business people. Unlike law firms, in-house departments usually do not isolate any attorneys, even juniors from the client.").

[14] *Evolving Role of In-House Counsel, supra* note 10, at 6–7.

[15] *See* Heineman, *In the Beginning*, Corp. Couns. (Apr. 2006).

[16] *See id.*

[17] *Id.*

"Whether it's an elevator conversation or walking down the hall or even inviting somebody for a cup of coffee, it always helps."[18]

When in-house counsel get to know their business colleagues, these clients are more likely to seek out corporate counsel when they have a need. Even if in-house counsel are physically integrated with their corporate client, they cannot be everywhere at once. So they must trust their internal clients to come to them for assistance. If the business colleagues view inside counsel as an integral component of their team, they will more often proactively email them and involve them in their decisions.[19] Being involved allows inside counsel to contribute and show their worth, while also keeping them "in the know" and allowing them to potentially head off issues before they become intractable problems.[20]

With some frequency, in-house attorneys are "stereotyped as difficult or uncompromising"[21] or "viewed as an expense to be minimized or avoided."[22] For this reason, it is imperative that in-house counsel—more so than others in the corporation—be someone with whom their business colleagues enjoy working. Being cooperative and pleasurable to work with can help overcome these stereotypes and allow internal clients to see in-house counsel as approachable and helpful.

David Starr, Chief Counsel and Chief Compliance Officer at Dean Foods Company, explains the importance of relationships with "internal clients": "In order to be an effective in-house counselor, it is critical to build solid relationships with the business people on multiple levels of the company and in all departments. The relationship must be based on trust, and in order to establish credibility, you have to learn the business and

---

[18] Vorro, *Coaching In-House Counsel Helps Perfect Their Game*, Inside Couns. Feb. 1, 2012.

[19] *See* Berman, *What to Consider When Considering an In-House Counsel Position (Part 1)*, Above L. Career Files, Nov. 29, 2012 (interview with Adam Heller, Senior Vice President of Legal Affairs at Geeknet), http://abovethelaw.com/career-files/what-to-consider-when-considering-an-in-house-counsel-position-part-1/, *archived at* https://perma.cc/XB43-KC5T.

[20] *Id.*

[21] Deanne Katz, Top 10 Tips for the New In-House Counsel, FindLaw Corporate Counsel Blog, http://blogs.findlaw.com/in_house/2012/08/top-10-tips-for-the-new-in-house-counsel.html (Aug. 28, 2012 5:56 AM), *archived at* https://perma.cc/WJC4-4WVV.

[22] Fox, *In-House Lawyers Also Work for a Client*, N.J. L. J., April 21, 1997 at 65.

listen to your colleagues' stories—their challenges, what makes them tick, what they view as successes, etc. It may take a while, but they have to know you are there for them at all times and can help them with any sort of legal issue they face."[23]

In the same way, Andrew Holywell, Senior Director & Associate General Counsel with Samsung Enterprise Solutions & Alliances, stresses the importance of developing relationships with internal clients: "You want a friend on the business side. Foster those relationships, particularly with those on the same level as you grow together in your careers."[24]

Needless to say, in-house counsel must be there for the business in good times and bad. Pam Justiss, Regulatory Counsel & Head of Compliance at American First Finance, understands this importance:

> As an in-house counsel, one way to become a trusted confidante is to be there for the business in both the highs and lows—to foster innovative ideas when growth is booming and to be there for the business when things didn't go like they planned. Having a servant heart can provide you with a deep sense of purpose while also making you invaluable to your colleagues. When you are in the trenches with the business when things are tough, they tend to remember that and entrust you with their most valued projects later.[25]

Even while inside counsel get to know their business colleagues, they are scrutinizing him: "How is 'this lawyer' going to work with everyone? How responsive will 'this lawyer' be? Although those questions will occasionally be verbalized, they are happening internally all the time."[26]

---

[23] Interview with David S. Starr, Vice President, Chief Counsel (Litigation, Employment & Risk) and Chief Compliance Officer, Dean Foods Company, in Dallas, Tex. (June 21, 2019).

[24] Interview with Andrew Holywell, Senior Director & Associate General Counsel, Samsung Enterprise Solutions & Alliances, in Dallas, Tex. (June 24, 2019).

[25] Interview with Pam Justiss, Regulatory Counsel & Head of Compliance, American First Finance, in Dallas, Tex. (June 28, 2019).

[26] Phillips, *Ethical Spark: Golden Rule Guides Chief Legal Officer's Approach, Even to Litigation*, Tex. Law (2013) (quoting email answers of Walt Holmes, Senior Vice President and Chief Legal Officer of Interstate Battery System of America Inc. on best practice questions at conclusion of article).

Some in-house lawyers function as members of their company's senior management team or, in large companies, as general counsel of a division of the company. In such cases, developing strong relationships with others on their management team is crucial. If practicable, it is desirable for inside counsel to office with or near the other members of the senior team. If not readily available, in-house counsel can miss a lot, including "hallway chatter" and may not be aware when a member of the management team develops a course of action that may be risky from a legal standpoint. Being close by can also provide valuable insight into the concerns of the leaders of the organization and the manner by which senior executives interact with each other.[27]

Relationships with other attorneys in the legal department, outside counsel, and corporate counsel at other companies are likewise important. Talking to other internal and external counsel helps inside counsel stay abreast of important legal issues. "Bouncing" ideas off other attorneys in the law department can be very helpful, particularly if the attorney whose advice is sought has handled a similar issue before. And when in-house counsel believes that a situation may involve an important legal or regulatory issue, other attorneys in the department or outside counsel can help confirm or deny this impression.

Some relationships within a corporation can be more difficult than others. Certain business people, albeit a minority, do not appreciate the legal function. They view the legal department as "overhead" and themselves as operators (i.e., the ones who generate revenue for the corporation and maximize shareholder value). Others view inside counsel as a roadblock. They avoid the legal department when possible unless directed by a supervisor to go there. Others will come solely so they can "check the box" that they asked legal. And finally, some send their transactions to legal at the eleventh hour to be "blessed," without having involved the department earlier in the process. Conversely, some internal clients may come readily to the legal

---

[27]   *See generally* Gutterman, *Top Ten Tips out of the Gates for New In-House Counsel*, Ass'n Corp. Couns., July 30, 2013, https://www.acc.com/resource-library/top-ten-tips-out-gates-new-house-counsel?Site=ACC, *archived at* https://perma.cc/3LER-J7V3.

department because they want a lawyer to make *all* their decisions for them in case something should go wrong later, they would be able to say, "The lawyer told me to do it that way."

Occasionally, in-house counsel will encounter a "company bully" who dares the legal department to push back. He may impose short deadlines on in-house counsel or communicate artificial deadlines. Although he is slow to respond to inquiries from the legal department, he demands an almost immediate response to something that may have been sitting on his desk for over a month.

Kellen McJunkins at Globe Life warns that in-house attorneys should anticipate pushback when trying to effect change within a business: "Implementing new rules and regulations can be like having a door slammed in your face multiple times. Don't take it personally, because as an in-house attorney you are only the messenger."[28]

Some internal clients have short memories. For this reason, it is prudent for in-house counsel to document conversations with business colleagues so they cannot later say that they were not advised or advised differently. Other business people may attempt to "forum shop" within the legal department. If they know that one attorney is likely to give them an answer they do not want, they will seek out a different attorney, hoping for a favorable answer.

More than ever before, lawyers are hired in a corporation to handle non-legal issues concerning compliance, labor relations, human relations, or contract negotiation matters. Although their law degrees and related skill sets can be very useful in these roles, difficult situations can arise when individuals hired to handle non-legal matters wrongly believe they as lawyers, can render legal advice to the corporation or try to influence or intimidate a new lawyer in the legal department. For this reason, many corporations caution employees with law degrees who handle non-legal matters not to render legal advice.

---

[28] Interview with Kellen McJunkins, Regulatory Attorney, Privacy Advisor, Globe Life, in McKinney, Tex. (June 24, 2019).

But thankfully, corporations tend to have few difficult people. Once in-house counsel develops strong relationships with her internal clients, they tend to work well with her.

Communicate Effectively

The most valued in-house lawyers are those who can communicate matters with the client in terms the client can understand.[29] People often assume lawyers are well-spoken professionals; however, speaking articulately and delivering information effectively are two different things.

Inside counsel should use commonplace words to get their points across to their internal clients. Where at times there may not be a plain English substitute, counsel should explain what a legal term or concept means when they first use it and spell out any acronyms.

Corporate counsel should avoid the use of "legalese,"[30] which Merriam-Webster defines as "the language used by lawyers that is difficult for most people to understand."[31] Some in-house lawyers may use legal jargon and concepts in an effort to demonstrate how smart they are to their business colleagues or to make the matter on which they are working seem more complicated. But when lawyers use legalese with internal clients, they merely succeed in alienating them. According to Walt Holmes, the Chief Partner Results Officer of Interstate Batteries, "Very few folks are really impressed with legal knowledge. In fact, that legal knowledge can be a barrier to working alongside folks. The challenge is . . . having the legal knowledge (which is essential) but being able to work with the [business] people . . . ."[32]

More importantly, legalese may keep internal clients, many of whom are sophisticated and highly intelligent, from grasping the message corporate counsel is trying to convey. Most business colleagues have not been to law school and will need inside

---

[29]   Fox, *supra* note 22.

[30]   *See* Beck & Byrne, *TopTier: The New R-3 100 Program Identifies Rising In-House Talent*, Inside Couns., August 2013, at 29.

[31]   Merriam-Webster Online: Dictionary and Thesaurus, http://www.merriam-webster.com/dictionary/legalese, *archived at* https://perma.cc/KZ8G-YAT2.

[32]   Phillips, *supra* note 26.

counsel to simplify complicated legal matters in terms they can comprehend.

In addition to using plain English in oral and written communications with internal clients, counsel should whenever possible eliminate legal jargon in contracts they draft. Some government regulations, including various state laws, now mandate the use of plain English in certain contracts, such as insurance contracts and consumer agreements.[33] Similarly, the U.S. Securities and Exchange Commission (SEC) regulations require its filings to be written in plain English.[34] In the preface to the SEC Plain English Handbook, Warren E. Buffet offers attorneys a very useful tip for writing in plain English:

> Write with a specific person in mind. When writing Berkshire Hathaway's annual report, I pretend that I'm talking to my sisters. I have no trouble picturing them: though highly intelligent, they are not experts in accounting or finance. They will understand plain English, but jargon may puzzle them. My goal is simply to give them the information I would wish them to supply me if our positions were reversed. To succeed, I don't need to be Shakespeare; I must, though, have a sincere desire to inform. No siblings to write to? Borrow mine. Just begin with "Dear Doris and Bertie."[35]

Most in-house counsel rely heavily on email, texts, and instant messages to communicate with their internal clients. And these methods are usually excellent ways to communicate with people without the time and effort of calling them or seeing them in person.[36] And for certain in-house attorneys who work for global organizations with internal clients in different parts of the world, there is no way they could do their jobs without

---

[33]   *See* Whiteman, *Raising the Bar on Legal Writing,* 23 Legal Times 23 (2000).

[34]   *See* Maister, *The SEC Gets Passive Aggressive: Chairman Wants Filings Written in Plain English,* 22 Tex. Law. 404 (2006). *See generally* B. Garner, *Securities Disclosure in Plain English* (1999).

[35]   Office Investor Educ. & Assistance, U.S. Sec. & Exch. Comm'n., *A Plain English Handbook: How to Create Clear SEC Disclosure Documents 2* (1998) https://www.sec.gov/pdf/handbook.pdf, *archived at* https://perma.cc/M78T-VJ9B.

[36]   Johnson, *Top Ten Ways to Become a More Efficient (and Possibly Happier) In-House Attorney,* Ass'n of Corp. Couns., Mar. 5, 2014, https://www.acc.com/resource-library/top-ten-ways-become-more-efficient-and-possibly-happier-house-attorney, *archived at* https://perma.cc/AHP4-B745.

these tools.[37] But in some cases, email, texts, and instant messages are not the best ways to communicate. Sometimes chains of emails go back and forth causing recipients not to understand what is being discussed, not know the background of the emails, or misinterpret the email altogether.[38] Much can be lost in translation in emails. Preservation of the attorney-client privilege is also a continual concern. For questions that require explanation or are complex or sensitive in nature, counsel should pick up the phone or, when feasible, walk over to talk to her business colleague instead.[39] Counsel can often save hours with a three-minute in-person conversation.[40]

When communicating, corporate counsel should take their audience into account because that often dictates how information should be dispensed. To communicate effectively, counsel need to gauge the relative sophistication of the business colleagues with whom they communicate, considering their education level and job experience. While counsel's audience will often include sophisticated executives, such as high-level officers, at other times it will include less-sophisticated people, such as the sales force. Counsel will likely communicate in a very different manner with executives than with sales people.

The consequences of not communicating effectually with internal clients can be severe. Krystal Jones, a regulatory attorney at Globe Life, advises, "You must learn to communicate as both a lawyer and a business leader to be effective. While, the 'answer is no because the law clearly says xyz' may be convincing to a lawyer, a business partner will likely grow frustrated and shut down."[41]

Counsel should articulate answers to business colleagues in an upfront and concise manner instead of burying conclusions in a 20-page legal analysis. One executive communications coach cautions in-house lawyers not to "bury" their headline: "A lot of attorneys tend to qualify everything they say. There are huge

---

[37]   *See* Sellinger, *Roundtable,* Corp. Legal Times, June 2003.

[38]   Johnson, *supra* note 36.

[39]   *Id.*

[40]   *Id.*

[41]   Interview with Krystal R. Jones, Regulatory Compliance Attorney, Globe Life, in McKinney, Tex. (June 24, 2019).

numbers of parenthetical phrases in their sentence structure because that's part of legal training. Think about using a 14-word sentence and get the verb as close to the noun as you can."[42] Another expert advises inside counsel to: "Analyze, don't summarize. No one wants to hear you give a 10-minute lecture on the ins and outs of corporate mergers. Just tell them how it applies to this particular issue."[43]

Some general counsel actively promote the use of sales and marketing concepts within the legal function to communicate the value of their work, in terms of tangible results and, if possible, quantitative terms.[44] For example, lawyers may promote that they added value to the business in a variety of ways, such as by identifying new revenue opportunities created by a change in the law or by helping avoid costly problems before they arise. The more value attorneys demonstrate to the organization, the more credibility they achieve.

Know the Business

In addition to knowing and communicating well with business colleagues, inside counsel must know their company's business. While this sounds obvious, the more inside counsel knows about the business, the better. Every business is different and what is important or appropriate for one may not be for another. Whether counsel works for a corporation that builds houses, delivers natural gas, manufactures automobiles, provides cloud-computing infrastructure, or grows fresh fruit, it is critical they know the company's business.

According to General Electric's former general counsel, Ben W. Heineman, Jr., "Inside lawyers should strive to be full members of the business team. Yes, the lawyers must, first and foremost, bring their legal skills, experience, and analysis to the business problems. But they must also have (or should have) the intelligence and breadth to learn and understand the products, technology, competition, and most importantly, the public

---

[42]   Vorro, *Effective Communication for In-House Counsel*, Inside Couns., Feb. 1, 2012.

[43]   Katz, *supra* note 21.

[44]   *Evolving Role of In-House Counsel, supra* note 10, at 4.

dimensions of the markets in which the business operates."[45] In the same way, Theis Rice, Vice President and Chief Compliance Officer at Trinity Industries recommends, "If you want to be a business partner, know their business as well as they do—integrating your legal contribution(s) like a chef integrates spices."[46]

The former chief legal officer of Interstate Batteries, Walt Holmes, recommends that in-house counsel "go spend some time with the people that drive the success (or potential failure) of the business! Understand the business! Think of ways you can improve the business after you have a better understanding of all of its facets."[47] Michelle Banks, former General Counsel of Gap, Inc., purposefully spent time on the store room floor and in the back storage room folding shirts and clothing at Old Navy to truly understand her retail business.[48]

Don E. Hinderliter II, the Deputy General Counsel at Sky Chefs, Inc. d/b/a LSG Sky Chefs knows the importance of business acumen and offers the following insight:

> In order to be a better attorney and team member, you need to understand the business. You have to go out into the field and see the operations. This allows you as the attorney to ask questions, have questions asked of you, and lets the field personnel know that you really care about them and the business and that you are not just a suit sitting at headquarters in an 'ivory tower.' One short visit to the field builds trust and allows you to better understand some of the 'shop floor' risks or specific operational issues that may not be readily apparent or discovered otherwise, which in turn allows you to draft better agreements.[49]

---

[45]   Heineman, *supra* note 15.

[46]   Interview with S. Theis Rice, Senior Vice President and Chief Compliance Officer, Trinity Industries, in Dallas, Tex. (June 24, 2019).

[47]   Phillips, *supra* note 26.

[48]   Bulacan, *Top Ten Things I Know Now that I Wish I Knew Then*, Ass'n of Corp. Couns. Legal Resources, Aug. 1, 2012, https://www.acc.com/resource-library/top-ten-things-i-know-now-i-wish-i-knew-then, *archived at* https://perma.cc/54PA-PYFN.

[49]   Interview with Don E. Hinderliter II, Deputy General Counsel, Sky Chefs, Inc. d/b/a LSG Sky Chefs, in Irving, Tex. (June 28, 2019).

For this reason, legal interns and externs who work with LSG Sky Chefs visit the company's DFW Airport Customer Service Center, a.k.a. the "flight kitchen," during their time with the company. On one occasion, an extern participated in a "Chef's Challenge" with the general counsel and a junior attorney, and prepared two entrees using only ingredients from the pantry and the walk-in cooler. "Although it's fun playing 'chef' for a day, Hinderliter says, "it's more fun helping the business thrive by drafting and negotiating contracts with language that reflects the actual business operations' needs. The business needs can ultimately only be discovered by truly getting to know the business."

Counsel should develop a working knowledge of the overall company and its organizational culture. One source suggests that, where practicable, in-house counsel who are new to a corporation take the following steps to proactively educate themselves about the company:

1.	Obtain a summary of the company's business plan and an organizational chart.

2.	Learn about the company's history and its corporate culture.

3.	Study the company's industry and the markets in which it operates.

4.	Read the company's most recent annual Form 10-K, which provides an in-depth overview of the company's business and financial condition.

5.	Review other recent SEC filings, such as quarterly reports on Form 10-Q and current reports on Form 8-K.

6.	Study recent company disclosures on its products, services, and activities.

7.	Review any company "due diligence binders."

8.	Review the minutes from the most recent board of directors and board committee meetings.

9. Confer with the company's outside auditors and law firms about their relationship with the company.

10. Meet with senior managers from the company's key business units.[50]

Moreover, inside counsel should learn everything they feasibly can about the particular industry and markets in which the company operates and understand how the company is situated within its industry. It helps to get involved in the relevant trade association. For example, an in-house attorney in the restaurant business may want to join the local chapter of the National Restaurant Association. An attorney with a hospital system may consider joining the American Hospital Association. Through groups like these, inside counsel can get up to speed on competitive and regulatory conditions in the industry,[51] as well as form relationships with peers at other companies, which can be invaluable resources if an issue arises with which counsel is not familiar.

On a micro basis, in-house counsel should seek to understand the specific business units they will counsel.[52] A critical part of corporate counsel's job is making sure that the company's operations comply with applicable laws and regulations.[53] Understanding how a business unit makes money and its operational methods (e.g., procurement, research and development, manufacturing, distribution, sales, marketing, etc.) are critical in this regard. Counsel should also know any specific business drivers, economics, goals, and priorities related to any particular transaction or litigation matter on which counsel is working. Over time, inside counsel also needs to learn how each of the company's units interact with one another, who the key players are within each unit, and how decisions are made within different units.[54]

---

[50]   Gutterman, *supra* note 27.

[51]   *Id.*

[52]   Martin & Atteberry, *supra* note 12.

[53]   *Id.*

[54]   *See* Katz, *supra* note 21.

Be a Facilitator Whenever Possible

Most law students these days have probably never heard of Dr. No, the villain in a 1962 James Bond spy film bearing the same name who plotted to disrupt an early American manned space launch with a radio beam weapon.[55] In the context of this chapter, Dr. No refers to inside counsel, whose characteristic answer to his business clients' questions is a resounding "No" or "You can't do that." Counsel who act like "Dr. No" reinforce the idea that in-house counsel is a roadblock. One of the quickest ways for in-house counsel to lose credibility with internal clients is to constantly answer "no." If told "no" too many times, business people will either avoid the lawyer altogether or go directly to outside counsel.

According to Krystal R. Jones at Globe Life, "Legal should not be the department of 'no,' but "the department of 'know.' Educate, engage, encourage creative problem solving. If you want business partners to come to you when there is an issue (rather than find out after the fact when regulators or litigators are knocking at your door), make sure they know you are there to help."[56]

In-house lawyers add value by identifying alternative courses of action that meet their internal clients' business goals rather than just raising objections.[57] Consider the case of a faculty member who asked the legal department whether she could take graduate students to a remote location to collect data on a grizzly bear habitat.[58] While it would have been easy to deny the seemingly dangerous request outright, the university attorneys suggested some alternatives to help their client achieve her educational goals with lower risk:

> The faculty advisor could visit the area before the trip
> to determine if the site is accessible by cell phone or
> radio. The students might be required to travel in small

---

[55]   Wikipedia, *Dr. No* (film), http://en.wikipedia.org/wiki/Dr._No_(film), *archived at* https://perma.cc/N9T6-H9CH.

[56]   Interview with Krystal R. Jones, Regulatory Compliance Attorney, Globe Life, in McKinney, Tex. (June 24, 2019).

[57]   Currell, *supra* note 10, at 4.

[58]   *See* Ward & Tribbensee, *Preventive Law on Campus*, Change, May/June 2003, at 19.

groups rather than alone and they might be told to
'check in' every few hours. The lawyer might also
suggest that the student sign release forms that
describe potential risks in detail. The group could hire
a guide who is familiar with the area. They also might
consider contracting with an insured third party to
provide transportation and lodging. Finally, the lawyer
might ask the faculty member to consult with others
who have taken students on similar trips for
suggestions on other ways to manage the risks.[59]

Like university counsel in this example, in-house lawyers
must try to be facilitators whenever possible and not obstacles.
But in some cases, "no" is the appropriate and *only* answer, such
as when the client's approach is illegal. Counsel must *always*
retain the leverage to say "no" when appropriate.

Beyond any illegality, there are many other situations
where being a Dr. No is not appropriate. Inside counsel can
effectively respond to their internal clients in a manner that
takes potential risks and legal issues into account but still allows
clients to achieve their desired results. For example:

- No, we can't do that but maybe we can do ABC;
- Yes, if you do A, B, & C;
- No, but let me help you structure the transaction in
  a way that I believe still achieves your goals;
- Yes, but there are some considerations and some
  risks if you decide to do that.

Sometimes inside counsel will encounter situations where
she simply does not know the answer. In such cases, it is better
for counsel to admit she currently does not know the answer and
then follow up later with an answer. Most business people will
admire counsel's candor. Some potential ways to respond in
these situations are: "Let me get back to you on that" or "Let me
research that issue further and circle back to you."

In answering complex questions, inside counsel should
never feel the need "to go it alone." The worlds within which

---

[59]   *Id.*

corporations operate and the legal issues they face have become increasingly complex. Thus, it is appropriate for inside counsel to consult with other attorneys in the corporation or with outside advisors on complicated issues.

HELPING INTERNAL CLIENTS IDENTIFY AND EVALUATE RISK

In-house counsel are playing a larger role in evaluating risk in the companies they serve and translating those risks in order to help their business colleagues make educated decisions.[60] For in-house counsel, risk management is important because the risk management and legal process functions overlap.[61] Inside counsel who help their business colleagues manage risk in a cost-effective manner will assist the business in becoming more competitive, effective, and profitable.[62]

There are risks in every business, and each business has its own peculiar risks.[63] Consumer companies risk changing consumer tastes and increased competition from other companies.[64] The potential impact of new or anticipated laws and regulations is a significant risk for many companies.[65] A manufacturing company may face commodity risks while a global company may encounter exchange rate risk.[66]

Despite any risks, "[c]orporations can and do pursue strategies involving risk—and most worthwhile entrepreneurial activity entails risk."[67] In some industries, taking calculated risks moves the business forward and increases its competitive

---

[60]   *See* Veasey & Di Guglielmo, *The Tensions, Stresses, and Professional Responsibilities of the Lawyer for the Corporation*, 62 Bus. Law. 1 (2006).

[61]   *See* John A. Chamberlain, *Risk Management for In-House Counsel,* Mich. Bus. L.J. (2005) at 10, https://higherlogicdownload.s3.amazonaws.com/MICHBAR/ebd9 d274-5344-4c99-8e26-d13f998c7236/UploadedImages/pdfs/journal/spr05_Articles.pdf, *archived at* https://perma.cc/7S9V-T962; *see also* Brown, *Managing Risk In-House*, Can. Law. Mag. (2012), https://www.canadianlawyermag.com/author/jennifer-brown/ managing-risk-in-house-1688/, *archived at* https://perma.cc/SK6T-2KCE.

[62]   *Id.* at 10.

[63]   *Id.*

[64]   U.S. Securities and Exchange Commission, *How to Read a 10-K*, https://www. sec.gov/answers/reada10k.htm, *archived at* https://perma.cc/Y24A-N77S.

[65]   *Id.*

[66]   *Id.*

[67]   *See* Corp. Laws Comm. of the Bus. Law Section of the American Bar Ass'n, Corporate Director's Guidebook 33 (6th ed. 2011).

edge.[68] "A critical skill in business today is knowing how much risk to take to make sure the business is competitive, yet playing by the rules at the same time."[69]

When lawyers transition from law firm to corporate legal department, many have a difficult time understanding that the corporations for which they work are willing to take on some level of risk, even legal risks. Many lawyers, by their nature, are risk averse, ultra conservative, and uncomfortable with ambiguity. And those who come from law firms worked in an environment in which they were taught to minimize risk. Thus, a new in-house lawyer may have to develop a tolerance and appreciation for an acceptable level of risk.

In-house counsel should understand the particular risks facing the corporation. For publicly traded companies, a good starting point is the company's annual report (Form 10-K) filed with the U.S. Securities and Exchange Commission. It offers a detailed picture of the risks a company faces in the MD&A, short for Management's Discussion and Analysis of Financial Condition and Results of Operations.[70] The MD&A discusses management's views of key business risks and how it addresses them.[71] In addition to the Form 10-K, counsel should read any key reports describing the corporation's programs for identifying and managing risks and visit with the company's risk manager who can be particularly informative.[72]

Just like people, every corporate client has its own risk tolerance. For example, some corporations litigate matters "to the death," while some seek to expeditiously settle disputes.[73] Most take a position somewhere in between.[74] Counsel should assess and seek to understand his corporation's risk/reward appetite and risk tolerance.

---

[68] *See* Brown, *supra* note 61.

[69] *Id.*

[70] U.S. Securities and Exchange Commission, *supra* note 64.

[71] *Id.; see* discussion Chapter 9 *herein.*

[72] Chamberlain, *supra* note 61, at 10.

[73] *See* Stephen F. Ellman, *Cooperation, Not Conflict*, N.Y. L. J. Jan. 31, 2004.

[74] *Id.*

In-house counsel's job is to help identify, evaluate, communicate, and manage risk.[75] If inside counsel determines that a particular activity is too risky, he may advise his internal client to avoid the risk altogether, although this may not be practical since risk is attendant with many activities.[76]

Counsel should be part of building a risk management framework upfront in pace with growth instead of going back later to fill in gaps. Pam Justiss, Regulatory Counsel and Head of Compliance at American First Finance, believes "involving legal from the outset is beneficial to the business and facilitates creative solutions that incorporate sound risk management strategies from the very beginning. The legal costs to the business associated with merely looping in counsel for loss mitigation strategies can be substantial."[77]

Generally, in-house counsel assess the overall risk but the client makes the ultimate decision.

> The consensus view is that lawyers are expected to identify a range of risks, with details about the attendant risk impact and consequences and suggestions for alternative approaches, but leave it to the client to make the decision. Some general counsel suggest that this policy is somewhat driven by business managers' concern that lawyers may be too conservative if they have ultimate responsibility. They acknowledge that clients who manage a multitude of other business risks should be trusted to manage legal risk, as long as their lawyers have effectively provided advice and counsel.[78]

If the client understands and appreciates the risks involved yet ultimately decides to take on the risk, that is the client's prerogative, provided the proposed conduct is not illegal or fraudulent.

---

[75]   Martin & Atteberry, *supra* note 12.

[76]   Chamberlain, *supra* note 61, at 10.

[77]   Interview with Pam Justiss, Regulatory Counsel & Head of Compliance, American First Finance, in Dallas, Tex. (June 28, 2019).

[78]   *Evolving Role of In-House Counsel: Adding Value to the Business, supra* note 10, at 9.

In addition to identifying and quantifying potential risks, counsel may advise her client on how to manage or transfer risks, such as through insurance policies, damages caps, or contractional indemnification clauses. In certain cases, if risk cannot be transferred, the potential exposure may be reduced through risk awareness training sessions tailored to the business unit that is most exposed or best placed to handle the risk.[79]

Legal counsel, as business partner, should work with business people to evaluate risk, but this is just the beginning. According to Theis Rice at Trinity Industries:

> Once your job is done at this stage, business people need to be comforted that mitigation options have been identified and implemented, and that internal controls are in place to assure the mitigation options implemented will be effective when called upon. You will need to put back on your legal hat to provide the comfort.[80]

Inside counsel must keep in mind that companies often have other considerations, apart from risk, that enter into the decision-making process. For example, companies may have concerns about the potential for adverse press coverage, the time value of executives as well as long-standing relationships with business partners. These considerations may enter into business decisions such as the decision to settle a lawsuit quickly rather than require senior executives to spend days being deposed instead of running the business.

Andrea Scofield at Interstate Batteries thinks "the most challenging (and rewarding) aspect of being in-house counsel is striving to be viewed by your internal clients as a trusted advisor rather than a roadblock." Scofield explains,

> One way to accomplish this is to remember that in addition to considering any potential legal concerns, business people also have to contemplate various other

---

[79]   *See* Hatton, *5 Steps to Legal Risk Management*, In-House Law. Feb. 23, 2010, http://in-house-lawyer.blogspot.com/search?updated-max=2010-04-07T08:55:00-07:00& max-results=10&start=30&by-date=false, *archived at* https://perma.cc/R8XK-GZKZ.

[80]   Interview with S. Theis Rice, Senior Vice President and Chief Compliance Officer, Trinity Industries, in Dallas, Tex. (June 24, 2019).

types of risks (e.g., financial risks, customer relationship impacts, etc.) when making a decision. Legal is not the only risk manager when it comes to running a business. Therefore, my goal is to help our business people evaluate and balance both the legal points and other business concerns so that they can arrive at the best decision.[81]

James Nichols, Litigation Counsel with Hewlett Packard Enterprises, understands that legal risk goes beyond monetary damages and injunctions in litigation matters. Nichols counsels, "You also have to determine potential time cost to senior leaders, impact on other outstanding cases, and countless other business specific concerns. This is why exposure calculations should always be an interactive process between in-house counsel, outside counsel, and the business leader(s) involved."[82]

ALLOCATING RESOURCES

Due to limited resources, inside counsel is often required to allocate internal and external resources and the amount of effort that is devoted to a matter.[83] As Paul Ward, the Vice President of Legal Affairs and General Counsel at Southern Methodist University (SMU), states, "You always wish that you had more time. Out of 100 transactional matters that you are dealing with, you realize that only 5–10 of these are Cadillacs and the rest are Chevrolets."[84]

The general counsel's goal should be "to allocate work on a practice basis to the most appropriate resources based on skills and competencies, level of effort relative to the work's value or risk, and the most effective use of internal and external resources."[85] One consultant suggests taking an "inventory" of the kinds of matters handled (or anticipated to be performed in the future) by each lawyer in the legal department as well as

[81] Interview with Andrea Scofield, Managing Counsel, Interstate Batteries, in Dallas, Tex. (June 25, 2019).

[82] Interview with James Nichols, Litigation Counsel, Hewlett Packard Enterprise, in Plano, Tex. (July 17, 2019).

[83] *See Ten Practical Tips for the New General Counsel*, Huron Legal Inst. 2012.

[84] Interview with Paul Ward, Vice President for Legal Affairs and Government Relations, General Counsel and Secretary, Southern Methodist University, in Dallas, Tex. (June 21, 2019).

[85] *Ten Practical Tips, supra* note 83.

outside counsel, and then categorizing the matters by their complexity or value.[86] The general counsel can use such an analysis to determine whether a particular matter should be sent to internal or external counsel; if external, what firm or vendor; and for both, the most suitable person to handle the work (e.g., in-house counsel, senior associate, partner, legal assistant, law intern, or non-lawyer).[87]

Finding the right work mix is critical to achieving good results and optimum effectiveness, and the trend shows companies keeping more work inside the company. A recent study showed:

> 36% of all law departments are bringing some work previously done by law firms in-house to be done by their own lawyer staff instead. They are also making use of contract and temporary lawyers to do in-house work on an as-needed basis, and pushing work down from in-house lawyers to paralegals and other para-professionals.[88]

The top reason for keeping more work in-house is to cover an increased workload.[89] Other reasons include "to fill open positions, handle new areas of expertise, handle new department responsibilities, and expand the workforce geographically. [Other law departments] . . . will hire new lawyers in an effort to save money on outside counsel."[90]

Chief legal officers must also apportion their time. According to research, chief legal officers spend 37% of their time advising their organization's executives and assisting with corporate strategy, 22% practicing law, 20% on other corporate management responsibilities, and 18% of their time managing the legal department.[91]

---

[86]   *See id.*

[87]   *See id.*

[88]   *See* 2018 Chief Legal Officer Survey: An Altman Weil Flash Survey, at iii, http://www.altmanweil.com//dir_docs/resource/154F22DC-E519-4CE2-991D-492A0448 C74F_document.pdf, *archived at* https://perma.cc/WTW6-3PRG.

[89]   *Id.* at i–ii.

[90]   *Id.*

[91]   *Id.* at i.

Finally, each attorney within the legal department should learn the culture of the organization and calibrate how much work is appropriate on a particular matter. The goal should be to efficiently resolve issues at the earliest opportunity in the most appropriate and cost-effective manner.

IN-HOUSE COUNSEL IN BUSINESS MEETINGS

Corporations operate in a "meeting culture," where business people and lawyers routinely attend meetings and participate on conference calls. But unfortunately, in many corporations, ineffective meetings rank as one of the top three time-wasters.[92] One survey of 38,000 workers in the United States found that workers spend 5.5 hours each week in meetings, yet only 29 percent felt the meetings were productive.[93] This section addresses why it is important that in-house counsel attend meetings, and provide ideas on how in-house counsel can be more effective and efficient in those meetings.

Inside counsel's presence and participation in meetings are important for a variety of reasons. Perhaps the most important is to enable in-house counsel to be sufficiently informed about what is happening in the company. Having "a deep and broad knowledge of the corporation's business" is crucial because inside counsel "does not deal with legal issues in a vacuum. They have to be considered in the context of the corporation's business."[94]

Meetings also allow in-house counsel to develop better working relationships with their internal clients. Participating in meetings helps the lawyer be seen as part of the team and not an obstacle.[95] As previously discussed in this chapter, that kind

---

[92]   *See Survey Finds Workers Average Only Three Productive Days Per Week,* Microsoft Off. Pers. Productivity Challenge, Mar. 15, 2005, https://news.microsoft.com/2005/03/15/survey-finds-workers-average-only-three-productive-days-per-week/, *archived at* https://perma.cc/4GXP-FNWZ.

[93]   *Id.*

[94]   *See generally* Editor, *General Counsel: The Glue Between the CEO and the Board*, 15 Corp. Couns. Bus, J (Nov. 2006) (interview with The Hon. E. Norman Veasey, former Chief Justice, Delaware Supreme Court about importance of general counsel attending board meetings, committee meetings, and executive sessions of independent directors), https://ccbjournal.com/articles/general-counsel-glue-between-ceo-and-board, *archived at* https://perma.cc/534L-UNVF.

[95]   *See generally* Hatton, *supra* note 79.

of relationship and accessibility encourages business colleagues to come to them with questions and look to them for solutions.[96] According to Pam Justiss at American First Finance,

> The best business decisions are made when all pertinent stakeholders are involved, including both the business and legal teams. Some legal departments pride themselves on being the "Department of No," but lawyers are uniquely skilled to provide invaluable insights that foster innovative growth and solve deeply-rooted problems. In my experience, in-house counsel cultivate business development much more than hinder it.[97]

James Nichols at Hewlett Packard Enterprises says great in-house counsel distinguish themselves from good in-house counsel at meetings with business leaders:

> As in-house counsel, your primary duty is to identify and mitigate risk the business may not even be aware of—even if it means being the sole voice of dissent about otherwise profitable products or innovations. A good in-house attorney will be able to clearly present the risk to non-legal experts [but] a great in-house attorney will go beyond and posit solutions.[98]

Another reason for in-house counsel to attend meetings is to identify potential legal issues and red flags before they become problems. Corporate counsel's business colleagues are often not capable of spotting potential legal issues because they do not know the applicable law, do not have the required experience or judgment, or have not been trained in critical thinking skills. In-house counsel, on the other hand, as a result of their training and experience can often recognize potential issues in specialized areas, such as intellectual property, environmental, or securities disclosure, even if they are not specialists in those areas.[99] And in situations where corporate counsel may not have

---

[96]   *Id.*

[97]   Interview with Pam Justiss, Regulatory Counsel & Head of Compliance, American First Finance, in Dallas, Tex. (June 28, 2019).

[98]   Interview with James Nichols, Litigation Counsel, Hewlett Packard Enterprise, in Plano, Tex. (July 17, 2019).

[99]   *Id.*

specific knowledge concerning an issue, they can at least recognize where potential legal issues or circumstances may require specialized lawyers.[100]

An additional reason for the presence of in-house counsel in meetings is to facilitate the invocation of the attorney-client privilege. In-house counsel's confidential communications with corporate employees in business meetings made for the purpose of obtaining or providing legal assistance will generally be privileged, although any business advice or underlying facts will not be shielded.[101]

In-house counsel cannot feasibly attend all meetings with business units. And not all meetings will require the input of counsel. Some will be very detailed and highly technical. Before any significant decisions are implemented, however, in-house counsel needs to be included in the decision-making process to ensure business colleagues are doing the right thing.[102]

Counsel should listen attentively in meetings and ask good questions. That means asking questions where appropriate and watching for indications that may indicate a larger issue—such as discussions about a disgruntled corporate employee, possible contract violations, or any other triggers of non-compliant behavior.[103]

"Most business meetings are not about solutions—they are about thought leadership. Listen, listen, listen, ask questions to clarify content, then go back to your office and think about what you heard and learned before you speak."[104]

In meetings, in-house counsel should try to make their internal clients feel like their matter is as important to them as

---

[100]   *Id.*

[101]   *See* Zeno & Root, *Preserving the Attorney-Client Privilege for In-House Counsel*, AHLA Connections, Dec. 2013, https://www.squirepattonboggs.com/~/media/files/insights/publications/2014/01/analysis-preserving-the-attorneyclient-privilege__/files/analysispreservingtheattorneyclientprivilegefori__/fileattachment/analysispreservingtheattorneyclientprivilegefori__.pdf, *archived at* https://perma.cc/SXB2-YW3W.

[102]   *Id.*

[103]   *See* Folsom, *10 Crucial First Steps For the CCO*, Inside Couns., Mar. 25, 2014.

[104]   Interview with S. Theis Rice, Senior Vice President and Chief Compliance Officer, Trinity Industries, in Dallas, Tex. (June 24, 2019).

it is to the clients.[105] For this reason, unless otherwise necessary, counsel should not answer their phones or check email during the meeting.[106] Their attention should be on the internal clients with whom they are interacting.[107]

If the lawyer is leading the meeting, she should first make sure that a meeting is appropriate; at times, other approaches will prove more beneficial.[108] One team-building consultant recommends only holding a meeting when there is a decision to be made or a problem to be solved.[109]

Before the meeting, inside counsel should also consider circulating an agenda, along with any relevant background materials before the meeting, including any PowerPoint presentations.[110] Some personnel wait until the meeting to share information, which often results in the first 20 or 30 minutes spent on "background."[111] Sending information in advance allows the parties to get into the substance of the discussion more quickly and allows more opportunity for pre-meeting preparation, formulating ideas, and asking colleagues questions to elicit a better decision.[112] At the conclusion of the meeting, counsel should summarize the accomplishments, decisions, and next steps and perhaps memorialize it in an email or one-page summary to share with meeting participants.[113]

CORPORATE MINUTES

Some corporate counsel are integrally involved in board of directors or board committee meetings.[114] They are involved for

---

[105]   Adyanthaya, *A Prescription for Productivity and Happiness*, 32 Ass'n Corp. Couns. 2, Mar. 2014, at 18.

[106]   *Id.*

[107]   *Id.*

[108]   Rogelberg, Scott & Kello, *The Science and Fiction of Meetings*, 48 MIT Sloan Mgmt. Rev. 2, Winter 2007, at 20.

[109]   *See* Daniel, *Eight Steps to More Effective Meetings*, CIO, Nov. 5, 2007, https://www.cio.com/article/2437983/eight-steps-to-more-effective-meetings.html, *archived at* https://perma.cc/3NKU-CEMN.

[110]   *See* Rogelberg, *supra* note 108.

[111]   Merchant, *Kill Your Meeting—The Future is in Walking and Talking*, Wired, Mar. 8, 2013, http://www.wired.com/2013/03/how-technology-can-make-us-stand-up/, *archived at* https://perma.cc/5PN3-VDNT.

[112]   *Id.*

[113]   Daniel, *supra* note 109.

[114]   Veasey & Di Guglielmo, *supra* note 60, at 13.

at least two reasons: first, to answer questions from board members and, second, to be a scrivener of the corporate minutes.[115] This section addresses the latter.

In many respects, board minutes are like a script for a play because they set forth who attended the board meeting, the location of the meeting, the points in time during the meeting when individuals entered and left the meeting, and a description of what the board and the attendees discussed or considered.[116] The Honorable E. Norman Veasey, the former Chief Justice of the Delaware Supreme Court, suggests that board minutes include at least the following:

- The date of the meeting and the names of the directors and other persons who attended the meeting;

- The times the meeting began and ended, and the times when persons entered and left the meeting;

- A description of the topics discussed or considered;

- Some general relationship between the length of the minutes devoted to a particular issue and the time devoted to the issue;

- Identification of anyone who provided information and advice at the meeting;

- A general description of the information provided to the directors before or at the meeting;

- A brief summary of the major terms and rationale discussed (without attributing particular words or points to any directors) in connection with significant transactions;

- The board vote on matters put to a vote, indicating any director who dissented, abstained, or absented herself or himself from the vote;

---

[115]   *Id.* ("Given the critical importance of the minutes, the general counsel should prepare the minutes or supervise the process of preparing the minutes so that they are professionally prepared and consistent from meeting to meeting.").

[116]   Interview with Paul M. Jolas, Vice President, General Counsel and Corporate Secretary, U.S. Concrete, Inc., in Dallas, Tex. (Nov. 4, 2013).

- If discussions were held or information exchanged among any directors before the meeting relating to matters considered at the meeting, those facts should be reflected; and

- The identity of the person preparing the minutes.[117]

A certain "balance" is required in preparing board minutes. There must be a requisite level of detail in the minutes but not too much detail. Each board, with the advice of the general counsel, should determine the level of detail to include in the minutes:[118]

> "[M]inutes should be sufficiently detailed to support the availability of the applicable protections provided by substantive law. Thus, minutes should summarize important discussions and actions, without generally purporting to provide a verbatim record or attributing specific words or points of view to particular directors. Minutes that do not reflect that an adequate deliberative process occurred can support an inference that directors failed to consider pertinent information fully and in good faith."[119]

Paul Jolas, the general counsel of US Concrete advises counsel to think about the board minutes as "Defendant's Exhibit 1" in a litigation matter in which the plaintiff alleges that the board of directors did not exercise its requisite duty of care.[120] According to Jolas,

> It is important to capture the fact that the directors exercised their duty of care by accurately reflecting in the minutes the matters discussed, references to the materials presented to the directors before or at the meeting, and that due consideration was given to the matter, including making sure adequate time was devoted to the matter.[121]

---

[117]   Veasey & Di Guglielmo, *supra* note 60. Reprinted with the permission of Chief Justice Veasey, Ms. Di Guglielmo, and the American Bar Association.

[118]   *Id.*

[119]   *See* Corporate Directors Guidebook, *supra* note 67, at 53.

[120]   Interview with Paul M. Jolas, *supra* note 116.

[121]   *Id.*

Properly prepared board minutes provide a contemporaneous record of the board's deliberative process and can deflect criticism regarding the adequacy of that process.[122] Consequently, the minutes should reflect the fact that the board engaged in a deliberative process, acted with the reasonable belief that its decisions were in the corporation's best interests, and duly considered other alternatives."[123]

Some in-house counsel will include a "start time" for each discussion point so that the length of the minutes devoted to a particular issue corresponds to the actual time devoted to the issue. But other corporate counsel are critical of this approach because doing so potentially opens directors up to questions about why they spent 30 minutes on "this" but only 15 minutes on "that." The amount of time spent on a matter may not necessarily indicate its level of importance.

When the board (or a committee) approves the minutes, the corporation should retain them as a corporate record as part of the company's minute books, along with files with the information provided to the board (or committee) in packets.[124] This information can help demonstrate the board's (or committee's) informed business judgment and help directors in recollecting past events.[125]

---

[122]   Veasey & Di Guglielmo, *supra* note 60.

[123]   *Id*. Note that most companies are now using electronic board portals, which allow board members to access board information on a paperless basis from a tablet device. *See, e.g., 10 Ways to Run More Effective Board Meetings: Running an Effective, Digital Board Meeting (Diligent 2019),* https://insights.diligent.com/wp-content/uploads/2019/02/10_ways_white_paper_letter_US.pdf, *archived at* https://perma.cc/SVF4-3B83.

[124]   *Id*.

[125]   *Id*.

CHAPTER 7

LAW COMPLIANCE

LAW COMPLIANCE—INSIDE COUNSEL'S ROLE

Law compliance has become an increasingly important aspect of in-house legal practice. In view of the serious adverse consequences that arise from illegal conduct, in-house attorneys today play a critical role in the practice of preventive law. One key way to effectuate this objective is the role that inside counsel plays in the implementation of effective and operational law compliance programs.

The extent of such law compliance programs depends largely on the operational practices and complexities of the corporation. For example, is the enterprise a publicly-held (and thereby a publicly-traded) company or a private enterprise? Does the company have multifaceted operations? Does the company conduct business outside of the United States? Does the corporation produce materials or otherwise engage in operations that raise environmental concerns? Not surprisingly, with respect to publicly-traded corporations, law compliance focuses on such areas as, for example, antitrust, environmental practices, the Foreign Corrupt Practices Act (FCPA), employment and hiring practices, intellectual property, taxation, and corporate/securities. Even privately-held enterprises that conduct business locally, producing (or selling) few products and having a small number of employees, are faced with law compliance issues—such as avoidance of discriminatory hiring and retention practices and compliance with the immigration laws.

ADVISING REGARDING LAW COMPLIANCE

When providing advice with respect to the company's law compliance objectives, the in-house lawyer may consider the following:

- The nature and scope of a company's law compliance program should reflect that enterprise's operations and the legal issues that the enterprise realistically may face.

- The law compliance program should be adopted by the company's board of directors and should be administered under its supervision as part of its monitoring function. The board of directors should revisit its law compliance program on a periodic basis for possible revision.

- Although no law compliance program is "bullet-proof," the company should ensure that the program's scope and implementation are sufficiently effective in view of the reasonably anticipated circumstances and risks.

- Corporate personnel, including officers and employees, should know and understand the applicable law compliance mandates. To integrate the program (such as a Code of Conduct) into the company's culture and facilitate compliance, educational sessions should be held on a periodic basis. Consideration should be given, where appropriate, to whether affected personnel should be required to certify on an annual basis compliance with applicable conduct and legal requirements.

- The law compliance program should be effectively administered. Lack of effective administration raises serious issues for adherence to applicable mandates and the adverse ramifications resulting from law violations.

- The law compliance program should be adequately enforced, such as spot checks, board of director (or delegated committee) review, "whistleblower" procedures, and the taking of meaningful disciplinary action (such as termination of employment) against those persons who fail to comply.

IMPACT OF SOUND LAW COMPLIANCE PROGRAMS ON GOVERNMENT PROSECUTION

Implementation of reasonably effective law compliance programs deter and help prevent wrongdoing. With the prevalence of government civil and enforcement actions being brought against corporations today, the presence of reasonably effective law compliance programs may dissuade government regulators from prosecuting and serves as a mitigating factor in determining the punishment to be assessed.

The importance of adequate law compliance policies is seen by the Department of Justice's decision not to prosecute Morgan Stanley for its employee's violations of the Foreign Corrupt Practices Act (FCPA). Declining to institute proceedings against Morgan Stanley, the Department of Justice explained:

> Morgan Stanley maintained a system of internal controls meant to ensure accountability for its assets and to prevent employees from offering, promising or paying anything of value to foreign government officials. Morgan Stanley's internal policies, which were updated regularly to reflect regulatory developments and specific risks, prohibited bribery and addressed corruption risks. . . . Morgan Stanley frequently trained its employees on its internal policies, the FCPA and other anti-corruption laws. . . . Morgan Stanley's compliance personnel regularly monitored transactions, randomly audited particular employees, transactions and business units, and tested to identify illicit payments. Moreover, Morgan Stanley conducted extensive due diligence on all new business partners and imposed stringent controls on payments made to business partners.[1]

---

[1]   Press Release, U.S. Department of Justice, No. 12–534 (April 25, 2012), *discussed in* McGreal, *Corporate Compliance Survey*, 68 Bus. Law. 163, 165 (2012). *See* U.S. Dept. of Justice, Antitrust Division, *Evaluation of Corporate Compliance Programs in Criminal Antitrust Investigations* (July 2019); Gruner, *General Counsel in an Era of Compliance Programs and Corporate Self-Policing*, 46 Emory L.J. 1152 (1997).

Hence, by adopting and implementing reasonably effective law compliance procedures and practices, Morgan Stanley avoided criminal prosecution.

The need for effective law compliance is not only on the federal level. Increasingly, the state attorneys general have become more active in pursuing enforcement actions against corporations, instituting proceedings, for example, based on consumer fraud, data breaches and identity theft, and lending practices. As stated by one source:

> [E]very corporate compliance program should include an affirmative strategy for becoming familiar with and working with AGs. In-house counsel and government relations personnel should actively engage in getting to know, understand and relate to AGs and their concerns. Additionally, in-house counsel and their government relations counterparts should strategically partner with outside counsel who have developed working relationships with AGs and who have the ability to communicate directly with the AG and his or her deputy. . . . AGs frequently rely upon counsel they trust and respect for advice and information on a wide range of issues—sometimes before initiating an investigation or filing suit. Successful AG relationships . . . also may help efficiently direct the scope of investigations or litigation and reach mutually acceptable resolutions.[2]

OVERSEEING THE COMPLIANCE FUNCTION

In many corporations, the inside general counsel oversees risk management and compliance functions, including serving as the chief compliance officer. In other companies, the compliance function is not within the law department. In these companies, "the role of the general counsel ranges from providing legal advice pertaining to compliance functions to hiring compliance officers and briefing senior managers and directors on compliance matters."[3] Irrespective of whether the

---

[2]   Sager & Nash, *The "New" Regulators: Why Corporate Compliance Strategies Must Address the Growing Influence of State Attorneys General,* 26 ACC Docket No. 7, at 66, 78 (Sept. 2008).

[3]   Duggin, *The Pivotal Role of the General Counsel in Promoting Corporate Integrity and Professional Responsibility,* 51 St. Louis L.J. 989, 1011–1012 (2007).

compliance function is directly overseen by the company's general counsel, the prevailing practice is that the general counsel as well as other in-house attorneys play an important role in seeking to effectuate the company's compliance with the law.[4] As stated by one source:

> With increased regulation of businesses by government agencies, in-house lawyers must take active steps to plan and implement programs to ensure corporate compliance with regulatory requirements. The in-house legal department shoulders much of the responsibility for developing formal compliance programs and educating personnel to prevent noncompliance with the law. In conjunction with this compliance function, inside lawyers also conduct or lead internal investigations when there are allegations of noncompliance or suspected problematic activities.[5]

The chapter next includes an excerpt of an article coauthored by the CEO of the Association of Corporate Counsel (Ms. Veta Richardson) focusing on the general counsel's role as an influencer of corporate culture.

The General Counsel as a Corporate Culture Influencer (2017)*
By Veta T. Richardson & Mary Blatch

Introduction

Corporate culture is widely acknowledged as adding value to companies, both in terms of improving financial performance and in creating an atmosphere that encourages ethical behavior. Evaluating and setting corporate culture is an important responsibility for boards and executive management, and because the board chooses the chief executive, ultimately culture emanates from the boardroom. Corporate culture is not a topic

---

4   *Id.* at 1012.

5   Kim, *Dual Identities and Dueling Obligations: Preserving Independence in Corporate Representation,* 68 Tenn. L. Rev. 179, 202–203 (2001). The subject of internal investigations is addressed in another chapter of this book.

*   Reprinted with the permission of the Association of Corporate Counsel, www. acc.com.

typically linked to a company's general counsel and legal department, but the failure to draw that link may prove shortsighted on the part of the board. Given the importance of the general counsel in matters of ethics, compliance, corporate governance, and risk and reputation management, the general counsel should be a key ally and partner in establishing a corporate culture that supports corporate performance without compromising ethical behavior, and legal and regulatory compliance.

This thought leadership paper explores how the general counsel (a/k/a chief legal officer) can be leveraged as a corporate culture influencer, and how her standing and stature vis-à-vis the CEO and other C-suite executives should be a topic of board inquiry.

When the general counsel has a seat at the chief executive's leadership table, it sends a signal to the company's stakeholders (internal and external) that ethics, compliance, and other legal risk considerations are a top priority of the company. A direct reporting line between the chief legal officer and chief executive officer is important to corporate culture as a reflection of the "tone at the top," and through which the CEO sends a powerful message that business decisions are made with appropriate consideration of the ethical, legal, and reputational impacts. . . .

As the board meets its fiduciary duty to keep a critical eye on the company's culture, part of that examination must include how the general counsel functions within the company. Through talking with well-respected general counsel and our own research regarding the expectations of corporate directors and chief executives regarding the chief legal officer, the Association of Corporate Counsel (ACC) has developed five indicators that all directors, particularly non-executive directors, should look to in order to assess whether a company's general counsel is well positioned to have a positive influence on corporate culture.

Regulatory and Business Demands Expand the Need for General Counsel Influence

In 1991, the US government issued the United States Sentencing Guidelines for Organizations, which incentivized the creation of corporate compliance programs meant to prevent and detect violations of the law. This began a more systematic approach by companies to address regulatory compliance as well as ethics within their organizations. Ultimate responsibility for a company's regulatory compliance usually rests with its general counsel, and as regulatory scrutiny has increased, so has companies' need for regulatory compliance advice.

Although some companies have compliance functions that are separate from the legal department, many of the activities mandated by a compliance program require legal analysis, and any effective compliance program requires coordination with the general counsel.

The emphasis on the general counsel's role in ethics and compliance has made the position grow in professional stature and influence. Regulators recognize that in-house counsel have an essential role in promoting compliance and ethics in their companies. They have even included in-house counsel in regulatory regimes meant to deter corporate wrongdoing like the Sarbanes-Oxley Act of 2002. Both directors and general counsel are acutely aware of the importance of the general counsel role in promoting ethics and compliance within the company. In ACC's *Skills for the 21st Century General Counsel Survey*, 54 percent of directors ranked "ensuring a company's compliance with relevant regulations" as one of the top three ways general counsel provide value to the company. ACC's 2017 *Chief Legal Officers Survey* found that 74 percent of general counsel rated ethics and compliance as "extremely" or "very" important over the next 12 months—the highest ranked concern in the survey. This emphasis on the general counsel's role in ethics and compliance created the need for general counsel to exert greater influence within their companies in order to fulfill the compliance mandate from regulators and the board.

Even outside of compliance concerns, legal and regulatory issues are increasingly central to the implementation of sophisticated business strategies. For example, protecting innovation requires understanding intellectual property law; overseas expansion requires knowing the employment laws of other countries; advances in data analytics require knowledge of data privacy laws. Where outside counsel used to be the primary legal advisers to the CEO, general counsel have come to fill that role in every corporation, particularly the large multinational and/or publicly held company. As legal departments have evolved and attracted top-level talent below the general counsel, the general counsel has carved out more time to consider strategic business issues and contribute to setting strategies. This development is a positive contribution to corporate culture. . . .

When a general counsel is part of the executive leadership that makes strategic business and operational decisions, those decisions are informed by not only a legal perspective, but also by broad ethical and public policy considerations. The general counsel is a diverse and unique voice at the executive table. ACC's *Skills for the 21st Century General Counsel Report* suggests that boards are just beginning to perceive the value of the general counsel as a strategic advisor. Twenty-seven percent of the directors surveyed ranked the general counsel's "input into strategic business decisions" as a top-three value driver currently, with 37 percent anticipating it would be a top-three value driver in the future.

A Strong General Counsel Supports a Strong Corporate Culture

. . . .

It is curious that there has not been greater discussion of the general counsel's role in influencing or supporting strong corporate cultures, especially with ethics and compliance being the primary drivers of corporate culture efforts. Of the 12 companies that have made Ethisphere's list of the "World's Most Ethical Companies" each year it has been published, ACC found that the majority of them have general counsel who are well-positioned to influence corporate culture. For example in 91 percent of those companies, general counsel report to the CEO. In 83 percent, general counsel serve as the corporate secretary, indicating direct access to the board, and in 83 percent of those companies, general counsel are also responsible for compliance.

The preventative role of the general counsel and corporate legal department is key to their contribution to regulatory compliance and corporate culture. When the general counsel is included in discussions of business strategies before they are implemented, she can help the company assess and avoid legal and business risks.

As preventing violations of laws and regulations is preferable to mere detection of violations when they occur, the general counsel has become instrumental in improving a company's overall compliance, as well as protecting its reputation.

Much of the general counsel's value when it comes to supporting a strong corporate culture stems from the fact that the legal department's metric for success is not the company's quarterly performance. The general counsel promotes ethical behavior and integrity in corporate decisions by taking the view that short-term gain is not worth compromising long-term sustainability. This perspective can be important to informing what a company considers ethical. Experts consider corporate culture to be the intangible framework meant to guide individual and organizational behavior when there are gray areas.

. . . .

A strong general counsel can establish the practices that reinforce a corporate culture that values ethics and integrity. But this value can only occur if the general counsel is properly situated within the company, and the legal department has effective interactions with the company's business units. A management team that marginalizes the general counsel and the legal department not only loses out on this risk-management perspective, but also sends a company-wide message that legal risk, ethics, and compliance are not taken seriously. . . .

Five Indicators of General Counsel
Influence on Corporate Culture

Accepting the proposition that a strong general counsel will have a positive effect on corporate culture, we suggest five indicators a board might consider when evaluating whether the general counsel has sufficient influence on corporate culture, and whether corporate culture itself is indeed healthy.

#1—The general counsel reports directly to the chief executive officer and is considered part of the executive management team

Before the rise of the general counsel and the corporate legal department, general counsel were not considered C-level executives. They often reported to the chief financial officer (CFO), chief administrative officer (CAO) or another senior executive. As regulatory and business demands spurred the changes in the legal department detailed above, the role and relative authority of the general counsel increased. Per the *ACC Chief Legal Officers 2017 Survey*, 72 percent of respondents report directly to the CEO.

. . . .

The reporting structure of the general counsel position is an important indicator of the influence that the legal department has in the company. The ACC *Chief Legal Officers 2017 Survey* showed that general counsel who report to the CEO were much more likely to say that the executive team "almost always" seeks their input on business decisions.

General counsel who report to the CEO were also significantly more likely to report they "almost always" contribute to strategic planning efforts compared with those who don't. When the general counsel is consulted about business decisions and strategic planning efforts, there is a greater likelihood that those decisions and plans will take into account legal and regulatory risks. Pre-decision consultation helps the legal department fulfill its preventative role within the company.

In addition to providing the legal department with requisite influence, having the general counsel report to the CEO is an important part of setting the "tone at the top." When legal has a seat at the table, it sends a message to the rest of the company that compliance with laws and regulations is a company priority. It also says something about the CEO: that input from legal is valued, and that the CEO's vision for the company prioritizes ethics and integrity.

#2—The general counsel has regular contact with the board of directors

A board of directors that does not have a consistent relationship with the company's general counsel should be a cultural red flag and prompt further board inquiry. While the relationship between the general counsel and the board can take various forms, it is important that the relationship at least be consistent. After all, the board is the company's fiduciary representative, and the company is the general counsel's client (not members of the executive management team). A relationship between the general counsel and the board of directors enables the board to set the right tone for the company's legal, ethical, and compliance culture, and also helps maintain the independence of the legal function. . . .

Our data indicate that there is room for improvement in the relationship between boards and general counsel. In the *ACC Chief Legal Officers 2017 Survey*, 18 percent of respondents reported having a "direct' reporting relationship with the board of directors, and 67 percent reported that they "almost always" attend board meetings. However, a full 21 percent report that they seldom or never attend board meetings. While not every company requires a direct reporting structure between the general counsel and the board, at a minimum, the general counsel must have a mechanism to bring controversial issues to the board—without prior CEO consent.

In addition to raising issues directly with the board, an influential general counsel can be an ally in the board's efforts to set the tone for the company's compliance culture. The ACC survey shows that similar to the effect of direct CEO reporting by the general counsel, a board relationship imbues the general counsel with more influence over business decisions. General counsel who had a reporting relationship to the board were significantly more likely to be asked for input on business decisions; they were also significantly more likely to contribute to the company's strategic planning.

A relationship with the board also helps preserve the independence of the legal department. Much has been made of the independence, or lack thereof, of in-house counsel, because they depend on management for employment and compensation decisions. The board can serve as an important check on the potential conflict the general counsel might feel between her service to executive management, and her duty to the company as a client. Moreover, if a general counsel needs to report concerns to the board, finding a way to do so without formal access or a prior relationship with the board creates an obstacle to fulfilling her ethical duties. Ultimately, this leaves the board of directors unaware, and potentially exposed, to legal or compliance risks that require their attention.

#3—The general counsel is viewed as independent from the management team

The first two indicators state that general counsel should have a seat at the management table and a relationship with the board. If the general counsel fails to maintain her independence, neither of those relationships will benefit the company the way they should. The value the general counsel brings to the table is compromised if she is seen as lacking the courage to challenge management decisions when necessary. While general counsel are a part of the executive team, they must maintain a delicate balance between that position and their duties to the company as their client. Further, the board needs to satisfy itself that the general counsel is achieving that balance in order to have a healthy corporate culture. . . .

As mentioned above, the company is the general counsel's client, and if the general counsel is overly beholden to management, the result may be advice and counsel that does not prioritize what's best for the company.

Additionally, if such a perception is widely held throughout the company, it can erode the confidence that lower level employees place in the legal department. The general counsel should be seen as the senior executive most capable of pushing back on management decisions that put the company at legal or reputational risk. There must be a willingness by the general counsel to raise issues with the board, even if doing so may threaten her own standing with the CEO and other executives.

#4—The general counsel is expected to advise on issues that extend beyond the traditional legal realm, including ethics, reputation management, and public policy

. . . .

If the general counsel is to manage risk and support an ethical corporate culture, she must be empowered to advise on issues beyond traditional legal matters. In addition to rapid changes in the legal and regulatory landscape, companies are navigating issues involving public policy, politics, the media, and social pressure from consumers. The increasing importance of these "business in society" issues means they can pose formidable risks to companies. Someone needs to have official responsibility for these matters and the general counsel is well suited for this task. Effective lawyering has always left room for evaluation of non-legal considerations. With the intense scrutiny that companies face in today's world, it is important to consider how conduct that is technically legal can still be damaging to the company's reputation, community goodwill, or its relationships with stakeholders. Corporate decisions in these areas need to be evaluated against a company's risk appetite, integrity, and values.

Indeed there is a trend toward consolidating control of some of the corporate functions that address these legal-adjacent issues within the legal department. For example, the *ACC Law Department Management 2016 Report* showed that the legal department often oversees the government affairs function (44 percent); security (23 percent); public policy (21 percent); and communications (19 percent).

Even if the general counsel is not directly responsible for these matters, management should proactively seek the advice of the chief legal officer on these issues. The legal department cannot be left out of the decision-making on such matters if an ethical culture is to thrive.

#5—Business units regularly include the legal department in decision-making

If the CEO's and board's relationships with the general counsel set the cultural tone at the top, then the interaction between business units and the rest of the legal department create the mood in the middle. Companies must develop a culture where in-house counsel are regularly consulted in decision-making at levels below the general counsel. This ensures that legal and risk considerations are taken into account as new products, services, or business practices are developed.

Inclusion of the legal department in the decision-making process is especially essential as businesses expand into areas where the law is uncertain. It is those gray areas where legal counsel can be most helpful in guiding the company in a manner that follows its corporate ethical compass. Having counsel involved on the front-end of decisions is the difference between having a legal department that is engaged, involved, and actively preventative from a compliance standpoint, and one that just plays clean up after something goes wrong. Greater interaction between the business and legal teams also reinforces the idea that risk management is everyone's responsibility. In today's hyper-regulatory business environment, ignorance of the law will not shield an executive from indictment. The interaction between a business and its attorneys will look different across companies, but from the board's perspective, if such interaction is not occurring, that might be a sign that corporate culture is underemphasizing legal and compliance risk.

The need for communication and collaboration with other functions is not limited to outward-facing business units—the internal-facing business units should also have established relationships with the legal department. Data security, for example, involves the law department and IT; the human resources department should provide information to support legal conclusions on employment matters; lawyers should be involved with the government affairs team to help define regulatory and legislative goals. In fact, because the legal department is so integral to the operations of a company, its reach can be a good proxy by which to measure communication and effective risk management across functions. If the board cannot find evidence of such collaboration, it could indicate a "siloed" corporate culture that exposes the company to unnecessary risks.

One important caveat to the above: However a company determines to facilitate the legal department's involvement in decisions, it should not be done in a way that negates individual lawyers' accountability to the general counsel. Several of the notable corporate scandals have been blamed, in part, on a lack of accountability between the general counsel and the line attorneys who had often seen signs of questionable corporate conduct. In other words, the attorneys who reported directly to business leaders were less effective in elevating issues of concern to the appropriate levels within the company. There should be general counsel oversight—perhaps a dotted-line reporting structure—over lawyers assigned to the business units to ensure proper reporting of issues of concern.

. . . .

The following excerpt provides an example of a corporate law compliance program—namely, with respect to insider trading. Every publicly-traded company (and privately-held enterprise that is privy to confidential information relating to publicly-held companies) must be vigilant with respect to this prohibition. As such, the following provides a useful illustration of a law compliance program directed towards a specified illegality. Note that additional coverage of insider trading is provided in Chapter 9 of this book.

COMPLIANCE PROGRAMS FOR INSIDER TRADING*
By Marc I. Steinberg & John Fletcher
47 SMU L. Rev. 1783 (1994)

I.   Basic Requirements of Compliance Programs

Organizations should access the nature of their business to determine the risks of insider trading and the need for preventive policies. A key determinant is the extent that an enterprise's personnel come into possession of material, nonpublic information about publicly-traded securities during the course of their work. . . . At a minimum, any [such] organization should examine such factors as the size and nature of its business in the adoption of insider trading policies and

---

* Originally appearing in Vol. 47 SMU Law Review No. 5. Reprinted with permission from the Law Review, the authors, and the Southern Methodist University Dedman School of Law.

procedures. The organization should reexamine its findings in light of changed conditions on a periodic basis.

If an organization determines the need for an insider trading policy, the policy adopted may focus on three areas: (1) educating employees about the prohibitions and risks of insider trading; (2) implementing procedures to help prevent and detect abuses in this context; and (3) adopting mechanisms to limit access to confidential information. Even a very general policy should cover the first area of educating the organization's employees and disseminating a clear statement that articulates the basic prohibitions against insider trading (and tipping).

A.   Elements of an Education Policy

All insider trading policies should provide a concise, nontechnical definition of what constitutes insider trading. The definition of insider trading should make clear that both trading and tipping are prohibited and that the tipping prohibition covers spouses, members of households, and friends. Likewise, the definition should make clear that insider trading prohibitions apply to securities of non-clients. The policy, moreover, should provide definitions of key terms like "materiality" and "nonpublic." [The definitions of these terms are covered in Chapter 9 of this book.] It is also helpful to provide examples of inside information that an organization's personnel would be likely to encounter. The policy should outline the potentially severe consequences of insider trading, such as incurring substantial civil and criminal penalties. It should also specify the impact of violations on employment with the organization. Finally, the policy should provide the name of an individual who may be contacted to answer any questions about the policy.

B.   Administrative Steps to Implement Policy

An organization should adopt procedures only if it has the commitment to observe and to enforce them. The policies and procedures implemented should reflect the level of risk that insider trading in the organization may eventuate. [For example,] an enterprise whose operations involve relatively few opportunities for insider trading may have the need to adopt only a basic policy statement. . . .

To implement a basic education policy, an organization should distribute copies of the policy to all personnel. [Consideration should be given whether the company should] obtain signed acknowledgments that the policy was read, understood, and will be followed. The organization should consider holding training sessions to explain the policy. The organization should designate a person or a committee to monitor the implementation of the policy. This compliance official or committee should include high-level personnel [such as senior in-house legal counsel]. . . . Organizations should also [provide] employees with a mechanism that would allow them to ask questions about the policy and to report possible violations in an anonymous fashion and without fear of retribution [whistleblower procedures and protection].

Generally, the greatest flaws in existing compliance programs relate to enforcement and documentation. An organization whose compliance program lacks these attributes incurs the risk of substantial liability exposure. One study on the legal effectiveness of compliance programs shows that outside observers often view them with skepticism. Courts may well scrutinize the procedures adopted to assess their implementation, probable effectiveness, the timing of their implementation, and the seriousness of the organization's commitment to the procedures. An organization that cannot document the efforts taken pursuant to its compliance program will face a significant burden when trying to prove its effectiveness to an outside party. In this respect, an organization would be ill advised to adopt any nonessential component of a program that cannot be feasibly implemented. Stated succinctly, once a compliance program is adopted, the organization "must abide by it."

Any organization whose employees may have access to material, nonpublic information would be prudent to promulgate a basic education policy. Many organizations whose operations merit a compliance program will implement additional procedures that are aimed at the prevention and detection of insider trading. . . .

II. Elements of a Publicly-Held Corporation's Compliance Program

An insider trading compliance program for a publicly-held corporation should focus primarily on securities issued by that corporation and its affiliates. The program also should address the additional reporting requirements and trading restrictions imposed on statutory insiders by Section 16 of the Securities Exchange Act. Since these rules affect officers, directors, and ten percent shareholders, corporations should adopt additional policies to provide these persons with the necessary guidance for compliance. Moreover, corporate compliance programs should provide guidance to employees on how to respond to inquiries from outsiders to avoid risks of tipping material, nonpublic information [Regulation FD compliance].

1. Procedures and Policies Directed at All Corporate Personnel

A corporate compliance program with respect to insider trading should encompass the basic elements and administrative steps outlined earlier. . . . A policy directed at all personnel of a large [corporation] should be as clear and concise as practicable. Such a policy should stress that the prohibition on insider trading encompasses trading as well as tipping material, nonpublic information to others, including spouses, minor children, and other relatives residing in the same household, and securities issued by *any* publicly-held corporation. The policy should provide examples of insider trading that are tailored to the corporate context. As discussed below, the policy should instruct employees not to respond to inquiries from outsiders and to refer all such inquiries to a designated [inside attorney] or compliance official.

2. Specific Policies for Directors and Officers

The federal securities laws place certain restrictions on the conduct of officers and directors with respect to their securities transactions. Accordingly, a corporate compliance program should seek to provide guidance to such persons. . . .

As a general matter, the policy should require all officers and directors to consult with [an in-house attorney] or a designated compliance person before purchasing or selling securities issued by the corporation. This policy should extend to transactions in options or other derivative securities that relate to the issuer's securities. These measures should assist insiders to comply with the restrictions placed on them by applicable law.

The policy for high-level officials should provide a more detailed treatment of the basis for prohibitions on insider trading than the policy provided to all employees. For example, the policy may provide examples that such officials will be more likely to encounter than the average employee. The company should [also institute] "blackout periods" during which officers and directors would not be allowed to trade as a matter of company policy. For example, the company could prohibit trading three weeks before and forty-eight hours after public announcement (and dissemination) of the company's earnings. The policy may also provide guidance to officers and directors so that they may determine whether they are affiliates and thereby face restrictions on the resale of their securities.

a. *Reporting Requirements Under Section 16(a)*

Section 16(a) of the Exchange Act requires officers, directors, and ten percent beneficial holders of an equity security of certain publicly-held enterprises to report their ownership of such securities. Such publicly-held corporations should consider the adoption of a policy that explains the requirements under Section 16(a) and establishes procedures that help ensure that these statutory insiders file the required forms.... [T]he Commission [has] adopted rules under Section 16(a) that encourage such practices by requiring publicly-held companies to disclose any company procedures that assist insiders with Section 16 compliance and to disclose the names of any statutory insiders who failed to properly file the required forms.

The policy should explain the basic purpose of each form that must be filed under the Section 16(a) rules and the timing for the filing of each form. . . .

In addition to distributing a policy statement to all statutory insiders, companies also should consider establishing procedures designed to assist and monitor the compliance of these persons with Section 16(a) requirements. In connection therewith, the company should designate a senior person, such as a senior attorney in the compliance or legal department, to be in charge of assisting insiders and tracking their compliance. . . .

b. Avoiding Short Swing Liability Under Section 16(b)

The policy statement directed at the statutory insiders of a publicly-held corporation may include procedures designed to avoid Section 16(b) liability for short swing profits. [Generally, directors, officers, and shareholders owning more than ten percent of a class of equity security (such as common stock) must disgorge all profits made if they buy and sell or sell and buy such company's securities within a six-month period.] Such a policy statement should describe Section 16(b)'s application to short swing trading and its disgorgement of profit provision. . . . The policy also may explain key concepts underlying Section 16(b). These concepts include, for example, the grant and exercise of options, the concept of beneficial owner, and the requisite holding periods.

3. Public Disclosure Procedures

Insider trading compliance programs for publicly-held companies should address procedures that control public disclosures made by their officers and employees. [This is particularly true in light of SEC Regulation FD which prohibits the making of selective disclosure of material nonpublic information.] Such procedures should minimize the risk that officers and employees tip confidential, material information to outsiders when fielding inquiries from persons outside of the company. Companies should consider distributing a concise policy to all personnel, instructing them to refer all inquiries about the company to a designated corporate officer or spokesperson. It may be beneficial to include this policy in the company's insider trading compliance material so that employees may better understand the potential consequences of tipping information to outsiders.

. . . .

The policy adopted may provide specific guidance on responding to inquiries from investors and analysts. One such policy would be to refrain from disclosing material information

. . . unless it has already been publicly released in a prior disclosure. A policy may elect to guide the information officer's response in a variety of situations like responding to rumors not attributable to the company, inquiries into sensitive topics such as mergers and acquisitions, and inquiries about the accuracy of analysts' reports. Selective disclosure of material information to specified analysts, shareholders, or the media must be avoided and is illegal under Regulation FD.

The Sarbanes-Oxley Act (SOX) of 2002 and Dodd-Frank Act of 2010 enacted significant provisions with respect to whistleblowers. These provisions impact the in-house lawyer's role with respect to corporate law compliance. The excerpt of the following article provides an overview of this subject.

MINIMIZING CORPORATE LIABILITY EXPOSURE WHEN THE WHISTLE BLOWS IN THE POST SARBANES-OXLEY ERA*

By Marc I. Steinberg & Seth A. Kaufman
30 J. Corp. L. 445 (2005)

Over the past [two decades], numerous newspapers and magazines have featured stories discussing whistleblowers. From Sherron Watkins at Enron to Cynthia Cooper at WorldCom, employees who reported perceived corporate fraud have received widespread attention. With this increased public focus, Congress chose to provide statutory protection in the whistleblower corporate or securities law context through enactment of the Sarbanes-Oxley Act of 2002 (SOX). [This whistleblower protection has been enhanced by the enactment of the Dodd-Frank Act of 2010, such as the provision of a lucrative whistleblower bounty program.[6]]

Prior to SOX, federal and state statutes (as well as common law) existed to protect whistleblowers in specific settings. For example, the False Claims Act provides protection to individuals

---

* Reprinted with the permission of the Journal of Corporation Law and the authors.

6 *See Digital Realty Trust, Inc. v. Somers*, 138 S. Ct. 767 (2018) (holding that to be a "whistleblower" within the scope of the anti-retaliation provision of the Dodd-Frank Act, a subject employee must report original information regarding a federal securities law violation to the SEC).

who report fraudulent activities committed against the federal government. The Energy Reorganization Act provides similar protection for employees in the energy industry. Individuals who deal with issues concerning the manufacture, distribution, and disposal of toxic substances receive protection under the whistleblower provision in the Toxic Substance Control Act (TSCA). Whistleblower protection provided by the Clean Water Act protects employees who work in the water treatment industry. As another example, the Occupational Safety and Health Administration (OSHA) enforces whistleblower protection provisions under several different statutes associated with worker safety and environmental protection. States likewise provide some degree of whistleblower protection, but each state's laws can vary regarding the persons protected, the procedural requirements for establishing the existence of retaliation, the type of evidence required to prove retaliation, and the available remedies. In part to eliminate the "patchwork and vagaries of current state [whistleblower] laws," Congress enacted SOX.

In their scope of coverage, SOX [and the Dodd-Frank Act] provide greater consistency and protection for whistleblowers than state laws. [These Acts] also promote a more hospitable environment for whistleblowers in the corporate and securities context through a decreased threat of employer retaliation. This consequence is due to the fact that [these Acts extend to] employees who report covered corporate fraud that may violate several federal statutes while other federal whistleblower provisions generally provide more limited protection. Furthermore, [these Acts] hold employers, employees, and other specified persons both civilly and criminally liable for retaliating against whistleblowers.

CHAPTER 8

WORKING WITH OUTSIDE COUNSEL

WHY USE OUTSIDE COUNSEL?

Why do corporations even use outside counsel? After all, as discussed in a previous chapter, many talented law firm attorneys want to work in-house. And plenty of excellent students graduate from law school each year. Why not just hire enough competent attorneys internally to handle *all* a corporation's legal matters?

Corporations use outside counsel for many reasons. One reason is to acquire expertise and resources on complex, highly-specialized or significant matters that most in-house legal departments are not equipped to handle, such as mergers or acquisitions, "bet the company" litigation, large construction projects, bond issuances, or initial public offerings.

While lawyers at a firm typically specialize in a specific practice area, many in-house counsel are highly-skilled generalists, handling a varied workload.[1] While very adept at providing day-to-day legal counseling on core operations, they must rely on subject-matter experts in law firms for complex or highly-specialized legal matters.

Large firm lawyers handle the same types of matters day-in and day-out for multiple clients, and they have been well-trained to do so by other experienced attorneys in their firms. As a result, they become subject matter experts in their respective fields. In addition to this expertise, outside counsel bring the wider perspective gained from representing multiple clients on similar matters and can offer their clients insight into how they handled the same or similar matters for other corporations.

---

[1]   Fontaine, *So You Want to Go In-House?*, NALSC.org (Fall 2013), http://www.nalsc.org/wp-content/uploads/2018/05/NALSC-Newsletter-Fall-2013.pdf, *reprinted from* Corp. Couns. (Sept. 30, 2013).

Corporations also use outside counsel to handle matters that occur on a sporadic basis, like litigation and acquisitions. Litigation tends to come in waves. If a corporation hired enough in-house lawyers to handle all its discovery, pre-trial motions, trials, and appeals, it would have a huge staff, busy when the company had litigation but twiddling their thumbs when it did not. Using outside counsel allows corporations to be more flexible because they do not have to hire and fire attorneys internally as their workloads go up or down.

Similarly, if a company hired enough in-house lawyers to handle its acquisitions internally, the team would be busy at "peak" demand times when the company was actively acquiring businesses but would be sitting around during the "valleys," while waiting for another deal to come along. For this reason, most corporate legal departments staff for the "valleys" and not the "peaks."[2]

Attorneys in law firms, on the other hand, (at least in "good times") stay busy by working on several cases or transactions for multiple clients—sometimes simultaneously. When one case or deal slows down, they hope another one for a different client heats up.

Corporations also hire outside counsel when the volume of work on a particular matter is too great to handle internally. Law firms are excellent at providing bandwidth on labor- or time-intensive matters. Most law departments are staffed with very competent and experienced lawyers, but their staff are limited. For example, a publicly-traded company with $1 billion in revenue may only have 8–12 attorneys, including the chief legal officer.[3]

---

[2]   *See Law Department Metrics Benchmarking Survey 2013*, ALM Legal Intelligence (2013), at 14, http://www.lexisnexis.com/counsellink/documents/2013-ALM-Lexis-Law-Department-Metrics-Benchmarking-Survey.pdf, *archived at* https://perma.cc/LV4F-GCZX ("In deciding in-house staffing levels, it is first necessary to analyze the need for legal services and establish a 'steady state' of required services. A steady state of legal services can often be determined by taking a multi-year view of the matters handled and excluding the top (largest) five to seven matters each year. The resulting fees associated with the remaining matters can often help identify a steady state of legal services.").

[3]   *Id.* at 20 (reporting that companies with under $100 million in revenue have an average 2.5 lawyers in the law department; those with $100 to $999 million in revenue, an average 6.7 lawyers; those with $1 to 4.9 billion, an average 15.5 lawyers; and those with more than $5 billion in revenue, 49.2 lawyers); *see also Chief Legal Officer*

Law firms excel at providing surge capacity when needed and can bring in resources generally not available in the corporate setting. They can assemble teams of attorneys, legal assistants, executive assistants, and other staff on short notice and pull "all nighters," if necessary.[4] Additionally, law firms have the ability to quickly turn around multiple drafts of complex transactional documents, handle one-million-page document reviews, and expeditiously complete time-sensitive internal investigations in an expeditious manner. Sometimes, as discussed in Chapter 3, law firms may even "second" one of their attorneys to a client's office on a short- or long-term basis to assist with overflow work, special projects, or to fill in when an in-house attorney is on leave or departs suddenly. This type of relationship—known as a secondment—typically benefits both the corporation and the law firm.

Law firms also serve as an available and expert resource to provide needed consultations or "second opinions" to inside legal counsel where deemed appropriate. Consultations with existing outside counsel can be useful on crucial issues or when inside counsel is uncertain.[5] Second opinions, especially from independent attorneys, can help verify key decisions or legal theories, to help assess settlement values, or to reassess a strategy when confidence in primary counsel has been shaken.[6]

Some companies hire outside counsel because they do not have in-house attorneys. Indeed, many small, emerging, or fledgling companies have day-to-day legal issues but either do not need, or cannot afford, a full-time general counsel. Some of these companies rely exclusively on law firm counsel while others use "outsourced general counsel" services.[7] Outsourced

---

2011 Survey Results, Ass'n of Corp. Couns. (Oct. 2011), at 12 ("As would be expected, the number of lawyers is generally proportional to the size of the organization, as measured by the total number of employees and/or its annual revenue. Public corporations, whether foreign or domestic, have larger legal staffs than other types of organizations.").

[4]   *See Jawboning Key to Managing Outside Lawyers*, Corp. Legal Times (Aug. 1993).

[5]   *See* Toothman, *Managing Lawyers & Legal Fees: A Guide to Integrated Management of Legal Services*, The Devil's Advoc. (Feb. 2, 2014), http://www.devils advocate.com/manage.html, *archived at* https://perma.cc/LV4F-GCZX.

[6]   *Id.* (noting that "second opinions do not cost much; it takes far less time to review a file than it takes to build it").

[7]   *See* Robbins, *Options for Companies That Don't Employ GCs*, Tex. Law. (Apr. 4, 2005). Examples of such firms include Reiter, Brunel & Dunn, PLLC (http://www.

general counsel provide corporate counsel services on an as-needed basis at a fraction of the cost of hiring a full-time general counsel or relying solely on law firms.[8] Most outsourced general counsel charge on a project-by-project basis or use fixed-fee monthly engagements.[9]

The lion's share of companies, however, do not send 100% of their legal work to outside counsel. Generally, companies with annual revenues between $1 billion and $4.9 billion typically spend approximately 60% of their legal budgets on outside counsel and 40% of their budgets on lawyers inside the company.[10] These percentages, however, can vary significantly depending on variables such as the number of corporate employees served by the law department, the industry within which the company operates, and the size of the law department.[11]

A final reason why corporations may use outside counsel, at least in part, is for "cover." Large, name-brand firms can provide "CYA" insurance coverage for a general counsel if anything goes awry on a significant matter.[12] When reporting to the CEO or board of directors, the general counsel does not want to be second-guessed on his or her choice of outside counsel (assuming the general counsel has the authority to retain outside counsel). General counsels had rather report that they retained the "best" firm for the case but that for some reason (unrelated to the selection of counsel, of course) a bleak outcome resulted for the company. Many general counsel also believe that if they are

---

outsourcegc.com/overview-of-an-independent-general-counsel/, *archived at* https://perma.cc/XAJ3-6WRH) and Lancaster Helling (http://www.lancasterhelling.com/why-were-different/, *archived at* https://perma.cc/6532-QC7A).

8   *Id.*

9   *Id.*

10   Maleske, *How to Cut Outside Counsel Spend: How Pressured Law Department Leaders Have Cut Costs and Stuck to Budgets*, Inside Couns. (July 1, 2011), https://www.law.com/almID/4e09f528150ba0562c000248/, *archived at* https://perma.cc/36YW-4LZ4; *see also Law Department Metrics Benchmarking Survey 2013, supra* note 2, at 162.

11   *See* Maleske, *supra* note 10.

12   *See* Scherl, *Hiring a Law Firm: Does Size Really Matter*, Corp. Couns. (Jan. 3, 2014), http://www.corpcounsel.com/id=1202635942367/Hiring-a-Law-Firm:-Does-Size-Really-Matter, *archived at* https://perma.cc/8U27-XVZR ("[E]ngaging a very large, very well-known law firm may or may not be the right choice for the matter at hand but, invariably, if something were to go wrong and fingers were going to be pointed, it was usually assumed that the choice of a large law firm would insulate the decision-maker from any culpability, as he or she went with the known commodity.").

comfortable with a hire and have good reasons for hiring a firm, they will not be second-guessed by their boards.

WHAT TYPE OF WORK IS TYPICALLY SENT TO OUTSIDE COUNSEL?

For the reasons outlined above, matters requiring specialized legal expertise and knowledge are generally outsourced to law firms (at least in part) if they occur on an episodic basis, require more labor or time than the law department can supply, and/or involve significant risk or potential exposure for the company. These matters most often include:

- Complex Litigation
- Government Relations
- Employment/Labor
- Transactions
- Patent/Intellectual Property Work
- Due Diligence
- E-Discovery
- Environmental, Health and Safety
- Antitrust
- Tax
- Employee Benefits/ERISA
- Capital Markets
- SEC Filings
- Corporate Governance
- Bankruptcy
- Banking
- E-Commerce
- Cloud Computing[13]

---

[13]   *See 2015 ACC Global Census: A Profile of In-House Counsel*, Ass'n of Corp. Couns. (Dec. 2015), at 11, https://www.acc.com/sites/default/files/resources/vl/purchase Only/1411926_2.pdf, *archived at* https://perma.cc/4JUR-PD42; *ACC Legal Department*

Of these matters, litigation tends to be the most expensive for most companies (both monetarily and time-wise), followed closely by major transactions.[14] Many companies internally staff a number of the above matters, such as in-house counsel preparing the company's periodic SEC filings.[15]

Companies in different industries typically send specific matters to outside counsel more than companies in other industries.[16] For example, manufacturing companies with large research and development efforts, such as the pharmaceutical industry, may expend a great deal of outside "legal spend" to protect or defend their intellectual property. Conversely, companies that provide services, such as health care, may use outside counsel more on operational legal issues, while retail companies with many locations and employees may outsource more real estate and employment law matters. Finally, corporations operating in highly-regulated industries, like financial services that have operations abroad and that are publicly-traded, may spend more on compliance and government affairs.

CRITERIA FOR SELECTING OUTSIDE COUNSEL

Legal services are largely a commodity offered in an *extremely* competitive environment. Thousands of competent lawyers are experts in their respective fields and professionals in every sense of the word. So how does inside counsel decide to

---

Benchmarking 2018 Report: Large Company Supplement, at 17; *2013 Law Department Benchmarking Survey, supra* note 2, at 205. *See generally The Criteria In-House Counsel Use to Hire and Fire Outside Lawyers: A Roundtable Discussion*, N.J. L. J. (June 16, 1997) (listing litigation, commercial lending, environmental, trademark, arbitration, antitrust, tax, mergers and acquisitions, and ERISA matters as those typically outsourced).

[14]   Interview with John Torres, Executive Vice President and Chief Legal Officer, Lennox International Inc., in Dallas, Tex. (June 21, 2019).

[15]   Some corporations hire attorneys to handle matters historically assigned to outside counsel, including contract negotiation and administration, employment matters, employee benefits, and regulatory filings. *See* DeFelice, *Best Practices in Management of Outside Counsel*, 6 *International In-House Counsel Journal*, No. 23 (2013), at 1. According to experts, "the expansion in size and quality of in-house legal departments, some with dozens and even hundreds of lawyers has resulted in a dramatic influx of well-trained, highly skilled in-house attorneys who build strong attorney-client relationships with their clients in the business and provide a wide range of legal services with little or no involvement of outside lawyers," *id.*

[16]   *See Law Department Metrics Benchmarking Survey 2013, supra* note 2, at 166.

whom to send the work? This section examines the criteria and methods in-house counsel use in selecting outside counsel.

Top Quality Legal Work

Above all, corporations want attorneys who perform top quality legal work. John Torres, Executive Vice President and Chief Legal Officer at Lennox International Inc., describes this criterion as the "price of admission" or the "table stakes."[17] Legal skills are an "absolute expectation of attorneys by corporate counsel,"[18] and attorneys who do not excel will not even be considered.

The complexity and significance of the specific matter at hand may influence the selection of outside counsel.[19] "If it is a 'bet the company' issue, a client needs the best firm it can afford. But for commodity-type work, a client does not need a senior partner at an *American Lawyer 100* firm. Basically, a client should only pay for what it needs."[20]

Providing top quality legal work is more than just being competent. In today's highly competitive market focused on high-level productivity and cost effectiveness, a lawyer must also:

- Put the "client's interests first" and be "breathtakingly good when analyzing issues, negotiating settlements, preparing briefs, or appearing in court"[21]

- Exercise solid judgment

- Keep up with changes in the law and practice

- Provide excellent client service

- Develop strong relationships with clients

---

[17]   Interview with John Torres, *supra* note 14.

[18]   *The BTI Client Service All-Stars 2014*, BTI Consulting Group (2014), at 5.

[19]   *See* Burns, *The Still Imperfect Relationship Between In-House and Outside Counsel*, 24 Of Couns. 10 (2005).

[20]   *Id.*

[21]   Herrmann, *The 5 Deadly Sins of Outside Counsel*, Above the Law (Feb. 17, 2014), http://abovethelaw.com/2014/02/the-5-deadly-sins-of-outside-counsel/, *archived at* https://perma.cc/388Y-BF9C.

- Work closely with other professionals and outside vendors
- Provide business advice when requested in addition to legal advice
- Be skilled at budgets and project management
- Be flexible and open to new approaches to practicing law

Specialization

Corporations are looking for the best outside lawyers to serve their business needs. Twenty-five years ago, companies hired one large, full-service law firm to handle most of their legal needs. Today, because many corporations operate in highly regulated, increasingly complex, and global environments, they hire (in addition to large firms) several small, mid-sized, and boutique law firms that focus on a handful of highly-specialized practice areas. If corporations used to look for someone who made "bottles," today they want someone who makes "red bottles out of recycled glass in Italy." Specialization is a key consideration for inside counsel when hiring outside counsel.

No lawyer or firm is capable of learning or keeping up with all the constantly emerging and evolving fields of law. Since 1970, the number of practice areas has increased dramatically.[22] Entirely new areas of practice include:

- Class Action Litigation
- Product Liability Litigation
- Environmental Law
- Computer Law
- Historic Preservation Law
- Animal Rights Law
- Intellectual Property Litigation
- White Collar Criminal Law

---

[22]   Jones, *Forecasting the Legal Employment Market*, LSAC Annual Meeting and Educational Conference (May 31, 2012).

- Securities Fraud Litigation
- Employment Law
- Privacy Law
- Healthcare Law
- Telecommunications Law
- Securitization
- Privatization
- Hostile Takeovers
- Cross-Border Transactions
- Energy and Natural Resources Law
- Land Use Law
- Endangered Species Law
- Toxic Substances Litigation
- Cybersecurity
- E-Commerce[23]

Meanwhile, practice areas that existed in 1970—such as immigration law, patent prosecution, premises liability law, and entertainment law—have grown exponentially.[24]

As the practice of law becomes more specialized and lawyers concentrate in particular areas, the competence level of the specialists increases, only adding to an extremely competitive market. Lawyers who restrict their practices to one particular practice area and handle scores of matters per year in that area will, of course, be much more experienced and efficient than a general practitioner who might work on only one such matter over the course of a year.

Cost

Cost is an important factor because legal services are expensive. The hourly rate charged by lawyers within a particular firm, however, is only one part of the cost analysis.

---

[23]   *Id.*
[24]   *Id.*

Sometimes, a lawyer whose hourly rate is considerably higher produces better results more quickly than a "cheaper" attorney, and in the end, is more cost-effective. For example, an attorney who bills $750 per hour and who is experienced and focused on achieving her client's goals may be a better selection than a lawyer who bills $300 per hour, particularly if the "cheaper" lawyer is not experienced or is more focused on billing hours rather than helping the client reach its desired results.

Large firms traditionally raise their billing rates on an annual basis, typically by sending out a well-crafted letter announcing that rates have gone up (such as 5%)[25] over the previous year. But some clients are beginning to push back on rate increases by sending letters of their own to their outside counsel that they will not accept fee increases from any outside counsel in the coming year. In a buyer's market where the supply of legal services exceeds demand, most firms yield to these pressures in order to keep the work, realizing that if they do not secure the work, one of their competitors will.

Willingness to Enter into
Alternative Fee Arrangements

Some corporations consider a law firm's willingness to enter into innovative non-hourly billing arrangements when hiring outside counsel. More and more corporations are looking for firms that are more flexible in offering compensation methods where payments to them are based on something other than billable hours (i.e., use of alternative fee arrangements).[26] And many chief legal officers are encouraging their existing outside counsel to transition to alternative fee arrangements. Firms

---

[25]   *See Chief Legal Officer 2011 Survey Results, supra* note 3, at 41 (noting that the median rate increase for 2011 was 5%).

[26]   *See* 2018 Chief Legal Officer Survey: An Altman Weil Flash Survey, at iii, http://www.altmanweil.com//dir_docs/resource/154F22DC-E519-4CE2-991D-492A0448 C74F_document.pdf, *archived at* https://perma.cc/WTW6-3PRG. (noting that 63% of departments report they negotiate fixed, capped, or alternative fees); *see also Norton Rose Fulbright's 10th Annual Litigation Trends Report* (2013), at 24. For example, GlaxoSmithKline increased its use of alternative billing arrangements from 3% to 68%; United Technologies Corporations' use of such arrangements is more than 70%; Home Depot's more than 68%, and Pfizer uses only alternative billing arrangements. *See* Anderson, *Tug of War: Firm Profits vs. In-House Savings*, Esq. Recruiting, LLC (Mar. 19, 2013), http://esquirerecruiting.com/wp-content/uploads/2013/03/Tug-of-War-Firm-Profits-and-In-House-Savings76.pdf, *archived at* https://perma.cc/7JYB-CXQR.

open to alternative fee arrangements may find themselves getting work over those that are not.

Corporations favor non-traditional billing arrangements because they more closely align the law firm's interests with their own.[27] Because alternative fee arrangements eschew the billable hour in exchange for a more measurable model of compensation, they remove disincentives for efficiency.

Alternative fee arrangements are also attractive to corporations because they provide a more predictable model of compensation than the traditional hourly model.[28] Corporate clients are looking for ways to better predict their legal spend, which helps the corporate law department with its internal budgeting process.

When entering into an alternative fee arrangement, both parties must carefully consider the client's principal objectives and how to achieve them in a cost-effective manner. The arrangement should also be "fair" to both sides. Alternative fee arrangements should not be considered "zero-sum games" in which one party wins and the other loses.[29]

But some corporate counsel resist alternative fee arrangements. For example, Mark Evans, Executive Vice President at Nestle Waters North America Inc., does not use alternative fees because he is concerned that he would not have the "full buy-in" of outside counsel who might staff his matters with less-experienced attorneys.[30] Instead, because of his "intensely close" partnering relationships with outside counsel, he sets strict budgets and expects outside counsel to follow them.[31]

Personal Relationships

Personal relationships are paramount in the hiring of outside counsel. Indeed, most outside counsel hiring decisions are based, not on the law firm, but on the individual attorney,

---

[27]   See Shomper & Courson, *Alternative Fees for Litigation: Improved Control and Higher Value*, Am. Corp. Couns. Ass'n Docket 18, No. 5 (2000).

[28]   *See id.*

[29]   *Id.*

[30]   *Id.*

[31]   *Id.*

her talents and how she has proven herself over time. Often, when lawyers move laterally to other firms, their clients follow them and their expertise, rather than staying with their prior firm.

According to Gene DeFelice, the Managing Director and General Counsel and Corporate Secretary of Novo Strategic Partners LLC, outside counsel should "understand the real relationship is with individual lawyers and not the entire firm or the entire practice."[32] For this reason, DeFelice insists on interviewing and selecting the key lawyers with whom he will work.[33] "It does not help to be working with the firm that has the best lawyer in a particular field if one is not working with that lawyer."[34]

Outside counsel are sometimes selected, at least in part, due to their relationship with the general counsel or someone else in the company. Outside counsel may be a law school classmate, a former law partner, or a personal friend.[35] Inside counsel, who place great emphasis on their relationships with outside counsel, want to make sure outside counsel knows the company, the company's needs, and will respond expeditiously to the task at hand.

Even if corporate counsel will hire a new attorney— particularly one highly recommended by another general counsel—they would prefer to hire an attorney with whom they already have a relationship and in whom they have confidence, especially on matters with high stakes. A new attorney is untested. He may not be as equipped to handle a sophisticated problem, and he may need to devote significant time "getting up to speed" on the matter as well as learning how his new client wants things done.

---

[32]   DeFelice, *supra* note 15, at 2.
[33]   *Id.*
[34]   *Id.*
[35]   *See* Burns, *supra* note 19.

Diverse Staffing

When hiring outside counsel, many corporations devoted to furthering diversity in the legal profession[36] may consider whether a firm can staff its matters with diverse lawyers especially at senior levels.[37] Some companies that implement diversity initiatives require that a certain percentage of their legal matters go to lawyers in minority- and women-owned law firms.[38]

One way companies identify diverse firms is through websites that routinely report law firm diversity efforts. In 2009, Vault and the Minority Corporate Counsel Association (MCCA)[39] launched the Law Firm Diversity Database,[40] an online database developed in cooperation with Accenture, Bank of America, Microsoft, PPG Industries, Sara Lee, and Wal-Mart to support the Call to Action, an effort launched by top general counsel to advance diversity in the legal profession. The database contains benchmarking information about the diversity programs at more than 250 major law firms, including quantitative data on the numbers of attorneys who are minorities, women, LGBTQ, or individuals with disabilities, as well as qualitative information regarding firms' diversity plans and initiatives. This tool allows in-house counsel to make side-

---

[36]   This includes expanding the inclusion of minorities and women at law firms as well as in the legal department. Many companies also consider diversity when recruiting new lawyers for their legal departments.

[37]   *See Law Firm Diversity Panel Highlights Role of Corporate Legal Departments*, Blog of Legal Times, http://legaltimes.typepad.com/blt/2013/03/law-firm-diversity-panel-highlights-role-of-corporate-legal-departments.html, *archived at* https://perma.cc/T9VX-8EMM (quoting Joseph West, former associate general counsel for Wal-Mart Stores Inc., who said Wal-Mart's legal department prioritized diversity in hiring outside counsel and found that the quality of work got better: "A broad net that was cast yielded greater results") (Mar. 25, 2013).

[38]   *See* Robert, *In-House: Growing Diversity Exists in Corporate Law Departments*, Chi. Law (July 2011).

[39]   *See* Minority Corporate Counsel Association, *Advancing Diversity, Inclusion and Equity*, MCCA.com, http://www.mcca.com (last visited Sept. 18, 2019). MCCA was founded in 1997 to advocate the expanded hiring, retention, and promotion of minority attorneys in corporate law departments and law firms that serve them. MCCA furthers its mission through the collection and dissemination of information about diversity in the legal profession. MCCA takes an inclusive approach to the definition of "diversity." Therefore, its research addresses issues of race/ethnicity, gender, sexual orientation, disability status, and generational differences that impact the legal profession's workforce. *Id.*

[40]   *Law Firm Diversity Database*, MCCA.com, http://mcca.vault.com, *archived at* https://perma.cc/H985-BLZ5.

by-side comparisons of diversity metrics, measure firms' progress over time, and measure their performance against industry-wide benchmarks. Similarly, *The American Lawyer* publishes an annual Diversity Scorecard that records the average number of full-time-equivalent minority attorneys— Asian American, African American, Latino or Hispanic, Native American and self-described multiracial attorneys—at Am Law 200 and National Law Journal 250 law firms.[41]

Some corporate legal departments hold their outside counsel accountable with respect to the number of diverse attorneys on their matters. They push outside counsel to staff their matters with diverse attorneys and require them to report the actual hours billed to their matters by diverse attorneys.[42] Earl Barnes, the Executive Vice President and Chief Legal Officer at AMITA Health "insist[s] on having a diverse group of people working on [his] matters," saying "firms find ways to make sure they have a diverse group of people working on [his] matters."[43]

Many corporate legal departments are focused on increasing the number of diverse attorneys within their own ranks and helping those attorneys develop and progress within the company. Craig Glidden, EVP and General Counsel of General Motors, asserts that change should begin at the top, "General counsel should be focused on building pipelines of diverse future attorneys in their respective legal departments and should also seek to identify and provide opportunities for diverse candidates to showcase their skills and leadership capabilities."[44] He adds that each attorney should also take control of his or her career

---

[41]   *See* The 2019 Diversity Scorecard, https://www.law.com/americanlawyer/2019/05/28/the-2019-diversity-scorecard/, *archived at* https://perma.cc/E7CJ-EA5X.

[42]   *See* Robinson, *Encouraging Diversity in Outside Counsel*, Inside Couns. (June 1, 2010) (advocating quarterly monitoring of the billable hours of the lawyers working on a company's matters to gain an indication of who is actually working on its matters and what level of work they perform), https://ccwomenofcolor.org/wp-content/uploads/2019/03/press_Encouraging-Diversity-in-Outside-Counsel.pdf, *archived at* https://perma.cc/DC7N-TLKT.

[43]   Robert, *supra* note 38.

[44]   *Change is Coming*, Diversity & The Bar Mag. (2018 Winter Issue), at 56, http://www.diversityandthebardigital.com/datb/winterdb_2018/MobilePagedArticle.action?articleId=1465422&app=false#articleId1465422, *archived at* https://perma.cc/Z778-FAYP.

and seek out opportunities to showcase his or her individual skills and talent.[45]

Key Relationships with Third Parties

Key relationships outside counsel holds with relevant parties may be another factor when hiring, particularly in litigation or government affairs. In a highly-regulated industry like insurance, which is regulated on a state-by-state basis, a former state department of insurance commissioner or friend of the current commissioner can be instrumental in securing a meeting with the "right" parties when faced with a regulatory or agency issue in the state. Similarly, lobbyists (many of whom are lawyers) are often hired because of their relationships with, and access to, legislators or their staffs.

Relationships can also be important in litigation matters. For example, for a securities fraud case brought in Texas state court, a "local" lawyer is likely preferred to one from a large New York firm. The local lawyer is likely to be viewed more favorably by jurors, and her relationships with judges and court staff can be instrumental. Even in transactional matters, a local attorney who has worked successfully with the attorney on the other side of the deal may be a better choice than one who has not.

Geography and Other Local Considerations

For certain matters, such as multi-jurisdictional cases or cross-border transactions, the venue of the case or location of the parties may be a dominant factor in the selection of outside counsel. The firm must have enough attorneys in the appropriate locations, or affiliations with other firms in those locales, to handle the client's needs, geographically, functionally, and specifically.[46]

Other considerations, particularly with litigation matters, include prior experience with the same opposing counsel in other matters; knowledge of local procedural rules or styles of practice; and reputation in a particular legal market. Lawyers who are capable in global markets are in demand by many companies, depending on the location of their business operations, because

---

[45]　*Id.*

[46]　*See* Burns, *supra* note 19.

of their knowledge, experience, language skills, and cultural acumen in a particular market.

METHODS USED TO SELECT OUTSIDE COUNSEL

In-house counsel can be selected in a variety of ways, including via (1) requests for proposals (RFPs); (2) referrals; (3) inherited outside counsel; (4) networking or speaking engagements; and (5) management and board member recommendations.[47]

Requests for Proposals

For certain matters, some companies resort to Requests for Proposals (RFPs), giving a select number of well-qualified law firms the opportunity to present why they are the best firm to handle the matter.[48]

Only a minority of corporate counsel currently use the RFP process to select outside counsel, although that number is increasing as more in-house counsel put their work out for competitive bids in an attempt to lower costs.[49] In the past, many firms were reluctant to respond to RFPs because they required a considerable investment of time and expense without necessarily the prospect of securing work. Today, however, many firms welcome the RFP process as a way to peddle the quality of their legal work, past results, pricing models, and excellent customer service.[50]

Inside counsel may use the RFP process for a number of reasons. For example, when a significant litigation or transaction matter arises, inside counsel may invite a firm with which he has not had a previous relationship to submit a written proposal. Similarly, some companies will use the RFP process to

---

[47]   See id.

[48]   See Ecker, *Proper Proposals*, Inside Couns. (June 2008).

[49]   See Thomas, *2010 ACC/Serengeti Managing Outside Counsel Survey*, Ass'n of Corp. Couns. & Serengeti Law (Oct. 25, 2010), at 24; *see also* Green, *More Frequent, Elaborate RFPs Challenge Outside Counsel*, Miami Bus. Rev. (Sept. 13, 2012) (citing survey that 42% of law firms have seen an increase in requests for proposals from in-house legal departments).

[50]   *See generally* Abrahams, *RFPs Qualifying to Qualify: Marketing the Law Firm*, L. J. Newsl. (Oct. 2, 2010).

hire law firms to handle all or most of their work in a specific area, such as labor and employment litigation; for discretionary spending items like compliance training for employees; or for matters in a new geographical location.[51]

Because the RFP process can be very time-consuming, most corporations will only seek proposals from a limited number of firms, including firms with which the company is familiar, as well as a select number of reputable firms with which the company does not have a prior relationship.[52] The submitted proposals allow the corporation to compare and contrast new firms against ones with which it has worked before.

Once firms submit their proposals, inside counsel will review the proposals and select their top candidates based on their selection criteria.[53] Some corporations will ask prospective law firms to come in for a face-to face meeting at the company, either as the final step to narrow down the top candidates in the RFP process or without an RFP.[54] At this meeting, the firms will usually give a presentation on why they believe they would be the best firm for the matter, as well as answer any questions the company might have.[55]

Referrals

The process of selecting outside counsel in most instances is much more informal than an RFP. The first step many inside counsel take when selecting outside counsel is asking for referrals among other attorneys in the corporate legal department or trusted sources at other companies or law firms.[56] Referrals provide inside counsel with easy access to a short list of potential candidates who have been recommended by other

---

[51]   See Ecker, *supra* note 48.

[52]   See *id.*

[53]   See *id.*

[54]   *Id.*

[55]   See Booden, et al., *Best Practices in Hiring Outside Counsel*, Ass'n of Corp. Couns. (2003), at 9.

[56]   Lyne, *The Pressure Is On: Though Happy in Their Jobs, General Counsels Surveyed Feel Squeezed by Management Over Legal Costs*, 14 Nat'l L. J. 24 (Sept, 9, 1991) (Of 350 respondents to a general counsel survey, 16% said they seek recommendations for outside counsel from other lawyers within their own companies and 32% reported that they seek recommendations from general counsels at other companies. Thirty-nine percent said they ask other law firms they work with for recommendations.).

sophisticated users of legal services and are usually more effective than an RFP.

Daniel J. Di-Lucchio, a principal in the management consulting firm Altman Weil, says he finds that in-house counsel will seldom or never hire new outside counsel because they are impressed with their work for an opposing party: "When I ask in-house lawyers how they choose firms, it is almost always through word of mouth and networking. I imagine occasionally some opposing lawyer will strike a chord, but it's rare."[57]

Counsel should "push [their personal contacts] for 'the best' in a particular field who has a demonstrated track record of achieving results for the client."[58] Theis Rice, Senior Vice President and Chief Compliance Officer at Trinity Industries, advises inside counsel to "pick outside counsel not based on breadth or all things they are best at but on the one thing you need done well."[59] Some of the questions inside counsel may ask when seeking a referral might include ones centered on results achieved, the fee structure used, ease of doing business, and any other stories about the representation that might be helpful in evaluating the lawyer and law firm.

Many corporate legal departments will keep a list of approved lawyers by subject matter expertise and region, so that when a need arises they know whom to call.[60] According to one expert, "It is important to have a stable of high quality lawyers who know how you work, understand your expectations, and are committed to exceeding them, and in whom you have confidence personally, professionally, and regarding individual subject matter areas."[61] Because of potential conflicts, the list often contains more than one attorney or law firm who can be called on a particular subject. Such a list can also provide a useful reference sheet when inside counsel is called by an attorney at a different company for a recommendation.

---

[57]   *Id.*

[58]   DeFelice, *supra* note 15, at 2.

[59]   Interview with S. Theis Rice, Senior Vice President and Chief Compliance Officer, Trinity Industries, in Dallas, Tex. (June 24, 2019).

[60]   *See* Lyne, *supra* note 56.

[61]   DeFelice, *supra* note 15, at 2.

"Inherited" Outside Counsel

Sometimes, outside counsel is "inherited" from a preceding general counsel. A company may have a long-standing relationship with a particular lawyer or law firm. Over the years, a relationship of trust may have developed between the client and outside counsel. Moreover, due to the nature of this relationship, outside counsel may have gained institutional knowledge that would be difficult (and expensive) to replace.

For these reasons, a new general counsel may be reluctant to transition to a different firm when he begins.[62] In many cases, it may be easier to continue with the established firm than to educate a new law firm and pay for any mistakes that it might make.[63]

Discovered Through Networking or Speaking Engagements

Sometimes outside counsel is initially unknown to the company but is a good CLE presenter on an important issue central to the company or an effective rainmaker.[64] For this reason, it is important for law firm attorneys to speak to groups to demonstrate their expertise and to place themselves in situations where they may get to know inside counsel, such as bar activities, CLE programs, and community events.

Many times, lawyers speak only to other law firm lawyers at local bar associations. While such speaking engagements can be useful in client development, counsel should focus their efforts on speaking at events that are attended by general counsel and senior managing attorneys, such as the SMU Dedman Law Corporate Counsel Symposium[65] or The General

---

[62]   *See generally* Burns, *supra* note 19.

[63]   *See id.*

[64]   It is important to note that name recognition gained as a result of speaking engagements is not necessarily evidence of expertise. DeFelice, *supra* note 15, at 2.

[65]   SMU Law Review, SMU Dedman Law Corporate Counsel Symposium, SMULawJournals.org, https://smulawjournals.org/smulr/symposia/ccs-details-to-come (last visited Sept. 18, 2019).

Counsel Forum's Annual Conference of General Counsel,[66] both of which are attended primarily by inside counsel.

Management and Board Member Recommendations

It is not uncommon for corporate executives and board members to weigh in on whom they believe should be hired by the company as outside counsel. Management and board members are intelligent, business-minded people who have good connections and a wealth of knowledge from their previous and current employment experiences. As a result, they may have excellent recommendations on specific outside counsel. Indeed, in some companies, CEOs play a significant role in identifying and selecting outside counsel.[67] It is also not uncommon for the board of directors to choose outside counsel, with the inside lawyer being of persuasive influence in this process.

IS A BIGGER FIRM BETTER THAN A SMALLER ONE?

Bigger firms are not necessarily better than smaller ones. For some legal challenges, such as class action lawsuits or certain cross-border transactions, the "horsepower" that a large firm can provide may be needed. Moreover, many general counsel may believe that hiring a large prestigious law firm provides them with "cover" should the contemplated transaction or litigation prove unsuccessful—or even worse—a disaster.

But large firms do not have a monopoly on legal talent. There are excellent attorneys in many small, mid-sized, and boutique firms, and corporations are not hesitant to go shopping. Nowadays companies hiring outside counsel tend to hire a mix of small, mid-sized, and large firms.

Small and mid-sized firms can be attractive even to big companies. Because they are particularly adept at understanding the importance of relationships and the ease of

---

[66]   *See, e.g.,* The General Counsel Forum website for more information on the 21st Annual Conference of General Counsel, https://www.tgcf.org/annual-conference/, *archived at* https://perma.cc/SC8B-TR2Y.

[67]   *See* LexisNexis Martindale-Hubbell, *State of the Profession Report: How Corporations Identify, Evaluate and Select Outside Counsel* (May 2005), at 3, https://www.businesswire.com/news/home/20051024005216/en/CEOs-Involved-Selection-Law-Firms-LexisNexis-Martindale-Hubbell, *archived at* https://perma.cc/V5G7-EFBZ.

doing business, they may be able to provide more personalized service. Moreover, these firms tend to charge hourly rates less than their large firm competitors, due in part to their lower overhead. Because they may be hungrier for new work and not nearly as bureaucratic as larger firms, they are often more flexible and open to alternative billing arrangements and fixed fees.[68] Finally, unlike larger firms, smaller firms rarely have to turn new clients away for conflicts.

Boutiques—firms that specialize in areas such as employment law, intellectual property, or securities matters—often offer as much expertise as large firms but without the associated price tag. This may explain why many large firm partners and associates are leaving to open their own small firms or making lateral moves to boutique firms.[69]

"PET PEEVES"

In-house counsel often have a "love-hate relationship" with their outside firms.[70] They depend on outside counsel in emergencies, look to them for top quality legal work, and rely heavily on their legal advice.[71] Corporate clients could not conduct business without outside counsel, but in-house counsel certainly have common "pet peeves" when it comes to working with outside counsel, leaving them frustrated, angry, and in many cases, unsatisfied. According to one survey of chief legal officers and general counsel at large corporations, 70% of corporate clients are so unsatisfied with their primary law firm that they would not recommend the firm to others.[72] It is

---

[68]   Mid-size firms are also much more likely to use alternative fee arrangements to charge clients. Firms with 201 to 500 attorneys used such fee arrangements in about 6 percent of matters in the 12 months ending June 2013, while firms with 750 or more lawyers did so in only 3 percent of their matters. *See* Ho, *Big Law Firms Are Losing Fees to Mid-Size Firms*, Wash. Post (Oct. 29, 2013), http://www.washingtonpost.com/business/capitalbusiness/big-law-firms-are-losing-fees-to-mid-size-firms/2013/10/29/4c2ec2ec-3ce b-11e3-a94f-b58017bfee6c_story.html, *archived at* https://perma.cc/N6NR-BQX3.

[69]   *See* Curriden, *Bolting for Boutiques*, Dall. Morning News (May 10, 2012) ("In Dallas small firms with 30 or fewer lawyers are expanding and experiencing record revenues. Nearly every partner at [some new] boutiques previously practiced at a large full-service firm.").

[70]   Lyne, *supra* note 56.

[71]   *See id.*

[72]   *See How Clients Hire, Fire and Spend: Landing the World's Best Clients*, BTI Consulting Group (2006), at 2, 5 (BTI began with baseline data from over 1000 interviews with corporate counsel at large and Fortune 100 companies conducted from 2001 to 2005 and then supplemented the data with more than 200 individual, independent telephone

troubling that over an eighteen month period, more than half the corporations in the survey replaced or demoted one of their firms without saying anything to the firm directly.[73] They just sent less and less work to the firm, which did not recognize the drop in client billable hours as a red flag until it was too late.[74] A survey of chief legal officers revealed that the primary reason (57%) they shift a significant portfolio of work (worth $50,000 or more) is because of client service.[75]

This section examines some of the most common "pet peeves" inside counsel have about outside counsel. Attorneys who more fully understand what clients do not like and avoid these "pet peeves" in their own practices will be more valuable contributors to their clients and less likely to be demoted or replaced.

Poor Communication

Why were the corporate clients in the survey above so disappointed? Was it because their lawyers were dropping "the ball," losing cases, or charging too much? No, in many situations, the clients went shopping for new outside counsel for one reason: poor communication. When asked "What is the one thing your outside counsel does that just drives you crazy?" more than half of the general counsels gave answers that can be categorized as poor communication.[76]

Clearly, not all clients are alike and each has its own set of expectations concerning communication. Some examples of poor communication include:

- Not keeping the client in the loop concerning the status of deals or cases
- Failure to return phone calls

---

interviews conducted from July to October 2005. 27% of those surveyed in 2005 were employed by Fortune 100 companies and 9% were employed by Global 100 companies.).

[73]   *Id.* at 10.

[74]   *Id.*

[75]   *See An Altman Weil Flash Survey, supra* note 26, at 46.

[76]   *Id.* at 42 (53% of general counsels replied as follows: 21% for failure to keep the client adequately informed; 15% for lack of client focus, including failure to listen, non-responsiveness, and arrogance; 10% for making decisions without client authorization or awareness; and 7% for failure to give clear, direct advice.).

- Decisions or expenditures made without client authorization

- Disregard for the client's outside counsel guidelines for billing, expenses, matter staffing, or matter management

Good communication helps in-house attorneys manage the dozens or even hundreds of active matters for which they are responsible. Law firms that communicate with their clients proactively help corporate counsel work more efficiently, effectively report internally on the status of various matters, improve performance, and mitigate risk.[77]

At a minimum, outside counsel must keep in-house counsel informed on a regular basis about matters they are handling. This includes providing regular status updates; developing an early case assessment or strategic plan in appropriate circumstances; coordinating on budgeting and staffing; and seeking necessary approvals prior to making any strategic decisions or financial commitments not previously agreed upon.[78]

Krystal R. Jones, Regulatory Compliance Attorney at Globe Life, asks her outside counsel to "keep me in the loop." She says her favorite firms to work with are ones that: "(1) project a reasonable deadline to complete work at the initial point of discussion; (2) notify her the moment they see a potential delay; (3) perform a sample of the work then get back to her to ensure it is in the appropriate format; and (4) are always available same day for a quick call."[79]

If outside counsel is receiving questions from clients like, "Where are you on this?" or hearing comments such as, "I can never get ahold of Bob," those should be red flags.[80] In-house counsel should not have to call outside counsel to find out where

---

[77]   See id. at 43.

[78]   Firms may want to consider designating a relationship attorney to serve as a contact on all matters the firm is handling for the client. Although the relationship attorney will likely not work on every matter, he or she should have sufficient familiarity with the client, be able to answer questions from the client (either by himself or by prompt communication with other firm lawyers) and deal with any concerns.

[79]   Interview with Krystal R. Jones, Regulatory Compliance Attorney, Globe Life, in McKinney, Tex. (June 24, 2019).

[80]   See Burns, supra note 19.

things stand on a particular matter or have trouble tracking down a lawyer for an answer. It is outside counsel's job to keep the client updated.

One successful communication tactic is for outside counsel to work with her client in establishing communication protocols at the start of each matter.[81] Such guidelines should clearly delineate what types of information need to be communicated, how frequently, in what format, and by what method (*e.g.,* e-mail, phone, etc.). Absent a pre-determined communications protocol (or outside counsel guidelines governing communications), in-house counsel will have different communication preferences. Some will want to be copied on every piece of correspondence and receive copies of all communications from opposing counsel. Other clients will prefer brief, monthly e-mail updates on matters, even if they have not yet been billed.

If something significantly changes with a matter, outside counsel should let her client know immediately.[82] And, as a general proposition, sending bad news by e-mail does not foster good client relations. With significant issues or unexpected developments requiring strategic decisions, most inside counsel will prefer a phone call or voicemail over an e-mail. Inside counsel should never first learn of significant developments, either good or bad, in a time description on a legal invoice, or worse, in the newspaper. If outside counsel is not able to work on a matter that she has been asked to handle, she should let her client know as soon as possible so that other arrangements can be made. Finally, outside counsel should communicate upcoming deadlines to inside counsel and provide the client with ample time to respond (such as with respect to providing comments on a brief or compiling documents or answering written discovery).

Unresponsiveness

When asked to rank their biggest pet peeves about working with outside counsel, inside counsel will usually list

---

[81] *How Clients Hire, Fire and Spend: Landing the World's Best Clients, supra* note 72, at 19.

[82] *See* Thomas, *supra* note 49, at 14.

"unresponsiveness" right behind "poor communication." Some attorneys, although experts in their particular practice areas, may not return their clients' phone calls or reply to their e-mails. Their unresponsiveness to clients' phone calls and emails represents another manner of poor communication.

Law students may find it hard to believe that some practicing attorneys are not responsive to their clients. But according to William S. Lipsman, former Associate General Counsel of Sara Lee Corp., "It is amazing how many lawyers don't follow up."[83] Outside counsel's lack of responsiveness is indeed puzzling. After all, being responsive is one of the most important things outside counsel can do, and it is one of the easiest.[84]

According to one outside attorney, "This is a service profession. For crying out loud, your lawyer is the person with whom you would walk arm and arm through the gates of hell. You can't be trying to get him for three days when you need to talk to him today."[85] Outside counsel's goal should be to respond in such a manner that the client feels as if it is the attorney's *only* client.

Ideally, outside counsel will take her client's call immediately or reply to her e-mail within the hour; understandably, this is not always practicable. At the very least, outside counsel should seek to return clients' phone calls and e-mails by the end of the day.

If other responsibilities keep outside counsel from promptly returning a call or responding to an e-mail, sending a short e-mail message explaining the situation and stating a response will be forthcoming would be appropriate. Automatic "out of office" replies can be helpful in letting clients know that outside counsel's response time may be slower than usual, and it might even encourage the client to call another attorney in the firm if the matter is urgent.

Outside counsel should understand that there are relational aspects of phone calls and e-mails: there is another person (your

---

[83]   *Jawboning Key to Managing Outside Lawyers, supra* note 4.
[84]   *Id.*
[85]   *Id.* (quoting Theodore R. Tetzlaff, Partner at Jenner & Block in Chicago).

client's representative) on the other end of the phone or the other side of the laptop or smartphone who e-mailed you for what she believed was an important reason and is awaiting your prompt response. She may perceive your failure to timely respond as being ignored or slighted.

So, if in-house counsel requests weekly status updates on a litigation matter in a pre-determined format and receives them only sporadically in a completely different format, she may see the law firm as being non-responsive.[86] Similarly, if inside counsel asks for a monthly invoice but receives a bi-weekly one, she may come away feeling as if she is being ignored.[87] And, as the saying goes, perception may become reality.

Not Being Accessible

The hallmark of a good attorney is accessibility. A client must be able to either contact or receive a response from outside counsel within a reasonable period of time. In the era of smartphones, text messaging, laptops, tablets, and call forwarding, it is easier for clients to reach their outside counsel than ever before. Thus, some clients have come to expect much faster responses from outside counsel, even at night or on the weekends.

Missing Deadlines

To outside counsel, deadlines imposed by the client may seem unreasonable or they may appear to be artificial deadlines, but in-house counsel gets to set the timing.[88] "Missing deadlines is a deadly sin for outside counsel."[89]

Lawyers are human, and an illness or a death in the family may cause them to miss a client deadline. But no client should have to repeatedly call their outside counsel in an effort to extract work product that was promised on a certain date but not delivered. Clients must be able to trust their outside counsel

---

[86] *How Clients Hire, Fire and Spend: Landing the World's Best Clients, supra* note 72, at 34.

[87] *Id.*

[88] *See* Randell, *Notes From a New General Counsel on the Relationship with Outside Counsel,* Practical Law. (Aug. 2008).

[89] Herrmann, *supra* note 21.

to do things on time. Failure to do so will prompt clients to send their work to another law firm that will meet deadlines.

Billing Surprises

Corporate counsel do not like to receive higher-than-anticipated invoices. For this reason, the billing partner should phone or e-mail his client to discuss any billing-related issues that arise during the course of the matter, preferably *before* the bill for that time period is sent. A phone call—such as "I took time off this bill and here's why," or "You have a big bill coming; let me tell you why," or "If there are any value or efficiency issues, let's talk about them"—can go a long way toward establishing a good relationship.

Sharing Confidences

If a client hears its outside counsel revealing confidences of another client for whatever reason—either on an elevator, at lunch, or as part of an RFP—that attorney will likely find himself off the approved list. Attorneys may want to prove they are "in the know" or "rubbing elbows" with corporate insiders, but an attorney must adhere to her professional obligation to maintain the confidences and secrets relating to the representation.[90] Failure to do so leaves the corporate client wondering, "If this attorney is not keeping other clients' confidences, how can we trust him with ours?"[91]

Not Listening

Another "pet peeve" is not listening, another aspect of poor communication. Lawyers are generally great at talking, but it is much more difficult for them to be good listeners.

Outside counsel must be patient and listen, so they can understand what their client is saying. Being tuned into what inside counsel is saying allows outside counsel to provide targeted, specific legal advice that meets the client's goals.[92] Indeed, it is nearly impossible for outside counsel to be an effective advisor, negotiator, draftsman, or advocate for his

---

[90]   *See* ABA Model Rule of Professional Conduct 1.6.

[91]   *See* Herrmann, *supra* note 21.

[92]   *The BTI Client Service All-Stars, supra* note 18, at 3.

client if he does not understand the client's objectives, the transaction, or the case. Moreover, effectively listening to clients' changing needs and demands may reveal new opportunities for outside counsel as competitive environments shift and company strategies transform.[93]

There are many reasons why outside counsel may not listen carefully to her client: she is busy, she is not accustomed to hearing clients out completely, or perhaps she assumes she knows better than her client. The conversation may go something like this. After listening to only part of what her client says in an initial interview, counsel interrupts: *"I see what the problem is, and here is what we will do."* The attorney assumes from her past expertise that she has heard enough to "get the picture" and decide what needs to be done.[94]

This behavior is problematic for several reasons. The attorney was unable to discover what information her client considers important—not only because she cut off her client at an important point in the interview but because her attitude may make her client hesitant to express its views throughout the representation.[95] Not having complete information could lead to incorrect legal advice or an inappropriate strategy. Most in-house counsel are sophisticated consumers of legal services and know what they want. Outside counsel would be prudent to listen to in-house attorneys and executives carefully and respectfully.

According to a former in-house attorney: "[O]utside counsel should spend less time telling clients what they can do for them and more time asking what they can do for their clients. The only way to learn that information is to listen and ask questions. I saw many outside lawyers being all too willing to talk a lot, especially about themselves."[96]

---

[93]   *See How Clients Hire, Fire and Spend: Landing the World's Best Clients, supra* note 72, at 18.

[94]   *See* Cunningham, *What Do Clients Want From Their Lawyers,* 2013 J. Disp. Resol. 143, 148 (2013).

[95]   *See id.*

[96]   Needles, *GCs Want Firms to Be Extensions of In-House Departments,* Legal Intelligencer (April 1, 2014) (quoting John C. Ryan, attorney at Duane Morris who spent eight years in-house at Aramark Corporation).

Being Arrogant

The institutional arrogance displayed by some attorneys is another corporate counsel pet peeve. In one survey, general counsel identified "arrogance" as one of the two things they like least about lawyers in private practice.[97] Unfortunately, the legal profession is chock-full of attorneys with huge egos. Sometimes outside counsel wrongly believe that they know better than their clients and make it appear that the client is "lucky" to have hired them or their firm. And attorneys love telling "war stories" about what they have accomplished for other clients.

But most clients are not overly impressed, and they do not especially care about outside counsel's pedigree or past successes. Arrogant conduct impairs a lawyer's reputation and impedes a good working relationship with one's client.

Spotting Problems but Not Providing Solutions

There are two parts to providing good advice: spotting the issue (problem) and identifying a solution. Good attorneys identify issues *and* deliver advice and practical solutions to their clients. Inside counsel and corporate executives want a good, practical recommendation as quickly as possible.[98]

Corporate counsel express frustration with outside counsel who only identify issues. Usually, clients already know they have a problem, and for outside counsel to only identify a problem without suggesting a sound solution renders the advice inadequate.

Similarly, corporate clients complain about attorneys who "equivocate, back pedal or overcomplicate matters."[99] Law firms that cannot make up their minds or who qualify their advice in such a way as to make it meaningless are ineffective. When communicating advice, conclusions, or recommendations to a client in a letter, memorandum, or e-mail, outside counsel

---

[97]   *See* Lyne, *supra* note 56.

[98]   *See* Randell, *supra* note 88 (One general counsel explains that she wants "practical creative solutions" from outside counsel, which in her opinion is what "adds value to the work product").

[99]   *See How Clients Hire, Fire and Spend: Landing the World's Best Clients, supra* note 72, at 45.

ordinarily should include the advice, conclusion, or recommendation *before* the analysis. Having the "short answer" upfront is appreciated by busy in-house counsel.

Ineffective Law Firm Marketing

Client development is often difficult for outside lawyers, but it is a necessary evil and must be done. Many lawyers, however, are not very good at client development and pursue approaches which are either ineffective at best or pushy at worst.

What does not work from a client's perspective? Inside counsel view telephone sales calls and slick marketing materials focused on the law firm as the least effective law firm marketing techniques.[100] One general counsel sums up his views on law firm brochures as follows: "The two things that I find most offensive are the brochures that only talk about the firm's success and the newsletter that cover[s] five million topics in two pages."[101] Although not particularly helpful to inside counsel, law firms continue to create and mail these materials perhaps, in part, because their competition is doing so.

Likewise, corporate counsel are not swayed by publications where the law firms pay to be included.[102] In many cases, outside recognition is "nothing more than paid advertising."[103] Instead, attorney rankings by peers outside the firm and those based on client feedback are usually more meaningful and may be consulted in addition to other sources of information.[104]

The success of some marketing efforts may depend on the client. Some clients and potential clients view invitations from firms to dinner, professional sporting events, or concerts as ineffective from a client development standpoint. Michael R. Capone, Senior Vice President, General Counsel of CCS Medical, Inc., says, "I am not impressed with fancy dinners, great seats at sporting events, or the grandiose office space, and they don't make me want to pay several hundreds of dollars for outside counsel's time. Knowing that outside counsel does solid legal

---

[100]   Lyne, *supra* note 56.

[101]   *See Jawboning Key to Managing Outside Lawyers, supra* note 4.

[102]   DeFelice, *supra* note 15.

[103]   *Id.*

[104]   *Id.*

work, without wasting time or resources, will get me to hire them again, and to defend their rates to our finance department. While I may be hiring them to defend our company, I have to defend them to our internal constituents with the power of the checkbook, and only value/ROI [return on investment] will help me do that!"[105]

Other clients may appreciate specific invitations. For example, "closing" dinners at the conclusion of a successful transaction or litigation matter may be appreciated by clients; they serve as a reminder of a successful outcome, and they help cement a better relationship with outside counsel.

Marketing efforts should happen organically. The attorney who suddenly surfaces twenty years after law school to "reconnect" with one of his former law school classmates (who coincidentally now happens to be the general counsel of a company for which the lawyer wants to do legal work) falls in the "awkward" category. The general counsel knows exactly why the attorney now wants to "do lunch." Attorneys seeking outside counsel work are advised to stay in contact with their network, work to develop strong relationships, and show patience.

Putting the Law Firm's Interests Ahead of the Client's Interests

This "pet peeve" can take many different forms: going over budget, delivering poor invoices, overstaffing, and doing more than the client wants. Unfortunately, in-house lawyers all too frequently see outside counsel put their interests over those of the client.

Going over Budget

Previously ignored by outside counsel, budgets are fast becoming a requirement to working with Fortune 1000 clients.[106] Approximately 48% of legal departments require budgets for at least some of their matters handled by outside counsel and 83% ask for budgets on significant matters.[107]

---

[105]   Interview with Michael R. Capone, Senior Vice President, General Counsel, CCS Medical, in Dallas, Tex. (July 2, 2019).

[106]   *See* An Altman Weil Flash Survey, *supra* note 26, at vi.

[107]   *See* Thomas, *supra* note 49, at 28.

Budgets help the department predict its legal costs as well as provide milestones to help determine whether a matter is going as anticipated. Today, corporate counsel are under enormous pressure from management to accurately forecast their outside counsel spending, which usually accounts for the majority of a legal department's budget.[108]

Law firms, on the other hand, are notorious for not wanting to provide budgets or for providing budgets with so many assumptions and caveats that they are worthless. Moreover, even when they provide budgets, some law firms still generate and send invoices at the end of the billing period reflecting billings significantly over their original estimate. Sometimes, these invoices will be accompanied by a letter that attempts to explain the many reasons why costs exceeded the original estimate.

There can be serious consequences for the general counsel if the cost of running the law department budget goes over plan, including lower performance evaluations, and a diminished annual bonus. In one survey, a little more than a quarter of the general counsels who responded said their bonuses or compensation are tied to controlling legal costs.[109]

In defense of law firms, budgets can be difficult to create. It is hard to estimate how much time a given matter will take, especially when the lawyer does not know what unexpected issues may arise during the course of the representation. Clients should understand that, with their authorization, outside counsel must do whatever it reasonably takes to get a matter "done" successfully. Issues are often not as outside counsel thinks they are, or many times, as presented initially by inside counsel. Sometimes matters mushroom beyond what they were anticipated. Other times inside counsel does not know enough at the outset of a matter to give a complete and accurate picture to outside counsel. And in rare cases, in-house counsel may actually understate (or misrepresent) the actual scope of a matter in order to get a better budget and then act "surprised" when the matter goes over budget.

---

[108] *Id.*

[109] Lyne, *supra* note 56.

Outside counsel should provide the client with an accurate, well thought-out budget and work plan at the outset of a project, and make the client aware of any major risk factors or variables that may significantly impact budget estimates.[110] Once agreed to, it is important for both parties to review the plans and budget, take into account developments in the matter, the accuracy of prior assumptions, and any need for new ones.[111]

Sometimes estimates are exceeded for reasons beyond a law firm's control. For example, an overly zealous plaintiff's attorney may unexpectedly notice dozens of depositions that were not contemplated when the initial case assessment and budget were created. In this case, outside counsel should immediately notify its client of the unexpected events and work with the client to reassess the projected costs in light of the plaintiff's litigation strategy. But if law firms exceed their estimates for reasons within their control, they likely will not get any future work and should not get paid for the unnecessary time spent or expenses incurred.

Delivering Poor Invoices

Law firm billing practices are another source of aggravation for inside counsel. A typical chief legal officer at a Fortune 1000 company works with 52 law firms and more than 200 individual attorneys.[112] Each month, bills from these different firms must be processed internally, and counsel must review and approve each one of them.[113]

The process of wading through these invoices in order to feel comfortable enough to approve an invoice for payment can be frustrating. Inside counsel complain of error-ridden invoices (including ones with time entries or expenses belonging to another client of the law firm); untimely billing or multiple months bills submitted at the same time; time descriptions that either do not provide enough detail or are incoherent; billed

---

[110]   *See How Clients Hire, Fire and Spend: Landing the World's Best Clients, supra* note 72, at 41.

[111]   DeFelice, *supra* note 15.

[112]   *See How Clients Hire, Fire and Spend: Landing the World's Best Clients, supra* note 72, at 35.

[113]   *Id.*

amounts that exceeds the value; and excessive expenses or law firm overhead improperly presented for payment.[114]

Aspiring outside counsel should understand that when most corporate counsel receive bills from their law firms, they go straight to the summary page to see the total amount charged, the timekeepers on the matter, and how much each billed to the matter. Based on this, they will assess whether the amount charged passes the "gut" check based on what they know the law firm has been working on as well as the time descriptions provided.

This particular "pet peeve" is one of the most fatal for law firms.[115] It is also one of the more common areas in which clients want to see law firms improve. It is important to note that an invoice is often the last piece of communication that a client receives from a law firm at the end of a matter.[116] "Even the most masterful legal advice can be undermined by an invoice that fails to meet client expectations."[117]

Corporate counsel are keeping a close eye on law firm invoices, reviewing them for errors, failure to comply with the company's outside counsel guidelines, inefficiencies, and unauthorized expenses.[118] Many companies have adopted e-billing systems to help them track and manage law firm bills.[119] And some clients promote standardized guidelines that help to

---

[114] *See id.*

[115] *Id.* at 44.

[116] *Id.*

[117] *Id.*

[118] *Id.* at 39; *see also* An Altman Weil Flash Survey, *supra* note 26, at vi (noting that 79 percent of departments provide guidelines for billing, expenses, matter staffing and matter management and 66 percent enforce those guidelines).

[119] Although some in-house counsel still use paper invoices or internal billing management software, many are moving toward Internet-based systems that help them better communicate and collaborate directly with outside counsel. These systems allow firms and companies to exchange information on a regular basis, including electronic billing to track spending against budgets, real-time billing, and accruals. Budget management has become easier and more efficient as the result of technology, like Thomson Reuters Legal Tracker, an online platform that allows in-house counsel and external law firms to co-ordinate on legal projects and deadlines, exchange bills and budgets, collaborate on documents and run performance reports. *See An Altman Weil Flash Survey, supra* note 26, at v, 15–17.

align law firm invoices with their internal accounting systems.[120]

Time descriptions must be accurate, both in terms of the time spent and the tasks described,[121] but beyond that they should be written in such a way that validate the time spent and hopefully demonstrate that the timekeepers provided value.

A helpful viewpoint is for the billing lawyer to look at the bill from the perspective of her client and ask, "Would I be satisfied with writing this check?" or "Does this invoice demonstrate that we provided value to our client?" If the answer to either question is "no," then perhaps an adjustment is in order.

With respect to expenses, some attorneys make the mistake of believing that they have a virtually unlimited right to bill for costs, including costs that fall under the category of a firm's "cost of doing business."[122] Most corporations will not pay for certain law firm support staff (such as administrative assistants and librarians), air conditioning or heating, meals for attorneys working on their matters,[123] or staff overtime—all of which are typically viewed as part of outside counsel's normal overhead.

Regarding travel expenses, most companies will place restrictions on what are reimbursable costs, as well as when attorneys may (or may not) bill time when traveling in connection with a matter. Often, clients will refuse to pay for "windshield" (*i.e.,* travel) time unless the attorney is actively working on the client's matter while traveling. This should be a matter agreed upon as set forth in the engagement letter between the company and the law firm.

Staffing up

Another pet peeve is when outside counsel unilaterally increases the number of attorneys or staff working on a matter

---

[120]   *Id.*

[121]   In communicating the work completed, outside counsel must remember that billing records may be discoverable, so they should be cautious about what they disclose.

[122]   *See* Smith, *Law Firms Face Fresh Backlash Over Fees*, Wall St. J. (Oct. 22, 2012).

[123]   Note that if a client requests that a firm work overnight to complete its matter by a certain time, it will typically pay for meals for the attorneys and support staff working all night on the matter. *See id.*

with insufficient input from the client. Adding another timekeeper to a matter, particularly an attorney unfamiliar with the matter or the client, can increase legal invoices considerably. For example, in billing rates used by firms in large legal markets, just one additional legal assistant can add $15,000 per month to an invoice; another associate, $30,000 per month; and an extra partner, more than $45,000 per month.[124]

When questioned, law firms typically respond they believed additional staffing was appropriate under the circumstances. What a law firm believes is appropriate under the circumstances, however, may differ considerably from what the client thinks is appropriate.

On staffing, outside counsel should communicate in advance what attorneys are working on a particular matter, their experience level, and hourly rate. This is often done through a proposal or the engagement agreement. Normally, additional timekeepers should not be added to a representation (or removed) without in-house counsel's prior consent. If the billing attorney believes that an additional attorney is necessary, she should first consult with her client to let her know why.

Some general counsel will want more routine work "pushed down" to more junior associates, contract attorneys, or paralegals, whereas others may want more senior associates or partners on their matter because they do not want to "pay for training associates."[125] Some corporate counsel will limit the number of attorneys who may work on a particular matter, the experience level of attorneys who are able to work on their matters, or the number of firm lawyers who may attend a deposition, meeting, or hearing. Many clients have a general rule that no summer clerks or first-year associates may bill on their matters because they do not feel they should have to pay for their training.

Doing More than the Client Wants

Many times, outside counsel wrongly believe that they must "turn over every stone," exhaustively research every issue and

---

124   *See* Toothman, *supra* note 5.
125   *Chief Legal Officer 2011 Survey Results, supra* note 3, at 42.

sub-issue, and pursue every "rabbit trail."[126] "Scorched earth and no stone unturned" tactics, however, rarely lead to better outcomes and are completely inappropriate outside a "bet the company" matter.[127]

Paul A. Jorge, Senior Vice President and General Counsel at TRT Holdings Inc., explains, "Most outside counsel want to build (and bill) the client for a Cadillac, but in virtually all instances, the client only really needs a Chevrolet. An outside lawyer who understands what the client needs and is willing to build (and bill) the client only what it needs is invaluable."[128]

Often, outside counsel feel compelled to "document" their research in a formal memorandum that would make any law school legal research and writing instructor proud. In many instances, however, inside counsel view these tasks as wasted efforts and are "peeved" when they receive the concomitant larger legal bill they create.

Usually, a written memorandum is not necessary. With some frequency, a short e-mail to inside counsel is the preferred approach, and it is often prudent for outside counsel to record in a documentary manner the communications conveyed. Many corporate counsel prefer e-mails because they can easily forward e-mails from outside counsel as necessary within their companies or incorporate the advice into e-mails they themselves send to their business colleagues. As seen in countless litigation scenarios, however, due care should be exercised with respect to the contents of e-mails. Many times, attorneys put things in an e-mail communication that they would *never* put in a formal letter. At times, clients will want outside counsel to call with a conclusion or advice orally before putting the analysis in writing.

---

[126] Admittedly, striking a balance between thoroughness and budget-consciousness can be difficult for an attorney in a firm. *See* Maleske, *10 Tips to Strengthen Relationships with Outside Counsel*, Inside Couns. (Jan. 31, 2011). One partner who returned to private practice after serving as general counsel, found himself after a telephone call with in-house counsel wondering how much time he should spend on the work and trying to strike this balance. *Id.*

[127] *See* DeFelice, *supra* note 15.

[128] Interview with Paul A. Jorge, Senior Vice President and General Counsel, TRT Holdings Inc., in Dallas, Tex. (June 24, 2019).

The telephone is often the most efficient way of getting things done. For recent law school graduates, who are accustomed to e-mailing and texting their friends, the concept of using the phone is a foreign one. They need to discipline themselves to use the phone. Not surprisingly, with respect to certain matters, both inside and outside counsel will want to discuss sensitive issues over the phone rather than committing the discussion to a written e-mail, which might be discoverable (irrespective of the attorney-client or work product privileges) in litigation. When in doubt, outside counsel can always ask the client what type of work product, if any, is wanted.

When practicable, outside counsel should seek to *minimize* the amount of work they do. Although counter to the law firm model of maximizing revenues by billing hours, outside counsel should not do more than her client wants on a project or fail to ask questions that would tailor the project to the client's goals. Jorge suggests that, "outside firms need to get away from focusing so much on their firm's bottom line and focus more on the client's bottom line. All of the emphases on billable hours is leading to terrible results for clients and causing an overcomplication of transactions and litigation."[129]

Sometimes outside counsel have a difficult time "ratcheting down" their work when a matter slows. When a case or deal decelerates for whatever reason, outside counsel should inform the client that the matter is calm, for now, and that he will advise the client immediately should there occur a substantive change.[130]

WHAT SHOULD OUTSIDE COUNSEL DO?

That is enough about all the things outside counsel should *not* do. This section addresses some concrete, affirmative steps that outside counsel can take to become more effective, trusted legal advisors to their current clients, as well as distinguish themselves from the competition and make themselves more attractive to prospective clients.

---

[129] *Id.*

[130] Herrmann, *The Curmudgeon's Guide to Practicing Law*, 2006 ABA Sec. of Litigation 119.

As a starting point, appreciate that in-house counsel are incredibly busy people. Thus, anything outside counsel can do to reduce their work or stress levels will be greatly appreciated.

One way to do this is by viewing the matters you are handling through the client's "eyes." Learn as much as feasible about the client and matter at hand and what aspects of the matter keep your client awake at night. Think about the matter from your client's perspective and develop specific strategies to creatively address your client's biggest concerns. Make sure counsel knows your objective is to successfully resolve the problem in the most expeditious and cost-effective manner.

Consistent with the foregoing, outside counsel should also endeavor to:

- Be proactive in understanding the client's business issues. Alex Arellano, General Counsel at American Airlines Center, recommends in-house counsel "select outside counsel that know your business/ industry or are willing to learn your business/ industry without billing you to learn."[131]

- Knowing the law and understanding how the law relates to the client's unique business considerations is what makes an outside lawyer truly worthwhile.[132]

- Keep a trained eye on changes in the clients' needs, goals, and expectations.[133]

- Develop sound knowledge of the client's industry and related market trends.[134]

- Provide the client with relevant industry, or practice-area information (but do not bill them for this time).

- Draw on knowledge of the client's business operations, regulatory environment, and

---

[131] Interview with Alex Arellano, General Counsel, American Airlines Center, in Dallas, Tex. (June 24, 2019).

[132] Needles, *supra* note 96.

[133] *See How Clients Hire, Fire and Spend: Landing the World's Best Clients, supra* note 72, at 10.

[134] *The BTI Client Service All-Stars, supra* note 18, at 4.

competitive landscape to anticipate and fulfill their needs.[135]

- Ask the client for feedback at the conclusion of a matter, as well as feedback on counsel's communication and responsiveness.[136]

- Have a positive attitude and demonstrate a willingness to improve.

- Gauge client satisfaction regularly and systematically at least once every 18–24 months. Client satisfaction is a key driver in a client's decisions to hire or fire a law firm.[137]

- Deliver more than what was expected. This demonstrates value and helps corporate counsel justify cost-effectiveness.[138]

- Demonstrate creativity and flexibility in approaching legal services. Whether it's new billing methods, new approaches to communication, new deal structures or forward-thinking strategies, clients see innovative and strategic prowess as superior client service.[139]

- Understand where your client is going strategically. Ask, "Where do you see things going in the next 12 to 18 months, and how can we help?"[140]

- If asked by a client for a referral for a particular type of attorney (*e.g.*, OSHA attorney), refer them to a superior attorney at your firm or at another firm (whose firm will not pose a competitive threat

---

[135] *See How Clients Hire, Fire and Spend: Landing the World's Best Clients, supra* note 72, at 27.

[136] *See* Maleske, *supra* note 126; *see also* Altman Weil Flash Survey, *supra* note 26, at vi (noting that a surprisingly small number of departments—only 33 percent—provide post-matter feedback, even if reports show regular feedback has effectively improved the performance of 71 percent of law departments).

[137] *See How Clients Hire, Fire and Spend: Landing the World's Best Clients, supra* note 72, at 10.

[138] *The BTI Client Service All-Stars 2014, supra* note 18, at 5.

[139] *Id.* at 4.

[140] Needles, *supra* note 96.

to "steal" the client). Good referrals are appreciated and help develop trust. Bad referrals can come back to "bite" the referring attorney if the company does not have a good experience with the attorney to whom they were referred.

- Read and meet all standards of performance and expectations in outside counsel guidelines provided by the client.

- Run conflicts of interest checks *before* submitting a response to an RFP.

- Try to anticipate reasonably foreseeable problems and risks for the client's business and communicate them.

- Protect the client. Go beyond identifying current problems and putting out "fires" to preventing future legal risks.

- Fairly and timely resolve any invoice dilemmas.

- When feasible, avoid advance conflict waivers.[141]

- Identify problems early so they can be fixed before they become bigger problems.

- Be a subject matter expert *and* cost-effective—a powerful combination driving exceptional client service.[142]

- Develop a trusted, professional relationship with the client, one in which she feels comfortable telling you something in confidence about the management pressures she is facing, human capital issues on the legal team, or something about the relationship.[143]

Because the competition for legal services is fierce, attorneys should seek to establish themselves as experts in their fields and develop relationships with new general counsels. With visibility, inside counsel will recognize the outside counsel's

---

[141]   *See* DeFelice, *supra* note 15, at 3.

[142]   *The BTI Client Service All-Stars 2014, supra* note 18, at 10.

[143]   Maleske, *supra* note 126.

expertise, so that he will be considered when a need arises. There are several ways to become recognized. One of the best ways is by speaking to relevant industry groups, bar associations, or CLE programs.[144] Giving an excellent presentation says, "I know a lot about this area, and you should consider *me*."

Another more-focused approach is for an attorney (or law firm) to host a two-hour breakfast seminar or "lunch and learn" focused on a single legal topic at the corporation. This format allows in-house counsel to conveniently receive a broad overview of an important legal topic in a brief period of time. Moreover, the presentation is even more beneficial for the in-house lawyers if continuing legal education credit is provided. The presenting attorney, on the other hand, gets to meet multiple lawyers within a legal department and demonstrate her expertise on the topic. Of course, arranging this invitation with company counsel may prove challenging. If so invited, this access can serve as an effective client development tool.

Volunteering for non-profit boards is an excellent way for attorneys to meet and interface with corporate executives, in-house lawyers, and other attorneys—individuals with the capacity to hire or recommend attorneys. Working collaboratively with other board members also helps establish the attorney as caring, knowledgeable, and hardworking. Moreover, performing well in this capacity, particularly in an area that touches an attorney's practice area, can help the attorney earn respect and become recognized as an expert with the greater likelihood of procuring future legal business.

Regularly authoring "solid" articles on a substantive subject that relates to an attorney's practice area can also help establish the attorney's expertise and build credibility. As an attorney's name appears in by-lines of published articles, with such articles having effective visibility, the attorney enhances her status as an authority in her field, thereby improving her client-retention opportunities.[145]

---

[144]   Lyne, *supra* note 56.

[145]   For example, John Patton, an intellectual property attorney with Patton Law Group, wrote the book, *Intellectual Property Law in 26½ Steps*, as a resource for in-house attorneys. The book presents practical advice in an easy to understand and entertaining

As discussed earlier in this chapter, most in-house counsel believe that the glossy, self-serving brochures mailed out by law firms are generally ineffective client development tools and largely unpersuasive. On the other hand, a law firm's sending current or prospective clients relevant single topic articles or case updates written by its attorneys can be an effective client development tool. Even if such an article or case update has not been written, a short note like the following may be appreciated by in-house counsel:

> *"This case just came out, and I think it may apply to you. I've enclosed a copy of the case (with the relevant sections highlighted). Please call me if you have any questions. Hope all is going well."*

This approach may indicate to the client that this attorney is proactive and may be able to help the client if a need should arise.

Law firm lawyers and law students who eventually work in private practice will be more effective legal advisors when they truly understand the "client," its needs, and expectations. Understanding the criteria that corporations use when selecting outside counsel and the methods by which outside counsel is selected will enable them to better attract clients. And keeping their focus on what is important to their clients and avoiding the "pet peeves" that drive their clients crazy, will hopefully lead to successful, long-term partnerships with their corporate clients.

---

format. Patton gives the books to clients as well as prospective clients and has found that he has become known as the attorney who wrote the book that makes intellectual property law fun.

CHAPTER 9

FOCUSING ON THE SECURITIES LAWS

The vast majority of in-house attorneys do not practice securities law. In fact, they likely never took a law school course on the subject. Yet, a basic understanding of key securities law principles is important for an inside lawyer in his or her practice. The purpose of this chapter is to focus on these issues.

Yet, it is also the case that many publicly-held corporations continue to expand the number of in-house attorneys employed as securities specialists. This is due to the high costs of retaining outside law firms to perform the periodic reporting and other relatively "routine" tasks that traditionally were undertaken by law firms. Tired of paying these fees, an increasing number of publicly-traded companies have employed in-house lawyers who are experienced in securities law. These lawyers draft the periodic disclosure and other specified reports required by the SEC as well as render advice with respect to securities law matters. These in-house opportunities have enabled thousands of lawyers to leave law firms and pursue their specialty within the parameters of corporate inside practice.

This chapter, of course, is not intended to be a comprehensive resource on securities law. For that, other sources may be consulted.[1] Rather, the discussion that follows seeks to provide the non-securities in-house lawyer with a basic understanding of certain key problematic issues that affect his or her inside legal practice.

---

[1]   For books by one of the authors on securities law, *see, e.g.,* M. Steinberg, *Securities Regulation* (7th ed. 2017); M. Steinberg, *Securities Regulation: Liabilities and Remedies* (2019); M. Steinberg, *Understanding Securities Law* (7th ed. 2018).

MEANING OF "MATERIAL" AND "NON-PUBLIC" INFORMATION

Material Information

Under the securities laws, information must be publicly disclosed in certain circumstances if such information is deemed "material." What is the meaning of this term? Generally, materiality is based on whether a reasonable person would consider such information important in making her investment or voting decision.[2] The test is an objective one, looking at the reasonable investor. Note that the standard is not that of "but for" the fact misstated or omitted, the investor would have decided otherwise. Rather, the fact need only be "important" to one's decision-making process. Another way of stating this is that "there must be a substantial likelihood that the [accurate] disclosure of the [misrepresented or non-disclosed] fact would have been viewed by the reasonable investor as having significantly altered the 'total mix' of information made available."[3] Ordinarily, a significant change (such as 10%) in the stock's market price after disclosure of the truthful information (which previously had been misrepresented or omitted) is relevant evidence of the materiality of the information in question.[4]

In situations that are in a state of flux, such as merger negotiations or other situations involving uncertain events, the probability/magnitude test also has been applied in ascertaining materiality. This standard involves "a balancing of both the indicated probability that the event will occur and the anticipated magnitude of the event in light of the totality of the company activity."[5] Where the magnitude of a contingent event is high (such as a publicly-traded company purchasing 100% of the illiquid stock of a privately-held enterprise), the fact of

---

[2]   See, e.g., TSC Industries, Inc. v. Northway, Inc., 426 U.S. 438, 449 (1976).

[3]   Id.

[4]   See Amgen Inc. v. Connecticut Retirement Plans and Trust Funds, 568 U.S. 455 (2013).

[5]   Basic, Inc. v. Levinson, 485 U.S. 224, 238 (1988). The Supreme Court has upheld the propriety of the "fraud on the market" theory to provide a rebuttable presumption of reliance. See Halliburton Co. v. Erica P. John Fund, Inc., 573 U.S. 258 (2014).

preliminary acquisition discussions *may* be deemed material even if the likelihood of the "deal" being consummated is relatively low. This means that materiality is, at times, an elusive principle, presenting challenging counseling dilemmas.

As the U.S. Supreme Court has made clear, there exists no "bright-line" standard for assessing materiality.[6] Whether information is deemed material is a "facts and circumstances" approach. This means that, unless the pertinent confidential information is clearly not of a material nature, lawyers would be prudent to treat such information as being material. After all, materiality determinations are based with the benefit of hindsight, with the distinct possibility that significant adverse consequences will ensue if a finding of materiality is made.

Non-Public Information

For securities law purposes, the terms "inside," "non-public" and "confidential" information may be viewed as the same. But importantly, under the securities laws, information can be known by some persons outside of the corporation, yet such information is deemed to retain its non-public or confidential status. The same holds true for widespread rumors in the marketplace; rumors ordinarily are not the same as a company's public disclosure of facts—either confirming or denying the rumors. Moreover, information may be non-public even if it is of a more or less general nature and does not provide specific details regarding a particular event or contingency.

For securities law purposes, non-public information becomes public in one of two ways: first, the usual way is that information is broadly communicated to the investing public by the company (or its agents) and digested by the securities markets; or second, which occurs less frequently, the information, even if not publicly disclosed, is transmitted to the securities markets by other means and is fully impounded into the stock price for the subject security.[7] This means that, unless there has been widespread disclosure by the company (or its agents) to the investing public and adequate time allotted for the

---

6   *Matrixx Initiatives v. Siracusano,* 563 U.S. 27 (2011).

7   See *SEC v. Mayhew,* 121 F. 3d 44 (2d Cir. 1997); *In re Apple Computer Securities Litigation,* 886 F. 2d 1109 (9th Cir. 1989); SEC Regulation FD.

securities markets to absorb that information, a significant risk exists that the subject information remains non-public. To address this situation, publicly-traded companies today institute "black-out" periods, generally prohibiting purchases and sales of the subject company's securities by insiders (including directors and officers) until a specified period, such as three business days, after the public announcement of a material event, such as the announcement of quarterly earnings (or losses).

INSIDER TRADING

In-house lawyers—as professionals are in general—are favorite targets for SEC and criminal prosecution for engaging in insider trading and illegal tipping of material, inside information. In-house lawyers must be very careful when purchasing (or selling) their company's (as well as publicly-held customer's and supplier's) securities. Engaging in this high-profile prohibited practice is a dangerous path to ruining one's personal and professional life.

The law of insider trading is quite complex and is addressed elsewhere.[8] Suffice to say for our purposes here, directors, officers, and corporate employees should not knowingly trade based on material, non-public information. If they do so, and the government properly brings suit, they will be held liable under the federal securities laws.[9] As a fiduciary and employee, in-house lawyers therefore have a legal obligation to refrain from purchasing or selling securities based on material, inside information.[10]

What about conveying (or "tipping") the information to others? When an in-house lawyer transmits material non-public information to others for his personal benefit or conveys a gift to the recipient-tippee, liability will ensue.[11] Providing inside

---

[8]   See, e.g., M. Steinberg & W. Wang, *Insider Trading* (Oxford Univ. Press 3d ed. 2010). For the author's most recent book on insider trading—focusing on a high profile case—*see* M. Steinberg, *Securities and Exchange Commission v. Cuban—A Trial of Insider Trading* (2019).

[9]   See, e.g., *United States v. O'Hagan*, 521 U.S. 642 (1997); *Chiarella v. United States*, 445 U.S. 222 (1980).

[10]   See, e.g., *Dirks v. SEC*, 463 U.S. 646, 677 n. 14 (1983). For a recent case involving an in-house attorney, *see* Michael & Mickle, *Ex-Apple Lawyer Accused of Insider Trading*, Wall St. J., Feb. 14, 2019, at B1.

[11]   463 U.S. at 662–664.

information to relatives, lovers, and friends is an especially dangerous route.[12]

In the tender offer context (a tender offer generally is a bidder's offer to purchase shares of the target corporation made directly to the target's shareholders), the insider trading liability net is larger. There, the in-house lawyer's knowing transmittal of material, inside information to another person (even without receiving a personal benefit or making a gift), where it is reasonably foreseeable that the tippee-recipient will trade (or tip), will incur liability.[13]

In addition to the insider trading prohibitions, SEC Regulation FD prohibits disclosure by a publicly-held company's senior officials or company spokespersons of material, inside information regarding the company or its securities to, among others, financial analysts, certain institutional investors and current shareholders.[14] Because the company's general inside counsel and her deputies may be viewed as senior officials, they may be deemed by the SEC as coming within the purview of Regulation FD. Although not as serious as an offense as insider trading, violation of Regulation FD may trigger an SEC enforcement action and sanctions levied that are detrimental to inside counsel's reputation and career.

Stated succinctly, because of the severe adverse ramifications that may be incurred by in-house lawyers when they trade on (or tip) material, non-public information, such trading and/or tipping should not occur. Liability for insider trading may well result in an SEC enforcement action, criminal prosecution (and significant time in the slammer), and revocation of one's license to practice law.

Note that treatment of corporate law compliance programs that encompass insider trading is covered in Chapter 7 of this book. Three insider trading SEC enforcement actions brought against in-house attorneys are contained later in this chapter.

---

12   *See, e.g., United States v. Grossman*, 843 F. 2d 78 (2d Cir. 1988).

13   SEC Rule 14e–3.

14   SEC Regulation FD; Securities Exchange Act Release No. 43154 (2000).

SEC FILINGS

Filings by a publicly-held company with the SEC are a regular occurrence. When a company has a public offering of its securities, a Securities Act registration statement must be filed with the SEC. Likewise, once publicly-held, companies must file current (Form 8-K), quarterly (Form 10-Q), and annual reports (Form 10-K) with the Commission. In addition, proxy statements must be filed with the SEC when proxies are solicited from shareholders with respect to items to be voted on in shareholder meetings. Moreover, informal reports, such as the "glossy" annual shareholder report, are provided to shareholders on a periodic basis. The general point to be made here is that the communications made must be sufficiently comprehensive and accurate. Lawsuits may ensue (such as plaintiffs' class action litigation) if the document contains allegedly materially false or misleading information.

Insiders and others also are subject to SEC reporting obligations. For example, directors, officers, and shareholders (who own more than 10% of a class of the issuer's equity securities) of a publicly-held company must file with the SEC their amount of "stock" ownership and any change (e.g., purchases or sales) in that amount. The general inside counsel, who performs significant policy-making functions, may be viewed by the SEC as an officer within the scope of the securities ownership reporting mandate.[15]

In addition, as also discussed in Chapter 7 of this book, such persons (i.e., directors, officers, and "10% shareholders") cannot buy and then sell or sell and then buy a class of their company's equity securities within a six-month period. If they do so, they are strictly liable to disgorge all profits from the prohibited trades.[16] This rule of strict liability applies even if the insider can prove that he did not have material non-public information when he engaged in the trade(s) in question.[17]

---

[15]   Section 16(a) of the Securities Exchange Act; SEC Rule 16a–1(f). These reports must be filed with the SEC by the end of the second business day after the trade(s).

[16]   Section 16(b) of the Securities Exchange Act.

[17]   *See, e.g., Whiting v. Dow Chemical Co.,* 523 F. 2d 680, 687 (2d Cir. 1975) (opining that "the unwary who fall within [Section 16(b)'s] terms have no one but themselves to blame").

A number of other situations exist where individuals must file SEC reports. For example, persons relying on SEC Rule 144 with respect to the resale of their securities must file a form with the Commission when such sales during a three-month period exceed 5,000 shares or generate a sales price greater than $50,000.[18] With the presence of stock option, stock benefit, and related equity compensation plans in many corporations, in-house lawyers may own and subsequently sell within a three-month period the requisite amount of securities to trigger the SEC filing requirement. Such situations can occur, for example, when the in-house attorney needs access to funds for the down-payment on a home or to pay for a child's college tuition.

Another example is when a person (such as an individual or corporation) beneficially acquires 5% or more of a publicly-held company's outstanding stock. In that situation, the owner must file a detailed disclosure statement with the SEC setting forth, for example, the number of shares owned, the source of the funds used, the person's identity and background, and the reason(s) or purpose(s) for the purchases.[19] The general objective for this SEC filing requirement is to alert the investing public of a potential shift in corporate control.[20] The in-house lawyer should be aware of this requirement so as to timely advise the client with respect to the filing requirements and other issues that reasonably may arise upon reaching the 5% ownership level.

In-house attorneys specializing in securities practice should be well aware of the foregoing requirements. It is important that in-house lawyers, who are not securities specialists, also have a basic understanding of these concepts. For example, a periodic SEC filing, such as a company's annual report, may call for disclosure relating to contentious labor issues involving the

---

[18]   SEC Rule 144(h).

[19]   Section 13(d)(1) of the Securities Exchange Act; SEC Rule 13(d)(1); SEC Schedule 13D. This filing must be made with the SEC within ten days after the person or group reaches the 5% ownership level. Note that a number of persons may act in concert as a "group" and thereby trigger the filing obligation. Certain institutional investors who purchase for investment purposes only (and who do not own 20% or more of the subject company's stock) have less stringent disclosure obligations. See Section 13(g) of the Securities Exchange Act; SEC Schedule 13G. Moreover, in practical effect, the Hart-Scott-Rodino Antitrust Improvements Act will limit the extent of pre-notification purchases in many situations.

[20]   See, e.g., Treadway Companies, Inc. v. Care Corp., 638 F. 2d 357, 380 (2d Cir. 1980).

company's workforce. The individual who may be best suited to draft the initial disclosure may be the in-house labor lawyer, rather than corporate/securities counsel. When engaging in this drafting process, it is important that the in-house labor attorney understand the meaning of the term "material" under the securities laws. Without such an understanding, the risk arises that the disclosure drafted for the SEC filing will be deficient. In this situation, it is incumbent upon the corporate/securities lawyer to communicate with the in-house labor attorney and focus on pertinent securities law disclosure mandates. The securities specialist also should carefully review and revise if appropriate the disclosure drafted by the in-house labor attorney.

RESALES OF SECURITIES

In-house counsel who do not serve as securities lawyers also should have a basic understanding that securities held by insiders and others, including their own holdings, may be "restricted" securities. Generally, "restricted" securities include those sold in private offerings and pursuant to certain employment compensation plans.[21] These securities normally have a holding period in which they cannot be sold—generally, six months for publicly-held companies and twelve months for privately-held companies.[22] In addition to the holding period, if the prospective seller is deemed an "affiliate" of the company (e.g., being a "control" person of the company), then limitations on the amount of securities that may be sold during any three-month period will apply.[23]

These rules are rather complicated. In-house securities lawyers certainly should know these mandates. But it is also important that the general inside counsel (even if not a securities attorney) be aware of these general requirements as well as other in-house lawyers who render advice to directors and officers with respect to their securities holdings. Indeed,

---

[21]   Restricted securities, for example, include those sold pursuant to the Rule 506 exemption of Regulation D and pursuant to the Rule 701 exemption (which provides an exemption for privately-held companies selling securities to employees and consultants for compensation purposes).

[22]   Rule 144(d); Securities Act Release No. 7390 (1997).

[23]   Rules 144(b)(1), 144(e); Securities Act Release No. 8869 (2007).

some awareness of these SEC rules relating to securities sale restrictions may well be beneficial to any in-house lawyer who owns "restricted" securities issued by the corporation.

STATE SECURITIES LAWS

With certain exceptions, the state securities statutes (called "blue sky" laws) also apply to securities issued and disclosures made by companies and their agents. Even with respect to stock exchange listed companies, where registration and reporting requirements are preempted by federal legislation, state regulators police allegedly fraudulent conduct. Enforcement actions have been brought by state securities regulators against both publicly and privately-held companies as well as their directors, officers, and in-house lawyers.[24]

CONCLUSION

The foregoing discussion focuses on why non-securities inside lawyers should be aware of some basic key securities law concepts. Knowledge of these basic principles (e.g., the meaning of material and non-public information under the securities laws) should prove beneficial to both the corporation and the individual in-house lawyer.[25]

The following excerpt provides a succinct overview of the federal securities laws as well as the "work" of the U.S. Securities and Exchange Commission ("SEC").

THE "WORK" OF THE SEC
Available at http://www.sec.gov/Article/whatwedo.html,
archived at https://perma.cc/CYM4-VPMR

The mission of the U.S. Securities and Exchange Commission is to protect investors, maintain fair, orderly, and efficient markets, and facilitate capital formation.

. . . .

----

[24]   *See* J. Long, M. Kaufman, & J. Wunderlich, *Blue Sky Law* (2019).

[25]   For further explanation, see M. Steinberg, *Understanding Securities Law* (7th ed. 2018).

The laws and rules that govern the securities industry in the United States derive from a simple and straightforward concept: all investors, whether large institutions or private individuals, should have access to certain basic facts about an investment prior to buying it, and so long as they hold it. To achieve this, the SEC requires public companies to disclose meaningful financial and other information to the public. This provides a common pool of knowledge for all investors to use to judge for themselves whether to buy, sell, or hold a particular security. Only through the steady flow of timely, comprehensive, and accurate information can people make sound investment decisions.

The result of this information flow is a far more active, efficient, and transparent capital market that facilitates the capital formation so important to our nation's economy. To ensure that this objective is always being met, the SEC continually works with all major market participants, including especially the investors in our securities markets, to listen to their concerns and to learn from their experience.

The SEC oversees the key participants in the securities world, including securities exchanges, securities brokers and dealers, investment advisors, and mutual funds. Here the SEC is concerned primarily with promoting the disclosure of important market-related information, maintaining fair dealing, and protecting against fraud.

Crucial to the SEC's effectiveness in each of these areas is its enforcement authority. Each year the SEC brings hundreds of civil enforcement actions against individuals and companies for violation of the securities laws. Typical infractions include insider trading, accounting fraud, and providing false or misleading information about securities and the companies that issue them.

. . . .

Though it is the primary overseer and regulator of the U.S. securities markets, the SEC works closely with many other institutions, including Congress, other federal departments and agencies, the self-regulatory organizations (e.g. the stock exchanges), state securities regulators, and various private sector organizations. In particular, the Chairman of the SEC, together with the Chairman of the Federal Reserve, the Secretary of the Treasury, and the Chairman of the Commodity Futures Trading Commission, serves as a member of the President's Working Group on Financial Markets.

This article is an overview of the SEC's history, responsibilities, activities, organization, and operation.

Creation of the SEC

The SEC's foundation was laid in an era that was ripe for reform. Before the Great Crash of 1929, there was little support for federal regulation of the securities markets. This was particularly true during the post-World War I surge of securities activity. Proposals that the federal government require financial disclosure and prevent the fraudulent sale of stock were never seriously pursued.

Tempted by promises of "rags to riches" transformations and easy credit, most investors gave little thought to the systemic risk that arose from widespread abuse of margin financing and unreliable information about the securities in which they were investing. During the 1920s, approximately 20 million large and small shareholders took advantage of post-war prosperity and set out to make their fortunes in the stock market. It is estimated that of the $50 billion in new securities offered during this period, half became worthless.

When the stock market crashed in October 1929, public confidence in the markets plummeted. Investors large and small, as well as the banks who had loaned to these investors, lost great sums of money in the ensuing Great Depression. There was a consensus that for the economy to recover, the public's faith in the capital markets needed to be restored. Congress held hearings to identify the problems and search for solutions.

Based on the findings in these hearings, Congress—during the peak year of the Depression—passed the Securities Act of 1933. This law, together with the Securities Exchange Act of 1934, which created the SEC, was designed to restore investor confidence in our capital markets by providing investors and the markets with more reliable information and clear rules of honest dealing. . . .

Monitoring the securities industry requires a highly coordinated effort. Congress established the Securities and Exchange Commission [SEC] in 1934 to enforce the newly-passed securities laws, to promote stability in the markets and, most importantly, to protect investors. President Franklin Delano Roosevelt appointed Joseph P. Kennedy, President John F. Kennedy's father, to serve as the first Chairman of the SEC.

Organization of the SEC

The SEC consists of five presidentially-appointed Commissioners, with staggered five-year terms. One of them is designated by the President as Chairman of the Commission— the agency's chief executive. By law, no more than three of the Commissioners may belong to the same political party, ensuring non-partisanship. The agency's functional responsibilities are organized into [several] Divisions and Offices. . . . [The SEC] is headquartered in Washington, DC. The Commission's [employees] are located in Washington and in 11 Regional Offices throughout the country.

It is the responsibility of the Commission to:

- interpret federal securities laws;
- issue new rules and amend existing rules;
- oversee the inspection of securities firms, brokers, investment advisers, and ratings agencies;
- oversee private regulatory organizations in the securities, accounting, and auditing fields; and
- coordinate U.S. securities regulation with federal, state, and foreign authorities.

The Commission convenes regularly at meetings that are open to the public and the news media unless the discussion pertains to confidential subjects, such as whether to begin an enforcement investigation.

Divisions

Division of Corporation Finance

The Division of Corporation Finance assists the Commission in executing its responsibility to oversee corporate disclosure of important information to the investing public. Corporations are required to comply with regulations pertaining to disclosure that must be made when stock is initially sold and then on a continuing and periodic basis. The Division's staff routinely reviews the disclosure documents filed by companies. The staff also provides companies with assistance interpreting the Commission's rules and recommends to the Commission new rules for adoption.

The Division of Corporation Finance reviews documents that publicly-held companies are required to file with the Commission. The documents include:

- registration statements for newly-offered securities;

- annual and quarterly filings (Forms 10-K and 10-Q);

- proxy materials sent to shareholders before an annual shareholder meeting;

- annual reports to shareholders;

- documents concerning tender offers (a tender offer is an offer [made by a bidder to shareholders of a target corporation] to buy a large number of shares of [such target] corporation, at a premium above the current market price); and

- filings related to mergers and acquisitions.

These documents disclose information about the companies' financial condition and business practices to help investors make informed investment decisions. Through the Division's review process, the staff checks to see if publicly-held companies are meeting their disclosure requirements and seeks to improve the quality of the disclosure. To meet the SEC's requirements for disclosure, a company issuing securities or whose securities are publicly traded must make available [specified] information, whether it is positive or negative, that [is significant] to an investor's decision to buy, sell, or hold the security.

. . . .

Division of Trading and Markets

The Division of Trading and Markets assists the Commission in executing its responsibility for maintaining fair, orderly, and efficient markets. The staff of the Division provide day-to-day oversight of the major securities market participants: the securities exchanges; securities firms; self-regulatory organizations (SROs) including the Financial Industry Regulatory Authority (FINRA), the Municipal Securities Rulemaking Board (MSRB), clearing agencies that help facilitate trade settlement; transfer agents (parties that maintain records of securities owners); securities information processors; and credit rating agencies.

The Division also oversees the Securities Investor Protection Corporation (SIPC), which is a private, non-profit corporation that insures the securities and cash in the customer accounts of member brokerage firms against the failure of those firms. Importantly, SIPC insurance does not cover investor losses arising from market declines or fraud.

The Division's additional responsibilities include:

- carrying out the Commission's financial integrity program for broker-dealers;

- reviewing (and in some cases approving, under authority delegated from the Commission) proposed new rules and proposed changes to existing rules filed by the SROs;

- assisting the Commission in establishing rules and issuing interpretations on matters affecting the operation of the securities markets; and

- surveilling the markets.

Division of Investment Management

The Division of Investment Management assists the Commission in executing its responsibility for investor protection and for promoting capital formation through oversight and regulation of America's investment management industry. This important part of the U.S. capital markets includes mutual funds and the professional fund managers who advise them; analysts who research individual assets and asset classes; and investment advisers to individual customers. Because of the high concentration of individual investors in mutual funds, exchange-traded funds, and other investments that fall within the Division's purview, the Division of Investment Management is focused on ensuring that disclosures about these investments are useful to retail customers, and that the regulatory costs which consumers must bear are not excessive.

The Division's additional responsibilities include:

- assisting the Commission in interpreting laws and regulations for the public and SEC inspection . . .;

- responding to no-action requests and requests for exemptive relief;

- reviewing investment company and investment adviser filings;

- assisting the Commission in enforcement matters involving investment companies and advisers; and

- advising the Commission on adapting SEC rules to new circumstances.

Division of Enforcement

First and foremost, the SEC is a law enforcement agency. The Division of Enforcement assists the Commission in executing its law enforcement function by recommending the commencement of investigations of securities law violations, by recommending that the Commission bring civil actions in federal court or before an administrative law judge, and by prosecuting these cases on behalf of the Commission. As an adjunct to the SEC's civil enforcement authority, the Division works closely with law enforcement agencies in the U.S. and around the world to bring criminal cases when appropriate.

The Division obtains evidence of possible violations of the securities laws from many sources, including market surveillance activities, investor tips and complaints, other Divisions and Offices of the SEC, the self-regulatory organizations and other securities industry sources, and media reports.

All SEC investigations are conducted privately. Facts are developed to the fullest extent possible through informal inquiry, interviewing witnesses, examining brokerage records, reviewing trading data, and other methods. With a formal order of investigation, the Division's staff may compel witnesses by subpoena to testify and produce books, records, and other relevant documents. Following an investigation, SEC staff present their findings to the Commission for its review. The Commission can authorize the staff to file a case in federal court or bring an administrative action. In many cases [approximately 90% of such cases], the Commission and the party charged decide to settle a matter without trial [ordinarily with the defendant neither admitting nor denying the SEC's allegations].

Common violations that may lead to SEC investigations include:

- misrepresentation or omission of important information about securities;

- manipulating the market prices of securities;

- stealing customers' funds or securities;

- violating broker-dealers' responsibility to treat customers fairly;

- insider trading (violating a trust relationship by trading on material, non-public information about a security); and

- selling unregistered securities.

Whether the Commission decides to bring a case in federal court or within the SEC before an administrative law judge may depend upon the type of sanction or relief that is being sought. For example, the Commission may bar someone from the brokerage industry in an administrative proceeding . . . . Often, when the misconduct warrants it, the Commission will bring both proceedings.

- *Civil action:* The Commission files a complaint with a U.S. District Court and asks the court for a sanction or remedy. Often the Commission asks for a court order, called an injunction, that prohibits any further acts or practices that violate the law or

Commission rules. An injunction can also require audits, accounting for frauds, or special supervisory arrangements. In addition, the SEC can seek civil monetary penalties, or the return of illegal profits (called disgorgement). The court may also bar or suspend an individual from serving as a corporate officer or director [of a publicly-traded company]. A person who violates the court's order may be found in contempt and be subject to additional fines or imprisonment.

- *Administrative action:* The Commission can seek a variety of sanctions through the administrative proceeding process. Administrative proceedings differ from civil court actions in that they are heard by an administrative law judge (ALJ), who is independent of the Commission. The administrative law judge presides over a hearing and considers the evidence presented by the Division staff, as well as any evidence submitted by the subject of the proceeding. Following the hearing, the ALJ issues an initial decision that includes findings of fact and legal conclusions. The initial decision may also contain sanction[s]. Both the Division staff and the defendant may appeal all or any portion of the initial decision to the Commission. The Commission may affirm the decision of the ALJ, reverse the decision, or remand it for additional hearings. Administrative sanctions include cease and desist orders, suspension or revocation of broker-dealer and investment advisor registrations, censures, bars from association with the securities industry, civil monetary penalties, and disgorgement. [The Commission's decision may be appealed by the defendant to the U.S. Court of Appeals.]

Division of Risk, Strategy, and Financial Innovation

The Division of Risk, Strategy, and Financial Innovation was established in 2009 to help further identify developing risks and trends in the financial markets.

This new Division is providing the Commission with sophisticated analysis that integrates economic, financial, and legal disciplines. The Division's responsibilities cover three broad areas: risk and economic analysis; strategic research; and financial innovation.

The emergence of derivatives, hedge funds, new technology, and other factors have transformed both capital markets and corporate governance. The Division of Risk, Strategy, and Financial Innovation is working to advise the Commission through an interdisciplinary approach that is informed by law and modern finance and economics, as well as developments in real world products and practices on Wall Street and Main Street.

Among the functions being performed by the Division are: (1) strategic and long-term analysis; (2) identifying new developments and trends in financial markets and systemic risk; (3) making recommendations as to how these new developments and trends affect the Commission's regulatory activities; (4) conducting research and analysis in furtherance and support of the functions of the Commission and its divisions and offices; and (5) providing training on new developments and trends and other matters.

Offices

Office of the General Counsel

The General Counsel is appointed by the Chairman as the chief legal officer of the Commission, with overall responsibility for the establishment of agency policy on legal matters. The General Counsel serves as the chief legal advisor to the Chairman regarding all legal matters and services performed within, or involving, the agency, and provides legal advice to the Commissioners, the Divisions, the Offices, and other SEC components as appropriate.

The General Counsel represents the SEC in civil, private, or appellate proceedings as appropriate, including appeals from the decisions of the federal district courts or the Commission in enforcement matters, and appeals from the denial of requests under the Freedom of Information Act. Through its amicus curiae program, the General Counsel often intervenes in private appellate litigation involving novel or important interpretations of the securities laws, and the Office is responsible for coordinating with the Department of Justice in the preparation of briefs on behalf of the United States involving matters in which the SEC has an interest.

The General Counsel is also responsible for determining the adherence by attorneys in the SEC to appropriate professional standards, as well as for providing advice on standards of conduct to Commissioners and staff, as appropriate. It is responsible for the final drafting of all proposed legislation that the Chairman or the Commission choose to submit for consideration to the Congress or the states, and for coordinating the SEC staff positions on such legislation.

Office of the Chief Accountant

The Chief Accountant is appointed by the Chairman to be the principal adviser to the Commission on accounting and auditing matters. The Office of the Chief Accountant assists the Commission in executing its responsibility under the securities laws to establish accounting principles, and for overseeing the private sector standards-setting process. The Office works closely with the Financial Accounting Standards Board, to which the SEC has delegated authority for accounting standards setting, as well as the International Accounting Standards Board and the American Institute of Certified Public Accountants.

In addition to its responsibility for accounting standards, the Commission is responsible for the approval or disapproval of auditing rules put forward by the Public Company Accounting Oversight Board (PCAOB), a private-sector regulator established by the Sarbanes-Oxley Act to oversee the auditing profession. The Commission also has thorough oversight responsibility for all of the activities of the PCAOB, including approval of its annual budget. To assist the Commission in the execution of these responsibilities, the Office of the Chief Accountant is the principal liaison with the PCAOB. The Office also consults with registrants and auditors on a regular basis regarding the application of accounting and auditing standards and financial disclosure requirements.

. . . .

Office of Compliance Inspections and Examinations

The Office of Compliance Inspections and Examinations administers the SEC's nationwide examination and inspection program for registered self-regulatory organizations, broker-dealers, transfer agents, clearing agencies, investment companies, and investment advisers. The Office conducts inspections to foster compliance with the securities laws, to detect violations of the law, and to keep the Commission informed of developments in the regulated community. Among the more important goals of the examination program is the quick and informal correction of compliance problems. When the Office finds deficiencies, it issues a "deficiency letter" identifying the problems that need to be rectified and monitors the situation until compliance is achieved. Violations that appear too serious for informal correction are referred to the Division of Enforcement.

Office of International Affairs

The SEC works extensively in the international arena to promote cooperation among national securities regulatory agencies, and to encourage the maintenance of high regulatory standards worldwide. The Office of International Affairs assists the Chairman and the Commission in the development and implementation of the SEC's international regulatory and enforcement initiatives. The Office negotiates bilateral and multilateral agreements for Commission approval on such subjects as regulatory cooperation and enforcement assistance, and oversees the implementation of such arrangements. It is also responsible for advancing the Commission's agenda in international meetings and organizations. The Office also conducts a technical assistance program for countries with emerging securities markets, which includes training both in the United States and in the requesting country. Over 100 countries currently participate in this program.

. . . .

Office of Legislative Affairs and Intergovernmental Relations

The Office of Legislative Affairs and Intergovernmental Relations serves as the agency's formal liaison with the Congress, other Executive Branch agencies, and state and local governments. The staff carefully monitors ongoing legislative activities and initiatives on Capitol Hill that affect the Commission and its mission. Through regular communication and consultation with House and Senate members and staff, the Office communicates legislators' goals to the agency, and communicates the agency's own regulatory and management initiatives to the Congress.

The Office is responsible for responding to congressional requests for testimony of SEC officials, as well as requests for documents, technical assistance, and other information. In addition, the Office monitors legislative and oversight hearings that pertain to the securities markets and the protection of investors, even when an SEC witness is not present.

Office of Public Affairs

The Office of Public Affairs assists the Commission in making the work of the SEC open to the public, understandable to investors, and accountable to taxpayers. It helps every other SEC Division and Office accomplish the agency's overall mission—to protect investors, maintain fair, orderly, and efficient markets, and facilitate capital formation. The Office coordinates the agency's relations with the media and the general public, in this country and around the world.

. . . .

The Laws That Govern the Securities Industry

Securities Act of 1933

Often referred to as the "truth in securities" law, the Securities Act of 1933 has two basic objectives:

- require that investors receive financial and other significant information concerning securities being offered for public sale; and

- prohibit deceit, misrepresentations, and other fraud in the sale of securities.

Purpose of Registration

A primary means of accomplishing these goals is the disclosure of important financial information through the registration of securities. This information enables investors, not the government, to make informed judgments about whether to purchase a company's securities. While the SEC requires that the information provided be accurate, it does not guarantee it. Investors who purchase securities and suffer losses [may] have important recovery rights if they can prove that there was [materially] incomplete or inaccurate disclosure of important information.

The Registration Process

[Absent an exemption,] securities sold in the U.S. must be registered. The registration forms companies file provide essential facts while minimizing the burden and expense of complying with the law. In general, registration forms call for:

- a description of the company's properties and business;

- a description of the security to be offered for sale;

- information about the management of the company; and

- financial statements certified by independent accountants.

All companies, both domestic and foreign, must file their registration statements electronically. These statements and the accompanying prospectuses become public shortly after filing, and investors can access them using the Electronic Data Gathering, Analysis, and Retrieval System (EDGAR). Registration statements are subject to examination for compliance with disclosure requirements.

Not all offerings of securities must be registered with the Commission. Some exemptions from the registration requirement include:

- private offerings to a limited number of persons or institutions;

- offerings of limited size;

- intrastate offerings; and

- securities of municipal, state, and federal governments.

By exempting many small offerings from the registration process, the SEC seeks to foster capital formation by lowering the cost of offering securities to the public.

Securities Exchange Act of 1934

With this Act, Congress created the Securities and Exchange Commission. The Act empowers the SEC with broad authority over all aspects of the securities industry. This includes the power to register, regulate, and oversee brokerage firms, transfer agents, and clearing agencies as well as the nation's securities self-regulatory organizations (SROs). The various stock exchanges, such as the New York Stock Exchange and the American Stock Exchange, are SROs. The Financial Industry Regulatory Authority [FINRA], which operates the NASDAQ system, is also an SRO.

The Act also identifies and prohibits certain types of conduct in the markets and provides the Commission with disciplinary powers over regulated entities and persons associated with them.

The Act also empowers the SEC to require periodic reporting of information by companies with publicly traded securities. [For example, pursuant to its Securities Exchange Act authority, the SEC engages in regulating the following activities:]

Corporate Reporting

[Publicly-held companies under the Securities Exchange Act] must file annual and other periodic reports. These reports are available to the public through the SEC's EDGAR database.

Proxy Solicitations

The Securities Exchange Act also governs the disclosure in materials used to solicit shareholders' votes in annual or special meetings held for the election of directors and the approval of other corporate action. This information, contained in proxy materials, must be filed with the Commission in advance of any solicitation to ensure compliance with the disclosure rules.

Solicitations, whether by management or shareholder groups, must disclose all important facts concerning the issues on which holders are asked to vote.

Tender Offers

The Securities Exchange Act requires disclosure of important information by anyone acquir[ing] more than 5 percent of a company's securities by direct purchase or tender offer. Such an offer often is extended in an effort to gain control of the company. As with the proxy rules, this allows shareholders to make informed decisions on these critical corporate events.

Insider Trading

The securities laws broadly prohibit fraudulent activities of any kind in connection with the offer, purchase, or sale of securities. These provisions are the basis for many types of disciplinary actions, including actions against fraudulent insider trading. Insider trading is illegal when a person trades a security while in possession of material nonpublic information in violation of a duty to withhold the information or refrain from trading.

Registration of Exchanges, Associations, and Others

The Act requires a variety of market participants to register with the Commission, including exchanges, brokers and dealers, transfer agents, and clearing agencies. Registration for these organizations involves filing disclosure documents that are updated on a regular basis.

The exchanges and FINRA are identified as self-regulatory organizations (SROs). SROs must create rules that allow for disciplining members for improper conduct and for establishing measures to ensure market integrity and investor protection. SRO proposed rules are published for comment before final SEC review and approval.

Trust Indenture Act of 1939

This Act applies to debt securities such as bonds, debentures, and notes that are offered for public sale. Even though such securities may be registered under the Securities Act, they may not be offered for sale to the public unless a formal agreement between the issuer of bonds and the bondholders, known as the trust indenture, conforms to the standards of this Act.

Investment Company Act of 1940

This Act regulates the organization of companies, including mutual funds, that engage primarily in investing, reinvesting, and trading in securities, and whose own securities are offered to the investing public. The regulation is designed to minimize conflicts of interest that arise in these complex operations. The Act requires these companies to disclose their financial condition and investment policies to investors when stock is initially sold and, subsequently, on a regular basis. The focus of this Act is on disclosure to the investing public of information about the fund and its investment objectives, as well as on investment company structure and operations. It is important to remember that the Act does not permit the SEC to directly supervise the investment decisions or activities of these companies or judge the merits of their investments.

Investment Advisers Act of 1940

This law regulates investment advisers. With certain exceptions, this Act requires that firms compensated for advising others about securities investments must register with the SEC and conform to regulations designed to protect investors. . . .

Sarbanes-Oxley Act of 2002 [and Dodd-Frank Act of 2010]

On July 30, 2002, President Bush signed into law the Sarbanes-Oxley Act of 2002 [SOX], which he characterized as "the most far reaching reforms of American business practices since the time of Franklin Delano Roosevelt." The Act mandated a number of reforms to enhance corporate responsibility, [improve] financial disclosures, and combat corporate and accounting fraud. [SOX also] created the "Public Company Accounting Oversight Board," also known as the PCAOB, to oversee the activities of the auditing profession. [Similarly, the Dodd-Frank Act of 2010 impacts corporate governance by requiring, for example, a shareholder advisory vote on the level of executive compensation, greater disclosure with respect to

executive pay, and compensation committees being comprised
entirely of independent directors.]

---

*As discussed earlier in this chapter, the SEC has brought
several enforcement actions against in-house lawyers who
allegedly engaged in illegal insider trading or tipping. Three of
these cases follow.*

SEC v. ANDREW S. MARKS
SEC Litigation Release No. 18956 (2004)

The Commission announced that, on October 25, 2004, a
Massachusetts federal court, by consent, issued an order in an
insider trading case enjoining Andrew S. Marks, of Wayland,
Massachusetts, from violations of the antifraud provisions, and
barring him from acting as an officer or director of a public
company. Marks was also ordered to pay $53,000 in
disgorgement. Marks is currently in federal prison serving a
sentence of a year and a day as the result of a related criminal
proceeding.

In its complaint, filed December 3, 2002, the Commission
alleged that Marks, who at the time was Vertex's highest-
ranking attorney, learned on September 20, 2001, that Vertex
planned to announce the suspension of clinical trials of one of its
promising drugs on September 24. According to the
Commission's complaint, on September 21, Marks liquidated all
of his Vertex stock despite having previously acknowledged in
writing that the impending release would not be viewed
favorably by Wall Street and that he should not sell his Vertex
shares. The Commission alleged that, by selling his holdings
prior to the company's public announcement on September 24,
Marks avoided a loss of $105,999.

According to the Commission's complaint, at the time he
traded, Marks was the designated attorney for employees to
consult regarding compliance with Vertex's employee securities
trading policy. In that capacity, the Commission alleged, Marks
wrote Vertex's CEO an email on September 20, advising him to
make sure that an employee who had requested permission to

trade had no knowledge of the impending press release. In the e-mail, Marks wrote:

> I guess that I am troubled about any employee trading prior to that release because it is likely to have an effect on the stock (looks like I can't sell any shares) and, depending on the degree of that effect, could create the perception of insider trading.

On September 21, less than 24 hours after writing this email to the CEO, the Commission alleged, Marks sold 20,900 shares of Vertex at an average price of $22.81 per share, receiving $476,765. Vertex announced its decision to terminate clinical trials at approximately 7:10 a.m. on September 24. Vertex's shares closed that day at $17.74, down $5.33 from the previous close on volume of 9.8 million shares, more than eight times average daily volume.

In its complaint, the Commission alleged that Marks traded in breach of a fiduciary duty to Vertex and its shareholders not to trade in the company's stock while in possession of material, nonpublic information about the company. As a result of the conduct described in the complaint, the Commission charged Marks with violations of the antifraud provisions of the federal securities laws. . . .

. . .[I]n the related criminal action, Marks had pled guilty to a one-count information filed by the U.S. Attorney for the District of Massachusetts charging him with unlawful insider trading in connection with his sale of Vertex stock. On January 12, 2004, a federal judge sentenced Marks to a year and a day in prison for his conduct.

SEC v. MITCHELL S. DRUCKER
SEC Litigation Release No. 21233 (2009)

On September 21, 2009, the United States Court of Appeals for the Second Circuit affirmed a jury verdict finding Mitchell S. Drucker, an attorney and former associate general counsel at NBTY, Inc. ("NBTY"), a nutritional supplements manufacturer and retailer, and his father, Ronald Drucker, liable for violating the antifraud provisions of the federal securities and affirmed the remedies imposed by the federal district court. . . .

The Commission had charged that, while Mitchell Drucker was a lawyer at NBTY, and had learned that NBTY was about to announce lower than expected quarterly earnings, he and his father, a former New York City police detective, sold their entire holdings of NBTY stock just before the negative announcement. Collectively, the defendants avoided $197,243 in losses by selling in advance of the announcement. . . .

. . .Judge Colleen McMahon of the United States District Court for the Southern District of New York, entered final judgments. . . . The judgment against defendant Mitchell Drucker permanently enjoined him from violating the antifraud provisions, and barred him from serving as an officer and director of any public company. The judgment also ordered defendant Mitchell Drucker to pay disgorgement and prejudgment interest totaling $201,146, to pay, and be jointly and severally liable with his father, defendant Ronald Drucker for, disgorgement and prejudgment interest totaling $74,411. . . . The judgment ordered Mitchell Drucker to pay a civil penalty of $394,486, representing two times the combined ill-gotten gains obtained by defendants Mitchell Drucker and Ronald Drucker. . . .

SEC v. GENE D. LEVOFF

SEC Litigation Release No. 24399 (2019)

On February 13, 2019, the Securities and Exchange Commission filed insider trading charges against a former senior attorney at Apple whose duties included executing the company's insider trading compliance efforts.

The SEC's complaint alleges that Gene Daniel Levoff, an attorney who previously served as Apple's global head of corporate law and corporate secretary, received confidential information about Apple's quarterly earnings announcements in his role on a committee of senior executives who reviewed the company's draft earnings materials prior to their public dissemination. Using this confidential information, Levoff traded Apple securities ahead of three quarterly earnings announcements in 2015 and 2016 and made approximately $382,000 in combined profits and losses avoided. The SEC's complaint alleges that Levoff was responsible for securities laws compliance at Apple, including compliance with insider trading laws. As part of his responsibilities, Levoff reviewed and approved the company's insider trading policy and notified employees of their obligations under the insider trading policy around quarterly earnings announcements.

The SEC's complaint, filed in federal district court in Newark, New Jersey, charges Levoff with fraud in violation of Section 17(a) of the Securities Act of 1933, Section 10(b) of the Securities Exchange Act of 1934 and Rule 10b–5 thereunder, and seeks a permanent injunction, disgorgement, prejudgment interest, a civil penalty, and an officer and director bar.

In a parallel action, the U.S. Attorney's Office for the District of New Jersey today announced criminal charges.

. . . .

CHAPTER 10

CORPORATE INTERNAL INVESTIGATIONS

Corporate internal investigations occur with relative frequency. They may arise, for example, as a result of a company's internal control procedures (such as "spot" checks of problematic areas in which the company conducts business) or may be triggered by complaints made by whistleblowers alleging suspected illegal activity. If the concerns are shown to be valid, the adverse ramifications to the company may be substantial, including, for example, government penalties (including monetary fines) and the filing of private lawsuits (frequently shareholder derivative actions and securities class actions that may result in settlements amounting to millions of dollars).

FACTORS TO BE EVALUATED

In assessing the appropriate structure, parameters, and objectives of an internal investigation, a number of factors should be evaluated by in-house counsel, including: should the investigation be conducted by inside or outside counsel; do the allegations involve a systematic problem, a one-time incident or somewhere in-between; the perceived scope of the investigation (geographic locations, including foreign countries, and the number and rank of corporate personnel potentially implicated); the persons or department responsible for maintaining investigation data; the breadth of documents and related materials to be reviewed; the number of employees, including high level personnel, that should be interviewed; the need to gather pertinent information without certain personnel being aware of the internal investigation; the anticipated time-line for completing the internal investigation; and the probability as well as magnitude of the reasonably anticipated consequences ensuing from the investigation.[1]

---

[1]   *See* Rathbone & Rapa, *A Primer on Internal Investigations,* 46 Rev. Sec. & Comm. Reg. 69, 69–70 (2013).

CLIENT CONFIDENTIALITY

Inside counsel's ability to render effective legal advice largely depends on the corporate client's willingness to provide detailed and truthful information. Absent such candor, it frequently becomes impractical for the in-house attorney to conduct a meaningful analysis of the client's possible legal rights and remedies.

Generally, the ethical rules protect from revelation confidences and secrets of the client (including communications coming within the attorney-client privilege). As the commentary to the ABA's Model Rules explains, the protection of a client's confidential information facilitates the development of facts that are necessary for effective representation.[2] The principle of lawyer-client confidentiality encourages the client "to communicate fully and frankly with the lawyer even as to embarrassing or legally damaging subject matter."[3]

In the context of organizational representation, the principle of lawyer-client confidentiality (and the specific communications it protects) becomes more complex. When serving as an in-house lawyer, the attorney's professional duties generally run only to that entity, and not to the constituents through whom the entity communicates.[4] Generally, corporate clients receive the same level of protection of confidentiality as an individual client; however, difficulty arises due to the fact that the corporation must speak through its constituents.[5] Since it is the constituents who must speak on behalf of the corporation, communications between the corporation's attorney and the corporation (through the constituents) must receive some level of protection in order for the corporation to benefit from the attorney-client privilege.

---

[2]   See e.g., Model Rules of Prof. Conduct, Rule 1.6 & cmt. 2.

[3]   Id. See Willy v. Administrative Review Board, 423 F. 3d 483, 495 (5th Cir. 2005).

[4]   See e.g., Model Rule 1.13. See Orbit One Communications, Inc. v. Numerex Corp., 255 F.R.D. 98, 104 (S.D.N.Y. 2008). See generally S. Martyn & L. Fox, The Ethics of Representing Organizations (2009).

[5]   Mulroy & Thesing, Confidentiality Concerns In Internal Corporate Investigations, 25 Tort & Ins. L.J. 48, 49 (1989).

The U.S. Supreme Court examined the degree of protection these communications should receive in the landmark *Upjohn* case.[6] In its analysis, the Court focused more on the subject matter of the communications and less on the particular organizational constituent from whom the communications were made.[7] As the Supreme Court explained, "[t]he communications concerned matters within the scope of the employees' corporate duties, and the employees themselves were sufficiently aware that they were being questioned in order that the corporation could obtain legal advice."[8] As a result, the Court reasoned, "[c]onsistent with the underlying purposes of the attorney-client privilege, these communications must be protected against compelled disclosure."[9] Thus, the Supreme Court held that, while the constituents themselves were not in an attorney-client relationship with the corporation's attorney, their communications on behalf of the corporation were nevertheless protected by the privilege existing between the corporation and the corporation's attorney.[10]

---

[6]   *Upjohn Co. v. United States*, 449 U.S. 383 (1981).

[7]   *Id.* at 394.

[8]   *Id.*

[9]   *Id. See* J. Gergacz, *Attorney-Corporate Client Privilege* (3d ed. 2017); Schipani, *The Future of the Attorney-Client Privilege in Corporate Criminal Investigations,* 34 Del. J. Corp. L. 921 (2009).

[10]   The *Upjohn* Court also addressed the *work product doctrine's* application to documents prepared in connection with employee interviews conducted by an attorney during an internal investigation. To the extent that these documents reflect privileged communications, they are protected by the attorney-client privilege. To the extent that these documents reflect the mental impressions of the attorney conducting the interview, they are protected by the work product doctrine. *Id.* at 401. The Court did not, however, grant an absolute privilege to such documents; rather it held that the moving party is required to make a sufficient showing of necessity and unavailability in order to compel disclosure. *Id.* at 402.

In *Hickman v. Taylor*, 329 U.S. 495 (1974), the Supreme Court recognized the work product doctrine, which was subsequently codified in Rule 26 of the Federal Rules of Civil Procedure. The work product doctrine ultimately protects from compelled discovery tangible items that are prepared "in anticipation of litigation or for trial" (FRCP 26(b)(3)). Essentially, the doctrine has been interpreted to protect a lawyer's mental impressions and legal analysis. In conducting an internal investigation, attorneys will inevitably keep written records of information gathered during employee interviews. To prevent these tangible items from being subject to future discovery, some commentators have suggested that the attorney should attempt to mix as many mental impressions and legal analyses as possible among the acquired and recorded information. *See* Kenny & Mitchelson, *Corporate Benefits of Properly Conducted Internal Investigations*, 11 Ga. St. L. Rev. 657, 667 (1995). *See also, Redvanly v. NYNEX Corp.*, 152 F.R.D. 460, 466 (S.D.N.Y. 1993) (holding that the corporation's attorney's notes were discoverable because they were "a running transcript of the meeting" and failed to reflect the

Hence, the attorney-client privilege protects subject communications from compelled disclosure to an outside third party. Consequently, the *Upjohn* decision ultimately deals with the degree to which the attorney-client privilege protects communications made on behalf of an organizational client by the organization's constituents. The situation becomes more ambiguous, however, with respect to whether such communications also are protected from disclosure to other constituents within the organization. This issue may arise, for instance, in the context of an internal investigation within a corporation.[11]

PURPOSES OF INTERNAL INVESTIGATIONS

Internal investigations can assist a corporation's board of directors and management in ascertaining the advantages and disadvantages of certain corporate policies. In other instances, internal investigations may be aimed at uncovering suspected wrongful and/or criminal acts perpetrated by certain company employees during the course of employment.[12] In such a situation, the internal investigation can take on paramount importance in the corporation's attempt to fend off or minimize the imposition of criminal or serious civil sanctions as a result of the wrongful acts. Indeed, in the aftermath of the Sarbanes-Oxley Act of 2002 (SOX) and the Dodd-Frank Act of 2010, internal investigations have become more common due to: (1) the directive to audit committees to establish procedures that relate to complaints received by the company regarding accounting or auditing matters; (2) the protection given to whistleblowers who

---

attorney's mental impressions). Note, however, that if the corporation ultimately might waive the attorney-client privilege and work product doctrine pursuant to the applicable government regulator's (e.g., the Department of Justice's) "request," counsel should consider confining the interview notes to solely factual matters. *See also, Ryan v. Gifford*, 2008 WL 43699 (Del. Ch. 2008) (due to that defendant directors and their lawyers were present when the corporation's special committee and such committee's attorney met with the corporation's board of directors, work product protection held to be waived).

[11]   *See generally* ABA Task Force on the Attorney-Client Privilege, *Report of the American Bar Association's Task Force on the Attorney-Client Privilege*, 60 Bus. Law. 1029 (2005).

[12]   *See Ryan v. Gifford*, 2007 WL 4259557 (Del. Ch. 2007); Kenny & Mitchelson, *supra* note 10, 11 Ga. St. L. Rev. at 661; Lublin & Bennett, *GM Board Probing Information Gap*, Wall St. J., May 15, 2014, at B1; Mulroy & Thesing, *supra* note 5, 25 Tort & Ins. L.J. at 48.

suffer termination or other retaliatory consequences as a result of engaging in protected conduct; and (3) the payment of significant monetary awards to whistleblowers who voluntarily provide the SEC with "original" information concerning a federal securities law violation that results in a successful enforcement action.[13] Hence, as a consequence of an increase in the number of employee whistleblower complaints and the recognition by audit committees of their enhanced responsibilities after SOX and the Dodd-Frank Act, internal investigations today are conducted with greater frequency.

Thus, there are certain advantages for a corporation to conduct an internal investigation. These advantages, for example, include:

> [1] enabl[ing] a company to take control of the situation, not only by gathering relevant facts, but by implementing prompt corrective actions . . .; [2] a thorough and regimented investigation ultimately will produce sound, reliable conclusions . . .; [3] an investigation allows a company to document facts required to take action against an employee or third party, if necessary; [4] a company can demonstrate its commitment to compliance by conducting [a thorough and impartial] investigation; [and] [5] a [sound] investigation can reduce the likelihood of a government enforcement action, or serve to mitigate penalties.[14]

---

[13]   See SOX §§ 301(m), 806; Dodd-Frank Act § 922, *amending,* § 21 of the Securities Exchange Act; *Digital Realty Trust, Inc. v. Somers,* 138 S. Ct. 767, 772–773 (2018) (holding that to sue under the Dodd-Frank Act's anti-retaliation provision, the whistleblower "must provide information relating to a violation of the securities laws to the [Securities and Exchange] Commission"); Securities Exchange Act Release No. 64545 (2011); Steinberg & Kaufman, *Minimizing Corporate Liability Exposure When the Whistle Blows in the Post Sarbanes-Oxley Era,* 30 J. Corp. L. 445 (2005). For discussion on the role internal investigations play in helping an organization avoid criminal liability, *see Sentencing Commission Amends Guidelines, Calls for Improved Compliance Officer Access,* 42 Sec. Reg. & L. Rep. (BNA) 914 (2010); Valukas & Stauffer, *Internal Investigations Of Corporate Misconduct,* 6 Insights No. 2, at 17 (Feb. 1992).

[14]   Rathbone & Rapa, *supra* note 1, 46 Rev. Sec. & Comm. Reg. at 70. *See* McLucas, Wertheimer & June, *Preparing for the Deluge: How to Respond When Employees Speak Up and Report Possible Compliance Violations,* 44 Sec. Reg. & L. Rep. (BNA) 922, 923 (2012) ("Lawyers in the General Counsel's office may be in the best position in many organizations to conduct the initial assessment because of their substantive knowledge of the securities laws, experience in reviewing allegations and objectivity. When in-house lawyers make the initial assessment, that assessment should preserve applicable privileges.").

COMPONENTS OF AN INTERNAL INVESTIGATION

Internal investigations generally are comprised of two courses of action: a document review and employee interviews.[15] It is in the area of employee interviews that the investigating inside or outside attorney particularly must exercise caution with respect to statements (or the lack thereof) made to the individual employee. This is especially true where the individual employee's interests appear adverse to the interests of the corporation.

In conducting an internal investigation, the attorney should seek to obtain as much truthful and factual information from interviewees as practicable. The corporation and the subject attorneys nonetheless must not impede an employee being interviewed from communicating as a whistleblower to the government. In a number of SEC proceedings, companies have incurred money penalties as well as other sanctions for using confidentiality agreements signed by interviewees during their internal investigations that allegedly violated the Dodd-Frank whistleblower provision.[16]

While ABA Model Rule 1.13 provides that the attorney's loyalty is to the organizational client, the rule also obliges the attorney to "explain the identity of the client [namely, the corporation] when the lawyer knows or reasonably should know that the organization's interests are adverse to those of the constituents with whom the lawyer is dealing."[17] An internal investigation designed to uncover suspected employee wrongdoing may place the company's interests and certain employees' interests at odds, thereby potentially invoking the attorney's obligation to explain the identity of the client to the interviewee-employee.[18]

---

[15]   *See* Kenny & Mitchelson, *supra* note 10, 11 Ga. St. L. Rev. at 665–667.

[16]   *See, e.g., In the Matter of KBR, Inc.*, Securities Exchange Act Release No. 74619 (2015) (settlement). *See also*, Kahn, *Preserving the Confidentiality of Internal Corporate Investigations*, 1 J. Corp. Disclosure & Confidentiality 155, 155–158 (1989).

[17]   *See* Model Rule 1.13(f).

[18]   *Id. See* Rule 4.3 ("In dealing on behalf of a client with a person who is not represented by counsel, a lawyer shall not state or imply that the lawyer is disinterested.").

For example, employees who are interviewed may possess material information pertaining to the attorney's fact-finding investigation that they do not feel comfortable disclosing for fear of repercussions. If, for instance, an employee had done something that could jeopardize her position within the corporation, it is unlikely that the employee will share the information with the attorney, unless the employee knows, or at least thinks, that her communications are confidential and will not be disclosed even to other constituents. Nonetheless, as counsel for the corporation, the attorney is obligated to remain steadfastly loyal to the company's best interests, and act in a manner intended to further those interests. As one source explains:

> Counsel for the corporation owes an allegiance to the corporation as an entity rather than to the employee being interviewed. In many circumstances, the interests of individual employees may be adverse to the interests of the corporation . . . In the interest of candor, counsel should instruct employees that he represents the corporation, that he is not their attorney, that employees cannot assert the attorney-client privilege to bar disclosure of the interview, and that the corporation possesses the attorney-client privilege but may waive it and disclose the information.[19]

Hence, the in-house attorney conducting the interview may well be obligated to give the employee-interviewee a Miranda-style warning. Accordingly, the Association of Corporate Counsel recommends that, prior to their interviews, employees be required to sign an acknowledgment that they received this type of warning.[20] Indeed, if appropriate, the standard warnings may be augmented by a pointed disclosure referencing the risk of an obstruction of justice criminal charge.[21] Moreover, in certain factual contexts, an in-house attorney may incur liability

---

[19]   Mulroy & Thesing, *supra* note 5, 25 Tort & Ins. L.J. at 49.

[20]   *See* Hechler, *Upjohn Warning Is a Vital Tool,* Nat. L.J., Jan. 16, 2006, at 8; Martin, *When Corporate Counsel Get Caught in the Middle,* Cal. Law. at 75 (Dec. 1989).

[21]   *See* Strauss, *Company Counsel as Agents of Obstruction,* N.Y. L.J., July 1, 2004, at p. 1.

exposure for failing to provide a sufficient notice to a non-client third party.[22]

From the organizational-client's perspective, the problem is that such a warning could result in the employee being less than truthful, thus having a chilling effect on the employee's willingness to candidly cooperate with the investigation.[23] Consequently, warning the non-client employee with respect to the consequences of making unprivileged self-incriminating statements could compromise the attorney's ability to fulfill her investigative responsibilities. In other words, the constituents may "not confide information the attorney feels is critical to competent representation."[24]

Although not generally favored today, in the past, some inside counsel objected to giving employee-interviewees a warning regarding the limits of confidentiality. As the former Executive Vice President and Chief Legal Officer of the ITT Corporation explained:

> There has been a good deal of discussion among corporate counsel as to whether an employee should be given a 'Miranda' type warning before being questioned in an internal investigation, or if not that, be given an opportunity to consult his or her own lawyer before submitting to interrogation. I have concluded that carrying out my professional responsibility to the corporate entity requires that neither of such courses be followed. It is my task to find out what the facts are as fully and as quickly as possible. It is the obligation of an employee to respond truthfully to questions put to him by the corporation as to activities in the course of his employment for which the corporation may be held responsible, whether civilly or criminally.[25]

---

[22]   *See Pendergast-Holt v. Sjoblom and Proskauer-Rose, LLP,* 2009 WL 890343 (N.D. Tex. 2009) (complaint); *Parker v. Carnahan,* 772 S.W.2d 151 (Tex. App. 1989); *Collin County v. Johnson,* 1999 WL 994039 (Tex. App. 1999).

[23]   Pizzimenti, *The Lawyer's Duty To Warn Clients About Limits On Confidentiality,* 39 Cath. U. L. Rev. 441, 484 (1990).

[24]   *Id.*

[25]   Aibel, *Corporate Counsel and Business Ethics: A Personal Review,* 59 Mo. L. Rev. 427, 438 (1994). *See United States v. Int'l Brotherhood of Teamsters,* 961 F. Supp. 665, 673 (S.D.N.Y. 1997) (allowing an employee not provided with warning to invoke the

Nonetheless, today this view no longer has widespread acceptance.

NEED FOR *MIRANDA*-TYPE WARNING

As internal investigations are frequently initiated to uncover facts related to suspected wrongdoing within the corporation, it normally is in the company's best interest to retain outside counsel to conduct the investigation in an attempt to enhance the objectivity of the investigation and preservation of the privileged status of detrimental information.[26] Irrespective of whether the investigation is undertaken by in-house or outside counsel, to avoid potential ethical and malpractice issues, the investigating attorney ordinarily should avoid individual representation of an organizational constituent-employee. If the attorney acts as legal counsel for an individual employee, the attorney will be bound by additional confidentiality obligations to that employee.[27] Therefore, prior to conducting employee interviews, prudent counsel should provide a "Miranda-type" warning. As one court held, "[i]n the absence of any advice by [corporate counsel] to the contrary, defendants were justified in believing that [corporate counsel] were there to protect their individual interests as well as those of the corporation."[28] Hence, a key objective of providing a "Miranda-type" warning is to avoid the impression that the attorney somehow misled the individual employee to believe that the attorney represented such employee's personal interests as opposed to (or in addition to) those of the corporation.[29]

---

attorney-client privilege would preclude counsel "from disclosing the employee's communications . . . thus thwarting the investigation").

[26] As one source explains, "[t]he best method of ensuring that the results of the investigation remain within the company's control is to conduct the investigation in a manner specifically designed to maintain both the confidentiality of the investigative results and the attorney-client or work product privileges associated with them." Kenny & Mitchelson, *supra* note 10, 11 Ga. State Univ. L. Rev. at 663–664.

[27] *Id.* at 666.

[28] *United States v. Hart*, 1992 U.S. Dist. LEXIS 17796, at *5 (E.D. La. 1992). *Cf. In re Grand Jury Subpoena Under Seal*, 415 F.3d 333 (4th Cir. 2005) (concluding that employee interviewed in an internal investigation did not have attorney-client relationship with the attorney conducting the interview).

[29] *See, e.g., Westinghouse Electric Corp. v. Kerr-McGee Corp.*, 580 F.2d 1311 (7th Cir. 1978) (holding that the employees' communications to the corporation's attorney were privileged and confidential based on the reasonable belief that they were being individually represented by the corporation's attorney).

Nonetheless, in determining whether the individual corporate employee has an attorney-client relationship with the corporation's legal counsel, numerous courts adhere to a more rigorous standard, requiring that the individual employee establish that: (1) he approached the corporate attorney to procure legal advice; (2) he made it clear to the corporate attorney that he was seeking legal advice in his individual capacity; (3) corporate counsel communicated to the employee in his individual capacity while knowing of the conflict dilemma; (4) the conversations between corporate counsel and the employee were confidential; and (5) the substance of the conversations with the corporate attorney did not concern matters within the corporation or the corporation's general affairs.[30]

A relatively recent case highlights this dilemma. There, the subject employee claimed that he believed that corporate counsel also represented him when he gave incriminatory statements in an interview during an internal corporate investigation.[31] During that interview, the employee was not given notice that the law firm did not represent him. Subsequently, corporate counsel provided the employee's statements to the government. Prohibiting the government from using these statements, the district court asserted that the interviewee-employee "was never told, nor did he ever contemplate, that his statements to the lawyers [conducting the interview] would be disclosed to third parties, especially not the Government in connection with criminal charges against him."[32] The court also referred the lawyers to the State Bar Association for possible disciplinary action.[33] On appeal, the Ninth Circuit reversed.[34] Taking a very different view of the circumstances than the court below, the Ninth Circuit held that the employee's statements during the

---

[30]   United States v. Graf, 610 F. 3d 1148, 1159 (9th Cir. 2010), relying on, In re Bevill, Bresler & Schulman Asset Management Corp., 805 F. 2d 120, 123–125 (3d Cir. 1986).

[31]   United States v. Nicholas, 606 F. Supp. 2d 1109 (C.D. Cal. 2009), rev'd, United States v. Ruehle, 583 F. 3d 600 (9th Cir. 2009).

[32]   606 F. Supp. 2d at 1112. See Scannell, For Corporate Lawyers, There's Just One Client, Wall St. J., April 13, 2009, at p. B1 (stating that the decision in Nicholas suggests that attorneys "need to issue more explicit warnings during internal investigations that they don't represent individual employees").

[33]   606 F. Supp. 2d at 1121.

[34]   United States v. Ruehle, 583 F. 3d 600 (9th Cir. 2009).

internal investigation interview were not protected under the attorney-client privilege. This was due to the appellate court's conclusion that the employee's statements to the attorneys conducting the internal investigation interview "were not 'made in confidence' but rather for the purpose of disclosure to [third parties, namely, the] outside auditors."[35]

In view that (as a matter of customary practice) a warning is given to an employee being interviewed, the next question is what should the warning contain. Tension exists between providing sufficient information to the employee to render the warning effective, without deterring the employee from providing accurate and truthful information. The Association of Corporate Counsel recommends that the attorney use a written script. For example, the in-house attorney could communicate to the employee that she is not the employee's lawyer and solely represents the corporation. Alternatively, counsel could inform the employee that she represents the corporation, not the employee individually, and as such, the employee's statements may be provided to others, including "superiors" within the corporation, and possibly to the government.[36]

DISCLOSING THE INTERNAL INVESTIGATION

Should a company publicly disclose its conducting of an internal investigation? Generally, privately-held enterprises have no obligation to disclose non-public information. Accordingly, these companies normally do not reveal their conducting of internal investigations. A different situation involves publicly-traded companies because they are subject to the periodic reporting provisions of the federal securities laws (including current, quarterly, and annual reports required to be filed with the SEC).[37] If an internal investigation is deemed

[35]   *Id.* at 609. *See Gilman v. Marsh & McLennan Companies, Inc.*, 826 F.3d 69 (2d Cir. 2016) (holding termination of employment appropriate for employees who refused to be interviewed pursuant to company's internal investigation).

[36]   *See* Hechler, *Upjohn Warning Is a Vital Tool,* Nat. L.J., Jan. 16, 2006, at 8; Rathbone & Rapa, *supra* note 1, 46 Rev. Sec. & Comm. Reg. at 72. *See generally* American College of Trial Lawyers, *Recommended Practices for Companies and Their Counsel in Conducting Internal Investigations,* 46 Am. Crim. L. Rev. 73 (2009).

[37]   For further discussion, *see, e.g.,* M. Steinberg, *Securities Regulation* (7th edition 2017).

material (such as a material FCPA internal investigation), disclosure of such investigation in an SEC periodic report would be prudent.[38]

Moreover, there may exist other sound reasons for a company to disclose an ongoing internal investigation. One reason is that if the company declines to disclose the internal investigation, the existence of the investigation or the underlying alleged misconduct may be made publicly by a third party (e.g., whistleblower, news media source, or plaintiffs' law firm) in a manner more detrimental to the company. This possibility is more likely to occur today due to the Dodd-Frank Act of 2010 which provides a lucrative financial bounty for whistleblowers who provide "original" information to the SEC concerning a federal securities law violation that results in a successful enforcement action.[39]

The decision that follows from the U.S. Court of Appeals for the D.C. Circuit (authored by Justice Kavanaugh when he served on that Circuit) illustrates the invocation of the attorney-client privilege in the context of a corporate internal investigation.

IN RE: KELLOGG BROWN & ROOT, INC.

United States Court of Appeals
756 F.3d 754 (D.C. Cir. 2014)

KAVANAUGH, *Circuit Judge*: More than three decades ago, the Supreme Court held that the attorney-client privilege protects confidential employee communications made during a business's internal investigation led by company lawyers. *See Upjohn Co. v. United States*, 449 U.S. 383 (1981). In this case, the District Court denied the protection of the privilege to a company that had conducted just such an internal investigation. The District Court's decision has generated substantial uncertainty about the scope of the attorney-client privilege in the business setting. We conclude that the District Court's

---

[38]   *See* Warin & Logan, *Disclosing Pending FCPA Investigations,* 46 Rev. Sec. & Comm. 61, 65 (2013).

[39]   *Id.* at 65–66. *See Digital Realty Trust, Inc. v. Somers*, 138 S. Ct. 767 (2018); sources cited note 13 *supra*. Issues relating to "whistleblowers" also are addressed in Chapter 7 of this book.

decision is irreconcilable with *Upjohn*. We therefore grant KBR's petition for a writ of mandamus and vacate the District Court's document production order.

I

Harry Barko worked for KBR, a defense contractor. In 2005, he filed a False Claims Act complaint against KBR and KBR-related corporate entities, whom we will collectively refer to as KBR. In essence, Barko alleged that KBR and certain subcontractors defrauded the U.S. Government by inflating costs and accepting kickbacks while administering military contracts in wartime Iraq. During discovery, Barko sought documents related to KBR's prior internal investigation into the alleged fraud. KBR had conducted that internal investigation pursuant to its Code of Business Conduct, which is overseen by the company's Law Department.

KBR argued that the internal investigation had been conducted for the purpose of obtaining legal advice and that the internal investigation documents therefore were protected by the attorney-client privilege. Barko responded that the internal investigation documents were unprivileged business records that he was entitled to discover. . . .

After reviewing the disputed documents *in camera*, the District Court determined that the attorney-client privilege protection did not apply because, among other reasons, KBR had not shown that "the communication would not have been made 'but for' the fact that legal advice was sought.". . . KBR's internal investigation, the court concluded, was "undertaken pursuant to regulatory law and corporate policy rather than for the purpose of obtaining legal advice." . . .

KBR vehemently opposed the ruling. The company asked the District Court to certify the privilege question to this Court for interlocutory appeal and to stay its order pending a petition for mandamus in this Court. The District Court denied those requests and ordered KBR to produce the disputed documents to Barko within a matter of days. . . . KBR promptly filed a petition for a writ of mandamus in this Court. A number of business organizations and trade associations also objected to the District Court's decision and filed an amicus brief in support of KBR. We

stayed the District Court's document production order and held
oral argument on the mandamus petition.

. . . .

II

We . . . consider whether the District Court's privilege ruling
was legally erroneous. We conclude that it was.

Federal Rule of Evidence 501 provides that claims of
privilege in federal courts are governed by the "common law—as
interpreted by United States courts in the light of reason and
experience." Fed. R. Evid. 501. The attorney-client privilege is
the "oldest of the privileges for confidential communications
known to the common law." *Upjohn Co. v. United States*, 449
U.S. 383, 389 (1981). As relevant here, the privilege applies to a
confidential communication between attorney and client if that
communication was made for the purpose of obtaining or
providing legal advice to the client. . . .

In *Upjohn*, the Supreme Court held that the attorney-client
privilege applies to corporations. The Court explained that the
attorney-client privilege for business organizations was
essential in light of "the vast and complicated array of regulatory
legislation confronting the modern corporation," which required
corporations to "constantly go to lawyers to find out how to obey
the law, . . . particularly since compliance with the law in this
area is hardly an instinctive matter." The Court stated,
moreover, that the attorney-client privilege "exists to protect not
only the giving of professional advice to those who can act on it
but also the giving of information to the lawyer to enable him to
give sound and informed advice." That is so, the Court said,
because the "first step in the resolution of any legal problem is
ascertaining the factual background and sifting through the
facts with an eye to the legally relevant." In *Upjohn*, the
communications were made by company employees to company
attorneys during an attorney-led internal investigation that was
undertaken to ensure the company's "compliance with the law."
The Court ruled that the privilege applied to the internal
investigation and covered the communications between
company employees and company attorneys.

KBR's assertion of the privilege in this case is materially indistinguishable from Upjohn's assertion of the privilege in that case. As in *Upjohn*, KBR initiated an internal investigation to gather facts and ensure compliance with the law after being informed of potential misconduct. And as in *Upjohn*, *KBR's investigation was conducted under the auspices of KBR's in-house legal department, acting in its legal capacity.* [emphasis supplied] The same considerations that led the Court in *Upjohn* to uphold the corporation's privilege claims apply here.

The District Court in this case initially distinguished *Upjohn* on a variety of grounds. But none of those purported distinctions takes this case out from under *Upjohn's* umbrella.

First, the District Court stated that in *Upjohn* the internal investigation began after in-house counsel conferred with outside counsel, whereas here the investigation was conducted in-house without consultation with outside lawyers. But *Upjohn* does not hold or imply that the involvement of outside counsel is a necessary predicate for the privilege to apply. On the contrary, the general rule, which this Court has adopted, is that a lawyer's status as in-house counsel "does not dilute the privilege.". . . As the [American Law Institute] Restatement's commentary points out, "Inside legal counsel to a corporation or similar organization . . . is fully empowered to engage in privileged communications." 1 Restatement [The Law Governing Lawyers] § 72, cmt. c, at 551.

Second, the District Court noted that in *Upjohn* the interviews were conducted by attorneys, whereas here many of the interviews in KBR's investigation were conducted by non-attorneys. But the investigation here was conducted at the direction of the attorneys in KBR's Law Department. And communications made by and to non-attorneys serving as agents of attorneys in internal investigations are routinely protected by the attorney-client privilege. . . . *Third*, the District Court pointed out that in *Upjohn* the interviewed employees were expressly informed that the purpose of the interview was to assist the company in obtaining legal advice, whereas here they were not. The District Court further stated that the confidentiality agreements signed by KBR employees did not mention that the purpose of KBR's investigation was to obtain legal advice. Yet nothing in *Upjohn* requires a company to use magic words to its employees in order to gain the benefit of the privilege for an internal investigation. And in any event, here, as in *Upjohn*, employees knew that the company's legal department was conducting an investigation of a sensitive nature and that the information they disclosed would be protected. KBR employees were also told not to discuss their interviews "without the specific advance authorization of KBR General Counsel." . . .

In short, none of those three distinctions of *Upjohn* holds water as a basis for denying KBR's privilege claim.

More broadly and more importantly, the District Court also distinguished *Upjohn* on the ground that KBR's internal investigation was undertaken to comply with Department of Defense regulations that require defense contractors such as KBR to maintain compliance programs and conduct internal investigations into allegations of potential wrongdoing. The District Court therefore concluded that the purpose of KBR's internal investigation was to comply with those regulatory requirements rather than to obtain or provide legal advice. In our view, the District Court's analysis rested on a false dichotomy. So long as obtaining or providing legal advice was one of the significant purposes of the internal investigation, the attorney-client privilege applies, even if there were also other purposes for the investigation and even if the investigation was mandated by regulation rather than simply an exercise of company discretion.

The District Court began its analysis by reciting the "primary purpose" test, which many courts (including this one) have used to resolve privilege disputes when attorney-client communications may have had both legal and business purposes. But in a key move, the District Court then said that the primary purpose of a communication is to obtain or provide legal advice only if the communication would not have been made "but for" the fact that legal advice was sought. In other words, if there was any other purpose behind the communication, the attorney-client privilege apparently does not apply. The District Court went on to conclude that KBR's internal investigation was "undertaken pursuant to regulatory law and corporate policy rather than for the purpose of obtaining legal advice." . . .

The District Court erred because it employed the wrong legal test. The but-for test articulated by the District Court is not appropriate for attorney-client privilege analysis. Under the District Court's approach, the attorney-client privilege apparently would not apply unless the sole purpose of the communication was to obtain or provide legal advice. That is not the law. We are aware of no Supreme Court or court of appeals decision that has adopted a test of this kind in this context. The District Court's novel approach to the attorney-client privilege would eliminate the attorney-client privilege for numerous communications that are made for both legal and business purposes and that heretofore have been covered by the attorney-client privilege. And the District Court's novel approach would eradicate the attorney-client privilege for internal investigations conducted by businesses that are required by law to maintain compliance programs, which is now the case in a significant swath of American industry. In turn, businesses would be less likely to disclose facts to their attorneys and to seek legal advice, which would "limit the valuable efforts of corporate counsel to ensure their client's compliance with the law." We reject the District Court's but-for test as inconsistent with the principle of *Upjohn* and longstanding attorney-client privilege law.

   . . . .

In the context of an organization's internal investigation, if one of the significant purposes of the internal investigation was to obtain or provide legal advice, the privilege will apply. That is true regardless of whether an internal investigation was conducted pursuant to a company compliance program required by statute or regulation, or was otherwise conducted pursuant to company policy. . . .

In this case, there can be no serious dispute that one of the significant purposes of the KBR internal investigation was to obtain or provide legal advice. In denying KBR's privilege claim on the ground that the internal investigation was conducted in order to comply with regulatory requirements and corporate policy and not just to obtain or provide legal advice, the District Court applied the wrong legal test and clearly erred.

. . . .

In reaching our decision here, we stress, as the Supreme Court did in *Upjohn*, that the attorney-client privilege "only protects disclosure of communications; it does not protect disclosure of the underlying facts by those who communicated with the attorney." *Upjohn Co. v. United States*, 449 U.S. 383, 395 (1981). Barko was able to pursue the facts underlying KBR's investigation. But he was not entitled to KBR's own investigation files. As the *Upjohn* Court stated, quoting Justice Jackson, "Discovery was hardly intended to enable a learned profession to perform its functions . . . on wits borrowed from the adversary." *Id.* at 396 (quoting *Hickman v. Taylor*, 329 U.S. 495, 515 (1947) (Jackson, J., concurring)).

Although the attorney-client privilege covers only communications and not facts, we acknowledge that the privilege carries costs. The privilege means that potentially critical evidence may be withheld from the factfinder. Indeed, as the District Court here noted, that may be the end result in this case. But our legal system tolerates those costs because the privilege "is intended to encourage 'full and frank communication between attorneys and their clients and thereby promote broader public interests in the observance of law and the administration of justice.' "

We grant the petition for a writ of mandamus and vacate the District Court's . . . document production order . . . .

The following excerpt, authored by a seasoned and expert practitioner, highlights key issues facing in-house attorneys with respect to the conducting of internal investigations.

LAW SCHOOL DIDN'T PREPARE YOU FOR THIS:
TIPS FOR THE INTERNAL INVESTIGATION*

By Gary R. Brown
ACC Docket (May 2010)

It can be one of the most daunting tasks you'll be asked to perform as in-house counsel: Following an allegation of improper or illegal conduct, you've been asked to investigate. Management will look to you to decide whether it is a false allegation, a miscommunication or a crisis. You will likely perform your investigation under time constraints, and often with limited resources. Important decisions may turn on your conclusions and recommendations, including HR actions, changes to business processes and possible litigation consequences. Often, those conclusions will rest on one of the most elusive and difficult determinations: the credibility assessment. You'll have to decide who and what to believe, and why, and be prepared to justify your decision.

It is unlikely that your education and experiences have prepared you to make these determinations. Evaluating the veracity of witnesses is not easily taught, and few law schools even try. Even experienced prosecutors and seasoned civil litigators, accustomed to exhaustive documentary and testimonial records generated by criminal investigation and civil discovery, may struggle with making credibility assessments using the limited toolset available to internal investigators.

Yet there is good news: Your personal and professional life experiences have provided you with analytical and interpersonal skills which, when properly applied, will go far in helping you conduct and manage in-house investigations. Equally important, your role as in-house counsel and the insights you have gained into your company and its business will prove critical to the success of any investigation at your company. Thus, even if you decide to retain outside counsel, you will provide an important value-add by staying actively involved in the process.

---

*   Reprinted with the permission of the Association of Corporate Counsel, www. acc.com.

The Investigation

Staffing considerations

Usually, the first decisions surrounding an internal investigation involve staffing, and whether to retain outside resources to conduct or assist in the investigation. Frequently, the nature and magnitude of the issue raised, combined with resource considerations, will dictate the answer. While every allegation should be taken seriously, not all are equal. Matters that are generally small and straightforward—such as simple human resources (HR) complaints—can usually be investigated using in-house resources. Conversely, so-called "bet the farm" allegations, which could, if verified, disrupt mission-critical business functions or result in significant litigation or regulatory action, will usually require outside counsel to gather facts and provide advice. Potential conflicts of interest could also drive the retention of outside counsel.

Internal staffing

In many cases, you will have to staff the investigation using internal resources, which often means you. However, when investigating an allegation of potential wrongdoing, you should never conduct interviews alone. This deserves repeating, as it is one of the fundamental pitfalls of investigations: Never interview alone. Having an assistant witness in the interview process is a critical protection against later assertions of fabrication or improper conduct. While most interviewees will act appropriately, others may later deny admissions made during the interview, make claims of intimidation or allege other improprieties. It is a common strategy by individuals—particularly when an internal investigation leads to HR or legal action—to attack the investigation and the investigator. So be prepared by having a second person with you.

As an added benefit, your witness can also serve as a note taker. You will have to document the results of your interview, preferably in real time. While conducting an interview, you need to formulate and ask questions, consider responses, observe the interviewee's demeanor and reactions, adapt your outline, and review documents. It is, therefore, exceedingly difficult to simultaneously take notes, which will interfere with the flow of the discussion and prevent you from establishing a robust dialogue with the witness. Thus, having a good note taker with you will greatly increase your chances of success.

Depending on the allegation under review, you may have to consider other internal resources to add to the team. This could include HR or IT professionals, as well as other business or subject matter experts. You may wish to include these additional team members in the interview, or consult with them separately. Beware of making your interview team too large, as this may serve to intimidate the interviewee. There is no one-size-fits-all approach here; you'll need to exercise judgment on a case-by-case basis.

Going outside

Selection of outside investigators is a serious matter. Generally, when retaining external investigators, outside counsel offers a distinct advantage over non-attorney investigators: the results of the investigation may be protected by attorney-client privilege, which could become important if the matter becomes the subject of litigation or review by auditors or government regulators. Since, at the outset of an investigation, it is often impossible to know whether this will become important, outside counsel is generally a better choice than an investigative firm. Arguably, investigators may work at the direction of in-house counsel, thus subjecting the results to a claim of privilege.

Risks involved in using outside investigative firms

In-house counsel may choose an outside investigative firm—rather than a law firm—to assist and/or conduct an internal investigation. Depending on the nature of the investigation, such a firm may offer a value proposition, because of lower hourly rates or particular expertise needed for the investigation. However, in opting for an investigative firm you face additional risks:

- *Privilege.* If acting at your direction, there is an argument that an investigative firm's work could be protected under the work product doctrine. When retaining an outside law firm, the privilege argument is much stronger, and the investigative results may be subject to protection as attorney-client communications, as well as work product. Additionally, attorneys are more likely to be sensitive to privilege concerns and may take steps to ensure protection of their work.

- *Quality.* Personnel at investigative firms can vary widely in talent and experience.

- *Optics.* While the conduct of an interview depends largely on the skills of the interviewer, employees may be more comfortable talking to an attorney than a "private eye."

Thus, retaining an investigative firm rather than a law firm requires more diligence and oversight.

However, which law firm should you engage? Don't rush to call the lawyer who negotiated your last lease: not every firm has the skills or resources to effectively conduct internal investigations. Generally speaking, you should look for firms that have extensive experience conducting such investigations, and preferably, investigations of similar allegations. Lawyers who have previously served as prosecutors or held investigatory positions with other government agencies are often good choices. You may also have to consider whether external resources may be required to provide discreet support functions, such as forensic data review or financial expertise.

Even in those matters that require outside counsel to conduct the investigation, you should remain actively engaged. Except in the most unusual situations, outside counsel will lack your understanding of your company, its practices, systems and people. These insights can be critical to a successful investigation, so—barring any conflict—you should be actively involved in every interview.

Developing the allegation

Before conducting interviews (and particularly before interviewing the subject of the allegation), investigate the allegation as thoroughly as possible. Become as knowledgeable as time and resources permit. This will make you more effective in conducting an interview and hopefully eliminate the need to conduct repeated interviews.

While the precise steps will be dictated by the nature of the allegation, your pre-interview investigation will likely include gathering and obtaining documents, getting information from the business and examining physical locations. Many investigations can be greatly furthered by access to email. Depending on the IT capacities of your company, the difficulty and expense of this investigative step can vary greatly. If your company has a centralized email repository and an effective search tool, email searches will prove an efficient and effective means of investigating most allegations. In absence of such a system, you may be compelled to recover email through forensic imaging of individual computers—a costly, slow and disruptive method. Forensic imaging has the added disadvantage of alerting subjects, possibly prematurely, about your investigation. Asking an interviewee to produce her computer for imaging can be discomfiting, and should only be done either well in advance of an interview or at its conclusion.

The best person to ask for additional information about an allegation is its source. Unfortunately, in some cases, that individual may be unavailable to you. If an allegation comes through an anonymous call or email, it is unlikely that you will receive any additional information from the source. (Many ethics hotlines and weblines provide the capacity to post questions to a complainant through an anonymous email system or call-back arrangement, which can be valuable tools.) Similarly, allegations received from third parties or government agencies may not offer the opportunity for follow-up. By contrast, an allegation coming from an identified, internal party will afford you the best chance of further researching the allegation, though this avenue should be pursued carefully. You can approach a complainant for additional information—such as provision of documents or the identification of additional witnesses—which may greatly advance your investigation, conserving time and resources. You should deal carefully with the complainant, however, until issues such as possible motives and biases of the complainant can be ascertained.

Conducting the interview

Preparation

Once you have finished gathering and reviewing as much background information as possible, you'll want to prepare an outline to use for the interview. Your outline will serve only as a roadmap through the interview; you'll need to maintain flexibility in discussing the subjects that may come up. Make sure to have copies of all relevant documents available during the interview.

In structuring your outline, keep a few basic things in mind. First, you'll need to establish a relationship with the interviewee, making sure that she is comfortable with you before you proceed to delicate subjects. Thus, you should usually begin by discussing background issues, as a way of opening a dialogue. This may include a general description of the allegation under investigation—and it's important to explain to a witness that an unproven allegation is meaningless and that your job is to investigate and evaluate all the evidence. It is important to keep an open mind and communicate this to the witness. Second, in most investigations, it is helpful to establish a factual baseline: learning what a witness does in the normal course of business, her job responsibilities and ordinary procedures, can often prove helpful in evaluating an aberrational event or unusual occurrence. Finding out how things should have gone can often shed light on what went wrong. Finally, establishing a rapport with an interviewee will also provide a behavioral baseline, providing you insight about the interviewee's mannerisms, style and tone.

Upjohn

The very first thing you'll need to cover is the *Upjohn* warnings. Much can and has been written on this subject, and there are many fine resources to guide you through the process. Keep in mind that *Upjohn* warnings, though important, should not be intimidating. *Upjohn* is often referred to as "corporate *Miranda*," which is an unfortunate way to view this procedure, as nothing could poison the interview environment more than giving the impression that the interviewee is about to be prosecuted. If you think about it, *Upjohn* represents little more than a common sense explanation of the law—you are a lawyer representing the company, not the individual. As such, your conversation is privileged, but that privilege belongs to the company, which may choose to waive it. Presented as a matter that is obvious and logical, rather than dramatic, the *Upjohn* warning will not (and, indeed, should not) unnerve its intended audience.

Tone

To properly conduct an in-house interview, check your *Law & Order* fantasies at the door. In the world of police and prosecutorial dramas, interrogators often shout, pound tables and throw things in an effort to intimidate and break lying witnesses. In the real world, such tactics are ineffectual and have no place even in a criminal investigation. And in the in-house interview, this approach is simply unacceptable. The presumption in conducting an in-house interview must be that your employees are acting in a professional manner and that their intent is to assist you in your investigation. While the presumption is not irrefutable, you should always give the interviewee the benefit of the doubt.

This presumption should carry over into the tone of your interview and should begin with the invitation. Never summon an employee to an interview; rather, you should invite them to a meeting. The best interviews are collaborative, which suggests that you should share as much as possible with the employee, asking for her assistance in clearing up the problem. While there may be certain facts or information that you cannot share, try to keep the discussion as open as possible. Remember, more information is always better. Treat this, however, as an inquisition, and the employee is likely to shut down, effectively ending your interview.

It's only in the final parts of the interview—after you've established a healthy dialogue, gathered whatever background information you need and established necessary baseline facts—that you should proceed to confront the witness with seemingly incriminating documents or difficult facts. This will allow the witness the opportunity to fully explain her side of the story, and prevent your interview from ending prematurely. Again, it's always better to have more information and to base your determinations on the fullest possible record.

Before concluding your interview, you should ensure that you've explored other possible sources of information, including relevant documents and witnesses, which the interviewee can provide or identify. Often, simply asking about such sources can help a witness crystallize her thought process. Finally, you should ask a catchall question, such as "Is there anything else we should talk about today?" The importance of such a question cannot be overemphasized. Very often, such questions can elicit important information from the interviewee, including the identification of other compliance issues that may require your attention. In addition, the use of a catchall question prevents subsequent claims that you failed to inquire about a particular matter, and can help preclude later embellishments by the interviewee.

Evaluating credibility

After completing your interviews, you'll be confronted with a substantial body of information. How do you evaluate its reliability? What about resolving conflicting information? These are complex tasks, more art than science, and will vary with every interview and investigation. However, there are some common elements that you can consider in making these determinations. I have presented these in an analytical framework: the credibility pyramid. The pyramid divides commonly encountered elements of investigative interviews into three areas.

The Credibility Pyramid

Base of the pyramid: Observations and impressions

The base of the pyramid consists of information gleaned from observation of the witness during the interview process (and occasionally from the witness's statements). These include the investigators' impressions of the witness, the witness's reactions to questions, her demeanor, observed or expressed biases, and your overall "gut feeling" about the witness. Such observations draw upon the same skills we use in everyday life to determine reliability—the criteria we use to decide whether to trust someone, buy something, cast a vote or even enter a business relationship. Did the witness appear forthright or evasive? Were there unusual delays before responding or other affectations that cause concern? Was the individual nervous or matter-of-fact? In short, did you believe [him or her]?

The information at the base of the pyramid is the easiest to obtain and will be the most abundant. Experienced investigators will have a distinct advantage in both making these observations and properly interpreting them. However, these are the most subjective indicators of credibility and can prove the most unreliable. Styles vary with the individual personality, cultural factors and experiences. Some people are better presenters than others, so there are no hard and fast rules, and demeanor can be readily misinterpreted. For example, I once encountered a witness (not the subject of an allegation) who provided solid, corroborated answers to questions during the course of a low-key, hour-long interview. Nothing she said was questioned or questionable, yet tears streamed down her face throughout the interview. Further inquiry revealed that the witness had done nothing wrong and was completely candid, yet cried simply because she felt intimidated by the process. In short, while interpersonal observations can be instructive, if at all possible, you rarely want to make a credibility determination solely on this basis.

The middle level: Logic and common sense

The middle level of the pyramid requires analysis of the information provided during the interview. This level of review is based on the fact that the truth *usually* makes sense. (I emphasize "usually" here because, based on experience, I've heard some very strange things that have, in unusual circumstances, turned out to be true.) People generally act in ways that are rational and interactions should follow a specific logic. If a witness is relating an account that seems hard to believe, that should raise a question in your mind as to whether it should be believed. This is not foolproof and you should make sure you've asked enough questions to fully understand the context of the information presented. However, if the witness's account remains illogical after a full inquiry, this can become a significant factor in determining its reliability. In making these kinds of determinations, your insight as in-house counsel should provide helpful guidance in determining whether the information being offered makes sense in the context of your business and its industry.

The apex: Corroboration and inconsistencies

Finally, at the top of the pyramid is corroboration and inconsistencies. These elements will require the most work to develop and are generally in smallest quantities. However, like rare gems, these elements will prove invaluable in making a credibility determination. Corroboration usually consists of documents or accounts from other witnesses that bolster information provided by the interviewee. Inconsistencies come in two forms: internal inconsistencies, in which an interviewee provides shifting accounts or answers that vary during the interview; and external inconsistencies, in which witness accounts and interviewee statements are at odds with information contained in records, or other witnesses contradict the witness's account.

In any case, corroborative and contradictory information must be scrutinized carefully, and you must make every effort to allow the interviewee to fully explain inconsistencies. And, of course, documentary evidence is generally far easier to evaluate. Corroboration by other witness accounts must be assessed to ensure that witnesses have not had the opportunity or motive to share their recollections, or made some effort to mislead investigators. Inconsistencies between and among witnesses may be the most difficult to evaluate. Investigators must rule out the possibility that witness inconsistencies can arise from the different ways in which individuals perceive and recount events . . ., and must consider biases and comparative credibility. . . .

Using the pyramid

Build your credibility assessment one layer at a time. During the interview, gather your impressions of the interviewee's demeanor, and make sure to collect impressions from other members of the team. Next, evaluate the logic or illogic of the information being provided, making sure to follow up with questions as appropriate to understand the full context. Finally, using information that you've already gathered during the investigation, or based on post-interview investigation, decide whether you have evidence that corroborates or undermines the interviewee's account. . . .

Complete information won't always be available

Conducting interview and evaluating credibility can be one of the most difficult parts of an internal investigation. The tools provided [herein] can help you effectively gather and evaluate investigative information. In many, if not most instances, you will not have access to complete information—life is not that easy. Your investigative record will have gaps, and your ability to fill those gaps will be limited by practical, legal and resource issues. However, with considered effort, which sometimes will involve creativity and flexibility, you can usually develop a sufficient record upon which to base reliable conclusions. This, in turn, will allow you to properly advise your business leaders in a dependable, cost-effective and timely manner.

CHAPTER 11

EARLY CASE ASSESSMENTS[1]

In litigation, a client and its lawyers invest effort, money and years in a case, with choices to be made and risks to be taken along the way. I have had critical facts turn against me midway through a case, and I'll bet you have, too. Wouldn't you rather know before the case that Mr. Smith will say the light was red? Or that Ms. Jones has notes to prove that nobody intended to form a partnership at that meeting? If done right, an Early Case Assessment ("ECA") program can be well worth the time, effort and money it will require. In this chapter we will explore various aspects of ECA, including some of the ways in which I and others have found it to be effective in managing cases—in the very early stages, ultimately creating long-term savings in the process.

WHAT IS AN "EARLY CASE ASSESSMENT PROGRAM"?

New lawsuits rarely come at convenient times. At the outset, they are not anyone's first priority. Soon enough, legal wrangling sets in—deadlines approach, extensions are brokered, and the plaintiff's perspective advances unrefuted. The case becomes a problem everyone seems willing to pay tens of thousands of dollars a month for until they're ready to deal with it. There is a better way.

ECAs can impact when—and how—cases get resolved, whether by settlement or through the courts. And if they are done right, ECAs can eliminate the carrying costs of litigation as usual. Various ECA methods have support in both the legal and corporate communities. According to one early corporate ECA pioneer, DuPont, "ECA methodology has been a cornerstone of DuPont's success in reducing its docket, its legal defense budget

---

[1] By John DeGroote. Used herein with the permission of Mr. DeGroote. Mr. DeGroote is a former global company general counsel now serving as a mediator, arbitrator and court-appointed trustee in significant disputes. This chapter has been modified to a limited extent by the authors of this book.

and in reaching faster and better resolution of lawsuits";[2] more on its successful use of ECA can be found in the DuPont Legal Model.[3]

In contrast, "Early Case Assessment" does not mean the visceral reaction one gets when reading a newly-served complaint, and it's not what most people do when they claim they have an ECA program in place. There's no shortage of articles on how great ECA is, but few sources offer practical advice on how to implement an ECA program.

USING ECA TO DEVELOP A ROADMAP

Hall of Fame former Major League Baseball catcher, outfielder, and manager "Yogi" Berra is often quoted as saying, "You've got to be careful if you don't know where you're going because you might not get there." The same could be said about litigation. As this chapter continues, we will further explore the use of ECAs as a litigation management tool and how ECAs can be used effectively to evaluate a litigation matter, develop a litigation strategy and formulate a settlement plan (if appropriate)—so that you know where you are going.

AN IMPORTANT LESSON FROM THE PLAINTIFF'S PERSPECTIVE

Some of the more important lessons I learned about litigation come from the contingent-fee plaintiffs' cases I handled before going in-house. Investing your own money in someone else's case drives efficiencies, and we could all learn a lot from the pre-litigation discipline that large-scale contingency fee cases require.

For example, one seemingly great prospective case involved trade secrets, market shares, and corporate profits. Our law firm interviewed witnesses, reviewed the documents, researched the law, and the case looked more than promising. Many law firms would have filed a lawsuit at that point. But on the cusp of our

---

[2]   Courson, Gardner & Sager, *Metrics for Success in DuPont's Legal Risk Analysis*, CHIEF LEGAL OFFICER, Vol. 1 No. 3, Summer 2002, at 29–31.

[3]   *The New Reality: Turning Risks into Opportunity through the DuPont Legal Model* (S. DeCarli & A. Schaeffer eds.) (E.I. du Pont de Nemours and Company 2009), http://www.cba.org/cba/cle/PDF/10PM_Schmitt_Dupontchapt1-2.pdf, *archived at* https://perma.cc/N2R3-UYDN.

firm's own multi-million-dollar investment, the prospective case was assessed again. More documents, more research and more investigation followed.

The law firm's in-depth review revealed much more about the case; important questions emerged but, on even further review, satisfactory answers did not. The firm walked away from the case. This experience exemplified the efficiency that ECA can bring—no matter which side of the docket counsel is on.

KNOW 80% OF WHAT YOU WILL EVER KNOW IN 60 DAYS

Two outside attorneys define ECA as "making a concerted effort to complete all the major work within the first 90 to 120 days of a lawsuit's filing."[4] In one of the better summaries of ECA available, another attorney recommends "front-loading" case preparation within 3 to 6 months of the inception of litigation.[5]

Hence, ECAs should be done quickly and arguably should be completed within two months. What's magical about the first 60 days? What can an attorney know in just two months? A Schering-Plough lawyer says that "in 60 days . . . you will know 80 percent of what you will ever know about a case" with an effective ECA.[6] While the amount of time ECAs will take may vary, the ultimate goal of an ECA—an understanding of the case and a strategy consistent with that understanding—remains the same.

THE ECA PROGRAM—DEFINED

While more prolonged approaches to ECA will work in many contexts, many prefer a quicker route, with a focus on the tasks that will provide the most insight at the lowest cost. Under this approach, the definition of an "Early Case Assessment program" is a disciplined, proactive case management approach designed to assemble, within 60 days, enough of the facts, law, and other information relevant to a dispute to evaluate the matter, to

---

    4   Iskra & Woody, *Early Case Assessment,* COUNS. TO COUNS., Jan. 2006, at 9.

    5   Prignano, *Early Case Assessments: Rein in Costs and Identify Risks,* IN-HOUSE DEF. Q., Spring 2008, at 8.

    6   Editor, *Energizing A Litigation Group—Overview and Results—Part I,* 2006 METRO. CORP. COUNS. 51, 51.

develop a litigation strategy, and to formulate a settlement plan if appropriate.

THE EARLY CASE ASSESSMENT CHECKLIST

Agreeing on an approach is one thing. Executing on it is another. Individual approaches to ECA may vary, but the one thing I can tell you with confidence is what I look for in an ECA. Whether it's communicated in a notebook or in a meeting or at a presentation, I'm looking for that 80 percent of what I will ever know about a case—not just our side of the case or how we should win.

My approach to ECA seeks each of the sixteen items listed below, with two caveats: (i) in some cases a few of these items will be better discussed at a high level than circulated in written form; and (ii) the level of detail required for any of these is within the attorney's sound judgment.

An Early Case Assessment Checklist includes:

The Facts

1. *A Claims Summary*: An executive summary of the plaintiff's claims and the defendant's response;

2. *The Other Side's Position*: The complaint, demand letter, response, or whatever you may have containing the other side's position and perspective unfiltered and in their own words;

3. *A Timeline*: A timeline showing the relevant facts and key dates, linked to supporting documents;

4. *Interview Summaries*: Summaries of, and witness evaluations from, all key interviews, including interviews of witnesses who might not be friendly;

5. *The Documents*: The 10 best documents for each side of the case;

6. *Your Experts*: A summary of expert testimony required or desired and likely candidates to serve as consulting and testifying experts;

7. *The Themes*: A concise statement of each side's likely themes;

The Law

8. *The Jury Charge:* A draft jury charge;

9. *A Summary of Legal Issues:* A summary of legal issues and likelihood of success of legal motions (such as motions for summary judgment);

The Forum, Your Opposition and More

10. *A Venue Analysis*: A memo evaluating the court, the jury pool, past verdicts in similar cases, and the applicable appellate court's rulings on similar issues;

11. *The Opposition*: A memo analyzing opposing counsel, his/her team, his/her trial experience and any cases of note;

12. *Your Insurance*: An understanding of your policies and your carrier(s) and what you have to do to protect your coverage;

13. *Other Circumstances*: A memo highlighting other circumstances affecting all parties and stakeholders (customer impact, potential for similar cases, etc.);

The Plan

14. *Your Strategy:* An outline of the case strategy and recognize that formulating this strategy must be an interactive process between counsel and client;

15. *The Budget:* A realistic budget to take the case to (and through) trial, including relevant assumptions, a case timeline, and any potential for an alternative billing arrangement; and

16. *A Settlement Plan:* A settlement plan and supporting analysis.

This list might sound like a lot, and it is—but it's nothing more than your case will require at some point in the future.

PUTTING THE CHECKLIST INTO ACTION

A checklist alone isn't enough. How an ECA works in practice—actually getting what's on the ECA checklist done—isn't quite the paint-by-numbers exercise it might seem to be. The following are four important ideas that will make your ECA efforts more effective.

1. Agree on the Goal

The logical starting point for any case assessment is to gather the facts, but I have learned the hard way that a quick dash for the facts isn't really where to start. Since the effort will require information, documents and cooperation from a number of people, the first step in an Early Case Assessment is to educate witnesses and stakeholders—immediately—so that delay is no longer the strategy. Whether the client is a first-time litigant or frequently defends cases, everyone involved needs to understand that counsel will be giving as full a report as practicable on the case by a specified date in the near future.

2. Not Something for the Lawyers to "Go off and Do"

If your assessment is going to be effective, it will require cooperation between knowledgeable people working for the client and trial counsel—this isn't something for the lawyers to go off and do. The entire team must understand that objective evaluation, not planning "our" side of the case, is our primary goal. The assessment will come from an initial pull of the relevant documents, interviews of more than a few witnesses, targeted legal research, and—often—a second review of the documents, a few follow-up interviews, and another look at the research once you have a better idea about the case and where it's going.

3. Project Management Isn't Just for Consultants

One of the most neglected elements of ECA is project management, best maintained through a regularly updated Action Item List—a list that clearly states who will do what by when (and occasionally how and where they will do it), with regular updates to the Early Case Assessment team on what is getting done and what isn't. I have had the good fortune of working on several large cases under effective project managers, and I have learned that a document that remains on an individual's "to do" list that is distributed to the entire team—highlighted as "late" until your task is done—creates enough peer pressure and accountability to complete most tasks. More on project management is beyond the scope of this chapter, but I will say that I learned more from the first few pages of *Project Management for Dummies*[7] than I would care to admit.

4. Time to Think

One Friday morning before a long weekend I scheduled a whiteboard session with one of my most trusted counsel on an ugly case that was going nowhere. After 3 hours with caffeine and a whiteboard—and without laptops or telephones—we had worked through a serious problem in the other side's case and how to exploit it. We achieved a great settlement using this new "discovery" shortly thereafter. Based on this productive morning and dozens like it since, I believe the most important ingredient to an effective case assessment is in creating and carving out the time to actually think about the case. It's easy to say that the other side is irrational. Yet the fact that you can't figure out why they have made the choices they've made doesn't necessarily mean they don't know what they're doing. It's up to you to take the time to actually think, and ask: "Why did they . . .?" and "Why don't we . . .?"

BETTER SETTLEMENTS FROM BETTER INFORMATION

As we have discussed before, getting your ECA done—gathering the information required by the Early Case Assessment Checklist—requires an up-front investment.

I have settled cases I didn't know enough about and I have settled cases after Early Case Assessments, and I'm confident I got better deals in the disputes I knew more about. The settlement value of your case should have nothing to do with the other side's opening settlement demand, and I like to know what that value is before settlement discussions start. Early Case Assessments are the best way to get there.

---

[7]   Stanley E. Portny, *Project Management for Dummies* (3rd ed. 2010).

ECAs drive better settlements through better information and the savvier strategies that result from that information. Here are a few reasons why you'll likely be happier with your next settlement if you do an Early Case Assessment first:

Better Information Through Early Case Assessments:

- You'll know what additional information you will need—from your own client and from the other side—before settlement discussions begin;

- The realistic budget that results from your Early Case Assessment may impact your client's settlement position;

- Your client can't, or won't, get serious about settling the dispute until it understands the weaknesses in its case;

- You and your client will have an agreement on a reasonable settlement range before negotiations begin;

- Without the early settlement talks that your ECA will impact (and the information you'll share in those discussions), the other side will invest unnecessarily in the dispute as the case rolls on— and, like it or not, the other side's investment in the case often determines what they will settle it for; and

- What you learn about your dispute through your Early Case Assessment will give you a confidence that likely can't be developed any other way.

Savvier Strategies Through Early Case Assessments:

- You'll know when to seek settlement discussions (and when not to);

- You can tailor strategic discovery designed to lead the other side to its own weaknesses;

- You'll know what to say and how to say it, as settlement discussions begin;

- You'll know which of the other side's sensitivities— bad facts, financial needs, reputational concerns, and more—to emphasize as the negotiations proceed, whether they have anything to do with your case or not;

- As one source has reflected, the appearance of preparation that results from your ability to focus on detail may give your client's settlement position more credibility with the other side;[8] and

- You'll know more about what your dispute is worth to the other side, and you'll be in a better position to get there at every step in the process.

As the DuPont Legal Department makes clear,[9] an effective Early Case Assessment program can drive better settlements. I'll leave you with one final thought about valuing your dispute: If you and the other side value the case differently, at least one of you is wrong. Make sure it isn't you.

BETTER DOCKET MANAGEMENT THROUGH EARLY CASE ASSESSMENTS

If your Early Case Assessment doesn't help you settle your case, this section addresses why a thorough ECA is a good investment anyway. It takes time, effort and money to make your way through the Early Case Assessment Checklist, but Early Case Assessments mean better case management—and more responsible docket management—even if your case goes the distance. With ECAs, you'll save money and ultimately get better results overall, whether you settle or not.

When you do an Early Case Assessment you'll see an immediate return on the up-front investment it required in more than a few ways:

Better (and Cheaper) Discovery from the Outset

- You'll know what discovery to ask for;

---

[8] Nancy Hudgins, *Negotiation Preparation: Scripting Your Moves*, MEDIATE.COM (Mar. 5, 2012), https://www.mediate.com/articles/HudginsNbl20120305.cfm, *archived at* https://perma.cc/TE5Q-H5A6.

[9] *See* Courson, Gardner & Sager, *supra* note 2; *see also infra* note 15 and accompanying text.

- You'll know what areas to avoid in discovery because you don't want the other side to become educated in those areas;

- You'll know what noncontroversial facts to ask the other side to stipulate to, which will eliminate discovery on those points;

- You won't be seeking any discovery on claims or defenses you have decided to abandon;

- Your timeline and the demonstrative exhibits you prepare during your ECA can be used to prepare and examine witnesses during discovery; and

- Your employee witnesses are less likely to have moved to another job; therefore, if you interview them early in the case, their memories of the facts are more clear.

More Disciplined Case Management

- You'll be able to identify areas that aren't worth pursuing—because there are stones that can be left unturned;

- You'll be in a better position to negotiate an alternative fee arrangement for the rest of the case;[10]

- You'll learn about areas that may require the help of a consulting or testifying expert—and you can bring her into the case at a more beneficial time for your client;

- Your knowledge of the case will enhance your credibility among witnesses and clients as the case is being prepared, whether you are trial counsel or in-house counsel; and

- Your client is more likely to treat the "big case" like the important matter it is if it's identified early (assuming your client doesn't settle the matter in a

---

[10]   Prignano, *supra* note 5, at 6.

disadvantageous manner when it learns how significant the case actually is).

Better Business Results Outside the Legal Department

- Your CEO and the rest of your management team will spend less time on a well-managed case;

- Your clients will be happier, since ECA encourages lawyers to "define and consider [the client's] goals earlier and throughout the case";[11]

- You'll have a better idea about what your client will spend on the case, and when it will be spent (and management normally appreciates this);

- The client may learn—at the outset of the case instead of years down the road—of necessary changes to its products, processes or conduct that will help it avoid future litigation;[12]

- You are better prepared for any public relations fallout that may result from the case;[13]

- When early settlements are reached, trade secrets and sensitive company data typically are not produced;[14] and

- Insurers likely will appreciate your responsible docket management and proactive risk reduction efforts whether this specific case is settled or not, which can lead to lower premiums.

While the points above make it clear that Early Case Assessment is worth the investment, it's hard to say exactly how much a good ECA is worth in any case. No matter how convinced I might be of ECAs' benefits, I have heard more than one in-

---

[11] DiCarli & Michalowicz, *How In-House Litigation Counsel Add Value—Proving Your Case*, Ass'n of Corp. Couns. Annual Meeting (2006) at 7, https://www.acc.com/sites/default/files/resources/vl/public/ProgramMaterial/20076_1.pdf, *archived at* https://perma.cc/HPQ3-7TK7.

[12] Barnum, *An Introduction to Early Case Assessment*, PRAC. LITIGATOR 23 (2006), https://www.schiffhardin.com/Templates/Media/files/archive/binary/barnum_110706.pdf, *archived at* https://perma.cc/S4H9-DX6B.

[13] Prignano, *supra* note 5, at 5.

[14] Matt Chandler, *Early Case Assessment Can Save Time and Money*, BUFF. BUS. FIRST (Mar. 31, 2008), http://www.bizjournals.com/buffalo/stories/2008/03/31/focus8.html?page=all, *archived at* https://perma.cc/E6B4-NMRN.

house lawyer say that "you are what you measure." Fortunately, the DuPont Legal Team had the same thing in mind when it published objective measures of its results.

"The DuPont cases where ECA was rigorously followed resulted in higher satisfaction from the business unit, faster cycle times and an average of 28 percent less cost."[15] DuPont's 28 percent savings is supported by other ECA-driven data. Other statistics likewise quantify the benefits of Early Case Assessment programs:

- ECA and other initiatives allowed GE to reduce litigation costs from $120.5 million in 2002 to $69.3 million in 2005;[16]

- "More than three-quarters of cases are resolved favorably, and litigation expenses [are] cut in half in all cases, when thorough early case assessment is performed," according to a survey of 341 practicing litigators;[17]

- "Conducting early case assessment enables attorneys to reduce the litigation expenses in 50% of their cases on average;"[18]

- ECA and other legal management efforts at DuPont reduced the cycle time of litigation (from filing to resolution) from 39 to 22 months and the overall docket by half;[19] and

---

[15]   *See* Courson, Gardner & Sager, *supra* note 2. *But see* Posting of Rees Morrison to General Counsel Metrics, Law Department Management Blog (Mar. 15, 2006) (challenging Dupont's methodology to a degree), https://www.lawdepartment managementblog.com/savings_from_ea/, *archived at* https://www.lawdepartment managementblog.com/savings_from_ea/.

[16]   John Wallbillich, *GE Legal Takes the Lead,* WIRED GC, Apr. 18, 2007 (quoting *Corporate Counsel* magazine), http://www.wiredgc.com/2007/04/18/ge-legal-takes-the-lead/, *archived at* https://perma.cc/BL93-QJ5X.

[17]   Chandler, *supra* note 14, at 2 (quoting Cogent Research study).

[18]   *Survey: Early Case Assessment Results in Favorable Outcomes in 76% of Cases and Reduced Litigation Costs in 50% of Cases,* BUS. WIRE (May 16, 2007), http://www. businesswire.com/news/home/20070516005694/en/Survey-Early-Case-Assessment-Results-Favorable-Outcomes#.Uw0XCPldV_4, *archived at* https://perma.cc/47QX-Y3YW (citing survey of litigators conducted by Cogent Research on behalf of LexisNexis).

[19]   *Five Years into the Experiment: An Evaluation of DuPont's Legal Model Revisited,* ACCA Docket 24, 34 (1998).

- More than half (57%) of surveyed attorneys felt that ECA assisted in their ability to prepare a more accurate litigation budget.[20]

Whether the benefits are obvious or subtle, objective or subjective, Early Case Assessments can drive better case management—and better case resolutions.

---

[20]   Deacon & Fehrman, *Process Makes Perfect: Some Guidance on Mastering Early Case Assessment,* CORP. COUNS. (Oct. 21, 2010). *See also* Patrick Lamb, *Litigation and Service, In Search of Perfect Client Service,* IN SEARCH OF GREAT CUSTOMER EXPERIENCES (July 25, 2005), http://www.patrickjlamb.com/2005/07/25/litigation-and-service/ *archived at* https://perma.cc/KQH3-VF7Q.

CHAPTER 12

INSIDE COUNSEL AS DIRECTOR

The practice of the general counsel serving as a corporate director to a business enterprise, whether that person is an in-house lawyer or a partner in a law firm, has been the situation to some extent for decades. This remains the case in privately-held companies and "smaller" publicly-held enterprises. From the client's perspective, the specialized training, unique experience, and analytical skills of its corporate counsel are a valued resource to a board of directors when making business decisions.[1] Additionally, in-house counsel may view this dual role as a means of strengthening his position within the corporate hierarchy.[2]

Although the practice of corporate counsel serving as director occurs with some frequency today in privately-held and "smaller" publicly-held companies, the propriety of attorneys acting in this dual capacity has long been criticized. Because an attorney/director must play dual roles as counsel and director, this arrangement raises a variety of issues pertaining to professional responsibility, potential conflicts of interest, and enhanced liability exposure.

For example, the application of the attorney-client privilege will be assessed on an ad-hoc basis depending upon whether the attorney/director was acting as legal counsel or as a director. By assuming this dual function, therefore, the corporation's assertion of the attorney-client privilege may be subject to challenge.[3] Also, by serving as director, counsel incurs the risk of having diminished ability to exercise independent judgment.

---

[1]   *See* Carrey, *Corporate Lawyer/Corporate Director: A Compromise of Professional Independence,* 67 N.Y. St. B.J. at 6 (Nov. 1995); Kim, *Dual Identities and Dueling Obligations: Preserving Independence in Corporate Representations*, 68 Tenn. L Rev. 179 (2001).

[2]   *See* Cheek & Lamar, *Lawyers as Directors of Clients: Conflicts of Interest, Potential Liability and Other Pitfalls*, PLI No. B4–6940, 712 PLI Corp. 461, 463–464 (1990).

[3]   *Grimes v. LCC International, Inc.,* 1999 WL 252381 (Del. Ch. 1999). *See* M. Steinberg, *Corporate and Securities Malpractice* 251 (1992); Finklestein et al., *Attorney-*

POTENTIAL DRAWBACKS

In these dual roles, counsel has a conflict between being a "team player" while, at the same time, rendering dispassionate legal advice that will be received with respect and without hostility by the inside directors.[4] [An inside director generally is one who has a significant employment relationship, such as being an executive officer (e.g., President) of the corporation.] Moreover, the attorney/director may be denied legal malpractice insurance coverage by the carrier on the basis that the alleged impropriety did not involve the practice of law. Conversely, the directors' and officers' (D&O) insurance carrier may assert that, due to inside counsel's conduct, that she was acting as an attorney rather than as a director, and thereby deny coverage.

Further, when counsel steps out of her attorney's shoes and acts as director, counsel's personal liability exposure is magnified. In such circumstances, courts frequently apply enhanced standards to analyze the propriety of the alleged wrongdoing.[5] Indeed, it has been asserted that lawyers who agree to sit as directors "have to be 'certifiably nuts' because of the likelihood of being sued."[6]

BENEFITS OF THE DUAL ROLE

Despite the potential risks, however, some companies exhort corporate counsel to serve as a director, due to perceived advantages that accrue to the client corporation. An ostensible benefit is for inside counsel to be even better informed concerning the corporation's business affairs and to be in an even better position to provide legal advice when contemplated

---

Client Privilege: Potential Dangers of Having Corporate General Counsel Perform Multiple Roles, 33 Rev. Sec. & Comm. Reg. 49 (2000).

[4]   *See* Model Rules of Prof. Conduct, Rule 1.7 cmt. 35; Hershman, *Special Problems of Inside Counsel for Financial Institutions*, 33 Bus. Law 1435, 1439–1440 (1978); Lorne, *The Corporate and Securities Adviser, the Public Interest, and Professional Ethics,* 76 Mich. L. Rev. 425, 490–495 (1978); Riger, *The Lawyer-Director—A Vexing Problem,* 33 Bus. Law 2381 (1978).

[5]   *See, e.g., Escott v. BarChris Constr. Corp.*, 283 F. Supp. 643 (S.D.N.Y. 1968); Hershman, *supra* note 4, 33 Bus. Law. at 1440 (1978) (asserting that "as a director, the General Counsel is likely to be held to a higher standard of care than other directors because of his [or her] unique access to information and expertise").

[6]   *Lawyer-Directors Are Key Targets for Plaintiffs' Lawyers, ABA Group Told*, 21 Sec. Reg. & L. Rep. (BNA) 1272 (1989) (hereinafter "*Lawyer-Directors*"). *See* Stewart, *Lawyer Directors: Just a Bad Idea,* 189 PLI/NY 155 (2009).

actions are first presented or when problematic situations initially arise.[7] This enables counsel to be more effective in rendering advice to the board of directors, thereby preventing problems which could arise "due to the ... failure of management or the board of directors to recognize developing legal problems in their early stages."[8]

Because the attorney/director understands the legal implications of a potential decision, she can also act as a sounding board for corporate management.[9] This facilitates the flow of information between the board of directors and inside counsel.[10] Additionally, because the attorney/director, like the other board members, is subject to the same potential for liability as a director, the other directors may have greater comfort in the legal advice rendered by the attorney.[11]

From inside counsel's perspective, if asked to serve in this dual role, economic inducements may prompt counsel to accept. Inside counsel's dual role enhances his relationship with the board of directors and executive management, including, of course, the CEO. Indeed, in some situations, the CEO may insist that the inside general counsel should be an integral member of the "team," and thereby serve on the board.[12]

ETHICAL RULES

In general, applicable ethical rules contain no specific prohibition against inside or outside counsel serving as a corporate director. In fact, the only guidance offered by the ABA Model Rules is included in the commentary to Model Rule 1.7, which touches upon the potential conflicts of interest that may

---

[7]   *See* Thurston, *Corporate Counsel on the Board of Directors: An Overview*, 10 Cumb. L. Rev. 791, 792 (1980) (citing Forrow, *Special Problems of Inside Counsel for Industrial Companies*, 33 Bus. Law. 1453, 1461 (1978)); Hawes, *Should Counsel to a Corporation be Barred From Serving as a Director?—A Personal View*, 1 Corp. L. Rev. 14, 17 (1978).

[8]   Thurston, *supra* note 7, 10 Cumb. L. Rev. at 792.

[9]   *Id.* at 793.

[10]   *Id. See* Cheek & Lamar, *supra* note 2, 712 PLI Corp. at 464; Zaffirini, *The Challenges of Serving as an Attorney/Director*, 33 Tex. J. Bus. Law No. 3, at 43, 44–45 (Fall 1996).

[11]   Thurston, *supra* note 7, 10 Cumb. L. Rev. at 793; Zaffirini, *supra* note 10, 33 Tex. J. Bus. Law No. 3, at 45.

[12]   *See* Lorne, *supra* note 4, 76 Mich. L. Rev. at 490–495.

exist when counsel serves as a director of the corporate client. Specifically, the Comment states:

> A lawyer for a corporation or other organization who is also a member of its board of directors should determine whether the responsibilities of the two roles may conflict. . . . If there is material risk that the dual role will compromise the lawyer's independence of professional judgment, the lawyer should not serve as a director or should cease to act as the corporation's lawyer when conflicts of interest arise. . . .[13]

Likewise, the American Law Institute's (ALI) Restatement of the Law Governing Lawyers generally acquiesces in the counsel-director arrangement:

> A lawyer's duties as counsel can conflict with the lawyer's duties arising from the lawyer's service as a director or officer of a corporate client. Simultaneous service as corporate lawyer and corporate director or officer is not forbidden under this Section. . . . However, when the obligations or personal interests as director are materially adverse to those of the lawyer as corporate counsel, the lawyer may not continue to serve as corporate counsel without the informed consent of the corporate client.[14]

A formal ethics opinion issued by the American Bar Association[15] provides additional suggestions to help an attorney/director avoid ethical violations and other problems. For example, the ABA opinion states that an attorney/director should:

> reasonably assure that management and the board of directors understand: (i) the different responsibilities of legal counsel and director; (ii) that when acting as legal counsel, the lawyer represents only the corporate entity

---

[13]   ABA Model Rules of Prof. Conduct, Rule 1.7 cmt 35. See Committee Report, *The Lawyer as Director of a Client*, 57 Bus. Law. 387 (2001) (stating that "[t]here is no ethical prohibition against a lawyer serving as a director of a client").

[14]   *See* American Law Institute, *Restatement of the Law Governing Lawyers* § 135 cmt. d (2000).

[15]   *Lawyer Serving as Director of Client Corporation*, ABA Comm. On Ethics and Professional Responsibility, Formal Op. 98–410 (1998).

and not its individual officers and directors; and (iii) that at times conflicts of interest may arise under the rules governing lawyers' conduct that may cause the lawyer to recuse himself as a director or to recommend engaging other independent counsel to represent the corporation in the matter, or to serve as co-counsel with the lawyer or his firm.[16]

Nevertheless, as the following discussion illustrates, serving as an attorney/director for inside counsel remains fraught with risk, including: (1) the potential loss of the attorney-client privilege; (2) potential conflict of interest challenges and the perceived loss of independence; (3) a heightened duty of care; (4) increased liability risk under the securities laws;[17] and (5) and possible loss of liability insurance coverage.

RISKS OF SERVING AS ATTORNEY-DIRECTOR

The first principal area of risk is the potential loss of the attorney-client privilege. In general, the purpose of the attorney-client privilege is to encourage full and frank communication between attorneys and their clients and thereby promote broader public interests in the observance of law. In order to invoke the privilege while acting as both attorney and director, an attorney must render the advice in her role as a lawyer, rather than in her role as a director. If the information in question was primarily communicated in the role of director, the privilege may be lost.

Although many in-house attorneys/directors regularly render business advice as well as legal advice, no clear test has been articulated to determine the issue of whether an attorney is acting as a director or as legal counsel. Instead, courts traditionally have used a factual analysis.[18] For example, in

---

[16]   *Id. See* Task Force on the Independent Lawyer, ABA Section of Litigation, *The Lawyer-Director: Implications for Independence* (1998); Committee Report, *supra* note 13, 57 Bus. Law. at 387–395; Kim, *supra* note 1, 68 Tenn. L. Rev. at 219–246.

[17]   An attorney/director faces increased liability risk under both federal and state securities laws. For state securities laws, *see generally* Steinberg & Claasen, *Attorney Liability Under the State Securities Laws: Landscapes and Minefields,* 3 U. Cal. (Berk.) Bus. L. J. 1 (2005).

[18]   Thurston, *supra* note 7, 10 Cumb. L. Rev. at 811.

United States v. Vehicular Parking, Ltd.,[19] the defendant in an antitrust case attempted to invoke the attorney-client privilege with respect to certain communications involving an attorney/ director. The court, however, concluded that as a director, the attorney was involved in the promotion and management of the business so that "his communications involving business, rather than legal advice, were, therefore, not privileged."[20]

When an in-house or outside attorney serves as a director, he may be required to exercise a higher standard of care than that of certain other directors, thus resulting in greater personal liability exposure. In general, Section 8.30 of the Model Business Corporation Act requires that directors "discharg[e] their duties with the care that a person in a like position would reasonably believe   appropriate   under   similar   circumstances."[21] Developments in corporate and securities law signify, however, that attorney/directors must not only act with the due care ordinarily required of a director, but also must adhere to higher standards premised on the attorney/director's unique skills and legal expertise—or, in other words, the standard expected of an "ordinarily prudent attorney/director."[22]

A widely cited case dealing with the issue of an attorney/ director's duty of care (also called "due diligence" in certain contexts) is *Escott v. BarChris Construction Corp.*[23] In *BarChris,* the plaintiffs brought an action for damages under Section 11 of the Securities Act of 1933 against the company, its officers, directors, accountants, and underwriters, alleging that the company's registration statement used to sell securities contained materially false and misleading statements. Defendants in the suit included both the inside and outside counsel for BarChris. With respect to outside counsel who also served as a director, the court stated:

> [I]n considering [the defendant's] due diligence defenses, the unique position which he occupied cannot

---

[19]   52 F. Supp. 751 (D. Del. 1943).

[20]   *Id.* at 753–754. *See SEC v. Gulf & Western Ind., Inc.,* 518 F. Supp. 675 (D.D.C. 1981); *Federal Savings & Loan Ins. Corp. v. Fielding,* 343 F. Supp. 537 (D. Nev. 1972); Thurston, *supra* note 7, 10 Cumb. L. Rev. at 811.

[21]   Model Bus. Corp. Act § 8.30(b).

[22]   Cheek & Lamar, *supra* note 2, 712 PLI Corp. at 490–491.

[23]   283 F. Supp. 643 (S.D.N.Y. 1968).

be disregarded. As the director most directly concerned with writing the registration statement and assuring its accuracy, more was required of him in the way of reasonable investigation than could fairly be expected of a director who had no connection with this work.[24]

In *Feit v. Leasco Data Processing Equipment Corp.*,[25] another case involving the attorney/director's due diligence defense under Section 11, the court opined that an attorney/director must undertake the strict investigatory obligations of an "inside" director. The court reasoned that the attorney-director was "so intimately involved in this registration process that to treat him as anything but an insider would involve a gross distortion of the realities of [the corporation's] management."[26] Supporting *BarChris*, the court stated that what constitutes satisfaction of a director's duty will vary with "the degree of involvement of the individual, his expertise and his access to the pertinent information and data; . . . [w]hat is reasonable for one director may not be reasonable for another by virtue of their differing positions."[27] Thus, under the standards outlined in the Model Business Corporation Act and as enunciated in such cases as *BarChris* and *Feit*, the attorney/director "is measured by a higher standard that takes into account his 'superior knowledge of, and access to, the relevant information.' "[28]

Attorney/directors also may be held liable under the securities laws for "causing" a subject violation.[29] Inside counsel serving as a director should be especially wary of these

---

[24]   *Id.* at 690. The inside general counsel did not serve as a director. Under Section 11, except for the issuer which is strictly liable, all defendants have a due diligence defense. *See* M. Steinberg, *Understanding Securities Law* 230–244 (7th ed. 2018).

[25]   332 F. Supp. 544 (E.D.N.Y. 1971).

[26]   *Id.* at 576.

[27]   332 F. Supp. at 577–578. *See* Cheek & Lamar, *supra* note 2, 712 PLI Corp. at 495.

[28]   Thurston, *supra* note 7, 10 Cumb. L. Rev. at 821, *quoting*, Folk, *Civil Liabilities Under the Federal Securities Acts: The Barchris Case*, 55 Va. L. Rev. 1, 34–35 (1969).

[29]   *See, e.g.,* Sections 15(c)(4) of the Securities Exchange Act (a person who was the "cause" of a failure to comply with the Exchange Act's reporting, proxy, or tender offer rules may be subject to an administrative enforcement action); Section 21(C)(a) of the Securities Exchange Act (cease or desist order may be imposed on a person who was a "cause" of the violation). *See also,* Albert, *The Lawyer-Director: An Oxymoron?,* 9 Geo. J. Leg. Eth. 413, 460 (1996); Cheek & Lamar, *supra* note 2, 712 PLI Corp. at 500.

provisions because these dual roles make counsel more
vulnerable to being sued for "causing" a securities law
violation.[30] Indeed, since the enactment of the Sarbanes-Oxley
Act in 2002, the SEC has brought several enforcement actions
against in-house attorneys.[31] The presence of the attorney as a
director undoubtedly enhances the SEC's scrutiny.[32]

An attorney/director also faces problems involving
insurance coverage—in the event that an attorney/director
becomes involved in litigation, there exists a distinct possibility
that she will be denied coverage.[33]

Generally, an attorney/director has insurance coverage
under two different types of policies: (1) professional liability
insurance procured by the corporation (which insures the
corporation and its attorneys against liabilities arising from the
providing of legal services); and (2) directors' and officers' (D&O)
liability insurance procured by the corporation (which insures
the director from liability resulting from such person's conduct
in her directorial capacity).[34]

Because the demarcation between professional advice as
legal counsel and business conduct as director at times is not
clear cut, the risk arises that an attorney/director will be denied
coverage under the company's D&O insurance policy as well as
the law firm's professional liability insurance policy.[35] Indeed,
because professional liability insurance generally provides
coverage for acts, errors, and omissions in the rendering of
professional services when acting in the capacity of a lawyer, the
insurer may deny coverage by asserting that the attorney/
director's conduct was outside the scope of her role as legal
counsel. On the other hand, the D&O insurer may contend that

---

[30]   See Block, Meierholfer & Wallach, *Lawyers Serving on the Board of Directors
of Clients: A Survey of the Problems*, 7 Insights No. 4, at 3, 6 (April 1993).

[31]   See M. Steinberg, *Attorney Liability After Sarbanes-Oxley* §§ 4.01–4.06 (2018);
Callcott & Slonecker, *A Review of SEC Actions Against Lawyers*, 42 Rev. Sec. & Comm.
Reg. 71 (2009).

[32]   See Gill & Bautista, "An Overview of Recent Enforcement Actions By the
Securities and Exchange Commission Against Attorneys," in *Gatekeepers Under
Scrutiny: What General Counsel Need to Know About Lawyer & Director Liability*
(Practising Law Institute 2004).

[33]   See Block, Meierholfer & Wallach, *supra* note 30, 7 Insights No. 4, at 8.

[34]   See *id;* Cheek & Lamar, *supra* note 2, 712 PLI Corp. at 499.

[35]   See sources *supra* notes 7, 30.

the actions of the attorney/director were not within the purview of her obligations as a director. Therefore, it is distinctly possible that an attorney/director will be denied coverage under both policies.[36]

SUGGESTED ALTERNATIVE

A better alternative may be for inside counsel, rather than serving as a director, to attend all board of director and key committee meetings and meaningfully participate only in an attorney role. This route enables counsel to be informed and to provide advice as appropriate, but without losing her independence and facing the burdens accompanying a directorship. Indeed, this view was espoused by former SEC Chairman Harold Williams, who stated:

> "I am not convinced that it is possible to develop a conduct rule which adequately resolves the inherent conflicts in dual service. . . . I would suggest, however, that there is no impediment to having general counsel attend board meetings as an active participant. I believe it should be standard practice. Such a procedure would give the company and the board the benefits of counsel, without presenting the dilemma posed by dual service."[37]

---

[36]   *Id.*

[37]   Williams, *The Role of Inside Counsel in Corporate Accountability*, [1979–1980 Transfer Binder] CCH Fed. Sec. L. Rep. ¶ 82,318, at 82,375 (1979).

TABLE OF CASES

Adell v. Sommers, Schwartz, Silver and Schwartz, 38

Amgen Inc. v. Connecticut Retirement Plans and Trust Funds, 272

Apple Computer Securities Litigation, In re, 273

Aronson v. Lewis, 14, 109, 111

Banks, In re, 39

Basic, Inc. v. Levinson, 272

Bevill, Bresler & Schulman Asset Management Corp., In re, 310

Blakely v. Washington, 16

Bobbitt v. Victorian House, Inc., 40

Brennan v. Ruffner, 39

Brownstein, In re, 37, 39

Cady, Roberts, In re, 118

Carnegie Associates Ltd. v. Miller, 39

Carter and Johnson, In the Matter of, 40

Carter, In re, 11

Chiarella v. United States, 274

Collin County v. Johnson, 308

Cox Communications, Inc. Shareholders Litigation, In re, 111

Digital Realty Trust, Inc. v. Somers, 225, 305, 312

Dirks v. SEC, 274

Egan v. McNamara, 39

Escott v. BarChris Constr. Corp., 346, 350

Eurycleia Partners, LP v. Seward & Kissel, LLP, 38

FDIC v. O'Melveny & Myers, 13

Federal Savings & Loan Ins. Corp. v. Fielding, 350

Feit v. Leasco Data Processing Equipment Corp., 351

Flood v. Synutra International, Inc., 14

Franchard Corporation, In re, 119

Francis v. United Jersey Bank, 127

Galler v. Galler, 38

Garner v. Wolfinbarger, 8

Gilman v. Marsh & McLennan Companies, Inc., 311

Glover v. Libman, 40

Graf, United States v., 40, 310

Grand Jury Subpoena Under Seal, In re, 12, 309

Grimes v. LCC International, Inc., 345

Grossman, United States v., 275

Gutfreund, In re, 11

Halliburton Co. v. Erica P. John Fund, Inc., 272

Hickman v. Taylor, 303, 318

Hopper v. Frank, 38

International Brotherhood of Teamsters, United States v., 308

Jesse v. Danforth, 39

Kahn v. M&F Worldwide Corp., 14

KBR, Inc., In the Matter of, 306

Kellogg Brown & Root, Inc., In Re, 312

Law v. Harvey, 38

Matrixx Initiatives v. Siracusano, 273

McKinney v. McMeans, 39

Metropolitan Life Insurance Company v. The Guardian Life Insurance Company of America, 38

Nicholas, United States v., 310

O.P.M. Leasing Services, Inc., In re, 142

O'Hagan, United States v., 274

Occidental Petroleum Corporation, In re, 119

Orbit One Communications, Inc. v. Numerex Corp., 302

Parker v. Carnahan, 12, 308

Pendergast-Holt v. Sjoblom and Proskauer-Rose, LLP, 308

Redvanly v. NYNEX Corp., 303

Revlon, Inc. v. MacAndrews & Forbes Holdings, 106

Rosenblatt v. Getty Oil Co., 14

Rosman v. Shapiro, 40

Ruehle, United States v., 12, 310

Ryan v. Gifford, 113, 304

SEC v. Andrew S. Marks, 296
SEC v. Credit Bancorp, Ltd., 39
SEC v. David C. Drummond, 158
SEC v. Gene D. Levoff, 298
SEC v. Gulf & Western Ind., Inc., 350
SEC v. John E. Isselmann, Jr., 155
SEC v. Jordan H. Mintz and Rex R. Rogers, 153
SEC v. Mayhew, 273
SEC v. Mitchell S. Drucker, 297
SEC v. Nancy R. Heinen, 156
SEC v. National Student Mktg. Corp., 11
Skarbrevik v. Cohen, England & Whitfield, 37, 39
Texas Gulf Sulphur, 118
Treadway Companies, Inc. v. Care Corp., 277
Triggs v. Triggs, 38
TSC Industries, Inc. v. Northway, Inc., 272
Upjohn Co. v. United States, 35, 303, 312, 314, 318
Vehicular Parking, Ltd., United States v., 350
Walt Disney Company Derivative Litigation, In re, 14
Weinberger v. UOP, Inc., 14, 15
Westinghouse Elec. Corp. v. Kerr-McGee Corp., 12, 40, 309
Whiting v. Dow Chemical Co., 276
Wilkes v. Springfield Nursing Home, Inc., 39
Willy v. Administrative Review Board, 302
Wortham & Van Liew v. Superior Court, 38